LIBRARY OF NEW TESTAMENT STUDIES

499

Formerly Journal for the Study of the New Testament Supplement Series

Editor
Mark Goodacre

ATTITUDES TO GENTILES
IN ANCIENT JUDAISM
AND EARLY CHRISTIANITY

Edited by

David C. Sim and James S. McLaren

BLOOMSBURY

LONDON • NEW DELHI • NEW YORK • SYDNEY

Bloomsbury T&T Clark

An imprint of Bloomsbury Publishing Plc

50 Bedford Square	1385 Broadway
London	New York
WC1B 3DP	NY 10018
UK	USA

www.bloomsbury.com

Bloomsbury is a registered trade mark of Bloomsbury Publishing plc

First published 2013

British Library Cataloguing-in-Publication Data

A catalogue record for this book is available from the British Library.

ISBN:	HB:	978-0-56763-766-6
	ePDF:	978-0-56703-578-3

Library of Congress Cataloging-in-Publication Data

David C. Sim and James S. McLaren

Attitudes to Gentiles in Ancient Judaism and Early Christianity /

David C. Sim and James S. McLaren p.cm

Includes bibliographic references and index.

ISBN 978-0-567-63766-6 (hardcover) – ISBN 978-0-5670-3578-3 (ePDF)

Typeset by Forthcoming Publications Ltd (www.forthpub.com)

Printed and bound in Great Britain

CONTENTS

ABBREVIATIONS

ABR	*Australian Biblical Review*
AB	Anchor Bible
ABD	*Anchor Bible Dictionary*. Edited by D. N. Freedman. 6 vols. New York, 1992
ABRL	Anchor Bible Reference Library
AHR	*American Historical Review*
AJEC	Ancient Judaism and Early Christianity
AJP	*American Journal of Philology*
AJSRev	*Association for Jewish Studies Review*
AS	*Anatolian Studies*
AYBRL	Anchor Yale Bible Reference Library
BA	*Biblical Archaeologist*
BAR	*Biblical Archaeology Review*
BBB	Bonner biblische Beiträge
BBET	Beiträge zur biblischen Exegese und Theologie
BCH	*Bulletin de Correspondance Hellénique*
BETL	Bibliotheca ephemeridum theologicarum lovaniensium
BHT	Beiträge zur historischen Theologie
Bib	*Biblica*
BIS	Biblical Interpretation Series
BJS	Brown Judaic Studies
BNTS	Black's New Testament Commentaries
BSR	Biblioteca di Scienze Religiose
BTB	*Biblical Theological Bulletin*
BUS	Brown University Studies
BZNW	Beihefte zur *Zeitschrift für die neutestamentliche Wissenschaft*
CBET	Contributions to Biblical Exegesis and Theology
CBNTS	Coniectanea Biblica New Testament Series
CBQ	*Catholic Biblical Quarterly*
CBQMS	*Catholic Biblical Quarterly* Monograph Series
CIG	*Corpus Inscriptionum Graecarum*
CQS	Companion to the Qumran Scrolls
CRINT	Compendia Rerum Iudaicarum Ad Novum Testamentum
CSCT	Columbia Studies in the Classical Tradition
CSHJ	Chicago Studies in the History of Judaism
DJD	Discoveries in the Judaean Desert
DSD	*Dead Sea Discoveries*
EA	*Epigraphica Anatolica*
EJL	Early Judaism and its Literature
ETS	Erfurter Theologischer Studien
EUS	European University Studies
FRLANT	Forschungen zur Religion und Literatur des Alten und Neuen Testaments

FzB	Forschung zur Bibel
HCS	Hellenistic Culture and Society
HeyJ	*Heythrop Journal*
HSM	Harvard Semitic Museum
HTR	*Harvard Theological Review*
HTS	*Hervormde Teologiese Studies*
IBS	*Irish Biblical Studies*
IEJ	*Israel Exploration Journal*
IG	*Inscriptiones Graecae*
IGR	*Inscriptiones Graecae ad res Romanas pertinentes*
IJO	*Inscriptiones Judaicae Orientis*
IK	*Inschriftengriechischer Städte auskleinasien*
JAJSup	*Journal of Ancient Judaism*, Supplements
JBL	*Journal of Biblical Literature*
JJS	*Journal of Jewish Studies*
JPS	The Jewish Publication Society
JSJ	*Journal for the Study of Judaism*
JSJSup	*Journal for the Study of Judaism,* Supplements
JSNT	*Journal for the Study of the New Testament*
JSNTSup	*Journal for the Study of the New Testament*, Supplement Series
JSOTSup	*Journal for the Study of the Old Testament*, Supplement Series
JSPSup	*Journal for the Study of the Pseudepigrapha*, Supplement Series
LCL	Loeb Classical Library
LNTS	Library of New Testament Studies
LXX	Septuagint
MAMA	*Monumenta Asiae Minoris Antiqua*
MNTS	McMaster New Testament Studies
MT	Masorertic Text
Neot	*Neotestamentica*
NICNT	The New International Commentary on the New Testament
NIGTC	The New International Greek Testament Commentary
NovT	*Novum Testamentum*
NRSV	New Revised Standard Version
NTABh	Neutestamentliche Abhandlungen
NTL	New Testament Library
NTS	*New Testament Studies*
NTSI	The New Testament and the Scriptures of Israel
NTT	New Testament Theology
OTP	*Old Testament Pseudepigrapha*. Edited by J. H. Charlesworth. 2 vols. New York, 1983
PCPS	*Proceedings of the Cambridge Philological Society*
PRS	*Perspectives in Religious Studies*
RECAM	Regional Epigraphic Catalogues of Asia Minor
RevQ	*Revue de Qumrân*
SBEC	Studies in the Bible and Early Christianity
SBLDS	Society of Biblical Literature Dissertation Series
SCSS	Septuagint and Cognate Studies Series
SFSHJ	South Florida Studies in the History of Judaism
SHC	Studies in Hellenistic Civilization
SNTSMS	Society for New Testament Studies Monograph Series
SNTW	Studies of the New Testament and its World

SP	Sacra Pagina
SPhA	*The Studia Philonica Annual*
SPM	Studia Philonica Monographs
SPNT	Studies on the Personalities of the New Testament
STDJ	Studies on the Texts of the Desert of Judah
TAM	*Tituli Asiae Minoris*
TBLS	The Bible and Liberation Series
TDNT	*Theological Dictionary of the New Testament.* Edited by G. Kittel and G. Friedrich. Translated by G. W. Bromiley. 10 vols. Grand Rapids, 1964–76
THNTC	Two Horizons New Testament Commentary
TSAJ	Texts and Studies in Ancient Judaism
TynBul	*Tyndale Bulletin*
VC	*Vigiliae Christianae*
VTSup	*Vetus Testamentum*, Supplements
WMANT	Wissenschaftliche Monographien zum Alten und Neuen Testament
WBC	Word Biblical Commentary
WUNT	Wissenschaftliche Untersuchungen zum Neuen Testament
ZPE	*Zeitschrift für Papyrologie und Epigraphik*

LIST OF CONTRIBUTORS

Donald Binder is Rector of Historic Pohick Church near Mt. Vernon, Virginia. His most recent publication is *The Ancient Synagogue from its Origins to 200 C.E.: A Source Book*, co-written with Anders Runesson and Birger Olsson (Brill, 2008).

Alan Cadwallader is a Senior Lecturer in the Faculty of Theology and Philosophy, Australian Catholic University. He is the co-editor (with Michael Trainor) of *Colossae in Space and Time* (Vandenhoeck & Ruprecht, 2011).

John J. Collins is Holmes Professor of Old Testament Criticism and Interpretation at Yale. His most recent book is *The Dead Sea Scrolls: A Biography* (Princeton University Press, 2012).

Mary L. Coloe is an Associate Professor at Yarra Theological Union within the MCD University of Divinity, Melbourne. Her most recent book is *A Friendly Guide to the Gospel of John* (Garratt Publishing, 2013).

Elizabeth V. Dowling rsm is a Lecturer in the Faculty of Theology of Theology and Philosophy, Australian Catholic University. She is the author of *Taking Away the Pound: Women, Theology and the Parable of the Pounds in the Gospel of Luke* (Continuum, 2007).

Jonathan A. Draper is Professor of New Testament at the School of Religion, Philosophy and Classics of the University of KwaZulu-Natal. He is the co-editor (with Cynthia Kittredge and Ellen Aitken) of *Reading the Signs of the Times: Taking the Bible into the Public Square* (Fortress, 2008).

Ian J. Elmer is a Lecturer in the Faculty of Theology and Philosophy, Australian Catholic University. He is the author of *Paul, Jerusalem and the Judaisers: The Galatian Crisis in its Broadest Historical Context* (Mohr Siebeck, 2009).

James S. McLaren is a Professor and Associate Dean Research in the Faculty of Theology and Philosophy, Australian Catholic University. He is the author of *Turbulent Times?* (Sheffield Academic, 1998), and Editor of *Australian Biblical Review*.

David T. Runia is Master of Queen's College and Professorial Fellow in the School of Historical and Philosophical Studies at the University of Melbourne. He is the author of *Philo of Alexandria On the Creation of the Cosmos according to Moses: Translation and Commentary* (Brill, 2001), and has been since 1989 the editor of *The Studia Philonica Annual*.

David C. Sim is an Associate Professor in the Faculty of Theology and Philosophy, Australian Catholic University. His most recent book is the co-edited volume (with Pauline Allen) *Ancient Jewish and Christian Texts as Crisis Management Literature* (Continuum, 2012).

Michael P. Theophilos is a Lecturer in the Faculty of Theology of Theology and Philosophy, Australian Catholic University. He is the author of *The Abomination of Desolation in Matthew 24:15* (Continuum, 2012).

Christopher M. Tuckett is Professor of New Testament Studies, University of Oxford. His latest book is an edition and commentary on 2 Clement; *2 Clement: Introduction, Text, and Commentary* (Oxford University Press, 2012).

Sean F. Winter is an Associate Professor at MCD University of Divinity in Melbourne. He is the editor of *'Immense, Unfathomed, Unconfined': The Grace of God in Creation, Church and Community* (Uniting Academic, 2013).

PREFACE

This volume began as one project of a Research Support Team funded by the office of the Deputy Vice-Chancellor (Research) at Australia Catholic University. The editors would like to acknowledge the great assistance provided by Australian Catholic University towards the original project and the volume that it has subsequently created. Our thanks also extend to our international team of collaborators whose partnership with the ACU Biblical scholars has contributed enormously to the diversity and overall quality of this collection of essays. The editors owe a debt of gratitude to our colleague, Dr Dermot Nestor, who provided invaluable support on various technical issues. Finally, this volume has been delayed by a number of unavoidable factors, and we would like to offer our thanks to the team at Bloomsbury T&T Clark who liaised with us and who completely supported us when problems emerged. It needs to be said that we originally envisaged a chapter on 'the historical Jesus and the Gentiles' which would have formed a bridge between the Ancient Judaism chapters and the Early Christianity chapters, but the scholar allocated this chapter was unfortunately unable to complete it due to various reasons, and finding a suitable replacement would have delayed the volume even more. Our decision to proceed without this chapter leaves an obvious gap in the volume, but we ask for the indulgence and understanding of readers and reviewers alike. The chapters that deal with 'Early Christianity' reveal the diversity of ways in which the later followers of Jesus tackled the issues of Gentile nature, status and inclusion.

David C. Sim
James S. McLaren

INTRODUCTION

James S. McLaren

There are a number of well-trodden pathways traversed regarding the manner in which Jews and Christians in the ancient world interacted with the wider social contexts in which their respective religious traditions were situated. Some paths have highlighted the extent to which conflict and tension acted as the main frame of reference. Traditionally prominent here has been discussion of major flash points, such as those associated with the actions of Antiochus IV Epiphanes and the responses by Jews to his actions.[1] Some paths have focused on the possible cultural interaction, especially in terms of the extent to which Jews and/or Christians engaged with Greco-Roman society.[2] Some paths have been concerned to chart the types of formal interaction in terms of official policy and rulings and/or wider social perceptions regarding the status of Jews and Christians.[3] At the same time, there is a growing awareness of the importance of situating these discussions in the context of developments within the study of the ancient Roman world and of how its empire functioned.[4]

---

1 A notable example here is E. Schürer, *The History of the Jewish People in the Age of Jesus Christ (175 B.C.–A.D.135)* (rev. G. Vermes, F. Millar, M. Black and M. Goodman; 3 vols. in 4 parts; Edinburgh: T. & T. Clark, 1973–87), who uses the reign of Antiochus IV Epiphanes as one chronological boundary and the reign of Hadrian as the other boundary marker.

2 For example, see D. Mendels, *The Rise and Fall of Jewish Nationalism: Jewish and Christian Ethnicity in Ancient Palestine* (Grand Rapids: Eerdmans, 1992); E. S. Gruen, *Heritage and Hellenism: The Reinvention of Jewish Tradition* (HCS 30; Berkeley: University of California Press, 1998); and J. M. G. Barclay, *Jews in the Mediterranean Diaspora: From Alexander to Trajan (323 BCE–117 CE)* (Edinburgh: T. & T. Clark, 1996).

3 For example, see E. M. Smallwood, *The Jews Under Roman Rule, from Pompey to Diocletian: A Study in Political Relations* (Leiden: Brill, 1976), and P. Schäfer, *Judeophobia: Attitudes toward the Jews in the Ancient World* (Cambridge, MA: Harvard University Press, 1997).

4 For example, see G. Woolf, *Becoming Roman: The Origins of Provincial Civilization in Gaul* (Cambridge: Cambridge University Press, 1998); and R. MacMullen, *Romanization in the Time of Augustus* (New Haven: Yale University Press, 2000).

One of the issues common to each of these different pathways is the way that Jews and Christians viewed the people with which they were interacting. This interest in the *other* has covered instances where there is an active dialogue partner or where either Jews or Christians have found themselves needing to respond to a specific situation. Particular attention has been devoted to the question of how Jews and Christians interacted with one another, especially from the perspective of the latter community.[5] While there has been some consideration of how one or another of these faith communities understood themselves from the per-spective of being the *outsider* in a given situation, the bulk of discussion has focused on Jews and Christians as the *insider*.[6] This approach is clearly understandable. Drawing on biblical tradition there was a divide between the notion of Israel on one side and the nations (*goyim*) on the other (e.g. Exod. 33.16). Writing in the first century CE Paul expresses the dichotomy as 'Jew' and 'Greek' (Gal. 3.28), admittedly in the con-text of claiming such a divide no longer existed.

It has become relatively common to refer to the *outsider* by the term 'Gentile'. Although the term was never used by any specific group or community to identify itself, it is employed here as a term of conven-ience. It is deliberately broad in scope, referring to any person or com-munity that was not counted among the *insiders* by Jews. It could refer to cultic and/or social practices and to matters of conviction. For Christians, 'Gentiles' referred to people who had no link with the cultural and religious heritage of Israel.

The most important recent contribution regarding the place of Gentiles among Jews and among Christians is the work of T. L. Donaldson.[7] He notes a well-established tendency for Christianity to be depicted as a religion that was universalistic in outlook, readily welcoming and explicitly open to Gentiles. At the same time, Jews have been depicted as particularistic, concerned to protect their practices and beliefs in a way that made them wary of *outsiders*. Donaldson set about challenging the validity of this universalistic/particularistic paradigm in the approach of Jews and Christians toward interaction with Gentiles. His detailed study

5   For example, see S. Wilson, *Related Strangers: Jews and Christians 70–170 C.E.* (Minneapolis: Fortress, 1995), and W. Horbury, *Jews and Christians: In Contact and Controversy* (Edinburgh: T. & T. Clark, 1998).

6   For example, regarding the place of Jews in Rome, see D. Noy, *Foreigners at Rome: Citizens and Strangers* (London: Duckworth, 2000).

7   While some of the issues were addressed in T. L. Donaldson, *Paul and the Gentiles: Remapping the Apostle's Convictional World* (Minneapolis: Fortress, 1997), the key contribution is T. L. Donaldson, *Judaism and the Gentiles: Jewish Patterns of Universalism (to 135 CE)* (Waco, TX: Baylor University Press, 2008).

brought together an extensive collection of passages from primary sources that help show Judaism was universalistic. He identifies four key categories that display the universalistic nature: a range of 'sympathis-ers', Gentiles that participated in Jewish worship; converts to the Jewish way of life; ethical monotheists; and Gentiles as participants in eschato-logical redemption. Donaldson's detailed study has clearly exposed a major shortcoming in previous reconstructions of how to explain and compare Jewish and Christian attitudes toward Gentiles. However, it is also clear that in order to redress that shortcoming Donaldson focused on redrawing the picture within the existing universalistic/particularistic frame of reference. He deliberately concentrated on discussing passages that helped show the extent and manner of Gentile interaction with Jews and of how Jews were universalistic in their attitudes toward Gentiles. The picture constructed from the source material examined by Donald-son was intentionally a positive one that sought to redress past carica-tures of Jewish attitudes toward Gentiles. Although his study clearly helped dispel past distortions in comparisons of Jewish and Christian attitudes, its focus on positive interaction does not necessarily convey the full extent of how Jews thought of Gentiles. It is appropriate to go even further and to question the effectiveness of the universalistic/particularis-tic paradigm for explaining how Jews and Christians interacted with Gentiles.[8]

The point of departure for this collection of essays is to provide an overview of the attitudes expressed by various Jews and Christians regarding Gentiles in the ancient world *per se*, rather than as an expres-sion of a particular outlook. The subject matter examined in this study is grouped in two broad categories: the attitudes of late Second Temple period Jews (with some supplementation from the Rabbinic literature) and the attitudes of first- and early second-century CE Christians. The chronological timeframe covered in the former category ranges mainly from the early second century BCE through to the later part of the first century CE.[9] In the opening chapter D. Sim provides an overview of Jewish attitudes toward the place of Gentiles, God-fearers and proselytes. He focuses on the important issue of the boundaries that distinguished Gentiles from Jews. In particular, he discusses the shifts in attitude

8   See A. Runesson, 'Particularistic Judaism and Universalistic Christianity? Some Critical Remarks on Terminology and Theology', *Studia Theologia* 54 (2000), pp.55–75.

9   The chronological boundary for the study, therefore, does not extend into the post-Second Temple period of second century CE, early Rabbinic Judaism and post-apostolic Christianity.

toward the question of conversion to the Jewish way of life, charting changes from the biblical period through to the end of the second Temple period. In broad terms, he shows that although Jews were not actively seeking converts as engagement with the Greco-Roman world increased, their way of life did attract varying levels of interest from Gentiles. Some of those people became known as God-fearers, Gentiles that displayed a variety of levels of commitment to the Jewish way of life. They were, however, not converts, not members of the Jewish community. To convert, to become a proselyte, required three major actions: exclusive worship of the one God and the rejection of idolatry; full acceptance of the Torah, including circumcision for males; and incorporation into the Jewish community.

All the other chapters focus on a particular individual, group, institution and/or corpus of writings. Largely due to a shared religious-cultural heritage derived from the biblical tradition it will be evident there are various points of overlap between the attitudes expressed. At the same time, it is important that the variety and the distinctiveness of the attitudes are explored as articulated within the confines of the specific group or individual. For some the issue of interaction with Gentiles was a matter of explicit concern, even if not necessarily a major priority. For others, comments and thoughts regarding Gentiles was no more than a periphery subject matter. It is somewhat ironic that the latter approach is no more evident than in the case of Philo, as explained by D. Runia in his discussion of the copious writings of the Alexandrian Jew who lived at the turn of the era. Immersed in a social, religious and political setting where interaction with the Gentile world was an everyday reality, Runia examines how Philo employed the notion of the Gentiles in his efforts to affirm the validity of his own religious heritage. Runia examines a selection of key passages from Philo's biblical commentaries and from his other non-exegetical works. Although Philo draws upon the binary contrast of Jew and Gentile, he does so in terms primarily in an allegorical manner: contrasting the good soul with the evil soul. Philo rarely pairs Jew and Gentile as nations or ethnic groups that were in competition with one another.

The sectarian writings among the large corpus of the Dead Sea Scrolls offer a distinctive perspective on the topic. As J. Collins explains, the two branches of the sect represented in the surviving texts seek to separate themselves from other Jews as much as from any non-Jews. Working on the premise that reservation, if not open hostility, should be evident in the depiction of Gentiles, Collins examines two key categories referred to the scrolls, the kittim and the *geruim*. The kittim, foreigners most likely understood to be Romans, act as agents of destruction and will, in turn, also suffer a similar fate. As Collins notes, however, this negative depiction of Gentiles was not necessarily distinctive to the sect. Collins then reviews the presentation of the *gerim* in several of the sectarian texts. There he notes a change in the depiction, especially between CD and 4Q174. While the former appears to allow for the *ger* to be included in the community by the time of the latter text the *ger* are rejected. Collins proposes that the variation is best understood as a change in the attitude over a period of time within the sect. As Collins observes, the presence of even a minor inclusive approach to the place of Gentiles in CD helps affirm that the predominant depiction of Gentiles in the scrolls was negative.

The subject of the next chapter, Josephus, might be expected to be one Jewish writer from the period that would display a constructive attitude toward Gentiles. However, in his discussion of whether or not Josephus respected Gentiles, J. McLaren argues there is no evidence to suggest he did so. McLaren reviews the presentation of Gentiles in two of Josephus' texts, his account of the recent war and in his apologetic defence of the Jewish way of life, and of the occasions where Josephus had direct inter-action with Gentiles during his career. Josephus displays no particular interest or enthusiasm for Gentiles, their customs or their practices. While some Gentiles were depicted in a positive manner it was always in order for Josephus to draw a contrast with his main subject matter, the behaviour of fellow Jews.

Another large, important group of ancient Jewish texts is the apoca-lyptic literature. While clearly written over a long period of time and the work of many different people, there are shared characteristics that warrant considering the attitudes regarding Gentiles in these works as a corpus. M. Theophilos provides a review of passages from seven texts that reveal secrets regarding the future. Conscious of the importance of considering both the literary and the historical contexts in which various allusions to Gentiles occur, he observes a definite pattern: Gentiles will be subject to divine judgment and destruction in the future. In some instances Gentiles act as the agent of divine punishment and are also even capable of participating in the vision of the future restored rule of God. However, any such constructive views are situated in a broader context of punishment and demise.

The next two chapters focus on institutions directly associated with the functioning of communal worship and celebration of the Jewish way of life: the Temple at Jerusalem and synagogues. In Chapter 6, J. McLaren provides a reassessment of the current scholarly consensus that Gentiles were welcome to participate in the sacrificial activities of the Temple. He reviews the available evidence through the lens of what can be gleaned by the actual Temple structure, and goes on to review the function of the Temple as a place of sacrifice, the layout of the Temple, especially in terms of the major development undertaken by Herod, the decisions made regarding activities at the Temple, and examples of Gentiles interacting directly with the Temple. McLaren concludes that Gentiles were not afforded a place or a role in the ritual activity of the Temple. Taking a lead from the recent debate about the existence of God-fearers, D. Binder examines the interaction between Jews and Gentiles in general regarding synagogues. He draws attention to pertinent evidence from literary and epigraphical sources across various parts of the Mediterranean world. He examines the evidence in two basic categories: constructive relations and destructive relations, with the bulk of evidence falling into the former category. Evidence from diverse locations, including Egypt and the Bosporus region, indicates that Gentile authorities supported the existence of synagogues and their role within the functioning of the local community, even to the extent of acting as patrons. In contrast, the examples of destructive interaction noted by Binder are associated with decisions made by specific officials. In effect, the synagogue was a conduit through which Jew and Gentile engaged in public interaction.

The remaining chapters address attitudes associated with people that were directly linked with early Christianity. The first two deal with material from the earliest layers of the tradition, Q and Paul. In Chapter 8, C. Tuckett considers the manner in which the Q tradition refers to Gentiles. Focusing on what is regarded to be the final form of Q, Tuckett commences by reviewing the passages regularly cited as evidence in support of a positive attitude toward Gentiles and their inclusion in the new movement. He contends that those references are somewhat ambiguous in meaning and that, in fact, Gentiles are not really part of the story world of Q. He notes that Q presents a relatively conservative attitude regarding the Law and then comments on the possibility of Gentile believers comprising a small part of the Q community. Tuckett suggests there is insufficient evidence to establish on what basis that participation took place, possibly because it was not yet a matter of discussion or debate. Paul's reputation as 'apostle to the Gentiles' means his writings form another major source warranting examination. In Chapter 9, S. Winter examines a number of what he terms 'descriptive' issues related to Paul's inclusion of Gentiles among the covenant community and related 'explanatory' questions for why he did so. Winter argues that

Paul understood the mission to Gentiles as rooted in the Scriptures of his Jewish heritage. Much of his writing addressed issues pertinent to communities where Gentiles were already in the majority and the issues related to how they might participate in the inheritance of Israel. At the same time, however, Paul was very critical of practices and ideas associated with the Gentile world.

Each of the next four chapters address the attitude toward Gentiles found within the four canonical Gospels. In Chapter 10, I. Elmer examines Mark's Gospel, focusing on the role played by the disciples in the advent of the Gentile mission in Mark 1–8. He explores the meaning of the disciples' call to become 'fishers of people', contending that the phrase had an eschatological, judgment connotation and that the disciples act as a foil to much of what Jesus undertakes in starting the mission to Gentiles. Next, D. Sim provides a detailed critique of the notion that the Gospel of Matthew was largely positive in its attitude toward Gentiles. After briefly reviewing the material normally cited to support the positive outlook, he then discusses five key passages that are critical of Gentiles and examines the manner in which Gentiles are depicted in the Gospel narrative. He comments that ongoing observation of the Torah was essential for anyone who wanted to participate in the community. As such, while some Gentile converts were likely to be part of the Matthean community, it was on the basis that they had become Jews and adopted all the components of the Torah. In the next chapter, E. Dowling examines the presentation of Gentiles in Luke–Acts. Noting that the Gospel openly signals a mission to Gentiles from very early in the story of Jesus, she explores why two key Marcan stories associated with that theme are not used (Mark 7.24-30; 8.1-10). She notes that a major concern of Luke–Acts was to explain how the restoration of Israel formed a key part of the mission to the Gentiles. Working from this basis, Dowling contends that Luke–Acts inserts stories about the restoration of Samaritans as a key step in the process that preceded the mission to the Gentiles. She charts how this is achieved in the narrative of both the Gospel and the story of the work of the followers of Jesus in Acts. In the next chapter, M. Coloe addresses the one Gospel that seemingly offers little direct comment regarding Gentiles, the Gospel of John. Noting the lack of overt interest, Coloe offers a detailed reading of one of the key passages, Jn 12.20. She argues that by reading the reference to the 'Greeks' within a narrative-critical context, including its allusions to earlier biblical traditions, the reference is to the future inclusion of Gentiles within the Christian community. By the time the Gospel was written this mission had already commenced and Gentiles were now part of the community.

The final two chapters offer examples of specific communal contexts where the reality of the Gentile mission and its impact on the nature of the particular community was readily apparent. In Chapter 14, A. Cadwallader considers the situation in Colossae, drawing upon evidence from the epistle and from epigraphical material from the region. He argues that Colossae is a clear example of the shift from a 'Jewish matrix to Gentile dominance'. Noting the use of 'Greek and Jew' (Col. 3.11) rather than the widely attested 'Jew and Greek', Cadwallader examines the regional literary context. He observes how the local population readily placed value on being Greek above and beyond their own cultural heritage. As such, for the early Christian community allegiance to things Jewish was no longer valued as much as things Greek in order to become part of the Roman empire. In the final chapter, J. Draper examines the *Didache*. While precise details about the community responsible for the text are still debated, its purpose was clearly that of a manual. Commencing with the reference to not giving holy things to 'dogs' (*Did.* 9.5), Draper examines the concern for purity within the community. Using Qumran as a point of comparison, he places emphasis on the extent to which the *Didache* community saw itself as holy and the living Temple. As such, the dogs were Gentiles, outsiders that conveyed impurity. He then examines another trajectory preserved through the *Apostolic Constitutions* that indicates openness to Gentile converts, in a manner similar to that portrayed in the Rabbinic tractate *Gerim*.

Chapter 1

GENTILES, GOD-FEARERS AND PROSELYTES

David C. Sim

1. *Introduction*

The related topics of Gentiles, God-fearers and proselytes raise a number of significant issues. These include matters of Jewish identity, the relationship(s) between the Jewish people and the Gentiles, the boundaries that separated these groups, the manner in which outsiders could join the people of Israel and when the process of conversion became possible, and the nature and status of such converts. In this study it will be argued that in very early times conversion to the covenant community of Israel was not possible, but that the barriers between the Jews and Gentiles were relaxed considerably in the post-Exilic era due to the interaction between Judaism and Hellenism. In the late Second Temple period and beyond we find many Gentiles sympathetic to Judaism who followed some Jewish practices and who were closely affiliated with their local Jewish communities. These people are known today by the generic term 'God-fearers', although our sources use other names to identify them as well. The same period also witnessed some Gentiles taking advantage of the relaxation of the boundaries that separated the people of Israel from the other nations, and fully converting to Judaism. The very existence of such converts or proselytes presumes a mechanism by which Gentiles could cross the boundary and become a member of the Jewish people, and the process of conversion will be examined as well. A further issue of interest concerns the Jewish attitude(s) to these proselytes, as well as their status within the people of Israel.

The following analysis will focus largely on the Second Temple period and the relevant sources from that time. At some points, however, reference will be made to later evidence, particularly the Rabbinic literature. While the witness of later sources often confirms or supplements what is revealed in the Second Temple material, it sometimes reveals important developments as well in the topics under review, and some attention will be paid to these. Ancient Judaism was not a static religious tradition, and the subject of Gentiles, God-fearers and proselytes well demonstrates just how flexible and innovative this tradition was in the later Second Temple period and the centuries beyond.

2. *From Exclusion to Possible Inclusion: The Origins of Conversion in Second Temple Judaism*

In the period between the conquest/settlement (however this process is perceived) and the Exile, Israel was a tribal society with each tribal group living within specific boundaries of the promised land. According to ancient tradition, these tribes were descended from the twelve sons of Jacob (Israel). God had delivered the twelve tribes of Israel from oppression in Egypt, entered into a holy covenant with them at Sinai, and then given them the land originally promised to Abraham. In these early centuries membership of the covenant community of Israel was based strictly upon birth within an identifiable kinship group. The people of Israel shared their land with other groups, but they were careful to distinguish themselves from these 'resident aliens' or *gerim* (e.g. Lev. 17.8, 10, 13; 20.2; 22.18).[1] In an attempt to maintain this distinction, the Torah specified that the Israelites were not to intermarry with the seven Canaanite nations among which they lived (Exod. 34.11-17; Deut. 7.3-4), though this seems not to have extended to other nations (cf. Deut. 21.10-14).[2] Yet, even when intermarriage did occur, the offspring were not considered members of the Israelite community for a number of generations and in some cases never at all (Deut. 23.3-8).[3] This manner of identifying an Israelite on the basis of ancestry, kinship and tribal affiliation involved strict boundaries around the covenant community, and essentially precluded the possibility of conversion on the part of outsiders born to other racial groups.[4] The Torah itself reflects this reality by remaining silent on the subject of conversion.

1   See J. Milgrom, 'Religious Conversion and the Revolt Model for the Formation of Israel', *JBL* 101 (1982), pp.169–76 (170–1); and S. J. D. Cohen, *The Beginnings of Jewishness: Boundaries, Varieties, Uncertainties* (Berkeley: University of California Press, 1999), pp.120–1.
2   Cohen, *Beginnings of Jewishness*, pp.243–4, 255–6, 260–1.
3   Donaldson, *Judaism and the Gentiles*, p.486.
4   Milgrom, 'Religious Conversion', p.175; and S. J. D. Cohen, *From the Maccabees to the Mishnah* (Philadelphia: Westminster, 1987), pp.21, 50.

This situation, however, was not to last. The catastrophic events of the Assyrian conquest and deportation of the northern tribes, followed by the later Babylonian victory and deportation of the southern tribes, laid the groundwork for significant changes in Israelite or Jewish self-identification.[5] The original tribal basis structure of society had been seriously ruptured, and those who returned from Babylon placed less emphasis on their tribal ancestry and more on their status as Priests, Levites or (lay) Israelites. Tribal ownership of specific areas was now irrelevant, and this was further emphasised as more and more Jews migrated to areas outside the Israelite homeland. But despite these developments, the entrenched and traditional view of Israelite self-identity proved difficult to move, at least in official circles. In the mid- to late fifth century BCE, both Ezra and Nehemiah were horrified that many Israelite men had married women from foreign nations, and each took steps to force or convince them to send away their wives and children (Ezra 9.1–10.44; cf. Neh. 10.28-31; 13.1-3, 23-37). Even at this stage the national/racial definition of the people of Israel still held sway, and conversion for non-Israelites (or non-Jews) was not an option. Certainly no attempt was made to integrate these woman and children into the covenant community.[6]

This situation probably prevailed for the next two centuries or so. S. J. D. Cohen has argued that in the first half of the Second Temple period the Hebrew term *Yehudi* and the Greek equivalent 'Ιουδαῖος meant not 'Jew' but 'Judean'. This ethno-geographic term denoted either a member of the Judean people living in the traditional homeland or, in the Diaspora, a member of an association of people who originally hailed from Judah. During this period membership of the covenant people of Israel was still exclusively tied to birth and ancestry, and the conversion of other peoples remained impossible.[7] Cohen's analysis is supported by the little extant evidence we possess. No text from this period makes any clear reference to outsiders joining the people of Israel.[8]

---

5   Here I am following Cohen, *Maccabees to the Mishnah*, p.51.

6   So too L. H. Schiffman, *Who Was a Jew? Rabbinic and Halakhic Perspectives on the Jewish–Christian Schism* (Hoboken: KTAV, 1985), p.15.

7   Cohen, *Beginnings of Jewishness*, p.109.

8   It has been suggested that the book of Esther, which can be dated to the fourth century BCE, contains an allusion to Gentile conversion. The Hebrew version of 8.17 states that, after the Jews had been given permission to kill their enemies, many Gentiles declared themselves to be Jews (*mityahadim*) for they were afraid of the Jews. According to L. H. Feldman, this situation involves a conversion to the Israelite or Jewish tradition. See L. H. Feldman, *Jew and Gentile in the Ancient World: Attitudes and Interactions from Alexander to Justinian* (Princeton: Princeton

It is generally agreed that it was the interaction between the Judean tradition and Hellenism that significantly affected Judean self-identification which, in turn, loosened the strict traditional boundaries around the covenant people and paved the way for the possibility of conversion. The conquest of Alexander the Great had introduced the Greek notion of citizenship (*politeia*). Citizenship involved not merely membership in a given state or nation, but also a particular way of life. Alexander and his later successors encouraged non-Greeks to hellenise or to become Greek, which could be achieved by speaking the Greek language, worshipping the Greek gods and fully adopting the Greek lifestyle. In this schema, the emphasis was placed much more firmly on cultural and religious practices than on racial origins. As is well known, many Jews were attracted to Hellenism, while others rejected this path and remained faithful to their Jewish heritage.

But in countering the influence of Hellenism, these traditional Jews were inevitably and significantly affected by it. They saw themselves as citizens of the Judean state with its own distinctive lifestyle based upon the ancient laws of Moses. This attempt to counter Hellenism on its own terms led to a crucial change in Judean self-identification. Citizenship in the Judean state was no longer simply a matter of birth and kinship affiliation. While these elements were retained, greater emphasis was now given to the traditional Judean or Jewish lifestyle that was opposed to the Greek way of living. As a direct result of the opposition to Antiochus IV's enforced hellenising programme, the term 'Ιουδαϊσμός was coined to contrast the Judean or Jewish cultural and/or religious tradition with its Hellenistic counterpart (cf. 2 Macc. 2.21; 8.1; 14.38; *4 Macc.* 4.26). In similar fashion the word 'Ιουδαΐζω came into being to denote the act of living the Jewish lifestyle (Plutarch, *Cic.* 7.6; Esth. 8.17 [LXX]; Josephus, *B.J.* 2.454, 463). At the end of the first century CE, Josephus testifies to this change of stance by stating that the Mosaic tradition involves not simply the matter of birth but lifestyle as well (*C. Ap.* 210). J. M. G. Barclay describes these two factors together as 'ethnicity', a

---

University Press, 1993), pp.289, 337, 343. A better reading, however, is that these Gentiles, on account of their fear, pretended to be Jews. So Cohen, *Beginnings of Jewishness*, p.181; and T. K. Beal, *The Book of Hiding: Gender, Ethnicity, Annihilation and Esther* (London: Routledge, 1997), p.103. When Esther was translated into Greek in the late second century BCE, the text was expanded so that the Gentiles 'were circumcised and judaised' (περιτέμοντο καὶ ἰουδάιζον), a reading followed by Josephus (*A.J.* 11.285). This alteration suggests that the Greek translators understood this event as a true conversion, but by this time conversion to Judaism had become well established.

combination of both kinship and cultural practice.[9] One of the more important repercussions of this development was the relaxation of the boundaries around the covenant people of Israel. Since membership was now largely dependent upon observance of traditional Jewish practices and customs, it became possible to incorporate non-Jews or Gentiles into the Jewish community.[10] One could become a Jew by worshipping the God of Israel, and by following the Jewish way of life as dictated by the Torah.[11]

Precisely when and where this momentous shift occurred is not possible to determine. It was noted above in n. 8 that the Greek version of Esth. 8.17, composed in the late second century BCE, refers to the circumcision and conversion of Gentiles. An even earlier witness appears in the apocryphal book of Judith, which also provides an unambiguous account of a Gentile converting to Judaism. When Judith tells Achior the Ammonite how she beheaded Holofernes, he believed in the God of Israel, was circumcised and joined the house of Israel (14.8-10). The story of Judith, which is set in the time of Nebuchadnezzar, is clearly fictional, but its importance lies in the fact that it takes for granted the possibility of conversion to Judaism. If this text was written in the decades following the Maccabean revolt, then it suggests that conversion to the Jewish tradition had become an accepted practice by the mid-second century BCE. We can assume from this that at least some Gentiles had undergone the conversion process in the preceding decades, though we know nothing about them or the circumstances of their conversion.

The earliest concrete evidence for conversions to Judaism relates to the early Hasmonean period, but there is a discrepancy in our sources as to whether these instances were voluntary or forced. Josephus relates that in 128 BCE Hyrcanus defeated the Idumeans and offered them a choice – either be circumcised and live according to the laws of the Jews or be expelled from their land. The Idumeans agreed to be circumcised and to adopt the Jewish mode of life (*A.J.* 13.257-58). This policy was repeated by Aristobulus some twenty-five years later when he subjugated the Itureans (*A.J.* 13.318). That these conversions were made under extreme pressure is also attested by Ptolomy, whose original text on the history of Herod is no longer extant but who is cited by Ammonius (*De Adfinium Vocabulorum Differentia* 243). By contrast, the Gentile author Strabo, writing perhaps a century before Josephus, suggests that the conversions

9   Barclay, *Jews in the Mediterranean Diaspora*, pp.402–5.
10   Cohen, *Beginnings of Jewishness*, pp.125–9.
11   Cohen, *Beginnings of Jewishness*, pp.132–5.

of the Idumeans and the Itureans were completely voluntary (*Geogr.* 16.2.34; cf. Josephus, *A.J.* 13.319, where Strabo is said to be follow- ing the earlier account of Timagenes). Scholars are divided over which version of events is the more reliable,[12] but this need not detain us here. The important point for our purposes is that these events provide the first concrete historical record of Gentiles joining the people of Israel. The relaxation of boundaries around the covenant community that enabled this to take place would lead to the voluntary conversion of other Gentiles in the ensuing centuries.

3. *God-Fearers*

In the latter part of the Second Temple period, the attitudes of Gentiles to Jews were far from uniform. This applies both to official attitudes and to more popular sentiments. At one extreme of the official level is the action of Antiochus IV and his attempt to enforce hellenisation on the Jews and ban their traditional practices. The opposite end of the spectrum is represented by early Roman policy prior to the Jewish revolt in 66–70 CE. The Jews were granted complete freedom to practise their religion and to conduct their own affairs (cf. Josephus, *A.J.* 14.190-246; 16.162-73; 19.278-91; 20.1-14). But Roman policy was not always beneficent. On three occasions (139 BCE, 19 CE and 49 CE) the Jews were temporarily expelled from Rome, and in 41 CE the Emperor Caligula attempted to have a statue of himself erected in the Jerusalem Temple. At the unofficial level the close-knit Jewish communities were often perceived as misanthropists who despised their Gentile neighbours, and many of their distinctive rituals – especially circumcision, the dietary laws and Sabbath observance – were criticised and ridiculed.[13] These sorts of sentiments, usually allied to other factors, led occasionally to the persecution of local Jewish communities.

---

12   Those scholars who follow the view of Josephus and see the conversions as compulsory include Feldman, *Jew and Gentile*, pp.324–36; Schürer et al., *History*, III.1, pp.207, 217; and M. Goodman, *Mission and Conversion: Proselytizing in the Religious History of the Roman Empire* (Oxford: Clarendon, 1994), pp.75–7. For the alternative position that these Gentile peoples mainly volunteered to convert to Judaism, see Cohen, *Beginnings of Jewishness*, pp.110–19; and A. Kasher, *Jews, Idumeans and Ancient Arabs: Relations of the Jews in Eretz-Israel with the Nations of the Frontier and the Desert During the Hellenistic and Roman Era (332 BCE–70 CE)* (TSAJ 18; Tübingen: Mohr Siebeck, 1988), pp.46–85.

13   See the evidence in Feldman, *Jew and Gentile*, pp.123–76.

But not all Gentiles were negative towards the Jews and their religion. Some admired Judaism for its antiquity, its strict monotheism, its ancient wisdom, its code of morality and the close society of its practitioners.[14] While many of these Gentiles chose to admire the Jewish tradition 'from afar' with little or no formal contact, others opted to seek closer affiliation with the Jews and to make a practical commitment to their religious and cultural tradition. Needless to say, there were varying levels of affiliation and commitment, but for our purposes it is sufficient to distinguish only between the God-fearer (φοβούμενος τὸν θεόν) or God-worshipper (θεοσεβής or σεβόμενος τὸν θεόν) and the full convert or proselyte (προσήλυτος).

God-fearers or God-worshippers were Gentiles who were attracted to Judaism and who made a measure of commitment to the Jewish religion and to their local Jewish communities. Such sympathisers loom large in the Acts of the Apostles, where they act as a bridge between the Jewish and Gentile worlds as the Christian mission expands to incorporate all nations (10.2, 22, 35; 13.16, 26, 50; 16.14; 17.4, 17; 18.7). While it is clear that Luke uses the category of the God-fearer to suit his own theological agenda, there is no necessity to question the very existence of God-fearers or sympathisers to Judaism and view them as a mere Lucan invention.[15] There is plenty of other evidence that confirms the witness of Acts that in the ancient world there were many Gentiles who formed an attachment to Judaism.[16]

14   Feldman, *Jew and Gentile*, pp.177–287.

15   Some scholars, however, have done precisely this. See A. T. Kraabel, 'The Disappearance of the God-Fearers', in J. A. Overman and R. S. MacLennan (eds.), *Diaspora Jews and Judaism: Essays in Honour of, and in Dialogue with, A. Thomas Kraabel* (SFSHJ 41; Atlanta: Scholars Press, 1992), pp.119–30; and R. S. MacLennan and A. T. Kraabel, 'The God-Fearers – A Literary and Theological Invention', in Overman and MacLennan (eds.), *Diaspora Jews and Judaism*, pp.131–43.

16   The scholarly literature affirming and evaluating the evidence for God-fearers is extensive. The most comprehensive treatment is B. Wander, *Gottesfürchtige und Sympathisanten: Studien zum heidnischen Umfeld von Diasporasynagogen* (WUNT 104; Tübingen: Mohr Siebeck, 1998). Other major studies are Feldman, *Jew and Gentile*, pp.342–82; and I. Levinskaya, *The Book of Acts in its First Century Setting. V. Diaspora Setting* (Grand Rapids: Eerdmans, 1996), pp.51–126. Important but shorter analyses include, Schürer et al., *History*, III.1, pp.160–9; Cohen, *Beginnings of Jewishness*, pp.171–4; Donaldson, *Judaism and the Gentiles*, pp.469–82; P. Trebilco, *Jewish Communities in Asia Minor* (SNTSMS 69; Cambridge: Cambridge University Press, 1991), pp.145–66; J. A. Overman, 'The God-Fearers: Some Neglected Features', in Overman and MacLennan (eds.), *Diaspora Jews and*

The tradition in Acts is confirmed by the evidence of Josephus, who states that in Antioch many Gentiles were attracted to Jewish ceremonies and were incorporated with the Jews in some measure (*B.J.* 7.45). In other references he singles out large groups of female sympathisers. At the beginning of the Jewish war many of the women in Damascus became attracted to Jewish ways (*B.J.* 2.560), while in Charax-Spasini large numbers of women became worshippers of God (*A.J.* 20.34). On an individual level, Poppaea Sabina, the wife of Nero, is described by Josephus as a worshipper of God who acted on behalf of the Jews (*A.J.* 20.195), while Philo refers to Petronius, who had learnt some elements of Jewish philosophy and religion and had also assisted the Jewish community (*Legat.* 245). The Roman historian Dio Cassius notes that the Emperor Domitian exiled or executed many people, including the consul Flavius Clemens, because of their atheism, which is described as drifting into Jewish ways (*Hist.* 67.14.1-2). The Gospel of Luke refers to a Gentile centurion who loved the Jewish nation and built the local synagogue (Lk. 7.1-10).

The later Rabbinic literature refers to Heaven-fearers (*yirei shamayim*) and they are often contrasted with full converts (e.g. *Mek. de-Rabbi Ishmael* 18; *y. Meg.* 74a; *Gen. Rab.* 28.5).[17] Other Rabbinic texts prefer the more traditional *ger toshab* to describe the Jewish sympathiser (e.g. *b. Abod. Zar.* 64b-65a). Although there is no consistency of definition, this particular individual was likewise a Gentile who followed some but not all of the Mosaic laws.[18]

Diaspora Judaism in the Rabbinic period also testifies to the existence of Gentile God-worshippers. There are a number of Greek inscriptions that refer to θεοσέβεις, though some of these are difficult to date.[19] The most important of these is the large inscription from Aphrodisias, which is usually dated to the early third century CE. The stele has writing on two of its four sides. One side lists a number of significant donors to the Jewish community, who are described as members of 'the decany',

Judaism, pp.145–52; and J. Reynolds and R. Tannenbaum, *Jews and Godfearers at Aphrodisias: Greek Inscriptions with Commentary* (Cambridge: Cambridge Philological Society, 1987), pp.48–66.

17   For discussion of the relevant texts, see Feldman, *Jew and Gentile*, pp.353–5. Cf. too W. G. Braude, *Jewish Proselyting in the First Five Centuries of the Common Era: The Age of the Tannaim and Amoraim* (BUS 6; Providence: Brown University Press, 1940), pp.137–8.

18   See Feldman, *Jew and Gentile*, pp.353–6; and J. Bamberger, *Proselytism in the Talmudic Period* (New York: KTAV, 2nd edn, 1968), pp.135–8.

19   Feldman, *Jew and Gentile*, pp.358–62. Cf. too Trebilco, *Jewish Communities*, pp.152–64, for discussion of the inscriptions from Asia Minor.

clearly an institution of influence and importance even if its precise meaning is uncertain.[20] This list includes thirteen native-born Jews, three individuals specifically denoted as proselytes, and two who are each described as a God-worshipper (θεοσεβής). The other side of the inscription contains further lists of names, presumably of less prominent contributors to the same cause. It begins with a list of fifty-five Jews followed by the words 'and as many God-worshippers (καὶ ὅσοι θεοσεβῖς), although only fifty-two of these are named.

The degree of commitment to Judaism must have differed from location to location and even from individual to individual,[21] but all of these God-fearers must have had as a bare minimum a belief in the God of the Jews. This may not have been an exclusive belief that rejected the worship of other gods. In fact, the evidence points in the opposite direction. As we shall see shortly, one of the key elements in the process of full conversion to the Jewish tradition was monotheism and the complete rejection of idolatry. This assumes that prior to conversion, the potential convert probably continued to worship other gods in addition to the God of Israel. Further, no fewer than nine of the named God-fearers in the Aphrodisias inscription are described as councillors (βουλευτής), presumably of the city of Aphrodisias. In order to hold this leading civic position, these people must have participated in the local and state cults, and could not have worshipped the Jewish God exclusively.[22] As for the adoption of Jewish practices, our sources provide a good deal of information. The references in Acts spell out that many God-fearers attended the synagogue on the Sabbath (e.g. 13.13-16) and some prayed and gave alms (10.2), and both Philo and Josephus confirm these details and refer to further practices that at least some God-fearers embraced. Philo states that those of virtue in other nations have observed some aspects of the Jewish Law, particularly the Sabbath day and the fast during the Day of Atonement (*Mos.* 2.17-24). In a similar vein, Josephus remarks that many Gentiles have emulated the Jews by observing the Sabbath, fasting, lighting lamps and observing the dietary regulations (*C. Ap.* 2.282-84; cf. too 1.166-67; cf. Juvenal, *Sat.* 14.96-101). In other texts the Jewish historian notes that many of these sympathisers contributed to the payment of the annual Temple tax (*A.J.* 14.110; *B.J.* 2.463).

---

20   The various possibilities are discussed in Reynolds and Tannenbaum, *Jews and Godfearers*, pp.28–38.

21   Reynolds and Tannenbaum, *Jews and Godfearers*, pp.61–2.

22   Goodman, *Mission and Conversion*, pp.117–19. Cf. too Reynolds and Tannenbaum, *Jews and Godfearers*, pp.62–4.

While it is always dangerous to generalise when there is no definitive evidence, it can be assumed that for the most part the Jewish community had a positive view of these God-fearers.[23] Certainly Philo and Josephus are completely positive about these people, and all Jews must have deemed them to be superior to the majority of Gentiles who showed little interest in Judaism or who were critical of the Jews and their religion. In some cases God-fearers were permitted to hold important positions within the local Jewish community. The Aphrodisias inscription cites two God-fearers among the decany, which suggests that they enjoyed some prominence. But despite their close affiliation with Jewish groups and the fact that some could hold prominent positions, these God-fearers had not crossed the boundary that separated Jew from Gentile; they still remained outside the covenant community. The God-fearers always appear at the bottom of the lists in the Aphrodisias inscription, and Josephus emphasises their outsider status when he remarks that the God-fearers in Antioch were incorporated with the Jews only in some measure or to a limited extent.

There is one final point to consider. Did the Jews consider that God-fearer status was in and of itself acceptable for Gentile sympathisers, or did they view it as a preparatory stage towards full conversion? The evidence is meagre, but what exists suggests that God-fearers were not subjected to pressure to convert. While there is a late Rabbinic tradition that affirms that the God-fearer (*ger toshab*) had twelve months to decide whether or not to convert, and if no decision had been made he (or she) would be regarded as an unaffiliated Gentile (*b. Abod. Zar.* 65), there is no evidence that this view was common in Rabbinic circles or elsewhere in the Jewish world at any time. The large numbers of God-fearers compared to the small number of proselytes, implied in Acts and Josephus and corroborated in the Aphrodisias inscription, testifies that most or all Jewish communities were content to accept God-fearers as they were. They perhaps hoped these sympathisers would convert, but they were not obliged to do so.

4. Proselytes and the Process of Conversion

The Gentile who decided to cross the boundary and undergo conversion to Judaism was known in the Greek-speaking world as the proselyte – προσήλυτος. This Greek term is most often the preferred word in the LXX for the Hebrew *ger* or resident alien. Needless to say, the meaning

---

23   Donaldson, *Judaism and the Gentiles*, p.481.

of this word developed over time in accordance with the developments in Judaism, and the writings of Philo provide the earliest extant use of the term in the strict and technical sense of a Gentile convert to Judaism (*Spec.* 1.51-52; 308; *Somn.* 2.273). Later in the first century the Christian literature uses the term with precisely the same meaning (cf. Acts 2.10; 6.5; 13.43; Mt. 23.15)

Once the Jewish tradition had broadened its sense of self-identity to focus on lifestyle more than birth and heritage, the need inevitably arose to establish the mechanism by which Gentiles could join the covenant people of Israel and participate fully in the Jewish religion. The evidence testifies that quite early on Second Temple Judaism developed three definitive steps that were necessary for the process of conversion. These were the exclusive worship of the Jewish God and the complete renunciation of idolatry, full observance of the Mosaic Law as specified in the Jewish Scriptures, and total incorporation into the Jewish community with all the benefits and risks associated with this momentous step.[24] The conversion of Achior mentioned in the post-Maccabean book of Judith mentions these three elements. Achior firmly believed in God, submitted to circumcision in accordance with the Torah and joined the House of Israel. That these three elements remained constant throughout the next few centuries is attested in the writings of the Roman authors Tacitus and Juvenal, who both wrote in the early second century CE. The former states that those who embrace the Jewish way of life undergo circumcision, despise the (Roman) gods and affiliate themselves solely with the Jewish community (*Hist.* 5.5.1-2), while the latter mentions monotheism, observance of the Jewish Law (including circumcision) and hostility towards non-Jews (*Sat.* 14.96-106) The requirement of the rejection of idols and other gods and the exclusive worship of the Jewish deity needs no more discussion, but the other two elements require further attention.

While observing the Mosaic Law in full was obligatory for both men and women, for men this involved the ritual procedure of circumcision of the foreskin. Although practised by other peoples, circumcision was considered in the ancient world by Jew and Gentile alike to be the definitive mark of (male) Jewish identity, and it was a necessary requirement for male Gentile converts to undergo this operation. The necessity of circumcision is attested in the story of Achior in Judith, the Greek text of Esth. 8.17 (see n. 8 above), the writings of Tacitus and Juvenal, and in the conversions of the Idumeans and the Itureans by the Hasmoneans. In

---

24   Cohen, *Beginnings of Jewishness*, pp.156–7; and Donaldson, *Judaism and the Gentiles*, pp.488–9.

addition, Josephus relates that foreign male rulers who wished to marry into the Herodian household were expected to become Jews and be circumcised (*A.J.* 20.139, 145; cf. 16.225). He also recounts the case of the Roman general Metilius at the beginning of the Jewish revolt. Having witnessed the massacre of his soldiers, Metilius begged for mercy and promised to become a Jew by undergoing circumcision (*B.J.* 2.454).

Josephus relates a further interesting case of conversion, that of Izates the king of Adiabene (*A.J.* 20.34-47). Izates wished to convert to Judaism and supposed that to do so he would need to be circumcised. His mother, Queen Helena, though herself a Jewish convert, attempted to dissuade him from this decision on account of her belief that his subjects would not accept his conversion. Izates then consulted Ananias, a Jewish merchant who had taught the king and the royal household about Judaism. Ananias also saw the political complications that such a conversion would bring, as well as the dangerous situation that he would face himself, so he advised Izates that he could worship God without being circumcised and that, given the circumstances, God would forgive him this oversight. The king was later visited by a Galilean named Eleazar who upbraided him for not following what was clearly dictated by the Torah, and Izates finally submitted to circumcision. This episode also attests that circumcision was a necessary requirement for Gentile converts. Izates realises that his full conversion requires this procedure, Eleazar confirms that it is demanded by the Torah, and even Ananias acknowledges that the king must ask for God's forgiveness if he fails to submit to it.

But the case of Ananias does alert us to the fact that under certain circumstances, in this case an extraordinary political situation and a sense of self-preservation, individual Jews might be prepared to relax the requirement of circumcision for converts. Philo provides evidence of others who perhaps shared this view. He refers to some Alexandrian Jews who dismissed physical circumcision in preference to an allegorical understanding of this ritual. Although the subject of converts is not mentioned, it is reasonable to suppose that these Jews would have accepted Gentiles as proselytes without the physical procedure. Philo too accepts the allegorical understanding of circumcision, but he insists nonetheless that the physical aspect is still necessary and must be observed (*Migr.* 89-93).[25]

---

25   See the discussion in J. M. G. Barclay, 'Paul and Philo on Circumcision: Romans 2.25-9 in Social and Cultural Context', *NTS* 44 (1998), pp.536–56 (540–3).

These exceptions to the general rule must be put into proper perspective. Some scholars emphasise these particular cases and infer from them that, although circumcision was the normal requirement for proselytes, there was some diversity within Judaism on this issue.[26] This conclusion, however, exceeds the evidence. It turns these two very rare exceptions, occasioned either by expediency or local ideology, into representative accounts of a wider view within the Jewish tradition. Since these cases are rare and exceptional, most scholars accept that there was no meaningful diversity within Judaism on this issue. Almost every Jew and every Jewish community would have accepted that circumcision was expected of the male proselyte as a necessary condition of membership in the people of Israel.[27] Certainly the later Rabbinic literature prescribes the necessity of circumcision for the male convert.[28] It should be noted that in the ancient world the removal of an adult male's foreskin was a painful and dangerous procedure. In defending the Jewish practice of infant circumcision, Philo explains that men were understandably afraid of this procedure (*QG* 3.48), and it has to be assumed that this ritual requirement prevented many men from the ultimate act of conversion.[29]

In the case of female converts they too were expected to learn and obey the Torah, particularly the rules governing women, but it is unclear whether in the Second Temple period they were required to undergo a formal initiation rite akin to the male ritual of circumcision. Certainly, the little evidence we possess of female conversion makes no mention of one.[30] While Josephus refers to two female proselytes, Queen Helena of Adiabene and Fulvia of Rome (*A.J.* 18.82), in neither case does he elaborate on the precise manner of their conversion. The only detailed

26   For example, see S. McKnight, *A Light among the Gentiles: Jewish Missionary Activity in the Second Temple Period* (Minneapolis: Fortress, 1991), pp.79–82; and T. M. Finn, *From Death to Rebirth: Ritual and Conversion in Antiquity* (New York: Paulist, 1997), pp.94–6.

27   So correctly Cohen, *Beginnings of Jewishness*, pp.124–5, 137–8, 158, 169; Feldman, *Jew and Gentile*, pp.157–8, 298–9, 346, 350–1; Schürer et al., *History*, III.1, pp.169–70; Goodman, *Mission and Conversion*, pp.81–2; Donaldson, *Judaism and the Gentiles*, pp.489–90; and J. Nolland, 'Uncircumcised Proselytes?', *JSJ* 12 (1981), pp.173–94.

28   See Cohen, *Beginnings of Jewishness*, p.219; Braude, *Jewish Proselyting*, pp.75–7; and G. G. Porton, *The Stranger Within Your Gates: Converts and Conversion in Rabbinic Literature* (CSHJ; Chicago: University of Chicago Press, 1994), pp.139–41.

29   Feldman, *Jew and Gentile*, p.328.

30   So Goodman, *Mission and Conversion*, p.62; and Cohen, *Beginnings of Jewishness*, pp.169–70.

account of a female conversion to Judaism in this period is provided by the romantic tale *Joseph and Asenath*, which probably dates to the early first century CE.[31] According to this text, the conversion of Asenath involves the rejection of idolatry and the sole worship of the Jewish God (10.12-13; 11.4-5, 7-9), a long period of sincere repentance (10.1-8, 14-17) and the confession of sins (11.3–13.15). There is no mention of a formal rite of initiation.[32] If it was the case in Second Temple times that Judaism had not developed a formal rite of entry for Gentile women, then this was seen as a serious deficiency by the later Rabbis. By the Talmudic period, woman converts were required to undergo a compulsory rite of immersion (cf. *y. Yebam.* 8d; *b. Yebam.* 46a),[33] perhaps as a necessary purificatory rite to participate in the ritual life of Judaism. Some earlier Rabbinic texts testify that male converts too had to be ritually immersed in addition to circumcision (cf. *Sifre Num. Shelah* 108.2; *b. Ker.* 9a), but the later Talmudim suggest that there were continuing debates as to whether both initiation rites were applicable to male proselytes (cf. *y. Qidd.* 4.7; *b. Ber.* 47b; *b. Yebam.* 46a-b).[34]

The third necessary step in the conversion of the Gentile involved a total integration into the Jewish community.[35] The former Gentile would abandon completely his or her previous social identity and create a new one within the confines of the Jewish world. Philo makes the point that converts are to be praised and respected because they have left their country, friends, family and traditional customs to embrace the superior Jewish way of life. (*Spec.* 1.51-52; 4.178; *Virt.* 102–108, 182). Much of the Rabbinic literature presupposes that proselytes have fully abandoned their former Gentile identity. For example, a convert who died with no Israelite wife or children was deemed to have died without legal heirs; their former Gentile relatives were no longer considered blood relations and were not entitled to inherit.[36]

---

31   R. D. Chesnutt, *From Death to Life: Conversion in Joseph and Asenath* (JSPSup 16; Sheffield: Sheffield Academic, 1995), pp.80–5; and E. M. Humphrey, *Joseph and Asenath* (Sheffield: Sheffield Academic, 2000), pp.28–38.

32   Chesnutt, *Death to Life*, pp.118–50.

33   Porton, *Stranger Within Your Gates*, pp.144–5.

34   On the subject of ritual immersion for male converts in the Rabbinic corpus, see Porton, *Stranger Within Your Gates*, pp.141–8; and Cohen, *The Beginnings of Jewishness*, pp.220–3. These scholars disagree over a number of fundamental points, but these differences need not detain us here.

35   Barclay, *Jews in the Mediterranean Diaspora*, pp.408–10.

36   See Porton, *Stranger Within Your Gates*, pp.21–2, 36–9; and Braude, *Jewish Proselyting*, pp.128–35.

As new members of the covenant community, proselytes were expected to observe all the Torah, and they would be given all the privileges afforded to native-born Jews. According to Cohen, this meant in practical terms that they would be counted as an official member of the synagogue, would be able to partake of sacred meals, would be able to bring legal cases before the local Jewish authorities, would be expected to contribute to the Temple tax, would be allowed to sit with the Jews in the theatre, and would be permitted to be buried with other Jews.[37] The proselytes would almost certainly have moved into the Jewish section of their city to be closer to their fellow Jews and the local synagogue, and many or most would have taken Jewish names, though this practice may have originated after Second Temple times. Josephus give no indication of a change of name in the converts he mentions, and Nicolaus the proselyte referred to in Acts 6.5 still bears a good Greek name. Later sources, however, relate that a change of name was common among converts. The three proselytes mentioned in the Aphrodisias inscription are named Samuel, Joses and Joseph, while the dozens of God-fearers in almost every case have Greek or Latin names.[38] A funerary inscription from Rome refers to a certain Veturia Paulla who took the name Sara upon her conversion.[39] In the Rabbinic literature we find converts named Benjamin (*t. Qidd.* 5.4), Judah (*m. Yad.* 4.4) and Ket'iah ben Shalom (*y. Hag.* 77a; *b. Abod. Zar.* 10b).

We come now to a number of crucial issues. First, what was the Jewish attitude towards proselytes? The early literature is largely uniform in presenting converts in a positive way. Philo, as noted above, takes pains to emphasise that proselytes should be honoured and praised because of the sacrifices they have made, and Josephus shows no negativity towards genuine Gentile converts at all. The author of *Joseph and Asenath* depicts the Egyptian Asenath in an entirely positive fashion. This view is reflected as well in the Rabbinic literature.[40] In the Mishnah Rabbi Joshua accepts an Ammonite for conversion after arguing that the Biblical injunction against the Ammonites (Deut. 23.3) was no longer applicable (*m. Yad.* 4.4), while in *Mek. de-Rabbi Ishmael* 18, Rabbi

---

37   Cohen, *Beginnings of Jewishness*, p.159.

38   See the comprehensive discussion on the names on the inscription by Reynolds and Tannenbaum, *Jews and Godfearers*, pp.93–115.

39   Goodman, *Mission and Conversion*, p.133.

40   For detailed discussion of the relevant texts, see Braude, *Jewish Proselyting*, pp.11–25; and Bamberger, *Proselytism*, pp.149–61. Cf. too the briefer treatments in Porton, *Stranger Within Your Gates*, pp.217–8; and Feldman, *Jew and Gentile*, pp.338–9.

Simeon ben Yohai makes the remarkable claim that converts are more precious to God than native-born Jews. The same text makes the further point that Abraham was circumcised at the age of ninety-nine in order to demonstrate that Gentiles could convert at any age. Other texts affirm this positive view of Gentiles by highlighting that certain distinguished Rabbis were descended from converts (*b. Git.* 56a, 57a; *b. Sanh.* 96b). The acceptance of proselytes is reflected in the tradition attributed to Judah the Patriarch that Gentile converts were not to be reminded of his or her origins (*m. B. Mes.* 4.10; cf. *t. B. Mes.* 3.25; *Sifra BeHar Pereq* 4.2). Further evidence that proselytes were considered favourably is found in the Rabbinic exegesis of the Hebrew Bible, where converts are normally depicted in positive terms and Abraham is considered to the proselyte *par excellence*.[41]

On the other side of the ledger, there are Rabbinic texts that contain less flattering views about proselytes. An extreme position is found in the saying of the fourth-century Rabbi Helbo, which attests that converts should be compared with sores (*b. Yeb.* 47b; *b. Qidd.* 70b). Other opinions are that proselytes bring trouble on those who convert them (*b. Yeb.* 109b) and that they are partly responsible for the delay of the messiah (*b. Nid.* 13a). Some Rabbis believed that Gentiles had an inherently wicked nature that conversion could not eradicate (cf. *Mek. de-Rabbi Ishmael* 18; *b. B. Mes.* 59b). A very late Midrash presents the view that the entrenched wickedness of Gentiles remains in the offspring up to the twenty-fourth generation (*Midrash Ruth Zuta*). While some scholars have tried to alleviate the offensiveness of these views,[42] most others accept them for what they are and conclude that they comprise a minority view within the Rabbinic corpus.[43]

A related issue concerns the status of converts once they had undergone the conversion process and entered the people of Israel. Did their integration into the Jewish community entail equal status with native-born Jews, or were they deemed to be inferior because of their Gentile background? It is perhaps important to note that non-Jews tended to believe that the convert was a Jew in all respects and no different from one who was born into the people of Israel,[44] but what was the Jewish perspective? Philo held the view that the convert was of equal rank and honour with native-born Jews who shared equally all the privileges of the

41   Braude, *Jewish Proselyting*, pp.26–38.

42   Braude, *Jewish Proselyting*, pp.39–48.

43   So Bamberger, *Proselytism*, pp.161–5; Porton, *Stranger Within Your Gates*, pp.218–19; and Feldman, *Jew and Gentile*, pp.339–40.

44   See Cohen, *Beginnings of Jewishness*, pp.159–60.

covenant people (*Spec.* 1.51-53; *Legat.* 211; *Virt.* 102–103), and Josephus presents a similar view (*C. Ap.* 2.209-10).[45] In the Rabbinic literature the opinion is found that the proselyte becomes an Israelite in all respects (*b. Yeb.* 47a-b), and that a convert who renounces the Torah is to be regarded as an apostate Jew rather than as a Gentile (*t. Demai* 2.4). Many Rabbinic texts emphasise the complete transformation of the convert (cf. *m. Git.* 2.6; *y. Nid.* 49b; *y. Yeb.* 6a; *b. Ket.* 28b, 37; *b. Yeb.* 35a), and as many again contain the principle that proselytes are not accountable for their sins prior to their conversion (*y. Bik.* 65c; *y. Qidd.* 58c; *b. Sanh.* 71b; *b. Yeb.* 48b).

Despite these statements affirming equality between the native-born Jew and the proselyte, the practical reality was perhaps somewhat different. Some converts were probably stigmatised about their origins, as the injunctions against this practice imply, and there is a wealth of evidence that converts in general were considered of lesser status than those born as Jews. Even Philo, who is generally positive about proselytes, nonetheless affirms that local Egyptian converts must wait for three generations before full assimilation into the people of God (*Virt.* 107; cf. Deut. 23.8-9). The Christian book of Acts makes a distinction between Jews and proselytes (2.10; 13.43), and in many Jewish traditions they are listed as a particular sub-group within the people of Israel, and more often than not they are ranked near the bottom. An early list at Qumran places in order of importance priests, Levites, Israelites and proselytes (CD 14.3-6),[46] and this is repeated in a later Rabbinic tradition (*t. Qidd.* 5.1). In the lengthy list of categories in *m. Hor.* 3.8, they are ranked second last, coming only before the freed (Gentile) slave, while in *Mek. de-Rabbi Ishmael* 18 righteous proselytes are ranked above God-fearers and repentant (Jewish) sinners, but are still ranked below sinless Israelites.[47] One text goes so far as to say that even in Heaven there will be a distinction between native-born Israelites and proselytes (*y. Hag.* 66a). It is telling as well that Gentile converts often bear the title 'proselyte', which immediately identifies their origins and their different status to those born Jews. We find this title in the reference to Nicolaus the proselyte in Acts 6.5, throughout most of the Rabbinic literature and in the Aphrodisias inscription, which demonstrates that the sharp distinction between the native-born Jew and the Gentile convert was normative for

---

45 Donaldson, *Judaism and the Gentiles*, p.490.
46 Donaldson, *Judaism and the Gentiles*, p.490.
47 It may or may not be coincidental that in the list of seven (Jewish) Hellenists in Acts 6.5 Nicolaus the proselyte comes at the end of the list.

centuries.[48] The practical distinction between these groups is reinforced in a good many Rabbinic texts that maintain that proselytes were governed in some cases by different rules because of their ancestry. These related to a whole host of issues, including prayers, the second tithe and marriage.[49]

Yet, what applied in the Rabbinic world may not have held elsewhere. The three converts mentioned in the Aphrodisias inscription, though identified as proselytes, were all members of the decany. One of them, Samuel, is designated as the president (ἀρχιδέκανος) of that organisation, which means he must have had both status and authority. Moreover, in the list of names of the decany membership, the proselytes are not listed together after the native-born Jews but are rather intermingled with them, which suggests that the ranking reflects social standing rather than racial origins.[50] But this evidence must be approached with caution in terms of the overall status of proselytes at Aphrodisias and elsewhere in the Diaspora. The issues of correct prayer, marriage partners and a host of other matters pertaining to converts must have arisen in any Jewish community that was bound to follow the Torah, and proselytes would doubtless on occasion have been expected to observe rules and interpretations that were inapplicable to those of impeccable Jewish heritage.

5. *Conclusions*

It is clear from the evidence that the religion of Judaism underwent major and definitive changes over the course of many centuries in terms of its self-understanding and its relations with the Gentile world. Initially Israelite religion was tribal and membership in the covenant people was dictated by birth. In this system there was no possibility for outsiders to convert. Yet, there were significant developments in the post-Exilic period. The interaction with and conflict between the Jewish tradition and Hellenism created a new understanding of Jewish identity that still incorporated the aspect of birth or ancestral heritage, but which began to place more emphasis on living the traditional Jewish lifestyle. It was this development more than any other that made the boundaries between Jews and Gentiles more flexible and which effectively enabled the

---

48   Cohen, *Beginnings of Jewishness*, p.161.
49   For a comprehensive discussion, see Bamberger, *Proselytism*, pp.65–110; and Porton, *Stranger Within Your Gates*, pp.155–92.
50   Reynolds and Tannenbaum, *Jews and Godfearers*, p.43.

possibility of Gentile conversion. There is strong evidence that the Jewish communities attracted many followers or God-fearers, who observed some Jewish rites and attended the local synagogue. These God-fearers were not considered converts and still remained outside the people of Israel. Some of these did, however, proceed along the path to full conversion by worshipping exclusively the Jewish God, observing the Torah in full and integrating themselves within Jewish community. While we find in a variety of Jewish sources many statements that these converts or proselytes enjoyed equal status with native-born Jews, the reality was perhaps rather different. The early tradition that sharply differentiated between the people of Israel and Gentiles proved remarkably resilient, and even when the boundaries were relaxed to allow Gentiles to convert, there still remained important distinctions between the native-born and the convert.

Chapter 2

PHILO AND THE GENTILES[*]

David T. Runia

1. *Introduction: Philo in his context*

Philo, the learned and devout Jew from Alexandria, was a slightly older contemporary of Jesus and lived at the same time as the events described in the Gospels. He is thus a valuable witness to the world of Second Temple Judaism and his writings were already used as such by Josephus. This of course is the same epoch out of which the Christian religion grew, meaning that Philo's evidence is also useful for understanding that process. The first church historian Eusebius made a detailed study of the extensive collection of Philo's writings that was available to him in the Episcopal Library of Caesarea. During the past two centuries modern scholars have continued the study of Philo's writings for the under-standing of both Judaism and the New Testament, although it can be argued that he is often taken for granted and is not used nearly enough.[1] It is thus fitting that a collection of essays on the notion of the Gentiles in Second Temple Judaism and Early Christianity should contain a study that focuses on what Philo can contribute to its subject.

For an understanding of Philo's writings and thought it is crucial to recognise that, apart from a significant stay in Rome during his later years, he lived and worked all his life in the multi-ethnic and multi-cultural society of Alexandria, the great metropolis of the eastern

* I wish to express my thanks to David Sim and James McLaren for inviting me to contribute to this study, and in particular to Ellen Birnbaum for invaluable and sage advice on how to tackle the subject. Translations of Philonic texts are my own, but with some debts to those in the Loeb Classical Library edition of Philo's works (see n.16 below). For Septuagint texts I have made use of the New English Translation of the Septuagint (NETS).

1 As argued by A. Terian, 'Had the Works of Philo Been Newly Discovered', *BA* 57 (1994), pp.86–97; G. E. Sterling, '"Philo has not been used half enough": The Significance of Philo of Alexandria for the Study of the New Testament', *PRS* 30 (2003), pp.251–69.

Mediterranean seaboard. Growing up in an immensely wealthy and influential Jewish family, Philo held a leading position in the Jewish community of the city. During the Ptolemaic period the Jewish community had grown in size and influence and been granted the right to run their own affairs. Together with the Greek citizen body and the native Egyptian populace they formed the three main ethnic groups of the city. With the advent of Roman rule in the decade before Philo's birth, the political situation in the city underwent significant change. The Jews lost their protection and during Philo's lifetime tensions mounted between the three ethnic groups, reaching a climax in the riots of 38 CE, which have been called the first anti-Jewish pogrom in history and which led to the Jewish embassy to the Emperor Gaius in Rome that dominated the final period of Philo's life.

Philo was an immensely learned man, with a prodigious knowledge of Greek literature and philosophy, and he placed that learning in the service of his people and his religion. He saw it as his life's task to explain and expound the Jewish Scriptures, which for him were primarily the Pentateuch, the first part of the Septuagint translation produced in Alexandria more than two centuries earlier. His goal was to plumb the depths of the wisdom contained in Scripture and in carrying it out he was certainly influenced by the dominant Hellenised culture of the city in which he lived. At the same time, however, it is important to recognise the strong apologetic motive that underlay all of Philo's intellectual activities. He wished to explain and defend the traditions of his people, showing that if properly understood they were in fact superior to the cultures of the other ethnic groups in the city, including Greeks and Romans.

2. *Subject and Aim of the Present Study*

Philo's profound knowledge of the contents of Scripture will have meant that the notion of 'the Gentiles' (τὰ ἔθνη), the nations other than Israel or the Jews and often standing in opposition to them, cannot possibly have escaped his notice. He would have also been aware that many Jewish speakers and writers took over the term from its scriptural use and employed it in a general way to refer to people not belonging to the Jewish race or nation. Thus, the usage found in the New Testament, for example in the sayings attributed to Jesus in the Gospels (e.g. Mt. 6.32) or in the Pauline epistles (e.g. Rom. 3.29; 11.13), would not have been a surprise to him. But was this a way of thinking and speaking that he himself practised, or did he prefer to approach the question of the relationship between Israel and the Jews on the one hand, and the other nations and peoples on the other, in another way?

It is crucial to our subject to observe that, when we speak of Israel and the Gentiles (or nations) or the Jews and the Gentiles, we are using sets of terms that stand opposed to each other in a binary relationship. One either belongs to Israel or to the Gentiles; one is either Jew or a Gentile. This opposition has strong biblical roots in the opposition ʿam/goyim, or in the opposition between 'people' (λαός) and 'nations', well illustrated by the words of Moses in Exod. 33.16, 'and we shall be glorified, I and your people above all the nations (ὁ λαός σου παρὰ πάντα τὰ ἔθνη) that are on the earth'. The binary nature of these oppositions will be important as we try to understand Philo's conception of how Israel and the Jews relate to other ethnic groups.

The aim of this brief contribution, therefore, is to examine what use Philo made of the notion of the Gentiles and its concomitant terminology. Does it occur in his writings and is it useful when analysing his thought? In the main body of the present study I shall present the evidence on how Philo uses the term and its relation to other terminology used in ethnic contexts. The final part of this study will contain some limited remarks on how Philo expresses the relationship between Israel and the Jews on the one hand and other nations and ethnic groups on the other.[2] At the end I shall make some last remarks on the question of how useful the concept and terminology of 'the Gentiles' are for understanding and expressing Philo's thought.[3]

The term 'Gentile' came into the English language via the Latin word *gentes*, commonly used in the Vulgate, and was greatly popularised in the King James Version, where in the New Testament it is even used to translate 'Greeks' (e.g. Rom. 3.9). It is primarily used to render the term *goyim* in the Hebrew Bible, which is translated τὰ ἔθνη in the Septuagint. It is thus on the term ἔθνος and particularly its use in the plural that we

2   A full examination of this broader and highly complex theme will be beyond the scope of the present analysis.

3   The only scholarly article that directly addresses the question of the 'Gentiles' in Philo's work is N. Umemoto, 'Juden, "Heiden" und das Menschengeschlecht in der Sicht Philons von Alexandrien', in R. Feldmeier and U. Heckel (eds.), *Die Heiden, Juden, Christen und das Problem des Fremden* (WUNT 70; Tübingen: Mohr Siebeck, 1994), pp.22–51. This research formed part of a planned larger study that has so far not been published. After some pertinent remarks on terminology, Umemoto adopts a broader approach to the question than in the present study. For other publications that touch on the question of 'nation' and 'nations' in Philo, see below, Section 4.

need to concentrate. The literal meaning of the term is 'nation', a band or group of people possessing common cultural, religious and linguistic features, and when used in the plural it means 'the nations'. It is this more neutral rendering that I will use in the body of the present study, returning to the term 'Gentiles' at the end of this contribution. The term occurs very frequently in Philo's works. It is about twice as common in the singular (195 examples) as it is in the plural (92 examples).[4] In the singular it most often refers to the Jewish nation. In the plural it is frequently used in general references involving cities, peoples and lands, which are of little interest for our subject. A full lexical analysis of Philo's use of the term is not going to help us very much.[5] What we need to do is examine passages where Philo uses the singular to refer to Israel and the Jews and the plural to refer to nations or peoples other than Israel or the Jews.

In studying Philo's very large body of writings, it is important not to regard them as a single unified block. A century of scholarship has determined that they must be divided into five distinct groups.[6] Of these the first three, which make up the bulk of his writings, are series of commentaries on Scripture. The first is the celebrated Allegorical Commentary, in which the first eighteen chapters of Genesis are interpreted in terms of the history of the soul. The second is the Exposition of the Law, a presentation of the contents of the Pentateuch. It includes the lives of Patriarchs and a detailed examination of the Mosaic Law in the form of both the Decalogue and the Special Commandments organised under the headings of the Decalogue. The third is the Questions and Answers on Genesis and Exodus, a kind of repository of scriptural exegesis presented as in the form of questions on the text. Unfortunately, it has been preserved for the most part only in an Armenian translation. The remaining treatises do not focus directly on Scripture, but consist of a number of apologetic treatises that discuss contemporary issues such as

4   Besides ἔθνος, Philo also uses the biblical term λαός, but less frequently than ἔθνος. It occurs 90 times in his work, most often in biblical quotations and set phrases such as the Homeric ποιμένες λαῶν. He almost never distinguishes between the two terms. An exception is at *QG* 4.157, as noted by E. Birnbaum, *The Place of Judaism in Philo's Thought: Israel, Jews, and Proselytes* (BJS 290; SPM 2; Atlanta: Scholars Press, 1996), p.56 n.90. See also my comments on *Mos.* 1.290-91 in Section 3 below.

5   For some statistics, see Umemoto, 'Juden, "Heiden" und das Menschengeschlecht', p.23.

6   On Philo's writings and their division into groups, see J. R. Royse, 'The Works of Philo', in A. Kamesar (ed.), *The Cambridge Companion to Philo* (Cambridge: Cambridge University Press, 2009), pp.32–64.

the pogrom in Alexandria and the embassy to Rome, and a number of purely philosophical treatises focusing on subjects of interest to Jewish thinkers.

3. *Some Philonic Passages*

We begin with the biblical commentary that always stands first in editions and translations of the Philonic corpus, the great Allegorical Commentary on Genesis, commencing at Gen. 2.4.[7] Although in the main biblical text that he is commenting on there is no substantial reference to 'nation' or 'nations' until Genesis 12,[8] Philo, following his usual method, introduces other biblical texts in his commentary. So at *Post.* 89-93 he cites the key text Deut. 32.7-9; 'Ask your father and he will inform you, your elders and they will tell you. When the Most High was apportioning nations, as he scattered Adam's sons, he fixed boundaries of nations according to the number of God's angels. And his people Jacob became the Lord's portion, Israel a measured part of his inheritance.' Philo does not think the literal meaning makes a lot of sense. What can our fathers tell us about how God scattered or settled the nations? It is best to allegorise: the father of our soul is right reason and the elders are its associates. They together fixed the boundaries of virtue and to them we must go for learning and teaching. God has dispersed the nations of the soul[9] and banished the sons of the earth (i.e. Adam),[10] but he fixed the boundaries of the offspring of virtue and made them equal in number to the angels, who are identified with the words of God. The second mention of 'nations' in the biblical text is explicitly identified with 'species of virtue'. These particular virtues become the portion of the angels, but the portion of God the leader is the chosen race (τὸ ἐκλεκτὸν γένος) of Israel, allegorised as the genus of virtue. The passage is complex, but it is clear that the contrast between the nations and Israel is given a deeper meaning in terms of philosophical allegory involving

---

7   It should be noted that *De Opificio Mundi*, which stands at the beginning of almost all texts and translations, in actual fact belongs to another commentary, the Exposition of the Law.

8   The only earlier references are in Gen. 10.5, 20 and 31. Though Philo quotes the first of these texts in *QG* 2.80, he ignores its mention of the 'nations'.

9   The reference here in *Post.* 91 is to the scattering of the nations in the Tower of Babel episode in Gen. 11, which Philo also allegorises in *Conf.* and elsewhere.

10   In *Congr.* 58 only this part of the text is cited and the sons of Adam are allegorised in terms of earthly ways of thinking (*tropoi*).

the life of the soul, in effect completely altering the biblical notion of a 'chosen race'.[11] In *Plant.* 58-60 the same biblical passage is again allegorised. The 'selected portion' (ἐξαίρετος κλῆρος) of God the universal Ruler is bestowed on the band of souls who possess the sharpest vision, a clear reference to Philo's usual etymology of Israel as 'he who sees God'. In contrast, the 'sons of Adam' are the children of the earth, a mob who are unable to follow the guidance of right reason. Here too the contrast between Israel and the nations is wholly subsumed under the allegory of the soul.

The first mention of a special *ethnos* occurs in Gen. 12.2, when God promises Abraham that he will make him into a 'great nation'. Philo reaches this text in his commentary at *Migr.* 53-61. The gift described in the text is interpreted as progress in the principles of virtue, with 'nation' indicating a large number and 'great' their improvement in quality. But Philo does not just have some kind of philosophical ethics in mind; 'The greatness and multitude of what is good and noble[12] has as its beginning and end the continual recollection of God and the summoning of assistance from him to oppose the native and confused and never-ending warfare of life' (56). Philo then quotes Deut. 4.6-7, in which 'this great nation' is called 'a wise and knowledgeable people' because it has God drawing near to it. But who are those worthy to receive these gifts? The text makes it clear that it is all lovers of wisdom and knowledge. Then, in a move that seems to contradict the original main text, Philo states that what is good and noble is in fact a rare commodity and he quotes another scriptural text, Deut. 7.7-8: 'It was not because you are more numerous than all the nations that the Lord chose and selected you – for you are very few in comparison with all the nations, but rather because the Lord loved you'. This text too is applied allegorically to the soul (60). The nations represent the crowd of passions and wickedness in the soul, as opposed to the one well-ordered rank, led by right reason. In the judgment of human beings the unjust multitude is preferred to the single just person, but in God's judgment the scarce good is preferred to the myriad unjust. Here again we see that Philo cites a key Pentateuchal text on the election of Israel over against the nations. He retains the binary contrast, but it is made between two ethical and religious categories, not between ethnic groups, whether in the past or in the present.

It is worth pointing out that in the entire Allegorical Commentary, which consists of twenty-one treatises, there is not a single reference to the Jewish nation. It is Israel that holds centre stage, interpreted as the

11   On this important passage, see further Birnbaum, *Place of Judaism*, pp.137–8.
12   I follow the LCL in translating τὰ καλά in this broad ethical sense.

person or the collective body of those 'who see God'. There can hardly be any doubt that there is a close link with contemporary Jews, for it is they who study the Scriptures and it is surely for well-informed members of the Jewish community that Philo is writing his allegories. Yet, as the text in *De Migratione Abrahami* makes clear, it is by no means certain that it is only the Jews who belong to the spiritual entity that is Israel. This is the conclusion reached by E. Birnbaum in her important monograph in which she carefully examines all the texts in which Philo speaks of Israel.[13]

The next major Commentary that I wish to discuss, the *Quaestiones et Solutiones in Genesis* and *Quaestiones et Solutiones in Exodum*, differs in its form quite markedly from the Allegorical Commentary, but in terms of its contents there is considerable overlap. In posing questions raised by the biblical passages in sequence, Philo almost always cites the text either in part or as a whole, and then proceeds to give both a literal and an allegorical interpretation. In at least seven chapters of the work Philo cites texts that speak of 'nations' and then generally gives an allegorical interpretation,[14] each differing from the other, whether it be in terms of 'inclinations' or 'evils', or 'senses and passions', or 'opinions' or 'encyclical studies'.[15]

Two passages that have been taken to refer to 'Gentiles' deserve closer examination. In *QG* 3.60, while interpreting Gen. 17.21, 'and my covenant I shall establish with Isaac, whom Sarah shall bear at this season in the other year', Philo comments on the second part of the text: 'Most wisely…it is said that "in the other year" she will bear Isaac, for that birth is not one of the life of the present time, but of another great, holy, sacred and divine one, which has an abundant fullness and is not like that of the nations'. The parallel text at *Mut.* 267 indicates that Philo is alluding to an interpretation in terms of the concept of αἰών, usually but probably erroneously translated 'eternity'.[16] R. Marcus, who translates

---

13   See Birnbaum, *The Place of Judaism*, pp.61–159, and her conclusions at pp.221–4. On p.222 she notes that Philo generally refers to Israel as a 'kind' (γένος) rather than a nation.

14   *QG* 2.80 (Gen. 10.2-5); *QG* 3.17 (Gen. 15.19-21); *QG* 3.42 (Gen. 17.3-4); *QG* 3.44 (Gen. 17.6); *QG* 3.59 (Gen. 17.20); *QG* 4.183 (Gen. 26.4); *QE* 2.22 (Exod. 23.27b).

15   *QG* 3.42; 3.17; 4.183; 3.44; 3.59, respectively.

16   On the concept of αἰών in Philo, see H. M. Keizer, 'Life Time Entirety: A Study of ΑΙΩΝ in Greek Literature and Philosophy, the Septuagint and Philo' (PhD diss., Amsterdam, 1999). She argues that the term is best translated 'the entirety of time'.

the final phrase 'not like that of the gentiles', indicates that the Greek is (τῶν ἐθνῶν) and comments: 'Philo does not often use ἔθνη in the biblical sense of "gentiles"'.[17] But is the translation appropriate in this case? It would seem that the mention of τὰ ἔθνη is prompted by the 'twelve nations' in the previous verse. Implicitly, Philo is asking why Isaac's time of birth is specified, but that of the twelve nations is not. To invoke a biblical notion of 'gentiles', as Marcus does, is misleading. The use of the term is quite specific to the particular exegetical context.

In the second text, *QE* 2.22, Philo asks the meaning of the words in Exod. 23.27b: 'I will confound all the nations into which you will come'. The entire passage of vv. 22-29 emphasises how, if the people (of Israel) serve the Lord and do not serve other gods God will drive out the various nations that are referred to by name in the text. It is quite striking how in the entire section dealing with this passage, *QE* 2.16-25 Philo at no stage draws attention to the promised special status of Israel (v. 22, 'a people special above all nations', 'a royal priesthood and a holy nation').[18] The passage discussed in 2.22 is the only one that speaks of the 'nations' in general. As part of his literal explanation Philo answers that God 'seems to bear testimony to the surpassing virtue of the nation in that it would convert not only its own members but also its enemies; and by "enemies" I mean not only those who commit acts of war but also those who are heterodox'. The term ἑτερόδοξοι is unusual in Philo, but here seems to combine both religious/ethnic and philosophical connotations.[19] But then Philo adds – in Marcus' translation – a 'deeper meaning', 'when there comes into the soul, as into a land, the prudence of a keen-eyed and seeing nature (i.e. Israel), all the Gentile laws which are in it become mad and rage and turn aside from worthy thoughts, for evil things are unable to dwell and live together with good ones'. The interpretation of the 'nations' in terms of evil thoughts coheres with Philo's usual allegorical schemes. But the reference to 'all the ethnic laws' (πάντες οἱ ἐθνικοί νόμοι, to judge by the Armenian) is unusual.[20] It may be prompted by the emphasis in the biblical passage on serving the God of

17   R. Marcus, in F. H. Colson, J. W. Earp, R. Marcus and G. H. Whitaker, *Philo of Alexandria* (10 vols. and 2 supplementary vols.; LCL; Cambridge, MA: Harvard University Press, 1929–62), Suppl. vol. I, p.263.

18   This passage is only found in the LXX, not in the MT (it is a doublet of Exod. 19.5-6). Philo cites the latter phrase in *Sobr.* 66 and could have derived it from either location.

19   Cf. *QE* 2.47, but there it is part of the allegorical explanation.

20   The adjective ἐθνικός is found only in *Mos.* 1.69 and 188, both with reference to the Hebrew nation.

Israel rather than the gods of the nations, which Philo translates into
doctrines of piety or impiety (cf. 2.26). Here too Marcus's rendering with
'Gentile' instead of 'ethnic' seems unjustified. The contrast is between
Israel and the other nations. As we also saw in the Allegorical Commentary, there is no attempt to specify the explanation in terms of contemporary relations between Jews and other nations. The only reference to the
Jews in this work, it would seem,[21] is at *QG* 3.48, where Philo notes that
not only the Jews practise circumcision, but also the Egyptians, Arabs
and Ethiopians and all those who live near the torrid zone.

Philo's remaining great commentary on Scripture, traditionally known
as the Exposition of the Law, is a very different work from the two previous ones. It is generally recognised that when compiling it Philo had a
different audience in mind. In the case of the two other commentaries
their readers would have needed to be initiated into the complexities of
the allegorical interpretation of Scripture in order to benefit from them.
They are works for 'insiders'. The Exposition of the Law employs a
more didactic method, taking care to explain key concepts of the Jewish
religion as it goes along. Philo has 'outsiders' in mind as at least part of
the readership of the work, whether these be non-Jews unfamiliar with
the Jewish sacred writings or members of the Jewish community who
wished to be better informed about their religious heritage. A key
indicator for the difference in purpose and audience is the terminology he
uses for his references to Jews and non-Jews.[22]

The first reference to 'nation' or 'nations' in the Exposition is at *Abr.*
56-57. Summarising the history of humanity so far, Philo states that
Noah was the father of a new race (γένος) of humans, but that the three
Patriarchs Abraham, Isaac and Jacob were the parents of a species of that
race, which is called 'a royal priesthood and a holy nation' (Exod.
19.6).[23] He adds that the special status of this nation is shown by its name
'Israel', explained as 'he who sees God'. Apart from a reference to Jacob
being named Israel at *Praem.* 44, this is the only time that Philo speaks
about Israel in the entire work. The Exposition is much more ethnocentric in its terminology than the two other commentaries. There are
countless references to 'the nation' and quite a few to 'the nation of the
Jews'.[24] In this work Philo assumes a direct continuity between the nation

---

21   Marcus notes that the Armenian term renders 'Hebrews', but it is likely that
the original had 'Jews'.
22   As argued by Birnbaum, *The Place of Judaism*, pp.25–9, 221–2.
23   See the discussion above at n.17.
24   *Decal.* 97; *Spec.* 2.163, 166; 4.179, 224; *Virt.* 212, 226.

described in the Pentateuch and the contemporary nation of the Jews. The key to this continuity is the Jewish observance of the Law revealed to Moses. That nation has a special status. 'Of nations', Philo writes, 'it is the one dearest to God (ἐθνῶν τὸ θεοφιλέστατον), which in my view has received the gift of priesthood and prophecy on behalf of the entire human race' (*Abr.* 98).

Apart from very general references such as the one just cited, there are only a few that mention 'nations' in the plural. In telling the story of the *Aqedah*, the attempted sacrifice of Isaac, Philo responds to critics who say there was nothing remarkable about Abraham's intended action. Greeks and barbarian nations, including the Indian gymnosophists, have done the same (*Abr.* 180-81). We have here the familiar categories of Hellenistic ethnography, to which we shall return. In a subsequent passage at *Spec.* 3.110-11 he discusses the practice found 'in many other nations' of exposing infants. This is condemned as being against the Mosaic Law. At *Spec.* 4.176-81, as part of a special section devoted to justice, Philo is proud to say that God reserves for himself the dispensation of judgment to the guest, the orphan and the widow (Deut. 10.18). Indeed, the whole Jewish nation might be regarded as having the position of an orphan when compared to all the other nations. In their case, if disasters strike, they may receive assistance through their international networks (διά τὰς ἐν τοῖς ἔθνεσιν ἐπιμιξίας). Yet, because the Jews live under exceptional laws, they lack help, and so the Ruler of the universe took pity on its orphaned state and made it his portion. There is an echo here of Deut. 32.7-9, the same text which Philo used in the Allegorical Commentary.[25] It is applied directly to the Jewish nation. In *De Praemiis et Poenis*, the book that concludes the Exposition, Philo gives an account of the rewards and blessings that the nation will receive from God if they fulfil the Law, as well as the punishments if they do not. One of the blessings will be the absence of war, or if it does occur, the enemy will be destroyed to a man. Philo cites from the prophecy of the seer Balaam that 'there will come forth a man' (Num. 24.7) who will subdue great and populous nations with God's aid. The passage presents biblical exposition and no link is made to the Jews' contemporary situation.[26]

---

25   See above on *Post.* 89-91, *Plant.* 58-60.

26   This account of rewards and punishments in *De Praemiis et Poenis* (and the text in *Mos.* 1.278-91 about to be discussed) is the closest that Philo gets to what might be called an eschatology. It is based on Pentateuchal texts and remains rather vague. See further P. Borgen, '"There Shall Come Forth a Man": Reflections on Messianic Ideas in Philo', in J. H. Charlesworth (ed.), *The Messiah* (Minneapolis: Fortress, 1992), pp.341–61.

The same theme and text also occur in *De vita Mosis* 1–2, Philo's biography of the Jewish lawgiver. The majority of scholars agree that the biography of Moses is not an integral part of the Exposition of Law, but is meant as a general introduction either to all the exegetical works or more specifically to the Exposition.[27] Like the Exposition, this treatise is very ethnocentric. Philo generally refers to the people of Israel as 'the Hebrews' (never Israel) and explicit connections are made with the situation of contemporary Jews in Alexandria. In the long section devoted to the Balaam episode, the prophet is said to declare (1.278): 'I would not be able to harm the people (λαόν) who live on their own and are not counted with other nations (ἑτέροις ἔθνεσιν), not through a difference of location or a severance of land, but in virtue of the peculiar nature of their separate customs'. He then (1.290-91) paraphrases Num. 24.7: a man will come forth who will exert power over many nations (ἔθνη); this people (λαός) has had God as its guide and 'it will devour the many nations (ἔθνη) of its enemies' (quotation of Num. 24.8). We have here a clear opposition between the Hebrews and the other nations, and unusually Philo appears to use the terminological distinction between the terms 'people' and 'nations' to express it.[28] In the second book Philo talks at some length about the Mosaic Law. Not only the Jews but almost all other people admire it. Throughout the world of Greeks and barbarians virtually every city and nation reject foreign institutions, but they are attracted to the Jewish laws (2.17-20, 25). A few pages later, however, Philo has to admit, somewhat contradictorily, that at present his own nation is not flourishing. Yet if their fortunes took a turn for the better, he claims, then others would abandon their own ancestral customs and honour the Jewish laws alone (2.43-44).

Finally we should say a few words about Philo's non-exegetical works. For the most part these are apologetic in intent, presenting and defending various aspects of Jewish life and thought. The best known are the two which describe the events that befell the Jews in Alexandria in 38–40 CE, *In Flaccum* and *Legatio ad Gaium*. It is very likely that these treatises were written at about the same time as the Exposition of the Law.[29] Like that work they are very ethnocentric, but instead of focusing on the Law in a fairly abstract way, they vividly describe current events

27   According to Royse, 'The Works of Philo', p.51, it belongs to the apologetic and historical works, though differing because it treats the distant past. Its exegetical basis brings it closer to the exegetical works.

28   It is remarkable that Philo never cites classic texts in Exodus in which this distinction is made: 19.5; 23.22a and 33.16.

29   As indicated by the famous autobiographical passage at *Spec.* 3.1-6, that is, midway through writing the Exposition.

and the anguish of the Jewish people and their leaders (of whom Philo was one). In both works the doctrine of divine Providence is central. At the beginning of *Legatio ad Gaium*, in a famous passage (1-7), Philo introduces Israel as the race that the Father and king of the universe has taken for his portion. The reference to Israel is unique in Philo's apologetic words and recalls the single passage in the Exposition at *Abr.* 56-57. Elsewhere he speaks frequently of the Jews and also of the Jewish nation (e.g. at *Flacc.* 170; *Legat.* 210). Particularly telling are the final words of both treatises. At *Flacc.* 191 he concludes that the Egyptian governor's grim fate was 'indubitable proof that the Jewish nation was not deprived of the assistance that God can give'. In *Legat.* 373 he states that 'a summary account has been given of the cause of the hatred that Gaius had towards the entire nation of the Jews'.

In a few passages in *Legatio ad Gaium* Philo also speaks of other nations. The emperor despised the Jews, because they alone opposed him on principle when he wished to receive the honours due to the gods. All other men, women, cities, nations, countries, regions of the earth, although they groaned at what was happening, nevertheless flattered him and worshipped him beyond what was appropriate. Only the nation of the Jews stood apart, for they were prepared to accept death rather than submit to destroying any of their ancestral traditions (115-17). What a contrast Gaius' behaviour formed with that of the emperor Augustus, who 'brought civilisation and harmony to all unsociable and beastlike nations, enlarged Greece with many a new Greece and hellenised the barbarian world in its most essential regions' (147). In this generalising context, without specific reference to the Jews, Philo again uses the conventional classical antithesis between Greece and the barbarian nations. Alarmed by the violation of the Temple proposed by Gaius, the body of Jewish elders speed to the Governor of Syria, Petronius, and supplicate him to allow them to send an embassy to the emperor: 'Perhaps…we will persuade him…not to treat us worse than all the other nations – even those in the most distant parts – who have preserved their ancestral customs' (240). The argument is that Jews should be set alongside the other nations who also have their own laws and they beg to receive the same treatment.

4. *How Philo Speaks about Nations and Ethnic Groups*

The selection of Philonic passages we have discussed is sufficient to allow us to draw some conclusions on how Philo speaks about the various ethnic groups in his world, his own Jewish people on the one hand and the broad spectrum of nations both in Scripture and in the Greco-Roman world on the other.

It has emerged that there is a clear division that runs through the entire corpus of Philo's writings. When he is expounding Scripture for an internal audience of readers with a deep knowledge of scriptural and Jewish traditions, Philo focuses on the concept of Israel, the spiritual entity of those 'who see God', who have an understanding of the one true God and of the religious and ethical way of life that flows on from that knowledge. As E. Birnbaum has shown in detail in her monograph on the subject, Israel cannot simply be equated with the Jewish people. It is a broader concept. Because its 'membership requirement' is the ability to see God, it appears to include not only Jews but also, it seems, non-Jews, such as Persian Magi and other unnamed sages from Greek and foreign lands.[30] Philo at all times remains quite vague about who can be reckoned to belong to this group. It is thus significant that in his more 'esoteric' writings Philo never speaks about the 'Jewish nation' and never addresses the question of the relation between Israel and the Jews. On the other hand, in his writings for 'outsiders', whether less well-informed Jews or non-Jewish readers, Philo (with the two exceptions noted above[31]) does not speak of Israel. Instead, both in his Exposition of the Law and in his more overtly apologetic treatises, he very frequently refers to the 'Jews' and quite often to the 'Jewish nation'. The reader of these works is left in no doubt that there is a direct connection between being a Jew (or a proselyte who has been welcomed into the Jewish fold) and following the ancestral customs of the nation as enshrined in the Mosaic Law of Scripture.

In the more 'esoteric' writings Philo regularly cites texts which make reference to Israel and 'the (other) nations'. We saw that in many, if not most, cases they are allegorised in terms of the history of the soul (or the sage) who makes progress towards virtue and the knowledge of God. The chosen 'nation' is the noble soul, the 'nations' represent various allegorical figures or entities. Some of these are troublesome and have to be overcome, such as evil inclinations or passions or the diverting senses; others are more neutral, such as opinions and encyclical studies that the soul meets on its path. In the case of an exegesis of Deut. 32.7-9, the 'nations' are even allegorised as 'species of virtue', as opposed to Israel as the generic form. Philo's allegories certainly very often have a binary structure, opposing the good and noble soul (or person) against the evil

---

30   Birnbaum, *The Place of Judaism*, p.224.
31   *Abr.* 56 and *Legat.* 4.

soul (or person), and this structure can sometimes be sensed in his treatment of the 'nation' versus the 'nations' as they appear in Scripture, without there ever being a direct equivalence between them.

It is thus primarily in the more exoteric and explicitly apologetic works that we find copious references to the Jewish nation and the other nations that constituted the ethnic map of Philo's world. It is quite striking that when wishing to speak of humanity in very general terms,[32] Philo most often uses the conventional hellenising categorisation of 'Greek and barbarians', and so also 'Greek and barbarian nations' (*Cher.* 91; *Plant.* 67; cf. *Abr.* 191; *Legat.* 147). Very recently K. Berthelot has analysed Philo's use of this conventional categorisation in a fine article.[33] She concludes that, contrary to what we might expect, Philo never includes the Jews among the barbarian nations, even though their original language is non-Greek.[34] Jews are to be placed on the Greek side of the equation. No doubt Philo is encouraged to do this because his own social group of upper-class Jews in Alexandria spoke Greek and in some cases even possessed Alexandrian citizenship. Indeed, as Berthelot points out, Philo even claims that the Jews are older than the Greeks, and that the latter are indebted to Moses for some of their key philosophical doctrines.[35] The other group that falls outside the categorisation are the Romans, who just before Philo's birth became absolute rulers of Egypt. As M. Niehoff has pointed out,[36] Philo sees important affinities between the Jews and the Romans. But it is to be agreed with Berthelot that, in Philo's eyes, the two nations are competing for the same space, albeit

32   These also include some general references in Allegorical Commentary and the *Quaestiones*.

33   K. Berthelot, 'Grecs, Barbares et Juifs dans l'œuvre de Philon', in B. Decharneux and S. Inowlocki (eds.), *Philon d'Alexandrie. Un penseur à l'intersection des cultures gréco-romaine, orientale, juive et chrétienne* (Monothéismes et philosophie 12; Turnhout: Brepols, 2011), pp.47–61.

34   E. Birnbaum points to a possible exception at *Mos.* 2.27 (part of the passage discussed in Section 3), where she remarks that the translation of the Jewish laws was undertaken so as not to restrict the laws only to the barbarian or non-Greek part of the world; see E. Birnbaum, 'Philo on the Greeks: A Jewish Perspective on Culture and Society in First-Century Alexandria', in D. T. Runia and G. E. Sterling (eds.), *In the Spirit of Faith: Studies in Philo and Early Christianity in Honor of David Hay (= The Studia Philonica Annual 13 [2001])* (BJS 332; Providence: Brown University Press, 2001), pp.37–58 (47).

35   Berthelot, 'Grecs, Barbares et Juifs', p.52.

36   M. R. Niehoff, *Philo on Jewish Identity and Culture* (TSAJ 86; Tübingen: Mohr Siebeck, 2001), esp. pp.6–13, 111–36.

from very different vantage-points.[37] Both claim a very special status, with universalist pretensions. The Romans dominate the world politically. The Jews would dominate the world culturally and religiously, if the uniqueness of their God and the superiority of their laws and customs were finally to be recognised.

All these apologetic considerations belong to what K. Goudriaan has most aptly called Philo's 'ethnical strategies'.[38] He is writing in an environment in which there are considerable tensions between the three main ethnic groups in Alexandria, Greeks, Jews and Egyptians, with the Romans exercising absolute power from above.[39] As we just saw, when speaking in the most general terms Philo uses the conventional Greek method of ethnical categorisation. Yet Goudriaan rightly emphasises that this does not mean in the least that Philo does not see an opposition between Jews and all other nations or peoples. It is in fact all-pervasive, certainly in the half of his writings that have a more overt apologetic intent.[40] The Jews are set apart from all other nations in two respects, the one religious and the other cultural. The unique God whom the Jews worship (but who is also recognised by the practitioners of the most reputable philosophy[41]) has chosen them as his portion and appointed them the suppliant race on behalf of all humankind. Their laws and customs are truly superior, although this is not (yet) universally recognised. Philo feels a strong obligation to expound the Law to both Jews and outsiders who are unaware or need to be persuaded of its superiority. He also addresses the current situation of the Jews in Alexandria, attempting to show how contemporary events confirm the special status of the Jews through the workings of divine Providence.

We may conclude, therefore, that Philo, when speaking about 'nation' and 'nations', works with three separate pairs of binary opposites: Israel versus 'nations', Greeks versus barbarians, and Jews versus all other nations. The first is almost always used in exegetical and philosophical contexts. Israel is a spiritual category with some universalist features.

---

37   Berthelot, 'Grecs, Barbares et Juifs', p.53.

38   K. Goudriaan, 'Ethnical Strategies in Graeco-Roman Egypt', in P. Bilde, T. Engberg-Pedersen, L. Hanestad and J. Zahle (eds.), *Ethnicity in Hellenistic Egypt* (SHC 3; Aarhus: Aarhus University Press, 1992), pp.74–99 (79–86).

39   On the important role of the Egyptians, both in Philo's exegesis and in his contemporary situation, see S. J. K. Pearce, *The Land of the Body: Studies in Philo's Representation of Egypt* (WUNT 204; Tübingen: Mohr Siebeck, 2007).

40   Although Goudriaan's analysis in 'Ethnical Strategies' is excellent, he fails to take sufficient account of the different kinds of exegetical works in Philo's *œuvre*.

41   See especially the well-known text at *Virt.* 64-65.

It appears not to be confined to the Jewish nation, but may include thinkers who are able to contemplate God. The second is a very general and non-controversial way of categorising ethnic groups, leaving the special status of Jews and Romans unstated. As Goudriaan remarks, Philo avoids a direct opposition between Jews and Greeks.[42] The third opposition is crucial to Philo's apologetic strategy and dominates his thinking when he looks at the place of the Jewish nation in its contemporary situation.

There are a number of scattered texts in which Philo expresses an opposition between Jews and others and between the Jewish nation and other nations. We have cited some of these in the key passages discussed above. But in spite of the importance of the binary categories of Jews and non-Jews for his thinking, Philo in fact does not have anything like a fixed terminology for this opposition. As we just saw, it is not captured by the formulas opposing either Greeks and barbarians or Jews and Greeks. There is no equivalent in his writings for the opposition *'am/goyim* in the Hebrew Bible or the opposition Jew/Gentile in the New Testament. The remarkable conclusion which the evidence constrains us to reach is that, although the binary opposition of Jew and non-Jew is certainly central to his thinking in the religious, political and cultural domains, he has not developed a clear and constant terminology to express it.

This absence is surprising and even counter-intuitive. If we should look for reasons for it, I would argue that these will have been both theoretical and strategic. It is clear that Philo has been impressed, seduced if you will, by the cosmopolitan strain that runs through Greek philosophy, and that it leads to tensions within his work. As we saw, Philo does not confine knowledge of the one God to the Jewish religion, in spite of the special status that he, following Scripture, accords to the Jewish nation. He keeps the contours of the spiritual category of Israel, which encompasses those people who are able to see the God who *is*, deliberately vague, but it appears to be larger than the Jewish people and thus may also include non-Jews. To illustrate this, we can cite a striking text from an overtly apologetic treatise, *De vita contemplativa*. Its main aim is to describe the community of the Therapeutae who live outside Alexandria. But Philo first speaks about the group of contemplatives in a rather general way, using the examples of the Greek philosophers Anaxagoras and Democritus to illustrate those who abandon their properties, but then overtrumping the philosophers with the example of those who form a community of contemplatives (14-20). He then adds, 'This kind (γένος)

---

42   Goudriaan, 'Ethnical Strategies', p.85.

exists all over the inhabited world, for it is necessary that both Greece and the barbarian land share in perfect goodness, but it abounds in Egypt in each of the nomes as they are called, and especially in the vicinity of Alexandria. The best of these contemplatives journey from everywhere to make their colony in a certain most suitable location...' (21-22). The reader surely knows that these people are Jews, but they are nowhere called as such in the treatise. Instead, he uses the conventional antithesis of the Greeks and barbarians to denote a broader category to which they belong. True to his apologetic purpose Philo calls them the 'best', but he rejects exclusivism. We might compare Philo's strategy with that of a younger Jewish contemporary. The apostle Paul writes that in the sight of the Lord, 'there is no distinction between Jew and Greek' (Rom. 10.12). Both theologians wish to transcend the twin ethnic categories, but their aims are very different. Paul wants to move beyond the distinction to identify a new group of believers. Philo admits that a larger and higher group of people exists, a multi-ethnic category of 'those who see and know the one God'. But his real interest is in the one imperilled group of Jews. He understands that in his Alexandrian situation, with enemies such as Isidorus and Lampo,[43] there will be no value in a direct confrontation between the categories of Jew and Greek. In the power play between the two groups, the trump cards would always be in the hands of the Greeks, as events indeed confirmed when the new emperor Claudius ascended to the throne.

5. *Philo and the 'Gentiles':*
A Not Very Useful Formulation

On the basis of the evidence presented in this study, our final conclusion can now be drawn. There is little to be gained by using the biblical term 'Gentiles' in relation to Philo's thought and writings. There were plenty of opportunities for Philo to use and develop the antithesis between ʿam and goyim, between Jews and Gentiles, but he declined to do so. Instead he often allegorises Pentateuchal texts that discriminate between Israel and the 'nations'. The handful of texts in the *Quaestiones* where translators from the Armenian are tempted to translate 'Gentiles' in English are isolated and dubious. In the case of the apologetic writings Philo

---

43　*Flacc.* 20; and *Legat.* 355. On these enemies of the Jews, see A. Kerkeslager, 'The Absence of Dionysios, Lampo, and Isidoros from the Violence in Alexandria in 38 C.E.', *SPhA* 17 (2005), pp.49–94; P. W. van der Horst, 'Two Short Notes on Philo', *SPhA* 18 (2006), pp.49–55.

speaks only vaguely about 'Jews' and 'others' and avoids the direct antithesis of Jews and Greeks. There can be little doubt that his apologetic mission encouraged a binary thinking in terms of Jews versus the rest. There were, however, theoretical and above all strategic reasons for avoiding a clear binary terminology.

Quite rightly, therefore, most Philonic scholars avoid the terminological pairing of Jew and Gentile when discussing Philo's thought and prefer to speak of Jews and non-Jews. Two American scholars have taken a different path, the one in a classic study that gave rise to considerable controversy two generations ago, the other in a recent important monograph. The opposition between Jew and Gentile was so central to the main thesis of E. Goodenough in his famous study *By Light, Light* that he entitled a key chapter 'Moses as Presented to the Gentile Inquirer'.[44] 'Gentile' stands for the non-Jewish reader whom Philo addresses in his non-allegorical writings. Such readers are invited to enter in the hellenising mystery religion which Philo, in Goodenough's interpretation, had made out of Judaism. The term 'Gentiles' is built into the very title of Terence Donaldson's monograph *Judaism and the Gentiles: Jewish Patterns of Universalism (to 135 CE)*.[45] Its aim is to show that the conventional antithesis between Judaism as a particularistic and Christianity as a universalist religion is simplistic and flawed, as especially illustrated by the practice of proselytism. A lengthy chapter is devoted to Philo as a key witness for a particular kind of Judaism. The opposition between Jew and Gentile is the key terminology for the entire study, including the chapter on Philo. On the basis of the evidence put forward in the present study, we may conclude that both studies are using terminology that is not taken from Philo's own usage, but rather would seem to be inspired by a paradigm with a different source, which is none other than that most influential of all books written in Greek, the New Testament.

---

44   E. R. Goodenough, *By Light, Light: The Mystic Gospel of Hellenistic Judaism* (New Haven: Yale University Press, 1935), pp.180–98.

45   Donaldson, *Judaism and the Gentiles*. For his chapter on Philo (pp.217–78), see the judicious review of E. Birnbaum in *SPhA* 20 (2008), pp.213–21.

Chapter 3

GENTILES IN THE DEAD SEA SCROLLS

John J. Collins

The Dead Sea Scrolls are a corpus of some 900 manuscripts discovered in caves near the Dead Sea, around Khirbet Qumran, south of Jericho, in the years 1947 to 1956.[1] These manuscripts include multiple copies of two rules for sectarian associations, which are related, but distinct. Both of these rules describe associations that had multiple settlements, spread throughout the land. Most scholars believe that these associations were branches of the Essene sect described by Philo, Josephus and Pliny the Elder, although the identification is vigorously disputed by a minority. The Essenes, we are told, did not live just in one location, but had communities in many towns.[2]

The Scrolls include many compositions, including most of the books we know as the Hebrew Bible, that are not sectarian in themselves. The collection as a whole seems to have a sectarian character, because of the number of copies of works, such as the rule-books, that are clearly sectarian and the absence of literature that could be identified as either pro-Hasmonean or pro-Pharisaic. Despite the common tendency to refer to the Scrolls as 'the library of the Qumran community', it is very unlikely that this huge collection of manuscripts was the library of a single community. The presence of multiple copies of both rule books, in different editions, is more satisfactorily explained on the hypothesis

---

1   For an inventory, see E. Tov (ed.), *The Texts from the Judaean Desert: Indices and an Introduction to the Discoveries in the Judaean Desert Series* (DJD 39; Oxford: Clarendon, 2002).

2   Philo, *Prob.* 76; Josephus, *B.J.* 2.124. See further J. J. Collins, *Beyond the Qumran Community: The Sectarian Movement of the Dead Sea Scrolls* (Grand Rapids: Eerdmans, 2010); idem, 'Sectarian Communities in the Dead Sea Scrolls', in T. H. Lim and J. J. Collins (eds.), *The Oxford Handbook of the Dead Sea Scrolls* (Oxford: Oxford University Press, 2010), pp.151–72.

that the Scrolls belonged to the broader Essene movement, and were brought to the desert to be hidden for safe-keeping during the Jewish revolt against Rome.[3]

Our concern here is with Scrolls that are clearly sectarian. We must allow, however, that even these Scrolls are not entirely uniform. At the outset, it will be well to say something about the two forms of sectarian association described in the Scrolls.

The Damascus Document or Rule (CD) describes a 'new covenant', whose members 'live in camps according to the rule of the land, and marry and have children', although the existence of another order that does not live in this way seems to be implied (CD 7.6-7).[4] The quorum for a 'camp' is ten members (CD 13.1). They contribute at least two days' salary per month for the needs of the community (CD 14.12-14). The Community Rule (1QS), or *Serek ha-Yahad*, in contrast, makes no mention of women or children, and requires that members have their property in common.[5] This form of communal association is called a *yahad*, or commune. The *yahad* was thought to function as a substitute for the Temple cult in making atonement for the land (1QS 8.1-10). Philo, Josephus and Pliny all claim that the Essenes were celibate, although Josephus also states that a second order of the sect accepted marriage. The Community Rule does not explicitly require celibacy, but the absence of any reference to women or children is extraordinary, especially in a text that is preoccupied with purity. Most scholars accept the view of G. Vermes that the Damascus Rule represents the 'marrying Essenes', while the Community Rule reflects the celibate branch of the sect.[6] It should be noted, however, that even the *yahad* had multiple communities, again with a minimum membership of ten.

Both forms of community that we find in the Scrolls had as their *raison d'être* an ideal of separation not only from Gentiles but from other Judeans. According to the Community Rule, 'when these become a

---

3   Compare A. Schofield, *From Qumran to the Yahad: A New Paradigm of Textual Development for the Community Rule* (STDJ 77; Leiden: Brill, 2009).

4   For a thorough analysis of the Damascus Rule, see Y. M. Gillihan, *Civic Ideology, Organization, and Law in the Rule Books: A Comparative Study of the Covenanters' Sect and Contemporary Voluntary Associations in Political Context* (STDJ 97; Leiden: Brill, 2011), pp.133–275; and Collins, *Beyond the Qumran Community*, pp.12–51.

5   Gillihan, *Civic Ideology*, pp.277–453; and Collins, *Beyond the Qumran Community*, pp.52–87.

6   G. Vermes, *The Dead Sea Scrolls: Qumran in Perspective* (Philadelphia: Fortress, 1981), pp.107–8.

community in Israel...they are to be segregated from within the dwelling of the men of sin to go to the desert to prepare there His path' (1QS 8.13). The Damascus Rule envisions a less complete separation, but restricts the relations that members may have with outsiders. For example, 'none of those who have entered the covenant of God should buy or sell to the Sons of the Pit except hand to hand' (CD 13.14-15).[7] No one should stay in a place close to Gentiles on the Sabbath (CD 11.14-15). Also, the so-called Halachic Letter (4QMMT), after listing halachic issues on which the writer's party differed from other people, states that 'we have separated ourselves from the multitude of the people...and from being involved with these matters and from participating with them in these things'.[8] It has recently been argued that this passage should be read as saying that God has separated Israel from the multitude of the nations because of these issues (mostly concerning purity).[9] An ideal of separation, especially from Gentiles, is implied in either reading. We should expect then the attitudes to Gentiles in the sectarian Scrolls would be at least reserved, if not hostile.

These attitudes can be illustrated by examining what the Scrolls have to say about two categories of people, the Kittim, or foreigners from the west, especially the Romans, and the *gerim*, or resident aliens (the term used for proselytes in Rabbinic literature). References to the Kittim occur especially in contexts of warfare, where relations with Gentiles are most likely to be hostile. The *gerim*, in contrast, were peaceful neighbors, and complicate somewhat the general impression of xenophobia in the Scrolls.

1. *The Kittim*

The word Kittim is derived from Citium in Cyprus, but is used as a general designation of foreigners from the west. In Gen. 10.4, the Kittim are sons of Javan (Greece). They are mentioned, without identification,

---

7   J. Baumgarten, 'The "Sons of Dawn" in CDC 13:14-15 and the Ban on Commerce among the Essenes', *IEJ* 33 (1983), pp.81–5, reads 'Sons of Dawn' instead of 'Sons of the Pit'. The phrase 'Sons of Dawn' occurs in 4Q298 ('Words of the Maskil to All the Sons of Dawn') apparently in reference to postulants and novices. See, however, C. Stroup, 'A Reexamination of the "Sons of the Pit" in CD 13:14', *DSD* 18 (2011), pp.45–53, who defends the reading 'Sons of the Pit'.

8   4QMMT, composite text C 7-8, in E. Qimron and J. Strugnell (eds.), *Qumran Cave 4 V: Miqsat Maʿase Ha-Torah* (DJD 10; Oxford: Clarendon, 1994), pp.58–9.

9   So E. A. Bar-Asher Siegal, 'Who Separated from Whom and Why? A Philological Study of 4QMMT', *RevQ* 25 (2011), pp.229–56.

in Balaam's oracle in Num. 24.14. In 1 Macc. 1.1, Alexander the Great is said to come from the land of Kittim. In Dan. 11.30, the 'ships of the Kittim', which encounter Antiochus Epiphanes in Egypt, are the Romans, who famously ordered him to withdraw from that country on 'the day of Eleusis'.[10] In the biblical commentaries, or pesharim, from Qumran, the Kittim are clearly the Romans. The reference in the War Scroll is less clear. There we read, in the opening column, of the Kittim of Assyria and the Kittim in Egypt, which sound suspiciously like the Seleucids and the Ptolemies.[11] The main surviving manuscript of the War Rule, 1QM, dates from the Roman period, and presumably the Kittim would have been identified as the Romans at that time.[12] It is quite possible, however, that the original formulation of the War Rule had the Seleucids and Ptolemies in view.[13]

In any case, the Kittim are cast in the War Rule as the followers of Belial, the quintessential 'Sons of Darkness'. They are destined for destruction: 'On the day on which the Kittim fall, there will be a battle, and savage destruction before the God of Israel, for this will be the day determined by him from ancient times for the war of extermination against the Sons of Darkness' (1QM 1.9-10).[14] A fragmentary text, 4Q285, that may belong to another recension of the War Rule describes how the messianic 'branch of David' will kill the king of the Kittim.[15] The reference here is probably to the leader of the Kittim in the final battle, whether this individual is envisioned as a Hellenistic king or, later, as a Roman general or emperor. The Kittim represent militantly

10   P. F. Mittag, *Antiochus IV Epiphanes. Eine politische Biographie* (Berlin: Akademie, 2006), pp.214–24.

11   B. Schultz, *Conquering the World: The War Scroll (1QM) Reconsidered* (STDJ 76; Leiden: Brill, 2009), p.129, thinks that the author is deliberately distinguishing between 'of Assyria' and 'in Egypt', and therefore that it is unlikely that the reference is to the Seleucids and the Ptolemies, but it is not clear that the distinction in terminology should bear any weight.

12   T. H. Lim, 'Kittim', in L. H. Schiffman and J. C. VanderKam (eds.), *The Encyclopedia of the Dead Sea Scrolls* (New York: Oxford University Press, 2000), pp.469–71, takes the view that all references to the Kittim refer to the Romans, and that the king of the Kittim is the Roman emperor.

13   Schultz, *Conquering the World*, p.156, thinks that the reference is only to the Seleucids, and the mention of the Kittim in Egypt echoes the reference to the invasion of Egypt by Antiochus IV in Dan. 11.

14   Translation F. García Martínez, *The Dead Sea Scrolls Translated* (Leiden: Brill, 1996), p.95.

15   M. G. Abegg, 'Messianic Hope and 4Q285: A Reassessment', *JBL* 113 (1994), pp.81–91.

hostile Gentiles, and their destiny in the eschatological battle is complete and utter destruction.

The Kittim also figure prominently in the pesharim. The clearest historical reference is found in 4QpNahum, frags. 3-4, 1.2-4, in the interpretation of Nah. 2.12b: 'The interpretation of it concerns Demetrius, King of Greece, who sought to enter Jerusalem on the advice of the Seekers-After-Smooth-Things, (but God did not give Jerusalem) into the power of the kings of Greece from Antiochus until the rise of the rulers of the Kittim; but afterward (the city) will be trampled and will be given into the hands of the rulers of the Kittim'.[16]

The Demetrius mentioned is the Seleucid king Demetrius III Eukairos (or Akairos) who was invited by the Pharisees (the Seekers after Smooth Things) to attack Alexander Jannaeus. The attack did not succeed. The Antiochus mentioned is Antiochus Epiphanes, the last foreign king to conquer Jerusalem before the coming of the Romans. The reference to the Kittim in this passage is simply factual, although we might expect that the pesherist would not have a very positive view of the foreign power that conquered Jerusalem.

There is a possible second reference to the Kittim in 4QpNah frags. 1-2.3-5a: 'He rebu(ked) the sea and dried (it up. The in)terpretation of it: "the sea" – that is all the K(ittim, whom God will rebuke,) so as to ren(der) a judgment against them and to wipe them out from the face of (the earth. And he dried up all the rivers.) (The interpretation of it: "the rivers" are the Kittim,) with (all) their (ru)lers, whose dominion will be ended'. If the passage is correctly restored, the pesher is consistent with the War Scroll in expecting, or hoping, that the Kittim would eventually be destroyed. There is also a fragmentary reference to rebuke in 1QpPsalms, where Ps. 68.30 is interpreted as follows: 'The interpretation of it concerns all the ru(lers of) the Kittim, (who) before him in Jerusalem. You rebuked...' The passage is too fragmentary to be informative, but it seems to fit the pattern according to which the Kittim would eventually be rebuked and destroyed.

There are several references to the destruction of the Kittim in 4QpIsa[a], frags. 7-10. The biblical passage in view is Isa. 10.33-34, which is part of an oracle against the advancing Assyrians. The Kittim are identified with the lofty of stature who will fall, and the thickets of the forest that will be cut down with an axe. As G. J. Brooke has noted, there is virtually nothing in these brief comments that is not derived from the text of

---

16   Translation M. P. Horgan, *Pesharim: Qumran Interpretations of Biblical Books* (CBQMS 8; Catholic Biblical Association of America, 1979), p.163.

Isaiah.[17] The interpretation is a prediction of events that are anticipated, not yet fulfilled.

Isaiah famously allowed that while the Assyrians must eventually be punished they were also 'the rod of my anger', the instrument of God for punishing Israel (Isa. 10.5). A similar view is reflected in the pesher on Habakkuk, which provides the most extensive references to the Kittim in the Dead Sea Scrolls. Citing Hab. 1.6, 'For see I will mobilise the Chaldaeans, a cru(el and determined) people', the pesher continues: 'Its interpretation concerns the Kittim, who are swift and powerful in battle, to slay many (with the edge of the sword) in the kingdom of the Kittim'.

The pesher follows the prophetic text in emphasising the fear and dread spread by the Kittim: 'They deride the powerful and despise the honoured men... (They)...will garner their wealth with all their loot, like the fish of the sea'. The pesherist notes that they will not believe the precepts of God (2.15) and that they kill many without pity (6.10). It is clear that the Kittim serve a purpose in punishing 'the last priests of Jerusalem, who will accumulate riches and loot from plundering the peoples' (9.5). In the last days, their riches and their loot will fall into the hands of the army of the Kittim. Yet 'God is not to destroy his people at the hand of nations, but by means of his chosen ones God will judge all the nations' (5.4).

Brooke has emphasised the role of biblical allusions in pesharim. In the background is the mention of Kittim in Num. 24.23-24: 'Sea peoples shall gather from the north, and ships from the district of Kittim. I look and they afflict Eber; but they too shall perish forever.'[18] Balaam's oracle figures prominently in the eschatological predictions of the Dead Sea Scrolls, and provided a guarantee that the Kittim would eventually perish.

Brooke also notes allusions to Deuteronomy 28 and Leviticus 26. Deuteronomy 28.47-68 describes how God will punish Israel by bringing a nation swift as the eagle – apparently a reference to the Babylonians. Leviticus 26.27-45 also seems to be aware of the Babylonian destruction of Jerusalem. The Babylonian typology is integral to the identification of the Chaldeans as the Kittim. The pesherist drew on other biblical passages that mentioned the Chaldeans, such as 2 Chronicles 36. The oracle against Babylon in Isaiah 13 is cited in 1QpHab 6.11-12, and some motifs are drawn from the oracle about Gog in Ezekiel 38. Brooke

17   G. J. Brooke, 'The Kittim in the Qumran Pesharim', in L. Alexander (ed.), *Images of Empire* (JSOTSup 122; Sheffield: JSOT, 1991), pp.135–59 (140).
18   Brooke, 'The Kittim', p.156.

concludes, 'The use of the Babylon materials shows how far-sighted is the author's perception of the Roman presence, since, like Babylon, Rome was shortly to destroy the Temple'.[19]

Brooke allows that 'the writing of some of the pesharim may well have been motivated in part by uncertain memories of Pompey's action in Jerusalem, or by contemporary experience of Roman occupation'.[20] This is surely a gross understatement. The 'destruction' of the Temple that Pesher Habakkuk has in view is not the action of Titus, which lay in the distant future, but the profanation of the Temple by Pompey, an event which looms very large in the pesharim. The pesharim used biblical phraseology to describe the Kittim/Romans, and for that reason tell us nothing that we cannot confirm from other sources, but this should not obscure the historical realism of the allusions. The hope that the Kittim would be destroyed was confirmed by scriptural allusions, but it was rooted in historical experience of conquest and occupation that was all too real.

It has been suggested that the differences between the pesharim and the War Scroll in their depiction of the Kittim reflect a development in the views of the sect. The pesharim supposedly reflect an earlier stage, when the Kittim could be assigned a constructive role in punishing sinful Israelites. By the time the War Scroll was written, they had become the arch-enemy of the sect.[21] This view is too simple. The War Scroll had a complicated history, and cannot be dated later than the pesharim in its entirety. The references to the Kittim of Asshur require a date in the Seleucid period, before the coming of Pompey.[22] Moreover, the pesharim also envision the downfall of the Kittim, just as Isaiah had envisioned the downfall of the Assyrians.

The sectarians were not alone in hoping for the eventual destruction of Gentile power. Already Joel 4 (English ch. 3) summons the nations, indiscriminately, to the Valley of Jehoshaphat for a judgment, that is compared to harvesting. Even the generally irenic book of Ben Sira contains a prayer that God 'crush the heads of the hostile rulers' (Sir. 36.12; the passage is anomalous in Ben Sira and is probably secondary). The myth of an attack by the nations on Mount Zion, only to be utterly defeated, goes back at least to Assyrian times (e.g. Ps. 2) and is possibly

---

19   Brooke, 'The Kittim', p.157.
20   Brooke, 'The Kittim', p.158.
21   See Lim, 'Kittim', p.470, following the suggestions of G. Vermes.
22   Schultz, *Conquering the World*, p.102, dates 1QM1 'soon after the Maccabean revolt or early on in the Hasmonean dynasty'.

as old as the Davidic dynasty. It remains a staple of apocalyptic eschatology throughout the Second Temple period (see, e.g., *4 Ezra* 13). Insofar as the War Scroll targets the Kittim, rather than Gentiles in general, it is arguably less extreme than what we find in Joel. In any case, the hope for the eventual destruction of hostile Gentiles was widespread in Second Temple Judaism, and not a distinguishing feature of the sect known from the Scrolls.

That said, the references to the Kittim reflect a dim view of the Gentile world. The references to the *ger*, or resident alien, however, are more complicated.

2. *The* ger

The term *ger* is used in the Hebrew Bible with reference to Israelites living among foreigners and to foreigners living among Israelites.[23] Many laws in the Pentateuch are designed to protect the alien living in Israel, because Israel was an alien in Egypt.[24] The *ger* is often grouped with the widow and the orphan in this regard, although it is clear that the status is not defined by poverty, but by foreign birth. The alien is often treated like the Israelite, and bound to observe the same laws. The alien enjoys the Sabbath rest, and is invited to rejoice at Passover (Deut. 16.11). He may celebrate Shavuot (Deut. 16.11) and Sukkot (Deut. 16.14; 31.12). Two passages in Deuteronomy, 29.10 and 31.12, include the *ger* in the assembly of all Israel that is to enter into the covenant and hear the commandments.[25] At the same time, the *ger* evidently does not enjoy the same status as native Israelites. In the Ten Commandments in Exod. 20.10, the *ger* is listed after sons, daughters, servants and cattle. Several laws in the Torah indicate that the *ger* was not expected to observe the commandments as rigorously as the native Israelite. For example, Deut. 14.21 forbids Israelites from eating the carcass of an animal found dead, but it may be given to a *ger* or sold to a foreigner.[26]

23   J. R. Spencer, 'Sojourner', in *ABD*, VI, pp.103–4.

24   Exod. 23.9; Lev. 19.33-34; Deut. 10.19; 16.9-12. Several laws in Deut. 24 are designed to provide for the alien.

25   S. Hultgren, *From the Damascus Document to the Covenant of the Community* (STDJ 66; Leiden: Brill, 2007), p.169, regards these as late additions to Deuteronomy because of their greater integration of the *ger*.

26   Y. M. Gillihan, 'The גר Who Wasn't There: Fictional Aliens in the Damascus Rule', *RevQ* 25 (2011), pp.257–305 (276).

The status of the *ger* changes in the Priestly laws, and the term arguably takes on the meaning of proselyte.[27] The legislation for the Passover shows the new situation. According to Exod. 12.43, no foreigner (*ben nokri*) may eat the Passover, but 'if an alien who resides with you wants to celebrate the Passover to the Lord, all his males shall be circumcised; then he may draw near to celebrate it; he shall be regarded as a native of the land. No uncircumcised person may eat of it. There will be one law for the native and for the alien who resides with you' (12.48-49). The resident alien is also required to observe the Day of Atonement in Lev. 16.29. Moreover, both native-born and alien are equally rendered impure by eating the carcass of an animal found dead, according to Lev. 17.15.[28] The provision for the circumcision of the *ger* marks a significant development over against the laws of Deuteronomy. In pre-Exilic Israel, a *ger* was a foreigner living in the land of Israel or Judah. The Priestly laws, at least in their final redaction, envision a situation where Israel is a confessional community, shaped in significant part by the experience of life in the Diaspora, which foreigners may join, although distinctions remain. While the *ger* is permitted to observe the Passover (Num. 9.13-14), he is not obliged to do so.[29] Leviticus also relegates the *ger* to a lower status than the native born. The *ger*, like other Gentiles, may be enslaved on a permanent basis, unlike native Israelites (Lev. 25.35-46). Throughout the Pentateuchal laws, the *ger* remains at the bottom of the Israelite hierarchy (e.g. Deut. 29.9-12).[30]

Several texts among the Scrolls follow biblical precedent in referring to the *ger*.[31] A sapiential text, 4Q423, says that God will judge fathers and sons, *gerim* and native born. 4Q159 (4Q Ordinances) cites laws from Leviticus, Numbers and Deuteronomy on provision for the indigent, including the *gerim*, and their right to humane treatment. Neither of these texts is sectarian in character. The Temple Scroll (11QT[a]), which is also not considered to be a sectarian text, allows the *ger* who was born in the

---

27   C. van Houten, *The Alien in Israelite Law* (JSOTSup 107; Sheffield: JSOT, 1991), pp.109–57.

28   Hultgren, *From the Damascus Document*, p.168.

29   Consequently, Hultgren argues that the term should not be translated as 'proselyte' (*From the Damascus Document*, p.175). Compare the excursus on *ger* in J. Milgrom, *Numbers* (JPS Torah Commentary; Philadelphia: JPS, 1990), p.399. Cohen, *The Beginnings of Jewishness*, pp.109–10, argues that one can only speak of proselytes in the period after the Maccabean revolt.

30   See further K. Berthelot, 'La notion de *ger* dans les texts de Qumrân', *RevQ* 19 (1999), pp.172–9.

31   Berthelot, 'La notion de *ger*', pp.178–84.

land to enter the third, outer, court of the Temple, with the women.[32] The passage discussing admission to the second court (39.4-6) is very fragmentary, but it contains the words 'fourth generation'. It has been suggested that this refers to aliens who have been resident in the land for four generations (cf. Deut. 23.9, which allows Edomites and Egyptians to enter the assembly if they have lived in the land for three generations). In this case, however, the reading is very uncertain.[33] The Temple Scroll omits several passages relating to the *gerim*, leading some scholars to question whether it envisioned a place for aliens in the eschatological time.[34] In that case the reference in 40.6 would have to be regarded as an interpolation, but this seems unduly speculative. The Temple Scroll is not very interested in aliens, but it does not exclude them entirely.

3. *The* ger *in Sectarian Texts*

Gerim are also mentioned in several sectarian texts. 4QpNahum, frags. 3-4, col. 2, 7-10a interprets Nah. 3.4 with reference to those who lead astray 'kings, princes, priests and people, together with the *ger* attached to them'. There is no implication here that the *ger* is a member of a sectarian community, and the reference is simply to aliens resident in the land. A more distinctly sectarian reference is found in 4Q279 (4QLots), a very fragmentary text that states that 'the fourth lot is for the *ger*'. This text seems to provide a sectarian explanation of the existence of the different categories of people in Israel.[35] It does not necessarily imply that *gerim* were admitted to the 'new covenant' or to the *yahad*, although it may imply that some place would be found for them in the eschatological time.

Clearer provision for the inclusion of *gerim* in the sectarian community is found in CD. CD 14.3, the rule for the assembly of all the camps, says that members should be enlisted 'priests first, levites second,

32   11QT 40.6; Berthelot, 'La notion de *ger*', pp.182–3, mistakenly gives the references as 60.6.

33   Berthelot, 'La notion de *ger*', p.184.

34   Berthelot, 'La notion de *ger*', pp.194–5. Cf. M. O. Wise, *A Critical Study of the Temple Scroll from Qumran Cave 11* (Chicago: The Oriental Institute, 1990), pp.172–3.

35   Gillihan, 'The גר Who Wasn't There', p.271; and F. Schmidt, 'Gôral Versus Payîs: Casting Lots at Qumran and in the Rabbinic Tradition', in F. García Martínez and M. Popovic (eds.), *Defining Identities: We, You, and the Other in the Dead Sea Scrolls. Proceedings of the Fifth Meeting of the IOQS in Groningen* (STDJ 70; Leiden: Brill, 2007), pp.175–85 (179–80).

Israelites third and the *ger* fourth'.[36] K. Berthelot, who emphasises the
continuity of the Damascus Rule with the biblical tradition, suggests that
ger here is a social-tribal category within Israel, analogous to the Levites
(who are also sometimes called *gerim* in the biblical texts). She points to
Deut. 29.10-11, which refers to 'the aliens who are in your camp', and
concludes that the *ger* is accepted as part of Israel, with a particular
status.[37] Y. Gillihan argues more forcefully that the *ger* here must be
understood as a Gentile proselyte who has been circumcised, is ritually
pure and has passed inspection by the *mebaqqer*.[38] S. Hultgren compares
CD to 2 Chron. 30.25, where 'the whole assembly of Judah, the priests
and the Levites…and the resident aliens who came out of the land of
Israel and the resident aliens who lived in Judah rejoiced' when
Hezekiah celebrated the Passover.[39] He suggests that the 'covenant for all
Israel envisioned by the Damascus covenant was, at its beginnings, not
unlike that envisioned by the Chronicler'. But the *ger* here can hardly be
the resident alien of earlier biblical legislation;: 'it is unlikely that a *ger*
who did not agree to observe the whole Law of Moses was admitted into
the "camps"'.[40] It seems likely then that CD continues the trajectory
found in the Priestly writings and allows for full integration of the
ger/proselyte into the community. There is another reference to the *ger*
in CD 6.31, which mentions the obligation to provide for 'the poor, the
needy and the *ger*', in typical biblical style, but that passage does not
necessarily require that the *ger* be a member of the new covenant.

The inclusion of the *ger* in the Damascus Rule, however, is at odds
with what we find elsewhere in the Dead Sea Scrolls. Most notable in
this regard is 4Q174 (Florilegium), which cites Exod. 15.17-18 ('The
sanctuary of the Lord which thy hands have established') and expounds
it as follows: 'that is the house to which shall not come…Ammonite nor
Moabite nor bastard nor stranger (*ben nekar*) nor *ger* forever, for his holy
ones are there…and foreigners shall not make it desolate again, as they
desolated formerly the sanctuary of Israel because of their sin'.[41]

---

36   The 4Q D fragments confirm the inclusion of the *ger*. See Gillihan, 'The גר
Who Wasn't There', p.264 n.27.
37   Berthelot, 'La notion de *ger*', p.193.
38   Gillihan, 'The גר Who Wasn't There', p.265.
39   Hultgren, *From the Damascus Covenant*, pp.196–7.
40   Hultgren, *From the Damascus Covenant*, pp.197–8.
41   Translation from G. J. Brooke, *Exegesis at Qumran: 4QFlorilegium and its
Jewish Context* (Atlanta: SBL, 2006; first published Sheffield: JSOT, 1985), p.92.

The list of excluded people is based on Deut. 23.2-4, which permanently excludes the Ammonite, Moabite, *mamzer* and Israelite with mutilated genitals from entering the assembly of the Lord. Whereas 11Q Temple grouped the *gerim* with the Edomites and Egyptians who were temporarily excluded, 4QFlorilegium grouped them with the Ammonites and Moabites, who were permanently excluded.[42] Also relevant here is Ezek. 44.6-9, which prohibits foreigners (*ben nekar*) from entry into the Temple.[43] The Florilegium extends the ban to the *ger*, whose status it equates with that of the *ben nekar*. There is room for debate as to just what the word 'house' connotes. At the minimum, it is the Temple and cultic assembly. Gillihan argues for a broader connotation, noting that the Florilegium emphasises 'the security, purity and covenantal fidelity of Israel as a whole – God's people in their holy land, both purified of all Gentile presence'.[44] In any case, it should be noted that the rationale for exclusion in 4QFlorilegium, the presence of holy ones in the congregation, is also cited in CD 15.15-16, which excludes people with various defects (but not *gerim*) from the congregation. The same rationale for excluding people with defects is cited in 1QSa, the rule of the congregation in the end of days. The contrast between 4QFlorilegium and CD with respect to the *ger* is all the more striking in view of the fact that 4QFlorilegium seems to draw on other parts of CD, especially CD 3.12–8.20.[45]

Gillihan has sought to relate the exclusion of the *ger* in 4QFlorilegium to the laws of 4QMMT, a text which lays out the basic halachic issues on which the sectarians differed from other Jews.[46] One of the concerns of that text is the principle of intermixing: animals of two kinds may not be mated, clothes may not be woven from two different materials, and so on. The people of Israel are 'children of holy (seed)', a principle found already in the book of Ezra.[47] The seed of priests is 'most holy'. The passage goes on to complain that some of the priests and some of the people were intermingling (4QMMT, composite text, B 80). The editors of 4QMMT, E. Qimron and J. Strugnell, took this as a reference to inter

42 Gillihan, 'The גר Who Wasn't There', p.289.

43 Gillihan, 'The גר Who Wasn't There', p.295.

44 Gillihan, 'The גר Who Wasn't There', p.295.

45 Brooke, *Exegesis at Qumran*, pp.205–9.

46 Gillihan, 'The גר Who Wasn't There', p.282–5.

47 Ezra 9.2. See C. Hayes, *Gentile Impurities and Jewish Identities: Intermarriage and Conversion from the Bible to the Talmud* (New York: Oxford University Press, 2002), pp.28–30.

marriage between priests and laity.[48] C. Hayes, however, has argued that this passage implies that any mixing of Jewish and Gentile seed was forbidden, since even lay Israelites had holy seed.[49] Since marriage with Gentiles was not common in this period (first century BCE), she argues that the prohibition is directed against marriage with *converted* Gentiles, or *gerim*. Hayes's argument is influenced by the precedent of the book of *Jubilees*, which is found at Qumran but is not regarded as a sectarian text. In its retelling of Genesis 34, the story of Dinah, *Jubilees* insists that the Shechemites were not rendered fit for marriage with Israelites by circumcision: 'and if there is any man who wishes in Israel to give his daughter or his sister to a man who is of the seed of the Gentiles, he shall surely die'.[50] Hayes comments, 'the polemical point of Jubilees' condemnation of intermarriage is not that sexual unions with unconverted Gentiles are prohibited (such a point would be uncontroversial in *Jubilees*'s day) but that even converted Gentiles are prohibited in marriage'.[51] The position of *Jubilees* on this issue was extreme. Other retellings of the Genesis 34 episode allow that marriage with the Shechemites after they were circumcised would have been permissible.[52] *Jubilees*, however, was an influential text in the sectarian movement. Not only are copies found at Qumran, but it is cited as authoritative in CD 16.3-4.

Gillihan further argues that the sacrifices of *gerim* would not have been acceptable, since 4QMMT (B 8-9) appears to reject Gentile sacrifices as whoredom.[53] He infers that there would have been little place for a converted Gentile in a community governed by the laws of 4QMMT. It must be admitted that 4QMMT does not explicitly address the status of the *ger*. Consequently this argument remains tentative. Logically, the view that the holiness of the people is genetically transmitted would appear to leave little room for conversion, but religious ideas are not always logically consistent. In light of the precedent of *Jubilees*, however, and the explicit exclusion of the *ger* from the eschatological 'house' in 4QFlorilegium, Gillihan's reading of 4QMMT is plausible.

48   Qimron and Strugnell, *Miqsat Maʿase Ha-Torah*, p.55, note to line 75.
49   Hayes, *Gentile Impurities*, pp.82–91; and Gillihan, 'The גר Who Wasn't There', p.283.
50   *Jub.* 30.7. Translation from R. H. Charles, 'The Book of Jubilees', in R. H. Charles (ed.), *The Apocrypha and Pseudepigrapha of the Old Testament* (2 vols.; Oxford: Clarendon, 1913), II, p.58.
51   Hayes, *Gentile Impurities*, p.81.
52   See especially J. L. Kugel, 'The Story of Dinah in the Testament of Levi', *HTR* 84 (1992), pp.1–34; and Hayes, *Gentile Impurities*, p.81.
53   Gillihan, 'The גר Who Wasn't There', p.284.

A number of other sectarian texts do not explicitly exclude the *ger*, but conspicuously fail to mention him at all. 1QSa, the rule for the congregation of Israel in the end of days, specifies that 'this is the rule for all the armies of the congregation, for all native Israelites' (1.6). The word for 'native', *ezrach*, is normally used in conjunction with *ger*, but there is no mention of *ger* here. Gillihan reasonably infers that 1QSa 'implies what the Florilegium predicts: the *ger* will not inhabit restored Israel'.[54] Neither is there mention of the *ger* in the War Scroll. While some Gentile peoples will survive the final conflict, to be subjected to Israel in the eschatological age, the 'seven nations of vanity' will be destroyed (1QM 11.8-9). The reference is to the Canaanite peoples whose destruction was commanded in Deut. 7.1-5. It appears then that there would be no place for Gentiles in the land of Israel in the final age. This idea was not peculiar to the *yahad* or the Essenes. The *Psalms of Solomon*, often thought to be Pharisaic, also anticipate the removal of all foreigners from the restored Israel (17.28).

1QSa and the War Scroll, like the Florilegium, are describing a future eschatological age. It should be noted, however, that the Community Rule, *Serek ha-Yahad*, does not acknowledge the existence of the *ger* either. All of this heightens the anomaly of the inclusion of the *ger* in CD 14. As Berthelot has emphasised, 'il faut souligner que de tous les textes de Qumrân, seul CD envisage le *ger* comme faisant partie de la communauté'.[55]

Scholars have attempted to deal with this anomaly in various ways. Hultgren would date the original Damascus covenant 'in circles close to the Chronicler, during or after the time of the Chronicler but before the Hasmonean period and probably before Ben Sira', most probably in the third century BCE.[56] But CD has little in common with Chronicles other than the inclusion of the *ger* in the community.[57] Even if the Damascus covenant is identified with the so-called parent community that is said to have been like blind people groping the way, before the arrival of the Teacher, in CD 1.9-10[58] it is only said to have been in this condition for twenty years. The arrival of the Teacher certainly cannot be dated before

54 Gillihan, 'The גר Who Wasn't There', p.297.
55 Berthelot, 'La notion de *ger*', p.215.
56 Hultgren, *From the Damascus Covenant*, p.205.
57 Hultgren, *From the Damascus Covenant*, p.196, claims that 'the structure of the Damascus covenant is almost identical to Asa's covenant in 2 Chr 15:9-15', but the only point of resemblance is the swearing of an oath. Asa did not inaugurate a new association distinct from the rest of Israel.
58 Cf. Hultgren, *From the Damascus Covenant*, p.57.

the Maccabean revolt, and should more plausibly be dated towards the end of the second century BCE.[59] Hultgren may be right to suppose that CD reflects an early stage in the development of the sectarian ideology, but it cannot be separated chronologically from the other scrolls to the extent that he proposes.

P. Davies has argued the reference is not to people of Gentile birth at all, but to 'a proselyte to the sect, and thus one in the process of initiation into it'.[60] There is no parallel for such usage. While the sectarians thought of themselves as the true Israel, they never dismissed other Jews as non-Israelites.[61]

K. Berthelot argues that the word *ger* in CD has its traditional connotation of resident alien in Israel, a recognised category in biblical law. In 4QFlorilegium, however, it takes on the meaning of proselyte. She suggests that the rejection of proselytes in 4QFlorilegium reflects a reaction to the forced integration of the Idumeans and others under the Hasmoneans.[62] As Hultgren has observed, however, it is hardly credible that the traditional *gerim* would be included in the congregation, unless they agreed to observe the full Torah of Moses, in which case they would in effect be proselytes.[63] It is apparent that some change occurred in attitudes toward the *ger*/proselyte between the formulation of the Damascus covenant and the Florilegium, whether this change was related to the policies of the Hasmoneans or not.

Most recently, Y. Gillihan, while accepting that CD provides for the presence of the *ger*, regards this as a legal fiction to conform to biblical precedent, but denies that any resident aliens would have actually been admitted to the community:

> I propose that the covenanters imagined the 'true' *ger* to be a righteous Gentile who accepted his eschatological exclusion from Israel. These fictional idealized resident aliens would attend assemblies for instruction

59   On the date of the Teacher, see Collins, *Beyond the Qumran Community*, pp.88–121; M. O. Wise, 'Dating the Teacher of Righteousness and the *Floruit* of his Movement', *JBL* 122 (2003), pp.53–87.

60   P. R. Davies, 'The "Damascus Sect" and Judaism', in J. C. Reeves and J. Kampen (eds.), *Pursuing the Text: Studies in Honor of Ben Zion Wacholder on the Occasion of his Seventieth Birthday* (JSOTSup 184; Sheffield: Sheffield Academic, 1994), pp.70–84 (75).

61   Gillihan, 'The גר Who Wasn't There', p.259.

62   Josephus, *A.J.* 13.257-58, 397. See Steven Weitzman, 'Forced Circumcision and the Shifting Role of Gentiles in Hasmonean Ideology', *HTR* 92 (1999), pp.37–59.

63   See above n.40.

but keep their distance from the cult. They would not seek to marry Israelites nor enter Jerusalem; they would live in their own cities and be prepared to evacuate Israel at the End of Days. In the meantime, should such *gerim* actually seek to live by sectarian law, they will be treated as the Torah requires: they will be present at assemblies, as in Deut 29–30 and Josh 8.[64]

To say that CD 14 is a legal fiction, however, only seems to finesse the problem. The legislation in CD may be utopian, but it indicates what was acceptable in principle. We do not know whether any proselyte to Judaism ever attempted to join the sect, but if any did, CD would seem to provide a place for them. It is difficult to believe that the covenanters would have accepted *gerim*, in principle, into their congregation, only to expect them to evacuate Israel at the End of Days. Gillihan is driven to this solution because he wants to harmonise CD and the Florilegium. In my view, it would be better to recognise that they are different, as Hultgren and Berthelot do in their respective ways. The difference may be due to chronological factors. CD represents an early formulation of sectarian ideology. The *yahad* described in the Community Rule expresses a stricter ideal of separation, both from Gentiles and from other Jews than did the Damascus covenant. The more negative attitude to proselytes in the Florilegium may have been influenced by the policies of the Hasmoneans, but this was not necessarily so. The stricter attitude may simply be a matter of religious ideology, an intensification of the ideology found already in the Damascus covenant and developed over time. Whether the more inclusive attitude was preserved in the movement of the new covenant, even after the development of the *yahad*, is difficult to say. While the two forms of association are rightly regarded as branches of the same sect, they differed in some notable respects, such as their attitudes to marriage. They may also have differed in their attitude to Gentile proselytes.

This discussion of the *ger* in the Dead Sea Scrolls complicates somewhat the impression of antagonism to Gentiles in the Dead Sea Scrolls. Nonetheless, the overall impression is decidedly antagonistic. The rule for the assemblies in CD may be an exception, but it is an exception that proves the rule. The dominant tone in the Scrolls is separatist and xenophobic, with little place for Gentiles, at least in the land of Israel, in the End of Days.

---

64   Gillihan, 'The גר Who Wasn't There', p.301.

Chapter 4

JOSEPHUS AND THE GENTILES

James S. McLaren

1. *Introduction*

The writings of Josephus enable us to have direct access to the thoughts and attitudes of an individual who spent most of his adult life interacting with Gentiles. This interaction took place in the second half of the first century CE, in several geographical locations and in a number of different social contexts. Based on his own testimony about his career, however, it is readily apparent that how we are to interpret and evaluate what Josephus has written is very complicated. In particular there has been much debate regarding his allegiance to his own people and heritage, especially in relation to Rome and its new ruling family, the Flavians.[1] The following discussion is based on the premise that while Josephus' personal circumstances changed dramatically, his core values and commitment to the Jewish way of life remained constant.[2]

A range of topics has been examined in relation to Gentiles within the writings of Josephus. By far the most popular topic is Josephus' rewritten biblical paraphrase and the accompanying post-biblical history in his twenty-volume *Antiquitates Judaicae*. Clearly crafted with an audience located within the Greek-speaking Greco-Roman world in mind, there has been much discussion of the ways in which Josephus recast the biblical story.[3] A second major topic of interest has been the

---

1   See T. Rajak, *Josephus: The Historian and his Society* (Duckworth: London, 2nd edn, 2003), esp. pp.185–222; and S. J. D. Cohen, *Josephus in Galilee and Rome: His Vita and Development as a Historian* (CSCT 8; Leiden: Brill, 1979).

2   For example, see J. S. McLaren, 'A Reluctant Provincial: Josephus and the Roman Empire in *Jewish War*', in J. Riches and D. C. Sim (eds.), *The Gospel of Matthew in its Roman Imperial Context* (JSNTSup 276; London: T&T Clark International, 2005), pp.34–48.

3   For example P. Spilsbury, *The Image of the Jew in Flavius Josephus' Paraphrase of the Bible* (TSAJ 69; Tübingen: Mohr Siebeck, 1998); and L. H. Feldman, *Studies in Josephus' Rewritten Bible* (JSJSup 58; Leiden: Brill, 1998).

apologetic nature of much of Josephus' literary career. Here tensions between self-preservation, commitment to the Flavian family as his sponsor, and concern for fellow Jews have been debated.[4] A third, less prominent topic is Josephus' literary activity as an attempt to attract Gentiles to the Jewish way of life. Here the key issue is the extent to which Josephus' main target audience was interested, sympathetic Gentiles.[5]

A common feature of these three topics is that the discussion often highlights a positive engagement between Josephus and the Gentile world in which he was located. Indeed, Josephus readily undertook the task of fostering such engagement; it was a duty and responsibility incumbent on him due to his upbringing and standing in the Jewish community. The present study will adopt a different perspective and pursue a different line of inquiry. The focus is what Josephus reveals about Gentiles in his writings: about individuals, groups, and about aspects of the ways of living among Gentiles.[6] We will consider what Josephus actually has to say about Gentiles, the context in which those comments are made, and the type of interaction between Jews and Gentiles that he depicts. Aware of the general perception of a positive engagement claimed in the existing lines of inquiry, did Josephus respect Gentiles? If so, on what basis, and in what ways, did he display this respect?

The study will approach the question of Josephus' interaction with Gentiles in three parts. We will commence with an examination of the depiction of Gentiles in *Bellum Judaicum*. This work is a substantial narrative pertaining to recent events that directly involved interaction between the Jewish community in Josephus' homeland and Gentiles. The next part will examine Josephus' final work, *Contra Apionem*. In this treatise Josephus actively engages with views and attitudes he claims

4   See the works cited in n.1 and S. Schwartz, *Josephus and Judaean Politics* (CSCT 18; Leiden: Brill, 1990).

5   See T. L. Donaldson, *Judaism and the Gentiles: Jewish Patterns of Universalism (to 135 CE)* (Waco: Baylor University Press, 2008); and S. Mason, 'Should Any Wish to Enquire Further (*Ant.* 1.25): The Aim and Audience of Josephus's Judean Antiquities/Life', in S. Mason (ed.), *Understanding Josephus: Seven Perspectives* (JSPSup 32; Sheffield: Sheffield Academic, 1998), pp.64–103.

6   The use of the term 'Gentile' here does not imply that all 'foreigners' can and should be identified as a single, homogenous group. Rather, it is simply a way of labelling the various disparate people that fall outside the label of being Jews. See T. Rajak, 'Greeks and Barbarians in Josephus', in J. J. Collins and G. E. Sterling (eds.), *Hellenism in the Land of Israel* (Notre Dame: University of Notre Dame Press, 2001), pp.244–62.

were articulated by a number of Gentiles regarding the Jewish way of life. The final part will consider some of the information Josephus provides about his life where he has direct interaction with Gentiles. From the discussion of these three aspects of Josephus' career it will be argued that he was not interested in Gentiles *per se*. He was not complimentary of Gentiles, or of practices and beliefs associated with Gentiles, for their own sake. His engagement with Gentiles was borne out of necessity and was always undertaken from the perspective that his Jewish way of life had little to gain and/or learn from interaction with the Gentile world.

2. *Gentiles in* Bellum Judaicum

There is no single section in the work where Gentiles are a main subject matter. Instead, they appear in a number of different contexts as required. We will comment on five of the more notable ways in which Josephus draws attention to Gentiles in the narrative. The first occasion, within the preface, helps set the tone. Josephus is openly critical of the existing accounts of the recent war between the Jews and the Romans (*B.J.* 1.1-2, 7-8). Initially not explicitly identified, other than being accounts designed to denigrate the Jews, Josephus soon offers a direct, forceful criticism of Greek authors of his day (1.13-16). These works, Josephus argues, fail to mimic the skill of ancient writers, who addressed the history of their own day (1.14), and they display no skill in the task of being an historian. They do not value 'truth' (1.16). These comments all have important rhetorical value for Josephus. He needs to assert both the value and the necessity for his own version of the war to be read by others. Josephus is also careful not to name the existing accounts as being written by Roman authors. However, our first encounter with Gentiles is a negative characterisation. Gentile authors shy away from writing on important, contemporary subject matter. When they do take up the challenge it is without any respect for 'truth', writing instead distorted, polemical accounts.

The second manner by which Josephus makes Gentiles an explicit part of the work is as participants in the description of events. A number of these individuals are depicted in a positive manner. Examples of these good Gentiles include Augustus (*B.J.* 1.391-92, 395-96; 2.37-38), Petronius (2.198, 201-203) and Neapolitanus (2.340-41). It is important to note that the positive depiction of these Gentiles is directly linked to the way they interact with the Jews. In particular it the respect with which they interact with Jews and the respect they display for the Jewish way of life. The extent to which the depiction of a Gentile is dependent on their treatment of Jews is evident from those presented in a negative way: Florus (2.293-308), Gaius (2.184-85, 203) and Catullus (7.439-53). These men openly attacked the Jewish way of life and/or Jewish people. As such, Gentiles are respected and criticised by Josephus in *Bellum Judaicum* according to the way they were remembered for interacting with Jews, not for any inherent aspect of their own identity. This observation is pertinent for the other main way that Gentiles feature in the description of events. On a number of occasions Josephus refers to the reverence and respect for the Temple and the cult that was displayed by the Romans (e.g. *B.J.* 4.324; 5.15-18, 562-64; 6.124-28). The Romans actively wanted to preserve the Temple (1.28; 6.236-43).[7] However, these are not freestanding positive portraits. For Josephus, these Romans help to highlight the gross criminal behaviour of those Jews he says were responsible for God deciding to destroy the Temple. Josephus is not trying to present Romans as pious Gentiles in their own right. Rather they act as the counter to those people who should know better, rogue Jews (6.99-102).[8]

The third notable appearance of Gentiles in *Bellum Judaicum* is in terms of fighting between Jews and Gentiles that coincides with the war. We first encounter trouble in the narrative in the lead up to the war commencing, with Josephus describing a dispute at Caesarea Maritima between the Jewish residents and the 'Syrian' residents (*B.J.* 2.266-70). Josephus goes on to describe the latter group as 'Greeks', which is probably a label referring to their geographical origin.[9] At dispute was a civic rights issue centring on control of the city: the governor decided to have the matter referred to the emperor for resolution (2.270).

---

7   See J. von Ehrenkrook, *Sculpturing Idolatry in Flavian Rome: (An)Iconic Rhetoric in the Writings of Flavius Josephus* (EJL 33; Atlanta: SBL, 2011), pp.131–5. He argues that Josephus' main target is elements of Greek culture that allowed Josephus to place together Jews and Romans as holding a shared value system. The broad underlying purpose, however, is that Josephus uses other peoples to show the respectability of the Jewish way of life.

8   On the depiction of Titus see J. S. McLaren, 'Josephus on Titus: The Vanquished Writing about the Victor', in J. Sievers and G. Lembi (eds.), *Josephus and Jewish History in Flavian Rome and Beyond* (JSJSup 104; Leiden: Brill, 2005), pp.279–95. Cf. G. M. Paul, 'The Presentation of Titus in the *Jewish War* of Josephus: Two Aspects', *Phoenix* 47 (1993), pp.56–66.

9   Cf. *A.J.* 20.173. See T. Rajak, *The Jewish Dialogue with Greece and Rome: Studies in Cultural and Social Interaction* (Leiden: Brill, 2001), pp.140–1; and von Ehrenkrook, *Sculpting*, pp.126–7.

Josephus provides a carefully crafted account of the resolution (2.284-92). Although he briefly notes that the emperor decided in favour of the Greek section of the population (2.284), Josephus focuses on an incident linked with the synagogue at Caesarea. Responsibility for the trouble that ensues is mainly attributed to the various Gentile participants. The 'Greek' owner of the land next to the synagogue insulted the Jews by undertaking construction work very close to the synagogue (2.285-86). Florus accepted a bribe from the Jews to intervene and resolve the matter, but then did nothing to assist (2.287-88); in addition 'Caesareans' incited trouble by setting up an altar outside the synagogue on the Sabbath (2.289). The only disruptive action attributed to the Jews was an attack on the labourers by some rash youths, in an effort to stop the construction work (2.286). Josephus has provided an account whereby the culprits are Gentiles in an incident that he is ascribing as being the trigger for the war (2.285). Whatever the precise details of the events that took place in Caesarea, Josephus has chosen to present the incident in a way that devolves the Jewish section of the population from responsibility for the trouble. Even when the Jews decided to quit the city and seek refuge, they suffer at the hands of Florus (2.292).

The dispute at Caesarea provides the broad frame of reference for the stories of fighting between Jews and Gentiles that take place as the war unfolds. Jewish residents of cities find themselves the subject of attacks from their Gentile neighbours; Jews in Caesarea are massacred (*B.J.* 2.457).[10] News of the attack leads to Jews taking revenge, attacking the inhabitants of several cities in the Decapolis (2.458-60). Yet these actions are very quickly overshadowed by the description of Gentile attacks on Jews residing in the region. Two general summaries of the attacks (2.461-65, 477-80) act as the bookends for the detailed example of Scythopolis (2.466-76).[11] There is an effort to justify or downplay the brutality and viciousness of these attacks. While they certainly assist to present the region as a place in crisis and turmoil, Josephus shows no reservation in laying the vast bulk of responsibility with Gentiles.[12]

The two other ways that Gentiles feature require only brief comment. One is the presentation of the Roman army. Josephus provides a detailed

10   Although the incident immediately preceding this attack is the massacre of the Roman garrison in Jerusalem (*B.J.* 2.449-56), Josephus does not suggest there was a causal link. Rather, the connection was that two parallel heinous crimes took place at precisely the same time as one another.

11   See also *B.J.* 2.481-83, 487-98, 559-61.

12   Josephus reminds the reader of these atrocities during the speech by Eleazar at Masada (*B.J.* 7.361-68).

digression on the Roman army as he prepares to describe the campaign of Vespasian in Galilee (*B.J.* 3.70-109). There is an outline of the structure, discipline and tactics of the army. Each component helps make the Roman army powerful and successful. Josephus even signposts the digression as a way of assisting readers to understand the futility of going to war against the Romans (3.108-109). This abundant praise is, in fact, similar to a double-edged sword. As much as it can be used to help explain any success, it can also be used as a blueprint against which to assess the ability of the Romans to put into practice all that was allegedly common nature to them. While there are individuals who behave with valour (5.312-16; 6.81-91, 186-89; 7.13-17), these are more than matched by examples of Romans displaying poor judgment and a lack of discipline (5.291-95, 317-30, 331-43; 6.152-56, 157-63, 177-86). The most significant example of the inability of the troops to follow orders supposedly occurred in relation to the most important order, that the Temple not be set alight (6.251-66).[13]

The other element, the summary of the Jewish schools of thought, is an example of indirect reference to Gentiles. One of the main functions of the summary is to provide readers with some general information about aspects of the Jewish way of life that might be of interest to an outside. Hence, the decision to identify them as 'philosophies' and then to discuss only a few features of their outlook and behaviour. It is possible the lengthy account of the Essenes was constructed in order to evoke a positive response among a Gentile audience.[14] However, there is only one explicit parallel made by Josephus in the *Bellum Judaicum* version (cf. *A.J.* 13.171-73; *Vita* 12). The primary purpose of the summary is for Josephus to be able to isolate responsibility for the war to a marginal, non-representative new group.[15] In this instance, where there is an opportunity for Josephus to claim links between Jews and Gentiles, he chooses instead to keep the discussion within the broad confines of his own tradition. From the various occasions where Gentiles appear as part of the narrative, Josephus displays no particular interest in them or in

13   Of course, underpinning the whole account of the burning of the Temple was Josephus' claim that it was God that made the decision about what would happen, not Titus. See also *B.J.* 5.548-52 regarding the barbaric behaviour of some of the allied troops and Titus' response (*B.J.* 5.553-61).

14   See S. Mason, *Flavius Josephus: Translation and Commentary*. IB. *Judean War 2* (Leiden: Brill, 2001), pp.84–95; and Rajak, *Jewish Dialogue*, pp.219–40.

15   See M. Goodman, 'Josephus and Variety in First-Century Judaism', in idem, *Judaism in the Roman World: Collected Essays* (AJEC 66; Leiden: Brill, 2007), pp.33–46.

their customs and practices. Where they do appear in a positive manner it is always in the context of acting as a point of comparison to some people, normally Jews, that have defied their fellow Jews and their God.

3. *Contra Apionem*

Josephus' *Contra Apionem* displays the author's literary diversity. Even allowing for the likelihood that all his writings were thematic, it is a departure from the narrative-based structure of his other works. Here Josephus takes on the role of providing a direct response to criticisms of the Jewish way of life.[16] Much of the work is framed as a legal debate, with various witnesses speaking on behalf of the Jews in response to accusations by 'Greeks' against their way of life. The main aspects of Jewish life that are criticised pertain to their origins, their exclusive behaviour and their peculiar practices. The means by which Josephus offers his response is illuminating for the present discussion of his attitude toward Gentiles. We will comment briefly on four the major strategies that Josephus uses: pitting Gentile claim against one another, comparing Moses with other great figures, noting examples of imitation, and direct and open criticism of the accusers. In all of these lines of defence Josephus is consistent in upholding that the Jewish way of life in no way is inferior to any other way of life. In fact, it is the reverse; the Jewish way of life is superior to those espoused by Gentiles.

Largely in order to counter the claim that the Jews were not an ancient people Josephus uses other Gentiles witnesses (*C. Ap.* 1.69-72). He cites evidence from Egyptians (1.73-105), from Phoenician sources (1.106-25), Chaldean sources (1.128-60) and then turns his attention to evidence from Greek sources (1.161-214). The claims of the accuser are met with counter-claims by information derived from fellow accusers that confirm the antiquity of the Jews (1.215, 217). The second strategy Josephus employs is to hold up Moses as the figure *par excellence* in the ancient world. One of the key ways that the Jewish way of life was attacked was to target the integrity and the reputation of Moses (e.g. 2.145). Josephus compares Moses with figures within 'Greek' traditions. He asserts that Moses is superior to all other philosophers, a view

16   For more detail regarding the following outline, see J. M. G. Barclay, *Flavius Josephus: Translation and Commentary*. X. *Against Apion* (Leiden: Brill, 2007), pp. xvii–lxxi. On Josephus' purpose, also see M. Goodman, 'Josephus' Treatise *Against Apion*', in M. Edwards, M. Goodman and S. Price (eds.), *Apologetics in the Roman Empire: Pagans, Jews, and Christians* (Oxford: Oxford University Press, 1999), pp.45–58.

affirmed by his antiquity (2.154, 158, 168-69). Admittedly, these comments are framed as part of an effort to defend his way of life, yet it is notable that Josephus actively engages in a ranking exercise, with Moses well out in front.

The third strategy involves a slightly different approach to the argument by comparison. Josephus also defends Moses and the laws by which the Jewish people live by showing how his teachings have been imitated. Plato 'imitates' Moses (*C. Ap.* 2.256-57), as do the Lacedaemonians (2.259). Josephus even asserts that although Jews do not try to imitate others they are very happy for other people to emulate them (2.261, 279-84).[17] The fourth and final strategy to note is use of a direct attack on the integrity of the accusers. At the outset of the work Josephus issues an open critique of 'Greek' history writing (1.6-7).[18] He even employs rhetorical questions to undermine the credibility of 'Greeks' given the lack of antiquity in their writings (1.15, 22); Josephus adds to the level of criticism by challenging the willingness of 'Greek' authors to undergo hardship in order to provide an accurate account of events (1.44-45). In short, 'Greeks' are not interested in ancient history (1.58) and by implication are not in a position to make claims about the antiquity or otherwise of Jews.[19]

In a work devoted to defending the Jewish way of life Josephus is likely to engage in rhetorical techniques and to try to undermine the arguments of his opponents. It is significant that in so doing Josephus finds little of value from outside his own heritage. Hence, he can ask the question, 'why would we emulate other people's laws when we see that they are not preserved even by those who laid them down?' (*C. Ap.* 2.273).[20]

4. *Josephus' Own Career*

The other perspective important to consider is the way Josephus presents his own interactions with Gentiles. There are three occasions that warrant discussion.[21] One is made public only in his short *Vita*: the trip he undertakes to Rome prior to the war. The story is clearly used by Josephus as

17   See Barclay, *Against Apion*, p.326 n.1125.
18   See Barclay, *Against Apion*, p.13 nn.29 and 30.
19   See also the comments on Greek mythology at *C. Ap.* 2.239-49.
20   Barclay, *Against Apion*, p.323.
21   Josephus' military encounter with the Romans as his opponent at Jotopata and his subsequent role in the Roman camp up to the capture of Jerusalem will not be discussed.

part of the process of affirming his credentials as a worthy public figure. He survives a shipwreck *en route* and is successful in achieving the purpose of the trip, the release of some fellow priests detained in Rome (*Vita* 14-16). Although Josephus does not offer any detailed commentary on his experience in Rome, nor of any direct influence the trip had on his way of thinking, it has been generally viewed as a positive encounter with the Roman world for Josephus.[22] However, it is notable that the means by which Josephus describes himself as being successful were not necessarily complimentary in nature. His two points of contact were not esteemed. One was a Jewish actor and the other was a woman, admittedly the wife of the Emperor (*Vita* 16). If anything, the fact that these two people were the means by which Nero was influenced Nero calls into question the integrity with which Rome was administered during his reign. As such, there is no particular reason to conclude that Josephus went away from Rome impressed by the people that claimed to rule much of the Mediterranean world.

The second interaction is the account of Josephus' surrender to the Romans at the end of the assault on Jotopata (*B.J.* 3.340-408). It is a very detailed and lengthy story given its relative small role within the larger narrative of the war. No doubt, this level of attention is due primarily because it was such a pivotal event in Josephus' life. The concern here is not so much the veracity or otherwise of the account but the way that Josephus explains what takes place. The named Romans all behave in a laudable manner; they apparently want to capture Josephus alive (*B.J.* 3.344-49, 351, 396-98) but there is no noticeable commentary.[23] Instead, what is particularly important is the way that Josephus seeks to explain the decision to surrender. Attention is often placed on the message that Josephus claims to have given to Vespasian about his impending rise to power (*B.J.* 3.399-402). It is clear that Josephus uses his role as a messenger as a way of providing a justification for his decision (*B.J.* 3.352, 354, 362). The significant point to note is that the whole means of defending his course of action is Jewish in origin. Josephus does not portray himself as using the type of arguments put into the mouth of Agrippa II about the futility of taking up arms (*B.J.* 2.345-401). Rather, Josephus claims that it was his duty as a priest capable of interpreting dreams to ensure that the message was delivered to Vespasian. Josephus draws upon a thoroughly Jewish reason to try to place himself among the

22   For example, Donaldson, *Judaism and the Gentiles*, pp.279–80.

23   Even this positive account of the key Romans has its counterpart later in the narrative, when news of Josephus' capture is greeted by the Jews of Jerusalem with criticism (*B.J.* 3.438-42).

Romans. There is no attempt to present what took place in a Roman guise.[24]

The third occasion is the immediate aftermath of the capture of Jerusalem. By that time Josephus had spent several years living directly under Roman control. He saw how Titus worked and watched as the Romans went about the task of crushing the Jewish forces that opposed them. As with the trip to Rome, it is only in *Vita* that Josephus describes his actions amidst the turmoil. Again, clearly with the intention of presenting himself in a very positive manner, Josephus displays piety and compassion.[25] His concern is for fellow Jews and for the Temple, not any desire for self-gain (*Vita* 418-21). Irrespective of whether or not this is an accurate account, it is insightful for the way that Josephus seeks to portray himself. In the narrative, and presumably still at the time he was writing *Vita*, Josephus wanted readers to look upon him as a Jew, one concerned for his religious heritage and for his compatriots.

5. *Conclusions*

Josephus appears to be a prime candidate for a Jew that would be accustomed to working with Gentiles. He was an educated Jew based in Jerusalem, who, as a priest, would have been familiar with the presence of Romans in his homeland. It is even likely that his education involved some basic Greek language study.[26] His move to Rome after 70 CE, sponsored by the new ruling family, also meant that most of his adult life was spent as a Diaspora Jew. However, being among Gentiles does not necessarily mean an interest in or affiliation with them. The question posed at the beginning of this chapter was: Did Josephus respect Gentiles? From a review of the way Gentiles are depicted in two of his works and the occasions from his own career where Josephus came into contact with Gentiles, it is apparent that Josephus did not display any particular interest in or affinity with them.

---

24   This approach is also evident in the core explanation for why the Jews were defeated and the Temple destroyed; it was the decision of the God of the Jews to use the Romans as instruments of divine punishment. See J. Price, 'Josephus and the Dialogue on the Destruction of the Temple', in C. Böttrich and J. Herzer with T. Reiprich (eds.), *Josephus und das Neue Testament. Wechselseitige Wahrnehmungen. II Internationales Symposium zum Corpus Judaeo-Hellenisticum 25.–28. Mai 2006, Greifswald* (WUNT 209; Tübingen: Mohr Siebeck, 2007), pp.181–94.

25   S. Mason, *Flavius Josephus: Translation and Commentary. IX. Life of Josephus* (Leiden: Brill, 2001), p.166 n.1718.

26   Rajak, *Josephus*, pp.46–64.

Chapter 5

THE PORTRAYAL OF GENTILES
IN JEWISH APOCALYPTIC LITERATURE

Michael P. Theophilos

1. *Introduction*

The portrayal of Gentiles in Jewish apocalyptic literature is variegated, rich and complex. Various scholarly attempts to navigate this diverse subject area have been prone to problematic methodological assumptions, ranging from issues in textual criticism, dating, authorship and provenance, to questions of historical and theological significance, particularly the extent to which a document is taken as normative of Jewish perspective and practice for the wider Mediterranean world. Notwithstanding these significant concerns, the subjects of which have filled many volumes, there is considerable merit in examining the relevant primary source material at the broader level, with the intention of possibly identifying any characteristics across the heterogeneous Jewish apocalyptic traditions. One such recent discussion is that of T. L. Donaldson,[1] wherein he attempts to expunge almost every aspect of the particularism of judgment in the ancient texts under discussion. The present study, in part, is a response to Donaldson's optimism regarding the portrayal and fate of the Gentiles in the Jewish apocalyptic texts. My intention is not to deny or underplay the streams of Jewish tradition that are replete with positive references to Gentiles participating in Israel's (eschatological) reward (Gen. 12.1-3; Exod. 12.38; 19.3-6; Isa. 2.2-4; 45.20-22; 51.3-5), but rather to note that distinct historical circumstances engender distinct literary responses. Jewish apocalyptic literature, composed during historical periods of turmoil, often functioned as a sharp invective and rebuke of the Gentile nations. This powerful element of polemical discourse is not surprising given that the

---

1 Donaldson, *Judaism and the Gentiles*.

predominant feature of the apocalyptic genre is to 'express an interpretation of historical situations (often political crises) and to shape the human response to those situations'.[2] The historical catastrophe that many of the Jewish apocalyptic texts wrestle with during this period is the destruction of Jerusalem in 70 CE. The primary departure point for Jewish attitudes towards Gentiles in this period is the assumption that Jews are 'set apart from Gentiles and that this separation is of divine origin'.[3] Often taking the role of the consummate 'other', Gentiles are frequently portrayed as archetypal idolaters and enemies of Yahweh who oppress the Jewish population and as a result stand under divine judgment.[4] However, even this pre-emptive summary requires some qualification and nuance, and will be noted in the analysis below. My discussion will centre on the following texts: *Testament of Moses*, *Sibylline Oracles* 3-4, *Jubilees*, *1 Enoch*, *4 Ezra*, *2 Baruch*, and *Apocalypse of Abraham*.

2. *Testament of Moses*

The genre of the *Testament of Moses* has traditionally been identified as a 'testament', that is, a farewell speech of a person who is soon to depart from their earthly existence. Indeed, M. G. Reddish definitively asserts in his analysis that the *Testament of Moses* is not an apocalypse.[5] Other more nuanced approaches have identified the apocalyptic elements in the work as significant for contributing to its multivalent genre.[6] Despite the absence of the traditional feature of the author as recipient of a revelation mediated by an otherworldly being, there are three features that justify its inclusion in our analysis of Jewish apocalyptic literature.

2   J. J. Collins, 'Apocalyptic Literature', in R. A. Kraft and G. W. E. Nickelsburg (eds.), *Early Judaism and its Modern Interpreters* (Atlanta: Scholars Press, 1986), pp.345–70 (360).

3   G. Gilbert, 'Gentiles, Jewish Attitudes toward', in J. J. Collins and D. C. Harlow (eds.), *The Eerdmans Dictionary of Early Judaism* (Grand Rapids: Eerdmans, 2010), pp.670–73 (670).

4   It is no surprise, then, that within those portions of the Hebrew Bible which were composed in periods when historical adversity threatened to erode Jewish national identity, one finds similar negative portrayals, most notably in the apocalyptic literature of Dan. 2 and 7.

5   M. G. Reddish, *Apocalyptic Literature* (Nashville: Abingdon, 1990), p.214. However, Reddish does later admit to there being 'apocalyptic eschatology' present in the work (p.216).

6   See, for example, L. H. Helyer, *Exploring Jewish Literature of the Second Temple Period* (Downers Grove: InterVarsity, 2002), pp.112–47.

First, the apocalyptic elements implicit within the text include *ex eventu* prophecy, cosmic catastrophes, stylised recollection of the past composed during a period of persecution, and significant elements of judgment and reward. Second, the distinct and severe division between the righteous and wicked is a common motif in apocalyptic works.[7] Third, the text includes important material related to our discussion of the portrayal of the Gentiles from a Jewish standpoint.

The work itself consists of a prophecy delivered by Moses before his death, and in this manner it effectively represents an alternative version to Deuteronomy 31–34. By appealing to Moses' authority, further *gravitas* is added to the discourse. The text opens with Joshua being summoned and appointed as the successor of Moses (ch. 1), who then proceeds to offer a proleptic account of the history of Israel (chs. 2–9), including reference to a return to the land because of the pity of a foreign king (i.e. Cyrus the Persian, 4.6). Reference is also made to a 'rash and perverse...wanton king' (6.2), who rules for 'thirty-four years' (6.6). The consensus of scholarship is that this figure refers to Herod the Great, the half-caste Idumean-Jew.[8] It is significant to note that this king is presented as God's instrument of judgment, specifically through his cruel administration. Herod's subsequent heirs follow, as does a 'powerful king from the west' (6.8), which eventually results in Jerusalem's destruction (6.9). In the final sequence of the vision (chs. 10–11), there are cosmic upheavals: '...the earth will tremble...the mountains will be made low...the sun will not give its light...it will be turned wholly into blood' (10.4-5). The apocalyptic language of that section (10.1-15) includes reference to the nations being punished (10.2, 7) and faithful Israelites receiving heavenly rewards (10.8-9). In this process, there is a significant element of triumphal gloating on behalf of the victorious Israelite: 'And you will behold from on high. You will see your enemies in Gehenna, and recognising them, you will rejoice' (10.10).

---

7   R. A. Kugler, 'Testaments', in D. A. Carson, P. T. O'Brien, and M. A. Seifrid (eds.), *Justification and Variegated Nomism*. I. *The Complexities of Second Temple Judaism* (WUNT 2.140; Tübingen: Mohr Siebeck, 2001), pp.189–213 (195).

8   G. W. E. Nickelsburg, *Jewish Literature between the Bible and the Mishnah* (Minneapolis: Fortress, 1981), pp.212–14, has cogently argued that there were essentially two stages of composition and hence two distinct crises that it seeks to address. The first was under the persecution of Antiochus Epiphanes IV, in the mid-second century BCE, with *T. Mos.* 5 and 8 directly addressing concerns of this period. Approximately two centuries later the work was revised and material was inserted between what is now chs. 5 and 8. Material in ch. 6 conspicuously refers to the Hasmonean period (6.1) and the rise of Herod the Great (6.2-4).

A distinctive feature of this work is the tension in which the author holds determinism on the one hand, and human freewill on the other. The introductory chapter clearly states that God 'created the world on behalf of his people, but he did not make this purpose of creation openly known from the beginning of the world, so that the nations might be found guilty' (1.12-13). All that happens is determined and foreordained by God (3.11-12; 12.4-5).[9] This robust determinism is strengthened during times of persecution and encourages confidence in God's ultimate providence.[10] However, there are also strong elements of Deuteronomic theology: 'Therefore, those who truly fulfil the commandments of God will flourish and will finish the good way, but those who sin by disregarding the commandments will deprive themselves of the good things which were declared before' (12.10-11a).[11] This is evident in the cycle of (1) sin (*T. Mos.* 2; 5.1–6.1; cf. Deut. 28.15; 32.15-18); (2) punishment (*T. Mos.* 3.1-4; 8; cf. Deut. 28.16-68; 32.19-27); (3) repentance (*T. Mos.* 3.5–4.4; 9; cf. Deut. 30.2; 32.28-34); (4) salvation (*T. Mos.* 4.5-9; 10; cf. Deut. 30.3-10; 32.35-43).[12] In this process, the Gentiles are the instrument of divine judgment: 'they (sinners), indeed, will be punished by the nations with many tortures' (12.11b). However, characteristically, the Gentiles themselves do not escape ultimate divine judgment and destruction (1.12-13).

3. *Sibylline Oracles*

The work known as the *Sibylline Oracles* is evidently an adaptation of a genre from earlier Greco-Roman literature.[13] Owing its derivation to

9   Despite the misgivings by Collins that the actions of Taxo in ch. 9 have the capacity to change the course of history (J. J. Collins, 'Testaments', in M. Stone [ed.], *Jewish Writings of the Second Temple Period: Apocrypha, Pseudepigrapha, Qumran Sectarian Writings, Philo, Josephus* [Philadelphia: Fortress, 1984], pp.325–55 [347]), human action in the *Testament of Moses* should be seen, as a whole, within the purview of divine control.

10   See further J. Priest, 'Testament of Moses', in *OTP*, I, pp.919–35 (922–23).

11   The theology of the *Testament of Moses* is identified as such by Kugler, 'Testaments', p.193.

12   See further, Nickelsburg, *Jewish Literature*, pp.81–3.

13   See J. J. Collins, 'The Jewish Adaptation of Sibylline Oracles', in I. C. Colombo and T. Seppilli (eds.), *Sibille e linguaggi oracolari: Mito, storia tradizione. Atti del Convegno Macerata-Norcia, Settembre 1994* (Rome: Istituti Editoriali e Poligrafici Internazionali, 1998), pp.369–87; J. J. Collins, *Seers, Sibyls, and Sages in Hellenistic-Roman Judaism* (Leiden: Brill, 2001), pp.1–19; A. Momigliano, 'From

the Greek σίβυλλα (prophetess), the genre is dominated by prophetic oracular utterances of doom, and in particular, woes and disasters on humankind, often brought on by ritual offences or ethical violations. R. Bauckham notes that the original intention of the *Sibylline Oracles* 'must have been to gain a hearing for their message from Gentile readers who would take them seriously as ancient prophecy'.[14] Similarly, J. J. Collins has noted: 'the use of the sibyl's name was intended to lend the weight of a venerable pagan authority'.[15] Whether such efficacy was enhanced by the genre is, of course, debatable. Despite the elements of propaganda that have frequently been noted in the work,[16] the extent to which this text functioned as an apologetic for outsiders is unresolved.

The *Sibylline Oracles* have been preserved as a series of twelve books.[17] Book 3 (dated to the mid-second century BCE) is generally considered to be the oldest of the identifiable Jewish portions,[18] and will be the focus of our attention here due to the unambiguous and explicit interest in its portrayal of Gentiles.[19] In it the Sibyl denounces various forms of idolatry. The Mosaic Law[20] is referred to in 3.256-59, and, as

the Pagan to the Christian Sibyl', in R. DiDonato (ed.), *Nono Contributo: alla Storia degli Studi Classici e del Mondo antico* (Rome: Edizioni di Storia e Letteratura, 1992), pp.725–44; and H. W. Parke, *Sibyls and Sibylline Prophecy in Classical Antiquity* (London: Routledge, 1988).

14   R. Bauckham, 'Apocalypses', in Carson, O'Brien and Seifrid (eds.), *Justification and Variegated Nomism*, I, pp.135–87.

15   J. J. Collins, *The Apocalyptic Imagination* (Grand Rapids: Eerdmans, 2nd edn, 1998), p.125.

16   Distinctive negative attitudes toward Rome and the positive portrayal of Egypt suggest that portions of this work functioned as explicit propaganda for the Ptolemaic King. See Bauckham, 'Apocalypses', p.186.

17   Collins uses the conventional numbering system (Books 1–8, 9–14) in his translation and notes in J. J. Collins, 'Sibylline Oracles', in *OTP*, I, pp.317–472. As Books 9 and 10 repeat previous material verbatim (cf. chs. 7–8), they are generally omitted in modern editions.

18   Book 3 is typically dated to the Maccabean period, predominantly on the basis of the reference to the seventh king of Egypt (3.193, 318, 608). Although the number seven may be functioning here to idealise the king, Collins ('Sibylline Oracles', p.335) notes 'the number could not be introduced, with any credibility, later than the reign of the seventh Ptolemy'. See also R. Buitenwerf, *Book III of the Sibylline Oracles and its Social Setting* (Leiden: Brill, 2003), pp.124–34; and J. Geffcken, *Komposition and Entstehungszeit der Oracula Sibyllina* (Leipzig: Hinrichs, 1902).

19   Book 4 will briefly be noted as one conspicuously antagonistic example of Jewish attitudes to Gentiles in the post-70 CE period.

20   Buitenwerf, *Sibylline Oracles*, pp.202–3.

is evident in the subsequent sections of Book 3, all people (including Gentiles) are required to keep the 'just ordinances on the two tablets' (3.257; cf. 3.195). The nations, however, have failed miserably, and hence stand under divine judgment (3.599-600). Gentile ignorance of the Law makes them only more culpable:[21] 'Because they knew neither the Law, nor the judgment of the great God, but with mindless spirit you all launched an attack and raised spears against the sanctuary' (3.686-88). The author presents this as a series of 'woes' against virtually all known ancient Near East and Mediterranean regions, including Babylon (3.300-313), Egypt (3.314-40), Asia Minor (3.341-49, 381-485), Rome (3.350-80), Greece and surrounding regions (3.401-572). In the future age, Gentiles will 'ponder the Law of the Most High God' (3.719), and acknowledge that they 'have wandered from the path of the Immortal... [and] revered things made by hand, idol and statues of dead men' (3.721-22). This results in God putting 'in effect a common law for men throughout the whole earth' (3.757-58), and judging those who do not acknowledge that 'he himself alone is God and that there is no other' (3.760), condemning them to being 'burnt with fire' (3.761).[22]

Book 4 was written in the wake of the destruction of Jerusalem,[23] and so in large part has the events of 70 CE explicitly on the horizon of its apocalyptic outlook. In addition to the exhortation to repentance for all humanity (4.162-70), and explicit reference to the destruction by fire of those evil-doers who persist in impiety (4.171-78), there appears to be an implicit polemic, specifically directed toward Rome for the intentional destruction of Jerusalem. *Sibylline Oracles* 4.130-32 states that one of the various disturbances resulting from the destruction of Jerusalem (described in 4.115-29) would be as follows: 'But when a firebrand, turned away from a cleft in the earth in the land of Italy, reaches to broad heaven, it will burn many cities and destroy men'. Commentators have often seen here a veiled reference to the eruption of Vesuvius which

21   Buitenwerf, *Sibylline Oracles*, p.264.

22   The theme of Gentile nations worshipping the God of Israel also reappears in 5.265 and 357. *Sib. Or.* 5.484-511 consists of a denunciation of Egypt's deities (Isis, *Sarapis*), and their conversion to the true God; 'Come let us change the terrible custom we have received from our ancestors'. *Sib. Or.* 3.702-31 anticipates that a portion of the Gentile nations will acknowledge the God of Israel and undergo religious conversion. See Buitenwerf, *Sibylline Oracles*, p.189. It should be noted that the specific requirements of the Law stated in 3.762-66 are not the Jewish laws of circumcision or dietary restrictions, but common ethical principles such as the avoidance of idolatry, homosexuality, arrogance, greed, astrology, augury and divination.

23   Bauckham, 'Apocalypses', p.187; Collins, 'Sibylline Oracles', pp.381–3.

destroyed Pompeii in 79 CE as divine retribution against Rome for the destruction of the Jerusalem Temple in 70 CE.[24] Destruction by fire is consistent with the theme of the punishment of the wicked in Jewish apocalyptic sources, and further demonstrates the author's view that the God of Israel is ultimately providential, not just over political and military manoeuvrings, but over all things, including natural forces.

4. *Jubilees*

Palaeographic dating of extant fragments of *Jubilees* from Qumran would suggest that the work was composed not later than the late Has- monean period (c. 165–63 BCE).[25] Within the fifty chapters of *Jubilees*, the biblical story is creatively retold, selectively covering material from Creation (Gen. 1) through to the confirmation of the covenant (Exod. 24). The name of the work is derived from the schema of divisions it presents (fifty successive forty-nine year Jubilee periods), and is cast as an apocalyptic revelation combining elements of *ex eventu* prophecy, persecution, eschatological upheavals, judgment and destruction of the wicked, judgment of other worldly beings, and cosmic transformation.[26]

The interest of the work is twofold. First, it seeks to advocate a 364- day solar calendar (as opposed to the solar-lunar calendar), the implica- tions of which are explicated in 6.32-38; 'but if they are transgressed, and they do not observe them according to his commandment, then they will corrupt all of their (fixed) times, and the years will be removed from within this (order), and they will transgress their ordinances' (6.33).

Second, considerable liberty is taken in re-writing the early Penta- teuchal traditions, especially in regard to the whitewashing of several accounts.[27] The emphasis throughout is on the exclusive nature of Jew- ish thought and practice, including the rejection of intermarriage and

24 Collins, 'Sibylline Oracles', p.387.
25 G. C. Carey, *Ultimate Things: An Introduction to Jewish and Christian Apocalyptic Literature* (St. Louis: Chalice, 2005), p.69; O. S. Wintermute, 'Jubilees', in *OTP*, II, pp.35–142 (43); and J. C. VanderKam, *Textual and Historical Studies in the Book of Jubilees* (HSM 14; Missoula: Scholars Press, 1977).
26 See further Collins, *Apocalyptic Imagination*, p.7.
27 For example, J. H. Charlesworth, *The Pseudepigrapha and Modern Research* (SCSS 7; Ann Arbor: Scholars Press, 1981), pp.143–4, notes that, 'Rebecca is com- manded by Abraham, who saw Esau's deeds and knew Jacob was the true heir, to love and cherish Jacob more than Esau (19.16-31)… The patriarchs are perceived as the innovators of culture; writing, medicine, and plowing originated respectively with Enoch, Noah, and Abraham.'

separation from Gentiles. In Abraham's blessing of Jacob in 22.16 he states: 'Separate from the nations, and do not eat with them. Do not act as they do, and do not become their companion for their actions are something that is impure, and all their ways are defiled and something abominable and detestable.' Although this passage has often been taken as evidence that Gentiles themselves are intrinsically impure,[28] J. Klawans has argued that in light of the permission granting the ownership of Gentile slaves (15.12-13, 24), and the negative emphasis on the Gentile behavior (1.9; 12.2; 20.7; 21.15; 22.17-22), separation is on the basis of Gentile *actions* rather than their intrinsic nature.[29] *Jubilees* 30.7 reiterates the prohibition of intermarriage and explicitly outlines the punishment for such action as stoning for men and burning for women.[30] Above all else, Gentiles in *Jubilees* are ritually impure because of their detestable acts, the emphasis being on their idolatry.[31]

The rationale for the portrayal of the Gentiles in this fashion can be attributed to the perceived vulnerability of Jewish identity in light of Ptolemaic and Seleucid threats during the late second and early first centuries BCE. Despite attempts to restore the nation to its former glory by expanding Jewish territory and securing political autonomy, the Hasmonean rulers became increasingly hellenised, corrupt and insensitive to Jewish religious traditions. In this light, the author of *Jubilees* sought to strengthen Jewish ethnic identity by 'restoring a proper relationship with his (God's) people and to call the readers to obedience'.[32]

5. *1 Enoch*

The text of *1 Enoch* is a composite work of five books: (1) the Book of Watchers (*1 En.* 1–36, c. third century BCE); (2) the Similitudes of

28   For example, J. D. G. Dunn, 'The Incident at Antioch (Gal. 2:11-18)', *JSNT* 18 (1983), pp.3–57 (18); and J. H. Neyrey, 'The Idea of Purity in Mark's Gospel', *Semeia* 35 (1986), pp.91–128 (100).

29   J. Klawans, 'Notions of Gentile Impurity in Ancient Judaism', *AJSRev* 20 (1995), pp.285–312 (294).

30   See further J. C. VanderKam, *The Book of Jubilees* (2 vols.; Leuven: Peeters, 1989), II, p.193.

31   The isolated references to the 'kittim' in *Jub.* 24.28-29; 37.9-10 (cf. 1QM) are most plausibly understood in relation to their geo-political reference as people who live across the Mediterranean. So Schultz, *Conquering the World*, p.146. Less likely is the view of Y. Yadin, *The Scroll of the War of the Sons of Light against the Sons of Darkness* (Oxford: Oxford University Press, 1962), p.24, that the term has an eschatological meaning.

32   Wintermute, 'Jubilees', p.41.

Enoch (*1 En.* 37–71, c. first century BC); (3) the Astronomical Book (*1 En.* 72–82, c. third century BCE); (4) the Book of Dreams (*1 En.* 83–90, c. 170–163 BCE); (5) the Epistle of Enoch (*1 En.* 91–105, c. second century BCE). Significant material pertaining to the portrayal of Gentiles is found in all but the third book (*1 En.* 72–82). We will proceed with an analysis of each.

The Book of Watchers (*1 En.* 1–36) obliquely introduces the Gentiles with apparent charity: 'all the sons of men will become righteous, and all peoples will worship me; all will bless and prostrate themselves' (10.21). However, this polemically presupposes that their current state is 'unrighteous', since they 'become righteous' (10.21). This is clearly indicated in the following verse: 'And all the earth will be cleansed from all defilement and from uncleanness' (10.22a). Indeed, in earlier chapters a strict division is drawn between the righteous and the sinners (1.7-9; 10.17; 22.13), presumably on the basis of those who have or have not transgressed the commandments of God (21.6a).[33] The consequences of this consist of being 'bound in this place (of punishment) until the completion of ten million years, according to the number of their sins' (21.6b). One must presume that this tension can only be held on the basis of interpreting 10.21 as referring to nations who accept the command-ments of the Lord (21.6). Donaldson's conclusion is perhaps too opti-mistic, or at least requires significant tempering: 'the passage belongs to the broader category of texts in which Gentiles are expected to turn to the God of Israel in the last days and share in the blessings of the end time'.[34] Nonetheless, G. W. E. Nickelsburg does note that 'The motif of the conversion of the nations...may have been derived exegetically from Isa 66:18-23'.[35]

A key text Donaldson discusses regarding Jewish attitudes toward the Gentiles is the second (*1 En.* 45–57) of the three parables of the Simili-tudes of Enoch (*1 En.* 37–71) with reference to a certain Son of Man (48.2). Within the parable, the Son of Man functions as (1) righteous judge (39.6; 48.2; 53.6); (2) revealer of righteous and unrighteous deeds (46.3; 49.2, 4); and (3) distributor of justice (48.4, 7; 51.5; 53.6; 57.7-8, 14-15). In 48.4 he is described as 'the light of the Gentiles', but precisely in what manner this occurs remains unclear. What does seem apparent is that the Son of Man serves as a support to the righteous (48.4a). This

33 Although 'Gentiles' are not explicitly mentioned, the context of 10.18-22 strongly implies such identification.

34 Donaldson, *Judaism and the Gentiles*, p.80.

35 G. W. E. Nickelsburg, *1 Enoch 1* (Hermeneia; Minneapolis: Fortress, 2001), p.228.

may refer to an eschatological context, but could just as easily apply to the circumstances of oppression, which would certainly be consistent with identifying the Son of Man with Enoch, as does 71.14. The tacit elements of hope held out to the Gentiles in 48.4 must be balanced with the strong words of condemnation in 48.8.[36] The author does not seem to be concerned to overstress the universal role of the 'Elect Son of Man as *lux gentium*'.[37]

The implicit eschatological participation of *select* Gentiles in the final portion of the Book of Dreams (*1 En.* 83–90), namely 90.30-38, occurs sequentially after the section detailing the destruction of Gentile oppressors (90.18-19). Presumably those Gentiles who escape this fate are those who have been 'gathered in that house' (90.33) because they have not participated in the oppression of Israel or shown contempt for God. Donaldson notes: 'The Gentiles join with the redeemed Israel in the "house" (Jerusalem), to share in the blessings of the eschatological era'.[38] Taken in conjunction with 90.37-38, 'what is undone in the end-time transformation is the initial degeneration of the family of Noah' (89.9).[39]

The Epistle of Enoch (*1 En.* 91–105) contains two passages relevant for our discussion. The eschatological participation of Gentiles is hinted at in 91.14, but must be carefully considered in context to appreciate its nuanced nature. Taken in isolation, 91.14b certainly supports some kind of universalism which incorporates Gentile participation; 'all human-kind will look to the path of eternal righteousness' (91.14b). However, it should not be overlooked that in the immediately preceding section of the verse there is a reference to their eternal destruction (91.14a; cf. 91.9). This calls into doubt Nickelsburg's conclusions that the verse pertains to the 'conversion of the Gentiles and the restoration of all things',[40] primarily because the text seems to imply that there will be a preceding judgment of the whole world (91.14a), which will act as a purification before 'all humanity will look to the path of eternal right-eousness' (91.14b). Donaldson concurs when he notes the ambiguity of this passage, which, for him, 'is not concerned to determine the status of these Gentiles with any precision'.[41]

---

36   Indeed this is also evident in 50.2-5 where the Son of Man heaps 'evil upon the sinners'.

37   Black, cited in Donaldson, *Judaism and the Gentiles*, p.95.

38   Donaldson, *Judaism and the Gentiles*, p.87.

39   Donaldson, *Judaism and the Gentiles*, p.87.

40   Nickelsburg, *1 Enoch*, p.415.

41   Donaldson, *Judaism and the Gentiles*, p.187.

The second passage in the Epistle of Enoch which deserves attention is 105.1-2, which again might seem to have elements of eschatological participation – that is, at least from E. Isaac's translation: 'In those days, he says, "The Lord will be patient and cause the children of the earth to hear"'.[42] However, of the Ethiopic manuscript evidence, Isaac himself notes that 'this text is [only] partially illegible'.[43] Nickelsburg, citing the superior textual support of 4Q En^c 1 translates the Aramaic of 105.1a as 'In those days, says the Lord, they will summon and testify against the sons of earth...'[44] In verses immediately preceding 105.1-2, the righteous are defined as those who 'have' (104.12) and 'believe' (104.13) 'my books' (104.12), namely, the books of Enoch. This distinct element of threat against Gentiles is reminiscent of 98.10, and relates to strengthening the identity of the Jewish community during the years immediately preceding the Maccabean crisis and Seleucid threat.[45]

6. *4 Ezra*

Although *4 Ezra* claims to be written by Ezra in Babylon thirty years after the destruction of 'our city' (Zion) (3.1), it is clearly an apocalyptic, pseudonymous piece of Jewish literature written one generation after the destruction of the Jerusalem Temple within the last decade of the first century CE. D. J. Harrington writes: 'the Babylonian exile of the sixth century B.C.E. becomes the literary occasion for exploring the theological issues raised by the recent destruction of Jerusalem and its temple in 70 C.E. under the Romans'.[46] In this light, the main theme of *4 Ezra* is the incongruent nature of the catastrophe which had come upon Israel in light of its election and covenantal status as Yahweh's chosen people (3.30, 32).

4 Ezra is structured into seven visions/episodes, in which the seer has revelatory encounters in an attempt to explain this conundrum. The third vision (6.35–9.25) concludes Ezra's first series of triplicate lament/

---

42   E. Isaac, '1 (Ethiopic Apocalypse of) Enoch', in *OTP*, I, pp.5–89 (5).

43   Isaac, '1 Enoch', p.86.

44   Nickelsburg, *1 Enoch*, p.335.

45   Isaac, '1 Enoch', p.7.

46   D. J. Harrington, *Invitation to the Apocrypha* (Grand Rapids: Eerdmans, 1999), pp.189–90 (185). On the basis of external evidence it is difficult to be any more definitive. However, on the basis of the rather complex imagery in the apocalyptic fifth vision, the 'middle head' is to be identified as Domitian (81–96 CE). As there is no evidence within *4 Ezra* that Domitian had died, many claim the document was composed before 96 CE.

complaint by recounting the story of creation and asking, 'If the world has indeed been created for us, why do we not possess the world for our inheritance?' (6.59). Although the author seems to conclude that God's ways are inscrutable and reserved for unique divine knowledge (4.21; 5.40), there are several hints that the rationale for Jerusalem's destruction rests at the feet of *both* its inhabitants *and* the Gentile nations. Additionally, any hint of henotheism or monolatrism is displaced by the emphasis on the God of Israel being the sole creator and sustainer of the physical realm (3.4-5; cf. 6.1-6, 38-55). Although the Law is portrayed as a divine gift to Israel (3.19; 9.31), 7.21 makes clear that *all* people (including the Gentile nations) were offered the Law but deliberately rejected it: 'For God strictly commanded those who came into the world...what they should do to live, and what they should do to avoid punishment' (7.21). These nations were not obedient (7.22), devised vain thoughts (7.22), declared that 'the Most High does not exist' (7.23), 'ignored God's way' (7.23) and scorned his Law (7.24).

The apparent tension between (1) the Gentiles' opulent wealth and prosperity, and (2) their oppression of God's people, becomes a significant literary aspect of *4 Ezra*. This is particularly evident in Ezra's lament within the first vision: 'For I have seen how you endure those who sin, and have spared those who act wickedly, and have destroyed your people, and have preserved your enemies' (3.30). The resolution to this pointed question of theodicy is *apparently* resolved in attributing pagan domination of the city and people of Jerusalem to their unfaithful adherence to the covenant. Uriel, Ezra's angelic companion, reveals that Israel is under judgment for its sin: 'If now that city is given to a man for an inheritance, how will the heir receive his inheritance unless he passes through the danger set before him? I said, "He cannot, lord". And he said to me, "So also is Israel's portion"' (7.9-10). Sin is defined as unfaithfulness to the Law (9.36), which has consequently resulted in alienation and estrangement from God (7.48). The fourth vision (9.26–10.59), although prefaced with echoes of a complaint (9.26-37), is a turning point in the narrative, in that Ezra accepts Israel's responsibility for her sin and consequent judgment: 'For we who have received the Law and sinned will perish, as well as our heart which received it' (9.36).

This, however, does not alleviate the coming judgment on the Gentiles for their mistreatment of God's people, nor for their wilful ignorance of the Law. They too will be subject to ultimate destruction; in the words of the author in 7.25, 'empty things for the empty, and full things for the full'. This idea is restated and emphasised in 7.36-44, wherein 'the pit of torment shall appear...and the furnace of hell shall be disclosed' (7.36).

Divine speech addressing the Gentiles pronounces fire and torments (7.38), as they are admonished to 'Look now and understand whom you have denied, whom you have not served, whose commandments you have despised' (7.37). Ezra probes further and enquires whether a righteous person could intercede for the ungodly as Abraham did for the Sodomites (7.102-15), a question to which there is a resounding negative response: 'No one will be able to have mercy on him who has been condemned in judgment' (7.115).[47] The fate of the mass of humanity causes significant distress to Ezra, and he laments that 'it would have been better if the earth had not produced Adam' (7.116), and compares the fate of the wicked to the reward of the righteous as 'a wave is greater than a drop of water' (9.15). Indeed, 'many have been created, but few will be saved' (8.3).

This apocalyptic scenario finds historical expression in the condemnation of the Roman political regime in the long and complex 'Eagle Vision' in 11.1–12.3, and the angelic interpretation in 12.10-36. In 12.11-12 Ezra's vision is identified with, yet supersedes, 'the fourth kingdom which appeared to your brother Daniel' (cf. 12.36). The theme of successive empires is also in the foreground of the Danielic apocalyptic material. Here, it serves Ezra as a prelude to the messianic fifth kingdom.[48] M. Stone notes that although in Daniel the fourth kingdom refers to the Greeks, 'here, it is Rome',[49] as it is in several other Jewish sources.[50] Within this identification, Stone notes that the three heads of the eagle would be the Flavians: Vespasian, Titus and Domitian.[51] The figure who puts down this beastly empire is the messiah, represented as a lion, presumably serving to arouse Davidic associations (12.31).[52] His role is to denounce (12.32), judge (12.32) and then destroy (12.33) the pagan enemies. What was impersonal and implied in 12.3 – 'the whole body of the eagle was burned, and the earth was exceedingly terrified' – becomes the explicit role of the messiah. Similar to the subsequent vision of 'the Man from the Sea' (13.1-13), and its interpretation (13.21-58), the messiah punishes his enemies by his pronouncement,[53] and 'will reprove

47   M. Stone (*Fourth Ezra* [Hermeneia; Minneapolis: Fortress, 1990], p.234) has noted that 'the idea that there is no mercy on the day of judgment is widespread throughout the book'.

48   This theme is common in Jewish apocalyptic literature (Dan. 2; 7; *2 Bar.* 39).

49   Stone, *Fourth Ezra*, p.361.

50   Josephus, *A.J.* 10.276; *Mek.* on Exod. 20.18; *Gen. Rab.* 42.2; *Pes. Rab.* 4; citations from Stone, *Ezra*, p.361 n.5.

51   Stone, *Fourth Ezra*, p.365.

52   Compare *2 Bar.* 39.8–40.3.

53   Stone, *Fourth Ezra*, p.365.

the assembled nations for their ungodliness…and will reproach them to their face with their evil thoughts and with the torments with which they are to be tortured' (13.37-38a). As noted by G. Carey in regard to the fifth and sixth visions, 'These two Messianic visions do not confirm each other point by point…[but] as poetic visionary literature, they reinforce each other by means of image and common aspiration'.[54] We can therefore affirm in essence, Donaldson's comments when he states, '*4 Ezra* is unrelentingly pessimistic about the ultimate fate of the Gentiles'.[55]

7. 2 Baruch

As with several late first-century apocalypses, *2 Baruch* depicts a fictional Babylonian setting as paradigm for the destruction of the Temple in 70 CE.[56] The main resolution to the question of theodicy consists of Israel being punished justly for transgressions. This, however, only sharpens the question by virtue of an even more corrupt pagan instrument used to inflict this punishment. Nonetheless, the nation of Israel is presented as privileged, having Abraham as her father (78.4) and possessing God's promises (78.7), and knowledge (14.5). As such, the author stresses Israel's greater responsibility: 'But now, because he trespassed, having understanding, he will be punished because he has understanding' (15.6); 'They, however, sinned and trespassed…although they knew they had the Law to reprove them' (19.3). Because they have now sinned (1.2; 77.8-10), deserved punishment will ensue (4.1; 6.9; 13.9; 78.3; 79.2) in the form of the destruction of the Temple by a foreign power (1.4).

Baruch's lament begins with a beatitude to those who will not experience Jerusalem's fate and anticipates the horrendous nature of the destruction: 'Blessed is he who was not born, or he who was born and died…' (10.6-7). Baruch then summons all creation to mourn Jerusalem's punishment.[57] R. Marks concludes that the downfall is attributed to 'the will of God rather than its conquerors' strength or defenders' weakness'.[58] This is a common theme in various Old Testament, inter-

54   Carey, *Ultimate Things*, p.154.

55   Donaldson, *Judaism and the Gentiles*, p.95.

56   Nickelsburg, *Jewish Literature*, p.287; Charlesworth, *OTP*, I, pp.616–17; P. M. Bogaert, *L'Apocalypse de Baruch* (2 vols.; Paris: Cerf, 1969), I, pp.294–5.

57   Cf. *2 Bar.* 10.18 which describes Vespasian and the destruction of the Jewish temple.

58   R. G. Marks, *Image of Bar Kokhba in Traditional Jewish Literature* (University Park: Pennsylvania State University Press, 1994), p.35 n.48.

testamental and Rabbinic sources,[59] and is employed here to emphasise the note of calamity. The attribution of the destruction of Jerusalem to Israel's covenantal infidelity shares thematic elements with Ezra's theodicy. However, *2 Baruch* develops this in a distinct fashion and includes a significant ironic twist. Rather than the emphasis being placed on a tyrannical pagan king, responsibility for divine judgment lies with the people of Israel: 'for the former tribes were forced by their kings to sin, but these two have themselves forced and compelled their kings to sin' (1.3). The seriousness of this is emphasised by the motif of God and his angels acting as the agents of destruction. Rather than merely allowing Jerusalem to fall, the divine forces are said to have destroyed the walls of the city, and invited Israel's enemies into the city 'because he who guarded the house has left it' (8.2). This constitutes the first of three visions in *2 Baruch*.

The second vision (chs. 36–40) consists of Baruch's fourfold revelation (forest, vine, fountain, and cedar). This pattern is distinctly reminiscent of the fourfold schemes in the apocalyptic genre (cf. Dan. 2; 7; *4 Ezra*). *2 Baruch* 40.1-3 explicitly notes that, 'the last ruler who is left alive at that time will be bound...convicted...and killed' by the Anointed One, who will then establish his own dominion forever.

The third vision is that of the 'Apocalypse of the Clouds' (53.1-12), which finds angelic interpretation (by Ramael) in chs. 54–74. The cloud which emerges from the great sea (53.1) poured down black water to earth (53.3-4), which then became bright, 'but there was not much of it' (53.5). The alternation between 'black water' and 'bright water' occurs twelve times (53.6), until it culminates in devastation and destruction (53.7). Carey describes the cloud vision as a 'historical review',[60] with the eleventh cycle corresponding to the Babylonian (i.e. Roman) disaster: 'For so far as Zion has been delivered up and Jerusalem laid waste... behold the smoke of impiety is there' (67.6). And, 'the one who has now destroyed Zion...will boast over the people and speak haughtily in his heart against the Most High' (67.7). The fate of the foreign nation who perpetrates this injustice will not escape, for 'he too will fall finally' (67.8), and 'the nations will be thoroughly punished...you nations and tribes, you are guilty' (13.5).

---

59   See a similar theme in 1 Chron. 21.15-16; 2 Sam. 24.16; and *1 En.* 56.5-8. In *Lam. Rab.* 4.15 God lowers the city walls for Nebuchadnezzar to enter. Cf. L. Ginzberg, *The Legends of the Jews* (6 vols.; New York: JPS, 1942), VI, p.392, where angels destroy the Temple.

60   Carey, *Ultimate Things*, p.164.

In this schema, Bauckham identifies a common pattern: (1) Israel disobeys, (2) God punishes by exile and destruction, (3) Israel repents, (4) God forgives and restores Israel, (5) God punishes Israel's enemies, that is, foreign nations and powers.[61] The difference, however, in the punishment of Israel and the punishment of the nations, is that Israel's current temporal punishment (destruction of the Temple) is undertaken to produce repentance – 'they were once punished, that they might be forgiven' (13.10) – while the future eschatological punishment of the nations is undertaken to cause annihilation and ultimate destruction.[62] Baruch's interpretation of the Mosaic covenant in 84.2 is typical: 'If you trespass the Law you will be dispersed, if you keep it, you will be planted'. Assuming repentance in 78.6, Baruch says they 'have suffered now for your good so that you may not be condemned at the end and tormented'. As Bauckham astutely notes, 'Israel is chastised in this age in order to be saved in the next, whereas judgement is withheld from her enemies in this age so that they may be punished finally'.[63] In Baruch's address to the people of Israel, he assures that better times are coming if they turn to the Law (32.1-2; 44.2-3, 6-7; 46.5-6).[64] This theme is well encapsulated in 32.2 ('For a short time the building of Zion will be shaken in order that it will be rebuilt') and 32.5a ('We should not, therefore, be so sad regarding the evil which has come now'). It is in this sense that *2 Baruch* is intrinsically more positive than *4 Ezra*. Future restoration in *2 Baruch* is on the horizon from the outset: 'And my people will be chastened, and the time will come that they will look for that which can make their time prosperous' (1.5). As Carey has noted, 'Zion's calamity is a necessary means to a blessed end'.[65]

It is clear however that the Law has an element of universality: 'For each of the inhabitants of the earth knew when he acted unrighteously, and they did not know my Law because of their pride' (48.40, 47). As Donaldson notes, 'Gentiles should have kept the Law, (and) are culpable for having spurned it'.[66] The genuine possibility of Gentile

---

61 Bauckham, 'Apocalypses', p.178.

62 Baruch's geo-political concern for the nation of Israel and God's reputation is evident in 3.5: 'If you destroy your city and deliver up your country to those who hate us, how will the name of the Lord be remembered?' This indeed is reminiscent of Moses' distress on Sinai in Exod. 32.12.

63 Bauckham, 'Apocalypses', p.178.

64 Clear distinction is made, however, between the righteous and the sinners. It is not simply 'ethnic' Israel that will receive salvation, but those that embrace Torah (21.11; 24.1-2; 51.1-5; 54.21).

65 Carey, *Ultimate Things*, p.160.

66 Donaldson, *Judaism and the Gentiles*, p.187.

adherence to the Law and the fate of 'those who have separated themselves from your statutes' (41.3) is explored in chs. 41–42. Baruch's
reflections by means of forty-one questions how those 'who left behind
their vanity [i.e. heathen idols], and fled under your wings' (41.4) –
presumably he is referring to proselytes – can receive appropriate
judgment since 'their time shall surely not be weighed exactly' (41.6).
The answer is given in 42.1-8, which Bauckham accurately summarises
as follows: 'the obedience of the apostates before their apostasy is not
counted in their favor, while the disobedience of the proselytes before
their conversion is not counted against them in the judgement'.[67]

The portrayal of Gentiles in *2 Baruch* includes threat and hope, and,
as Donaldson has noted, 'represents a strain of thought…that is
optimistic about the possibility of Gentiles becoming proselytes, and
treats proselytes as an important group in the overall scheme of salvation'.[68] However, how real this possibility was, and to what extent this
motif may function as a thematic literary device to further portray Israel
in a negative light, is unclear.[69] The theme of eschatological participation
of the Gentiles in 72.2-6 does not, however, necessarily offer support for
Donaldson's view. Although the passage starts positively, 'When…my
Anointed One comes, he will call all nations, and some of them he will
spare…' (72.2a), it also includes the corollary phrase 'and others he
will kill' (72.2b). *2 Baruch* also implies that the capacity in which the
Gentiles will 'participate' is for the purposes of being 'subjected to your
people' (72.5b).[70] Thus overall, there are isolated glimmers of hope
extended to the Gentiles, but overwhelmingly the perspective of the
writer toward the Gentiles is threat and judgment. This more nuanced
perspective, compared to *4 Ezra*, may be attributed to the later date of
this text (c. 100 CE) and the growing realisation by the Palestinian Jewish communities that imminent restoration was an increasingly remote
hope given the realities of the early second century CE.

---

67   Bauckham, 'Apocalypses', p.178.
68   Donaldson, *Judaism and the Gentiles*, p.189.
69   In the vision of the re-built Temple in 68.5-6, the nations are portrayed as
honouring Zion: 'And the nations will again come to honour it' (68.5). The nations
are clearly present as Gentiles, as opposed to proselytes, and again may function as a
thematic literary enhancement of the future glory of Israel. There is no indication
that they will, by virtue of being Gentiles per se, partake eschatologically, but are
rather present as recognition. Further intrigue is generated by the word 'again' in
68.5, in light of there being no discernable earlier circumstance where this might be
accurately applied, although one could appeal to 2 Chron. 9.23; 1 Kgs 8.41-43.
70   P. Volz, *Die Eschatologie der jüdischen Gemeinde im neutestamentlichen
Zeitalter* (Tübingen: Mohr, 1934), p.356.

8. *Apocalypse of Abraham*

R. Rubinkiewicz describes the *Apocalypse of Abraham* as concerned mainly with 'Israel's election and covenant'[71] presented in terms of a haggadic midrash 'based on the text of Genesis 15'.[72] The work, which was also written after the destruction of the Second Temple,[73] displays some similarities with the *Testament of Abraham*, but is differentiated by its 'greater sense of urgency that pervades its eschatological aspirations... [T]his...pondering of the ways of God and his justice...is aroused by the reactions of the writer to the destruction of the Second Temple.'[74] The work falls into two distinct parts. Chapters 1–8 consist of a narrative concerned with Abraham's tragic-comic discovery of God,[75] in which he turns from making idols for his father's family business to worshipping God.[76] Chapters 9–32 are an apocalyptic revelation granted to him in response to his prayer. The sequence is initiated with a vision of the divine court (God, his throne and attendants, chs. 17–18), followed by scenes of the cosmic order (chs. 19–21).

On Abraham's journey through the heavens, his angelic guide, Jaoel, discloses to him a vision 'in which all creation is reflected and humanity is divided into two parties',[77] that is, the 'chosen' and the 'Gentiles/ heathen'. When God speaks to Abraham in 22.4, reference is made to

71   R. Rubinkiewicz, 'Abraham, Apocalypse of', in *ABD*, I, pp.41–3.

72   R. Rubinkiewicz, 'Apocalypse of Abraham', in *OTP*, I, pp.681–8 (681).

73   J. H. Charlesworth dates the Apocalypse of Abraham to the last two decades of the first century CE; see *OTP*, I, pp.68–69. See too R. G. Hall, *Revealed Histories: Techniques for Ancient Jewish and Christian Historiography* (Sheffield: JSOT, 1991), pp.75–79. The *Apocalypse of Abraham* is preserved only in the Old Slavonic translation, but is unanimously believed to be derived from a Semitic original; see A. Kulik, *Retroverting Slavonic Pseudepigrapha: Toward the Original of the Apocalypse of Abraham* (Leiden: Brill, 2005); and R. Rubinkiewicz, 'Les sémitismes dans l'Apocalypse d'Abraham', *Folia Orientalia* 21 (1989), pp.141–8.

74   M. Stone, 'Apocalyptic Literature', in Stone (ed.), *Jewish Writings of the Second Temple Period*, pp.383–441 (416). Many similarities with *4 Ezra* and *2 Baruch* have been noted, to the extent that some have suggested a literary relationship between *4 Ezra* and the *Apocalypse of Abraham*.

75   For parallels of tales of Abraham's life, see G. H. Box and J. I. Landsman, *The Apocalypse of Abraham* (London: SPCK, 1918), pp.1–18.

76   Abraham's conversion was a popular theme in Second Temple literature (*Jub.* 11; Josephus, *A.J.* 1.154; Philo, *Abr.* 15). Collins, *Apocalyptic Imagination*, p.226, notes that this 'defines the religion of Abraham as the rejection of idolatry' and that 'idolaters are ultimately doomed to destruction as Terah is in ch. 8'.

77   Collins, *Apocalyptic Imagination*, p.226.

'those who are on the left side are a multitude of tribes who existed previously'. The divine voice continues 'some that have been prepared for judgement and restoration, others for revenge and perdition at the end of the age'. As Stone has commented, the 'later part of this revelation centers on the sin of Adam and its implications for mankind, as well as the destruction of the Temple and its aftermath'.[78] Within this schema, Gentiles are portrayed as those who both oppress and corrupt the purity of the Jewish faith. The references to idol worship in Abraham's pre-conversion should be seen as an oblique reference to the less than subtle Hellenistic influences threatening Jewish belief and practice of the time. In 27.1-12, Abraham looks at the panoramic vision of history in which 'from its left side a crowd of heathens ran out and…captured men, women and children who were on its right side' (27.1). The Gentiles are then portrayed as slaughtering some and imprisoning others (27.2), before burning the Temple with fire and plundering the holy things in it (27.3). In the light of this horrific scene, Abraham earnestly appeals to God: 'Eternal One, the people…are being robbed by the hordes of the heathen. They are killing some and holding others as aliens, and they burned the Temple…Why will it be so?' (27.4-6). Abraham's probing question of theodicy is only resolved when God responds in 27.7: 'Listen, Abraham, all that you have seen will happen on account of your seed who will continually provoke me because of the body which you saw and the murder in what was depicted in the Temple of jealousy'. In this schema, Gentiles are the divine instrument to punish wayward Israel, and also the recipients of divine wrath. In 31.1-3 the fate of the heathen who mocked 'my people' (31.1) is explicit: 'I will deliver those who have covered me with mockery, over to the scorn of the coming age, because I have prepared them to be food for the fire of Hades…and to be the contents of a wormy belly' (31.2-3). This scene is pre-empted by the earlier reversal of fortunes stated in 29.19: 'they will destroy those who have destroyed them…they will spit in their faces'.

The primary motivation for composing the *Apocalypse of Abraham* does not seem to stem from the exegetical concerns of Genesis,[79] but rather, (1) attempts to make sense of the Jewish worldview in light of the destruction of the Temple in 70 CE, and (2) acts as a clarification and re-statement of Israel's preferential status as God's people in the context of encroaching Hellenistic practices and foreign political rule during the late first and early second centuries CE.

---

78   Stone, 'Apocalyptic Literature', p.415.
79   Noted by Collins, *Apocalyptic Imagination*, p.227.

9. *Conclusions*

The overwhelming attestation of, references to, and portrayals of Gentiles in Jewish apocalyptic literature is that of their ultimate judgment and final destruction. As noted in the present analysis, the apocalyptic genre characteristically finds its origin in an attempt to resolve crises, be they questions of national identity and survival (Maccabean), or more particularly with regard to a specific historical event (the destruction of Jerusalem in 70 CE). By orienting the readers' attention on the future eschatological deliverance and vindication of Israel, and the consequent punishment of the Gentile nations oppressing Israel, Jewish apocalyptic offers the mechanism to ease the cognitive dissonance of the turbulent socio-political scenario. As Carey has noted, 'If a group perceives the world to be in moral disorder, then a final judgement provides one possible resolution to such injustice'.[80] If the perpetrators of this injustice are Gentiles, then it stands to reason that such hubris will be punished with divinely executed retributive justice.

---

80   Carey, *Ultimate Things*, pp.71–2.

Chapter 6

THE TEMPLE AND GENTILES

James S. McLaren

1. *Introduction*

In antiquity Jerusalem and its Temple attracted only minor, almost passing attention from non-Jewish authors. The general tenor of what little comment was offered ranged from being a neutral reference to its existence to being complimentary of its scale and significance in the region.[1] A similar situation prevails in modern scholarship regarding the relationship between the Temple and Gentiles. It has not been viewed as an issue that warrants much discussion, with the only topic of any note being the question of the ability of Gentiles to offer sacrifices in the Temple.[2] The consensus opinion is that Gentiles did have access to the cult; they were able to offer sacrifices and that, in effect, the 'exclusive Temple of Jerusalem became cosmopolitan'.[3] In large part this

---

1 Pliny the Elder's praise of Jerusalem is a high point in the way the city is viewed by non-Jews (*Nat.* 5.70). It is also notable that the Temple is not included among the aspects of the Jewish way of life often subject to ridicule and criticism. Although Tacitus notes some of the distinctive features of the Temple (*Hist.* 5.4-5) he does not regard them as reasons for mockery.

2 For example, the Temple does not feature as part of the discussion by M. Smith, 'The Gentiles in Judaism 125 BCE–CE 66', in W. Horbury, W. D. Davies and J. Sturdy (eds.), *The Cambridge History of Judaism. III. The Early Roman Period* (Cambridge: Cambridge University Press, 1999), pp.192–249.

3 Schürer et al., *History*, II, p.313. See also, for example, Donaldson, *Judaism and the Gentiles*, pp.289–359; S. J. D. Cohen, 'Respect for Judaism by Gentiles according to Josephus', *HTR* 80 (1987), pp.409–30 (412–15); and R. Albertz, 'Are Foreign Rulers Allowed to Enter and Sacrifice in the Jerusalem Temple?', in R. Albertz and J. Wöhrle (eds.), *Between Cooperation and Hostility: Multiple Identities in Ancient Judaism and the Interaction with Foreign Powers* (JAJSup 11; Göttingen: Vandenhoeck & Ruprecht, 2013), pp.115–19. I am grateful to Professor Albertz for kindly sending an advance copy of his essay. Due to time constraints it was not possible to incorporate a full discussion of his important contribution in this chapter.

assessment has been based on an examination of the available literary evidence, especially examples in narrative texts of occasions when Gentiles directly interacted with the Temple.[4] A by-product of such an approach is that the discussion is shaped primarily by examples of where it is the Gentiles who initiate the interaction. While such evidence is important, in the following investigation I am proposing that we should reorient the discussion by giving priority to a focus on what we can ascertain from the actual Temple. I contend that the physical layout of the Temple and its related activity indicate a different conclusion. Gifts and votive offerings were readily received from Gentiles but at no stage were they allowed to participate in the cult and offer sacrifices to the deity in their capacity as Gentiles.[5]

At the outset there are two important cautionary observations to note about adopting an approach that focuses on the Temple. The Temple was an inanimate institution, an edifice situated in a specific location. Any comment that can be made about the relationship between the Temple and Gentiles is tempered by the fact that it was always dependent on the attitude of the people that controlled the location. In other words, the Temple was subject to the decisions of people. It was people who determined what could take place within the confines of the Temple. Two somewhat extreme examples help explain the extent to which those in power could alter the function of the Temple: Antiochus IV's decision to dedicate the Temple to the worship of Zeus, and Eleazar b. Ananias' decision to cease offering sacrifices for the well-being of the emperor and Rome. The second observation is directly related to the first: as an institution there is no particular body of literature that articulates the views of the Temple. As a result, we are constantly faced with the need to derive meaning from the outside. The instructions regarding the functioning of the cult in the biblical narrative and the comments of the priest Josephus are important and helpful. However, they do not function in the same way that texts written by a specific group can be understood to be representative of its worldview.

---

4   See Donaldson, *Judaism and the Gentiles*, p.10. Schürer et al., *History*, II, pp.309–13, set out the model for the discussion of the issue, grouping the evidence according to sacrifices by and for Gentiles, sacrifices for Gentile authorities and votive offerings given to the Temple by Gentiles. It is also understandable that the main exponent of the counter-view critiquing this approach has done so by focusing on the very same literary evidence. See D. R. Schwartz, 'On Sacrifices by Gentiles in the Temple of Jerusalem', in idem, *Studies in the Jewish Background of Christianity* (WUNT 60; Tübingen: Mohr Siebeck, 1992), pp.102–16.

5   Schwartz, 'Sacrifices', p.109, makes a brief, passing reference to the physical structure and layout of the Temple but does not explore its potential significance.

The decision to focus on the actual Temple is predicated on the principle that the shape and design of physical structures conveys messages to all the people that come into contact with that location. The use of space can be shaped in order to create freedom and access. It can also be used to control and limit access, to constrain the engagement of people with a location. It is even possible that providing access and restricting access are shared objectives in the design of the one place.[6] The key question here, therefore, is as follows: Was the Temple constructed in a manner that allowed and/or enabled non-Jewish participation in its activities? We will examine this question by exploring four related issues. First, we will briefly review the function of the Temple in order to outline what type of activity took place there. Second, we will review the layout of the Temple, paying particular attention to any changes in its design. Third, we will examine the evidence of specific decisions by those overseeing the Temple regarding the activity and practices that took place there. A particular focus here will be whether or not there is any evidence for decisions regarding participation by Gentiles in any of the activities. The fourth and final issue will be a review of specific examples of occasions when Gentiles interacted with the Temple.

2. *The Function of the Temple*

On a very practical level the primary purpose of the Temple was that it operated as a place where homage was paid to the God of the Jews through the offering of animal sacrifices. All other activities were ancillary to that particular role. Other approved offerings, in the form of produce and money, as well as gifts and votive offerings, were presented at the Temple as a consequence of its role as a place of sacrifice. In this context, the Temple also became a depository of precious goods and money. The ritual activity associated with the cult functioned at a community and individual believer level.[7] Personal and communal sacrifices

---

6   For example, see J. Monnet, 'The Symbolism of Place: A Geography of Relationships between Space, Power and Identity', *Cybergo: European Journal of Geography* 562 (2011), online: http://cybergeo.revues.org/24747 (accessed 14 March 2013); and P. Richardson, *Building Jewish in the Roman East* (Waco: Baylor University Press, 2004), p.274.

7   See Josephus, *C. Ap.* 2.193. For more detail, see T. Wardle, *The Jerusalem Temple and Early Christian Identity* (WUNT 291; Tübingen: Mohr Siebeck, 2010), pp.13–45; and E. P. Sanders, *Judaism: Practice and Belief 63 BCE–66 CE* (London: SCM, 1992), pp.49–102.

were offered at the Temple through the agency of certain people delegated with responsibility of ensuring the sacrificial activity was maintained on an ongoing basis.

Its role as a place of sacrifice in worship of a deity meant the Temple in Jerusalem was essentially just like any other temple in the Greco-Roman world. Animal sacrifice as a form of worship and devotion was standard practice and any non-Jew visiting Jerusalem would have naturally associated the Temple with such activity.[8] However, apart from this shared basic function, there were two very important ways in which the Temple in Jerusalem was significantly different from other Greco-Roman temples. The first is the fact that the Temple was deemed to be the one and only place where sacrifices to the deity of the Jews could be offered. While there could be other places of worship, and rituals could be put in place in the home and community regarding aspects of daily life, the Temple in Jerusalem was *the* place where sacrifices could be offered.[9] The second key difference was that the Temple in Jerusalem was a sacrificial site dedicated to the worship of one deity. As a monotheistic religion there was no notion of the Temple being a shared sacred site. All sacrifices offered there were to the one and only God. Therefore, the Temple in Jerusalem was an exclusive site that was functioning as the *one* place where sacrifices could be offered to the *one* God.

The vast bulk of the sacrificial and related activity was based on instructions and rules derived from the Mosaic tradition within the biblical narrative. These rules and instructions were understood to be decreed by God, so that what was done at the Temple honoured God in the way that had been divinely sanctioned. Strict conditions applied regarding who could perform the sacrifice, what was to be sacrificed and from whom such sacrifices were expected and even permitted. Here an important point of clarification is required. The prayer associated with the dedication of Solomon's Temple sets the tone for future generations. There is a sense of expectation and anticipation that Gentiles were allowed and/or even expected to show respect and to pay homage to the sanctity and glory of the Temple (1 Kgs 8.41-43; Josephus, *A.J.* 8.116). However, respect and homage are not the same as being able to, let alone

---

8   As noted by Goodman, *Judaism*, p.47.

9   See Goodman, *Judaism*, p.48. S. Rocca, *Herod's Judaea: A Mediterranean State in the Classical World* (TSAJ 122; Tübingen: Mohr Siebeck, 2008), p.287, also notes a difference in the actual type of animal sacrifice. At Jerusalem whole animal offerings were accepted. The other key difference was the complete absence of statues and any iconic decoration in the Temple. It is notable that Tacitus draws attention to this feature (*Hist.* 5.4).

expected to, offer sacrifices. In fact, contrary to what some have claimed, there is no clear biblical precedent that allowed for Gentiles to offer sacrifices.[10] A key text is Lev. 22.25, where reference is made to offerings that were blemished not being acceptable, even when supplied by Gentiles. This passage does not imply that Gentiles could offer sacrifices if unblemished. Instead, the issue is the rules regarding sacrifices offered by Israelites (Lev. 22.18) and the reference to Gentiles was a way of emphasising that the use of any blemished offerings was totally unacceptable.[11] Indeed, given the extent of detailed instruction regarding how the Jews were to offer sacrifices and regarding the type of sacrifices they were to offer, the resounding absence of reference to Gentiles regarding the sacrificial activity is significant. The general silence of biblical accounts on involvement in the offering of sacrifices indicates that the ritual cult pertained only to those people who worshipped the God of Israel. In line with adherence to the core tenets encapsulated in the Decalogue, to be a worshipper of the God of Israel required allegiance to a monotheistic system of belief and practice.[12]

The business of being the one place where the one God could be worshipped through the offering of sacrifices was directly linked with the symbolic value of the Temple. It was sacred, holy ground. It functioned as the throne room of God, a place of wonder, awe and majesty.[13] In turn, the notion of the Temple as a holy space found expression in the decisions regarding the layout of the building and on the ability of people to access its various parts. It also meant that any concerns or questioning about how the activity of the Temple was performed had the potential to turn into highly charged disputes between competing groups. At one end of the scale was Josephus' criticism of Agrippa II's decision to allow Levites to wear linen robes (*A.J.* 20.216-17), and at the other end was the decision of those responsible for the views expressed in 4QMMT to separate themselves from the Temple and demand that correct practice be restored.[14]

---

10   For example, see Schürer et al., *History*, II, pp.309–10, Donaldson, *Judaism and the Gentiles*, p.291; and Mason, *Flavius Josephus*, p.314 n.2572.

11   See Schwartz, 'Sacrifices', p.107; and Albertz, 'Foreign Rulers', p.126 n.34. On the interpretation of Lev. 22.25 I am also grateful for the insights offered through personal correspondence by my colleague, Dr. Dermot Nestor. See also Ezek. 44.6-9; cf. Num. 15.14. Albertz, 'Foreign Rulers', pp.117, 120–22, argues that foreign participation in the cult was part of the biblical tradition.

12   The ability of Gentiles to offer gifts and votive offerings will be discussed below in Section 5.

13   See Wardle, *Jerusalem*, pp.16–18.

14   See Wardle, *Jerusalem*, pp.92–3.

There are two important observations to note in relation to the fact that the primary function of the Temple was the place where sacrifices were offered. One is that the Temple was a place for insiders of that religion. As much as Jews were expected and required to go to the Temple to offer sacrifices, the opposite also applies: there was no reason for Gentiles to engage with the activities of the Temple. They could not offer sacrifices to any other deity at the Temple and they could only offer sacrifices there as people that worshipped the God of Israel. As such, there is no reason to expect there to be any regular direct interaction between the Temple and Gentiles. The second observation is that there was no expectation that Gentiles would participate in the activities of the Temple. At best, any link between Gentiles and the Temple would fall into two main formats: a tourist-curiosity interest, especially given the distinctive aspects of the way the Temple functioned; and, as part of formal stately protocols of either a visiting dignitary or a ruler at times when the Jews were under foreign control wanting to pay respect to the major religious site of the local population. One final comment helps reinforce the exclusive nature of the Temple and the absence of any reason for interaction between the Temple and Gentiles to be a likely scenario. It is the location of the Temple. While its positioning in Jerusalem may have been justified and explained on the basis of being a divinely sanctioned choice, it had little connection with the practicalities of where people would be likely to travel through, let alone chose to travel through. Jerusalem was not on any major trade route and it did not have any particular resources that would attract interest. In fact, one of the only reasons to visit Jerusalem was to participate in the activity of the Temple. Indeed, for the non-Jew there were a number of sites of cultural and civic importance in the region that acted as likely destinations; such as Ptolemais and the cities in the Decapolis, like Damascus, Jerash and Pella. For a non-Jew to go to Jerusalem was to go out of the way from the vast majority of other places they would be more likely to visit in the region.

3. *The Physical Layout of the Temple*

Discussion of the actual layout of the Temple is complicated on two practical levels. One is the difficulty of having to reconstruct its shape and precise dimensions from incomplete archaeological remains and literary records that are contradictory to one another on several points of detail. The other difficulty is that the Temple underwent changes introduced by various rulers that had oversight of its activity. Fortunately, for the one key change, ushered in by Herod, we have sufficient resources

from which to examine what he did. We can also consider the significance of the changes he introduced for the relations between the Temple
and Gentiles.

Prior to Herod the Temple appears not to have undergone any significant alterations or expansions. In effect, the structure that stood from
soon after the return from Exile in the late sixth century BCE was the
one that had been built through Persian sponsorship. It was largely
modelled on the shape of the first Temple, with the altar located outside
(Josephus, *C. Ap.* 1.198-99). There was one designated area where Jewish men in a state of ritual purity could stand and watch the sacrifices
being performed. There were some minor changes made to the Temple,
with walls for fortification and a reservoir added under the direction of
Simon (Sir. 50.2-4), and then modifications made by Antiochus IV and
then by the Hasmoneans (Josephus, *A.J.* 17.162).[15]

It was Herod who instigated the most substantial redevelopment and
expansion of the Temple. Probably commencing in 20/19 BCE (Josephus,
A.J. 15.380; cf. *B.J.* 1.401), it took over nine years for the main parts of
the work to be completed and the whole project was not entirely finished
until the reign of Agrippa II in the early 60s CE. This was a project of
massive proportions. Fundamental to Herod's redevelopment was the
expansion of the Temple Mount, cutting into the landscape to the north
and building an artificial platform to the south. Once completed, the
platform measured approximately 488 metres along the western side, 315
metres along the northern side, 280 metres along the eastern side and 280
metres along the southern side. This work required massive retaining
walls that became the base of large porticoes enclosing the entire complex. A major fortress was built along part of the northern wall, new
elaborate entry points were constructed and a very large portico was
added that stood out for all to see on the southern end of the Temple
Mount, the so-called Royal Portico (Josephus, *A.J.* 15.412).[16]

Within the context of all these highly significant monumental elements
of the expanded Temple Mount, the work undertaken within the confines
of the actual platform is of particular importance. Herod added new
courts to the complex so that there were now four courts: the outer court
that was open to foreigners and to all Jews, except women in a state of
ritual impurity; the second court open to male and female Jews in a state

15   See Rocca, *Herod's Judaea*, p.293.

16   For a detailed description of Herod's redevelopments, see E. Netzer, *The
Architecture of Herod the Great Builder* (TSAJ 117; Tübingen: Mohr Siebeck,
2006), pp.136–78; and D. Bahat, 'The Herodian Temple', in Horbury, Davies and
Sturdy (eds.), *Cambridge History of Judaism*, III, pp.38–58.

of ritual purity; the third court open to male Jews in a state of ritual purity; and, the fourth court open only to priests, wearing their robes and in a state of ritual purity (Josephus, *C. Ap.* 2.103-4; *B.J.* 1.193-200; *A.J.* 15.410-20).[17] This addition of the outer court is the first explicit identification of a space where Gentiles could enter within the walls of the Temple Mount. Along with the introduction of a designated court for Jewish women, it is most likely that this court for Gentiles was an initiative of Herod. For the first time Gentiles were explicitly welcomed into the vicinity of the Temple in a designated area inside the walled porticoes that surrounded the entire complex.[18] The vast bulk of this outer court was located at the southern end of the Temple Mount, under the shadow of the Royal Portico.

Given the scope and the scale of the work undertaken by Herod in relation to the Temple Mount, there has been much discussion as to why he undertook such a large venture. First and foremost there were potential practical benefits. An enlarged facility that also allowed more groups of people to have access to the complex increased the chances of visitors going to Jerusalem. In turn, this increased the opportunity for revenue to be raised.[19] In the present context symbolic significance has also been attached to the inclusion of Gentiles within the confines of the walled Temple Mount. It was a deliberate action designed to make the Temple cult inclusive, to make Gentiles feel welcome.[20] It has also been proposed that Herod saw this new space as an opportunity for Jews to encounter the Roman world within the confines of the Temple, for Jew and non-Jew to connect with one another.[21] These largely positive inter-

17   On the issue of Gentile impurity, see J. Klawans, *Purity, Sacrifice, and the Temple: Symbolism and Supersessionism in the Study of Ancient Judaism* (New York: Oxford University Press, 2006); Hayes, *Gentile Impurities*; and Sanders, *Judaism*, pp.70-5.

18   On the association of these two new courts with Herod, see Richardson, *Building Jewish*, pp.287-94. See also Donaldson, *Judaism and the Gentiles*, p.208. Note also that the Temple described in 11QT xliv 5-8 has three courts, with Jewish women, along with children and proselytes outside the Temple proper in the outer court. There is no court for Gentiles. The reference to Antiochus III issuing an instruction that Gentiles were not to enter the Temple does not negate the likelihood that Herod initiated this means of giving Gentiles formal access to the Temple Mount (Josephus, *A.J.* 12.145). Antiochus III's instruction related to entering the actual Temple, something that Herod also forbade (see the discussion of the balustrade below).

19   See Goodman, *Judaism*, pp.61-5.

20   For example, see Richardson, *Building Judaism*, pp.293-4.

21   See B. R. McCane, 'Simply Irresistible: Augustus, Herod, and the Empire', *JBL* 127 (2008), pp.725-35 (732-3).

pretations of Herod's intentions are all premised on the notion that he was trying to be inclusive. It is clear that what Herod did by constructing the two new courts did mean certain groups could now feel they had their own space within the Temple complex. However, when considered within the context of his other actions, there are also a number of factors that indicate Herod was motivated by a concern to preserve the exclusive dimension of the Temple and its cult, rather than trying to make the Temple more inclusive and cosmopolitan.

Herod was particularly conscious of the need to provide appropriate locations where the religious practices of Gentiles could be fostered and celebrated. The three temples to Augustus and Rome constructed by Herod effectively reinforced the separation and the distinction between the religious activities associated with the Jewish cult from that of Greco-Roman religious activity. One further key architectural feature of the redeveloped Temple complex highlighted the separation between Jew and non-Jew, and the exclusive nature of the Jewish cult. The divide between the outer court and the rest of the Temple Mount was marked by a balustrade 1.5 metres in height (Josephus, *B.J.* 5.193). Notices, written in Greek or in Latin, were placed at several points along the length of the balustrade warning Gentiles not to go any further: 'No foreigner is to enter within the forecourt and the balustrade around the sanctuary. Whoever is caught will have himself to blame for his subsequent death.'[22] Reinforcing this limit placed upon Gentiles regarding where they could go within the Temple complex there was a small area beyond the balustrade and then the wall of the actual Temple where the three remaining inner courts were all located. In other words, Gentiles could now access a new enlarged open space within the Temple complex but they could still not go anywhere within the Temple. At one and the same time Gentiles were now being included and excluded. In the aftermath of the war, as he sought to affirm the value of the Jewish way of life in *Contra Apionem*, Josephus was conscious of not wanting to draw attention to the fact that Gentiles were excluded from the Temple (*C. Ap.* 2.104).[23] What Herod did was provide Gentiles with a place where they could go that was within the Temple complex that was also close to where his own prestige and status was celebrated – the Royal Portico. More than anything else, the new, large outer court had a very

22   See P. Segal, 'The Penalty of the Warning Inscription from the Temple of Jerusalem', *IEJ* 39 (1989), pp.79–84 (79). See also Josephus, *B.J.* 5.193-94; 6.124–26; *A.J.* 15.417; Philo, *Legat.* 212; *Spec.* 1.156; and *m. Kelim* 1.8.

23   See Barclay, *Flavius Josephus: Translation and Commentary*, X, p.222 nn.365 and 366.

practical role that related to the Jewish community. During the three major pilgrimage festivals it meant many of them could mingle with one another inside the Temple complex. Unable to rebuild an expanded Temple that could accommodate more people, Herod took the next best option, the provision of an expanded outer court where Jewish pilgrims could come and be close to the celebration of the activities in the Temple. From brief asides Josephus makes regarding the numbers of Jews that attended the festivals, it would appear Herod's construction of a large outer court was popular (e.g. *B.J.* 6.423-25; *A.J.* 20.106).[24]

There is no doubt that Herod's major redevelopment of the Temple complex provided a spatial change in the way Gentiles could interact with the Temple. In the vastly expanded Temple Mount area there was now a designated space where Gentiles could go; they passed through the outer retaining wall of the complex. However, as much as they were now able to be inside the complex, their position as people not allowed into the Temple area itself was formally reinforced. A barrier was erected outside the Temple beyond which they were not allowed to pass. This positioning on the outside of the Temple was made even clearer by the fact that within the actual Temple Herod had constructed a court where Jewish women in a state of ritual purity could now enter. As such, Herod did not change the fundamental reality of Gentiles not being part of the direct activity of the Temple. The physical layout of the Temple, and of the wider Temple Mount, gave practical expression to the primary function of the Temple as a place for insiders, the worshippers of the God of the Jews to offer sacrifices.

4. Decisions by Those Overseeing the Temple Regarding the Activity and Practices

Attention now turns to a consideration of specific occasions where the decisions made by the people responsible for administering the activity in the Temple had a direct impact on Gentiles.[25] There are three examples to consider: the decision to offer sacrifices for the well-being of the emperor and Rome; the case of Paul and his non-Jewish companion entering the area beyond the balustrade; and, the decision to cease offering the sacrifices for the well-being of the emperor and Rome.

24   See Netzer, *Architecture*, p.275 n.17.
25   The actions undertaken by Antiochus IV (1 Macc. 1.47-54) and the incursion into the Temple by Samaritans (Josephus, *A.J.* 18.29-30) both lie outside the scope of this study.

The decision to offer sacrifices at the Temple for the well-being of the emperor and Rome on a regular daily basis was made during the reign of Herod. It is an initiative that is best understood within the context of the imperial cult that was quickly emerging in parts of the Roman east. Along with the three purpose-built temples for Augustus and Rome, the introduction of a daily offering at the Jerusalem Temple meant the Jewish landscape and its cultic religious activity acknowledged the presence of Rome and could be regarded as supporting the interests of the empire. Josephus was certainly keen to assert such a view regarding this daily offering, even after the Temple had been destroyed (*C. Ap.* 2.73-77).[26] What makes this decision particularly noteworthy is that the offering was to occur twice daily: the regular routine of sacrifices offered at the Temple now had an added dimension. The offering was made to the God of the Jews but it was for the explicit purpose of aiding Gentiles. At a practical level there is no suggestion that a non-Jew had any direct association with the actual sacrifice; like all other sacrifices the priests on duty in the Temple carried out the sacrifice. What is not entirely clear, however, is who paid for the sacrifice. Philo claims that Augustus covered the costs (*Legat.* 157, 317), while Josephus states that the Jews paid for them (*C. Ap.* 2.77; *B.J.* 2.197).[27] It is even possible that both were correct, with Herod indicating his intention to establish the daily offering and with Augustus responding by expressing his willingness to help cover the costs of the initial offerings. Whatever the precise details regarding the funding of the offering, it is particularly important to note that this decision was a Jewish initiative. Apart from occasional interference from Pilate, and then Gaius, it helped control the level and the extent of non-Jewish involvement in the cult for much of the next 60 years.

The second example is the story of Paul visiting the Temple complex, allegedly with a non-Jewish companion (Acts 21.17-36). It is very difficult to establish the precise details of what took place, largely

26   For further discussion, see J. S. McLaren, 'Jews and the Imperial Cult: From Augustus to Domitian', *JSNT* 27 (2005), pp.257–78.

27   It has also been proposed that taxes from the province paid by Jews were used to fund the daily offering. See Smallwood, *The Jews Under Roman Rule*, p.198; and Donaldson, *Judaism and the Gentiles*, p.291. One of the difficulties with determining the historicity of these statements is that both authors had good reason to depict the financial sponsorship as they do. Philo was eager to contrast Gaius with Augustus as the role model *par excellence*, while Josephus wanted to affirm the integrity of the cult and of the non-standard way by which the Jews expressed their allegiance to Rome.

because of the way the author of Acts has woven the story into a larger narrative context: namely, regarding Paul's mission and of interactions within the emerging Christian community and between that community and the wider Jewish community and the Roman authorities. Paul was seized by Jews from inside the Temple complex (Acts 21.30), and accused of taking a non-Jew past the balustrade into the area where they were not allowed (21.28-29). It is not clear, however, who actually accompanied Paul into the Temple (21.26). A further complication is that in the course of the extensive account of hearings against Paul (21.37–26.32) the initial offence, escorting Gentiles beyond the balustrade, is only alluded to very briefly (24.13, 17-18; 25.8).[28] At best, what the story indicates is that the exclusion of Gentiles from the Temple was well attested and that a Jew thought to be aiding any such incursion beyond the balustrade was also liable for punishment.[29]

The third example is the decision to cease offering the daily sacrifice for the well-being of the emperor and Rome in 66 CE. This action reversed the decision made during the reign of Herod to set up the daily offerings. Josephus does not provide many of the details of what took place. Written after the destruction of the Temple, his account has commentary that is explicitly critical of the decision (*B.J.* 2.409) and it is carefully edited to include only the views of one side in the debate (*B.J.* 2.411-17). These factors are important to bear in mind when reflecting on the relevance of this decision for the place of Gentiles in the activity of the Temple. One of the most significant consequences of this negative depiction of the action is that it is easy to dismiss and/or downplay that it was a decision introduced by priests holding important roles in the community. In other words, it was deemed to be sufficiently popular and appropriate at the time for it not to be revoked.

At the outset Josephus is careful with how he depicts the decision. He states that a blanket ban on accepting any 'gift or sacrifice from a foreigner' (*B.J.* 2.409) was introduced. In turn, this meant the daily offerings for the well-being of the emperor and of Rome could no longer take place. In other words, Josephus avoided making the daily offering the direct focus of the action. Instead, it was merely a by-product of a more fundamental decision about the operation of the Temple cult. In order to reinforce this depiction of the event, Josephus then provides

28 Another puzzle regarding the story is the fate of the person that accompanied Paul. Note also that from the way the account is framed that it was no more than an accusation rather than a known offence (Acts 21.29).

29 See Segal, 'Penalty of the Warning Inscription', p.83.

some information about the arguments put forward to have the decision about gifts and sacrifices overturned. At first glance this appears to be evidence that Gentiles had been previously allowed to offer sacrifices at the Temple and that, in fact, it was the norm that they could do so. However, caution is necessary regarding exactly what Josephus describes as being at issue and regarding the way he has constructed the argument against what Eleazar and his associates did. Josephus provides no explanation of how a decision to stop accepting gifts or sacrifices from foreigners is linked with the cessation of the daily sacrifice offered for the well-being of the emperor and Rome.[30] The latter was a Jewish offering, possibly paid for by the Romans, but it was a sacrifice made by Jews on behalf of certain Gentiles. At best, the daily sacrifice could be viewed as a gift and only on the basis that it was the Romans who paid for the sacrifice. Josephus clearly wants the reader to have no sympathy for the action of Eleazar. A key part of his subterfuge here is to encourage the reader to find the decision totally unacceptable by linking the offering of sacrifices by Gentiles to the long-standing tradition of accepting their gifts to the Temple (*B.J.* 2.412, 414, 417).[31] Josephus has successfully deflected attention away from the core issue, the open rejection of Rome by the decision to cease the Jewish offering for the well-being of the emperor and Rome.[32]

These three examples are rather limited in their scope: two relate to the one practice, which was a Jewish activity undertaken on behalf of certain Gentiles, and the other example pertains to the treatment of a Jew in relation to a known feature of the Temple, the balustrade marking the point beyond which Gentiles were not to enter. They reinforce what has already been observed about the Temple and the place of Gentiles in relation to its activity. The Temple was a no-go zone for Gentiles and in 66 CE the cultic activity was also deemed a no-go zone to such an extent that a Jewish offering for the well-being of Gentiles was stopped.

---

30   For an alternative approach, see Albertz, 'Foreign Rulers', pp.115–17.

31   On the possible motivation of Eleazar, see Albertz, 'Foreign Rulers', pp.122–31; and J. S. McLaren, 'Going to War against Rome: The Motivation of the Jewish Rebels', in M. Popović (ed.), *The Jewish Revolt against Rome: Interdisciplinary Perspectives* (JSJSup 154; Leiden: Brill, 2011), pp.129–54.

32   For alternative views on the significance of this action, see Donaldson, *Judaism and the Gentiles*, pp.291–2; and Mason, *Judean War 2*, p.314 nn.2571 and 2572. As pointed out by Schwartz, 'Sacrifices', p.109, acceptance of gifts is quite different from allowing Gentiles to offer sacrifices. Furthermore, what Gentiles might deem to be a sacrifice the Jews could view as gifts.

5. *Specific Examples of Gentiles Interacting with the Temple*

The final aspect to consider includes the occasions where Gentiles are depicted as engaging directly with the activity of the Temple. It is understandable that the vast majority of the examples relate to leaders and to other prominent officials and individuals: they formed the bulk of the subject matter in what has been preserved in the surviving literature. We will discuss the examples in two parts: those occasions where the Gentiles are clearly offering a gift to the Temple, and those occasions where it appears the participation may be an example of offering a sacrifice.

There are numerous examples of gifts from Gentiles being presented to the Temple. This practice is well attested in a number of sources.[33] It is important to note that these gifts were acts of friendship, more often than not, given in the context of rulers and dignitaries seeking to win favour among the Jewish community.[34] Some are gifts offered while visiting the territory, while others are sent from afar. For the various Jewish authors that record these examples of precious gifts it offered an excellent way of depicting a sense of respect and even veneration for the Temple. Indeed, it is notable that for Philo and Josephus, the two main sources of information, they wrote in the immediate shadow of events that made the fate of the Temple a matter of urgency. For Philo it was the order of Gaius that his statue should be placed in Jerusalem, and for Josephus it was the aftermath of the destruction of the Temple and the question of whether or not it would be rebuilt.

In general, it is not possible to determine if there was any particular religious connotation to the decision to send gifts to the Temple. The one clear occasion where the gift is described as being motivated by personal piety and affection for the Jewish religion was the story of Fulvia, and she had already become a proselyte (Josephus, *A.J.* 18.82).[35] As such, strictly speaking, her gift was not really that of a non-Jew. Instructive here is the reference to Gaius not visiting Jerusalem while undertaking a tour of the region (Suet., *Aug.* 93). Augustus commends the decision of

33   For example, see 2 Macc. 3.35; *3 Macc.* 1.9; Philo, *Legat.* 157, 291, 297, 319; Josephus, *B.J.* 1.357; 5.262-64; *A.J.* 11.31-32; 12.78-84; 13.55, 242-43; 14.448; 18.82; *C. Ap.* 2.48; *m. Šeqal.* 7.6; *m. Menah.* 5.3, 5, 6; 6.1.

34   See Donaldson, *Judaism and the Gentiles*, pp.52, 470; and Schwartz, 'Sacrifices', p.109 n.22. Cf. Cohen, 'Respect', pp.412–15.

35   Another possible occasion of a personal gift is by Julia Augusta (Philo, *Legat.* 319).

Gaius not to visit Jerusalem. From the immediate context it is clear that Suetonius' comment related to being astute regarding where to offer veneration and where not to do so. It was appropriate for Gaius to make time to hear from the priests of Ceres and for him to avoid Apis in Egypt and Jerusalem in Judea. Implicit here is that any visit to the latter two locations would be a case of political expediency rather than an expression of appropriate religious piety and veneration.[36]

The second group of examples are the occasions where the offering of an actual sacrifice is depicted. It is significant that Josephus is the source of them all. They all feature in texts written during the reign of Domitian and they all serve to show the Jewish people, their Temple and the foreign dignitaries in the best possible light. Due caution is warranted in terms of ascertaining whether or not they have any value for describing actual historical instances of a non-Jew offering sacrifices. We will address each in turn, in chronological order. The earliest, the story of Alexander the Great visiting Jerusalem and offering sacrifices under instruction from the high-priest, is widely regarded as not being historical (*A.J.* 11.336).[37] It contradicts what Josephus makes quite clear on numerous other occasions: Gentiles were not allowed to enter the Temple. The second example is Ptolemy III deciding to celebrate his victory in Syria by forgoing the offering of sacrifices in Egypt and, instead, going to Jerusalem. There he allegedly offered sacrifices as well as numerous gifts (*C. Ap.* 2.48). There is reason to doubt the historicity of this story as well. It is very difficult to explain why the ruler of Egypt would offer thanks for the recent victory in Jerusalem rather than to the deities of his own homeland.[38] The third example relates to the visit of Marcus Agrippa (*A.J.* 18.12-26). Josephus describes Agrippa receiving numerous gifts from Herod and how the people of Jerusalem enthusiastically welcomed Agrippa when he arrived in Jerusalem, where he offered a very large sacrifice (18.14). Philo provides a slightly longer account of Agrippa's visit (*Legat.* 294-97). He has Agrippa display an even grander level of enthusiasm and delight regarding the Temple (296) than that assigned by Josephus. However, Agrippa does not offer a sacrifice; rather, he provides numerous gifts for the Temple (297). Philo is con-

---

36   A number of scholars have incorrectly read this story to imply that visiting Jerusalem was the norm and, therefore, that it classifies as a further example of Gentiles displaying homage and veneration of the Temple. For example, see Donaldson, *Judaism and the Gentiles*, p.400; and Mason, *Judean War 2*, p.317 n.2611.

37   See E. S. Gruen, *Heritage and Hellenism: The Reinvention of Jewish Tradition* (HCS 30; Berkeley: University of California Press, 1998), pp.189–203.

38   See Barclay, *Against Apion*, p.195 n.164.

cerned to show Agrippa as displaying respect for the Temple in a way that does not compromise its sanctity (297). If his respect for the Temple had entailed the offer of sacrifices, then there is no reason as to why Philo would have not included such an action.

The fourth example is the visit to Jerusalem by the legate Vitellius (*A.J.* 18.122). Josephus claims that Vitellius went to Jerusalem and that his plan was to join the Jews in the celebration of a festival where he would offer a sacrifice. This depiction of Vitellius intending to offer a sacrifice fits with the general way that Josephus depicts the legate, an official that displayed respect for the concerns and religious sensibilities of the Jews (18.95, 121). However, the primary reason for his visit to Jerusalem was to announce a change in the high priest (18.123), possibly as a response to the request that he alter the route by which his army was to march (18.121).[39] The final example appears to have taken place during Josephus' lifetime. In the context of explaining the enduring respect for Moses (3.317-18), Josephus refers to a recent occurrence. Although the details are not entirely clear there is no reason to doubt that Josephus is describing an actual event.[40] Some people had travelled from beyond the Euphrates River in order to go to Jerusalem to offer sacrifices (3.318). Although not made clear by Josephus it is likely these people were a mixture of Jews and Gentiles. Once in Jerusalem some offered sacrifices (3.318), some were unable even to enter the Temple and some decided not to offer sacrifices. These actions were all undertaken in order that they complied with Moses' instruction that only those who followed 'our laws' could partake of the sacrifice (3.318). The veneration and respect for the instruction of Moses that Josephus highlights here has an important bearing on how all the specific examples are to be viewed. While reverence and respect for the Temple by Gentiles, through such means as the offering of gifts, was something that Josephus, Philo and other Jewish authors wanted to promote, it did not mean that they were willing to compromise the principles by which the cult functioned. Moses had decreed that the sacrifices and, therefore, the Temple were for those people who adhered to 'our laws'.

39   The visit of Neapolitanus to Jerusalem (Josephus, *B.J.* 2.341) has also incorrectly been identified as an example of a Gentile worshipping at the Temple. For example, see Mason, *Judean War 2*, p.317 n.2611. Cf. Schwartz, 'Sacrifices', p.109.

40   For an alternative view, see Donaldson, *Judaism and the Gentiles*, pp.310–11.

6. *Conclusions*

The Temple was a sacred place and of particular significance for Jews. It was the one and only place where Jews could offer sacrifices to their deity. In no way could the sanctity of this sacred space be compromised. This situation was made very clear by the one major redevelopment that took place during this period, the expansion by Herod. His innovations associated with a desire to increase the number of pilgrims were both revolutionary and fully supportive of the existing boundaries and restrictions. Gentiles could now have access to part of the complex even if they were not allowed any greater access to the actual Temple than before the reign of Herod. Certain Gentiles were now made part of the explicit activity of the Temple through the daily offering for the well-being of the emperor and Rome. In time, even this allowance was deemed to be excessive and inappropriate and the Temple was restored to its proper purpose in 66 CE. Although Gentiles were welcome to provide gifts for the Temple, they were not part of its sphere of activity; it functioned exclusively for those who worshipped the God of the Jews. This situation prevailed until 70 CE, when Vespasian and Titus decided veneration and respect of the Temple as sacred space of the Jews no longer applied. Titus and his troops offered sacrifices to their gods on the site (Josephus, *B.J.* 6.316). He then took possession of many of the utensils associated with the cult (6.387-91). All of this behaviour stood in stark contrast to the choices made by Pompey (1.152-53). The circumstances were now very different; there was no place for an exclusive cult site that had been so instrumental in rejecting the Romans.

Chapter 7

THE SYNAGOGUE AND THE GENTILES

Donald Binder

1. *Introduction*

Throughout most of the twentieth century, the presence of Gentiles in the early synagogues was taken for granted, largely because of several references to 'God-fearers' (φοβούμενοι/σεβομένοι τὸν θεόν) in the Acts of the Apostles.[1] In the 1980s, however, Thomas Kraabel challenged this belief in a series of articles, arguing that the aforementioned references were a Lucan literary invention designed to justify the spread of Christianity:

> The God-fearers are a symbol to help Luke show how Christianity had become a Gentile religion legitimately and without losing its Old Testament roots. The Jewish mission to Gentiles recalled in the God-fearers is ample precedent for the far more extensive mission to Gentiles which Christianity had in fact undertaken with such success. Once that point has been made, Luke can let the God-fearers disappear from his story. That is just what they do, and that is why there is no further reference to them in the New Testament and no clear independent record of them in the material evidence from the classical world.[2]

---

1   Luke specifically mentions the presence of God-fearers in synagogues at Pisidian Antioch (Acts 13.16, 26, 50 [*AS* 174]), Philippi (Acts 16.14 [*AS* 185]), Thessalonica (Acts 17.4 [*AS* 186]), Athens (Acts 17.17 [*AS* 90]), and Corinth (18.7 [*AS* 91]).

2   A. T. Kraabel, 'The Disappearance of the "God-Fearers"', *Numen* 28 (1981), pp.113–26 (120–21). See also idem, 'Synagoga Caeca: Systematic Distortion in Gentile Interpretations of Evidence for Judaism in the Early Christian Period', in J. Neusner and E. S. Frerichs (eds.), *'To See Ourselves as Others See Us': Christians, Jews, 'Others' in Late Antiquity* (Chico: Scholars Press, 1985), pp.226–32; idem, 'The Roman Diaspora: Six Questionable Assumptions', *JJS* 33 (1982), pp.445–64; idem, 'Afterword', in Overman and MacLennan (eds.), *Diaspora Jews and Judaism*, pp.347–57; and R. S. MacLennan and A. T. Kraabel, 'The God-Fearers – A Literary and Theological Invention', *BAR* 12 (1986), pp.46–53.

As suggested in the above quotation, Kraabel's claim stemmed mainly from a presumed lack of support from the early epigraphic evidence. While some researchers initially shared Kraabel's skepticism regarding both the historicity of the Lucan accounts and the existence of God-fearers, others argued forcefully against this interpretation, citing either new evidence or evidence that Kraabel had overlooked.[3]

The weight of the latter arguments seems to have tipped the balance in favour of the pre-1980s construct in the view of most current research-ers. Nevertheless, the debate was useful, not only in grounding upon the wider array of evidence our historical understanding of these early Gentile sympathisers of the synagogues, but also in offering some addi-tional nuance to it. In view of these relatively recent discussions, the focus of this chapter will be upon the primary sources of our knowledge regarding early Gentile interactions with the synagogues: those literary, epigraphic and archaeological references that form the basis of our understanding of those relationships.

At the same time, the recent reaffirmation of Gentile sympathisers within the ancient synagogues must not obscure the historical reality that interactions between Gentiles and this leading Jewish institution were not always halcyon. Indeed, the religio-political tensions between Jewish monotheism and the polytheism of the wider Greco-Roman society eventually erupted into violence, leading to the destruction of many synagogues in the first and second centuries of the Common Era. The primary evidence reflects these interactions as well.

Thus the relationships between Gentiles and the ancient synagogues can broadly be divided into two major categories: constructive relation-ships and destructive ones. Since the former is associated with the rise of the early synagogues, we will begin our discussion there.

3　　L. H. Feldman, 'The Omnipresence of the God-Fearers', *BAR* 12 (1986), pp.58–63; R. F. Tannenbaum, 'Jews and God-Fearers in the Holy City of Aphro-dite', *BAR* 12 (1986), pp.44–57; J. G. Gager, 'Jews, Gentiles, and Synagogues in the Book of Acts', *HTR* 79 (1986), pp.91–99; Reynolds and Tannenbaum, *Jews and God-Fearers at Aphrodisias*; I. A. Levinskaya, 'The Inscription from Aphrodisias and the Problem of God-Fearers', *TynBul* 41 (1990), pp.312–18; P. Trebilco, *Jewish Communities in Asia Minor* (SNTSMS 69; Cambridge: Cambridge University Press, 1991), pp.145–66; J. A. Overman, 'The God-Fearers: Some Neglected Features', in Overman and MacLennan (eds.), *Diaspora Jews and Judaism*, pp.145–52; D. D. Binder, *Into the Temple Courts: The Place of the Synagogues in the Second Temple Period* (Atlanta: SBL, 1999), pp.301–7; L. I. Levine, *The Ancient Synagogue: The First Thousand Years* (New Haven: Yale University Press, 2nd edn, 2005), pp.123–4, 293–4, 374, 509; and D. Koch, 'The God-fearers between Facts and Fiction: Two Theosebeis-Inscriptions from Aphrodisias and their Bearing for the New Testament', *Studia Theologica* 60 (2006), pp.62–90.

2. Constructive Relationships between Gentiles and the Synagogues

While the precise origins of the synagogues are obscure and still a matter of scholarly debate,[4] it is clear that one of the places where they first flourished was the land of Egypt in the aftermath of Alexander's conquest. The Jewish Philosopher Philo, writing around the year 41 CE, attests this basic belief:

> The first is taken from the kings. There were about ten, or even more, kings in succession in three hundred years, and yet the Alexandrians did not dedicate a single portrait or statue of them in the prayer halls (προσευ-χαί), although the kings whom they regarded, described, and spoke of as gods were of the same race and species as themselves. (Philo, *Legat.* 138 [*AS* 140])[5]

Although the above passage is apologetic and thus prone to bias, the epigraphic record nevertheless strongly supports its claim of sustained tolerance by the Ptolemaic dynasty for the early synagogues: not only were the Jews of Egypt allowed to construct their synagogues, but they were also exempted from erecting idols within them – even images of the reigning, divinised monarchs.

The surviving inscriptions are instructive for understanding how they achieved such concessions. One of the earliest examples dates from the second half of the third century BCE from the city of Arsinoë-Crocodilopolis:

> On behalf of King Ptolemy, son of Ptolemy, and Queen Berenice his wife, and his sister, and their children, the Jews of Crocodilopolis dedicated the prayer hall (προσευχή) and... (*AS* 150)

---

4   For a review of the literature, see A. Runesson, *The Origins of the Synagogue: A Socio-Historical Study* (Stockholm: Almqvist & Wiksell, 2001), pp.67–168; Binder, *Temple Courts*, pp.163–80; Levine, *The Ancient Synagogue*, pp.22–8; idem, 'The First Century Synagogue: Critical Reassessments and Assessments of the Critical', in D. R. Edwards (ed.), *Religion and Society in Roman Palestine: Old Questions: New Approaches* (New York: Routledge, 2004), pp.70–102.

5   This translation and all others in this chapter are taken from *AS*. For use of the term προσευχή in reference to the ancient synagogue, see Binder, *Temple Courts*, pp.111–18; Levine, *The Ancient Synagogue*, pp.85–7; idem, 'The Second Temple Synagogue: The Formative Years', in idem (ed.), *The Synagogue in Late Antiquity* (Philadelphia: American Schools of Oriental Research, 1987), pp.7–31 (13–14).

While at first glance the inscription appears to be a typical dedication, in fact it employs phrasing that is distinctive to Jewish synagogue monuments of the period. Here, the key term is ὑπέρ, 'on behalf of'. Thus the synagogue is not dedicated *to* the members of the royal family, as such a wording would denote their divinity. Instead, the synagogue is dedicated to God, who is either implied or named in the lost portion of the inscription, *on behalf of* the royal family.

Another example dating more than a century later (about 100 BCE) makes this vital distinction even more apparent:

> On behalf of King Ptolemy and Queen Cleopatra, Ptolemy, son of Epikydes, the chief of police, and the Jews of Athribis dedicated the prayer hall (προσευχή) to God Most High. (*AS* 151)

Again we see that the synagogue is dedicated *to* God Most High (θεὸς ὕψιστος; cf., e.g., Gen. 14.18-22 LXX) *on behalf of* the king and queen. With this bit of diplomatic legerdemain, the inherent conflict between Jewish monotheism and the polytheism of the ruling Gentile class was largely side-stepped in the first three centuries of the synagogues' existence in Egypt.

The above inscription might also be an example of a Gentile contributing towards the construction of a synagogue, depending on the ethnicity of the high-ranking official, Ptolemy Epikydes, who is listed separately as a contributor. Since Egyptian Jews commonly took on Greek names, however, and could also serve in upper-level positions, it is unclear whether he was a Gentile benefactor or simply the principal Jewish donor.

Less uncertain is a similar gift made a century and a half later in the Phrygian city of Acmonia:

> This building was erected by Julia Severa; P(ublius) Tyrronios Clados, ruler of the synagogue for life (ἀρχισυνάγωγος διὰ βίου), and Lucius, son of Lucius, ruler of the synagogue (ἀρχισυνάγωγος), and Popilios Zoticos, ruler (ἄρχων), restored it with their own funds and with money which had been contributed: they painted the walls and the ceiling, and they secured the windows and made all the rest of the ornamentation; and the congregation (συναγωγή) honoured them with a golden shield on account of their virtuous disposition, goodwill and zeal for the congregation (συναγωγή). (*AS* 103)[6]

---

6   For use of the term συναγωγή in reference to the ancient synagogue, see Binder, *Temple Courts*, pp.92–111; Levine, *The Ancient Synagogue*, pp.21–6; and idem, 'The Second Temple Synagogue', pp.13–14.

Along with her husband, Lucius Servenius Capito, Julia Severa served as one of the city archons from 59 to 63 CE. In addition, she also functioned as the high priestess of the imperial cult at Acmonia during this same general period. This latter leadership position makes it unlikely that she was anything more than a patron of the local Jewish community. Nevertheless, her donation was a significant one. Whether the structure referenced was a newly constructed synagogue or a building that was renovated into one, her generous gift attests a positive relationship between the two parties.

From another quarter of the Roman empire, a similar amicable relationship between the Jewish synagogue and a governing Gentile official is attested by an inscription from Berenice in the Province of Cyrene (modern Benghazi) dating to 24 CE:

> In the year 55, on the 25th of Phaoph, during the assembly of the Feast of the Tabernacles, during the offices of Cleandros, son of Stratonicos, Euphranor, son of Ariston, Sosigenes, son of Sosippos, Andromachos, son of Andromachos, Marcus Laelius Onasion, son of Apollonios, Philonides, son of Hagemon, Autocles, son of Zenon, Sonicos, son of Theodotos, and Josepos, son of Straton. With regard to Marcus Tittius, son of Sextus, (from the tribe of) Aemilia, a noble and good man: whereas he has assumed the office of prefect over public affairs, he has exercised kind and just leadership and has always displayed a peaceful demeanor in his daily affairs; whereas he has not been burdensome to the citizens who petition him privately; whereas he has exercised helpful leadership with regard to the Jews of our community (πολίτευμα), both publicly and privately; and whereas he has not himself ceased to act worthily with his own noble kindness: therefore, it seemed well to the rulers (ἄρχοντες) and to the community (πολίτευμα) of the Jews in Berenice both to honour him and to crown him by name at each regular assembly (σύνοδος) and each new moon with an olive crown and woollen band, and that the rulers (ἄρχοντες) should inscribe the vote on a stele of Parian stone and place it in the most prominent place in the amphitheatre (ἀμφιθέατρον). All (stones) white. (*AS* 132)[7]

As can be seen, this inscription records a resolution, unanimously adopted, that the local prefect, Marcus Tittius, be commemorated with a stele placed prominently inside the synagogue (referred to above as the amphitheatre), as well as with special honours on his behalf at their

---

7   For use of the term ἀμφιθέατρον in reference to the ancient synagogue, see Binder, *Temple Courts*, pp.140–5; Levine, *The Ancient Synagogue*, pp.96–100; and idem, 'The Second Temple Synagogue', pp.13–14.

regular (likely Sabbath) and festival assemblies. The generous language of the resolution bespeaks of a congenial relationship between the synagogue and the Roman ruler, reminiscent of the one attested in Luke between the Jews of Capernaum and a local centurion who reportedly built the synagogue there (Lk. 7.4-5 [*AS* 6]).

These local examples of harmonious interactions between Gentiles and the early synagogues illustrate the larger pattern of tolerance generally emanating from most Greco-Roman rulers well into the first century CE. We have already seen evidence of this in the dedicatory inscriptions from Ptolemaic Egypt. A more specific example of the synagogues' protected status in that realm can be found in an inscription from the second half of the first century BCE that had replaced one from about a century earlier:

> On the orders of the Queen and King, in place of the previous tablet concerning the dedication of the prayer hall (προσευχή), let the following be written: King Ptolemy Euergetes proclaimed the prayer hall (προσευχή) inviolate. The Queen and King issued the order. (*AS* 171)

This warning monument indicates that this synagogue had received the same right of asylum as enjoyed by most Gentile sanctuaries in Egypt in this period. Several bits of literary evidence (*AS* 135-37; *3 Macc.* 3.27-29; 4.17-18 [*AS* 147]) suggest that this privilege was not confined to this lone synagogue, but was the norm throughout Ptolemaic Egypt. This meant that everything and everyone inside the synagogue precincts were legally protected from pillaging, plunder or arrest. As another Egyptian synagogue inscription attests, they were 'sacred precincts' (ἱερὸν περίβολον [*AS* 143]; cf. Philo, *Flacc.* 48 [*AS* 138]).[8]

During the Hellenistic period, the major offender of these generally friendly relationships between Jews and Gentiles was, of course, Antiochus Epiphanes, who defiled the Jerusalem Temple in 167 BCE. His successors, however, soon returned to the earlier policy of tolerance, as can be seen in a reference Josephus makes to their treatment of the synagogue at Antioch in Syria:

> For, although Antiochus surnamed Epiphanes sacked Jerusalem and plundered the Temple (ναός), his successors on the throne restored to the Jews of Antioch all such votive offerings as were made of brass, to be laid up in

8   On the use of the term ἱερὸν περίβολον in reference to the ancient synagogue, see Binder, *Temple Courts*, pp.131–2; Levine, *The Ancient Synagogue*, p.86; and idem, 'The Second Temple Synagogue', pp.13–14.

their synagogue (συναγωγή), and, moreover, granting them citizen rights on an equality with the Greeks. Continuing to receive similar treatment from later monarchs, the Jewish colony grew in numbers, and their richly designed and costly offerings formed a splendid ornament to the Temple (ἱερόν). Moreover, they were constantly attracting to their religious ceremonies multitudes of Greeks, and these they had in some measure incorporated with themselves. (Josephus, *B.J.* 7.44-45 [*AS* 190])[9]

Thus the plundered goods of the Jerusalem Temple were given a new home in the Antioch synagogue, which Josephus also calls a temple (ἱερόν), indicating its sacred status. Additionally, he mentions that the synagogue there was attracting Greeks to its religious ceremonies, implying that some were fully or partially converted to Judaism. We shall return to this topic below.

Before we do, we need to note that elsewhere Josephus cites several official letters or inscriptions granting the Jewish synagogues in the expanding Roman empire similar privileges as they enjoyed under their previous Greek overlords. One of the earliest of these was written by Julius Caesar:

Julius Gaius commander, consul of the Romans, to the magistrates, council and people of Parium, greetings. The Jews in Delos and some other Jews being dwellers there, some of your envoys also being present, have appealed to me and declared that you by statute prevent them from performing their native customs and sacred rituals. Now it is not acceptable to me that such statutes should be made against our friends and allies and that they are prevented to live according to their customs, to collect money for common meals and to perform sacred rituals: not even in Rome are they prohibited to do this. For in fact Gaius Caesar, our commander and consul, by edict forbade religious guilds to assemble in the city but, as a single exception, he did not forbid these people to do so, or to collect money or to have common meals. Likewise do I prohibit other religious guilds (θίασοι) exempting only these people whom I permit to assemble and feast according to their native customs and laws. And if you have made any statute against our friends and allies you will do well to revoke them because of their good service and goodwill toward us. (Josephus, *A.J.* 14.213-16 [*AS* 93])

9   For use of the term ἱερόν in reference to the ancient synagogue, see Binder, *Temple Courts*, pp.122–30; Levine, *The Ancient Synagogue*, p.23; and idem, 'The Second Temple Synagogue', pp.13–14.

Here, Caesar not only chastises the officials who were interfering with the religious rituals of the Jews (and perhaps Samaritans) of Delos,[10] but in doing so, he cites as a precedent his liberal policies with regard to the Jewish synagogues in the city of Rome itself.

Josephus goes on to quote a decree of Caesar's eventual successor, Emperor Augustus, which further extends the rights of the Jewish synagogues:

> Caesar Augustus, Pontifex Maximus with tribunician power, decrees: since the Jewish nation has been found well disposed to the Roman people not only at the present time but also in the past, especially in the time of my father the Emperor Caesar, as has their high priest Hyrcanus, it has been decided by me and my council under oath, with the consent of the Roman people, that the Jews may follow their own customs in accordance with their ancestral law, just as they followed them in the time of Hyrcanus, high priest of God the Most High, and that their sacred monies shall be inviolable and may be sent to Jerusalem and delivered to the treasurers in Jerusalem, and that they need not give bond (to appear in court) on the Sabbath or on the day of preparation for it after the ninth hour. If anyone is caught stealing their holy books or holy monies from a synagogue (σαββατεῖον) or a banqueting hall (ἀνδρών), he shall be regarded as sacrilegious, and his property shall be confiscated to the public treasury of the Romans. The decree which was given to me by them concerning the piety which I show to all mankind, and on behalf of Gaius Marcius Censorinus, I order that it and the present edict be set up in the most conspicuous part (of the Temple) assigned to me by the federation of Asia in Ancyra. If anyone transgresses any of the above ordinances he shall suffer severe punishment. (Josephus, *A.J.* 16.162–65 [*AS* 120])[11]

While this decree was specifically addressed to the Province of Asia, other evidence from the period makes it clear that the policy contained therein extended throughout the Roman empire.[12] The edict granted to the synagogues the same right of inviolability customarily bestowed upon Greco-Roman temples. Further, it protected the Jewish practice of

---

10   On the presence of a Samaritan synagogue on Delos, see *AS* 100, 101, 102; Binder, *Temple Courts*, pp.297–317, 471–4; Levine, *The Ancient Synagogue*, pp.107–13; M. Trümper, 'The Oldest Original Synagogue Building in the Diaspora: The Delos Synagogue Reconsidered', *Hesperia* 73 (2004), pp.513–98.

11   On the use of the term σαββατεῖον in reference to the ancient synagogue, see Binder, *Temple Courts*, pp.147–9; Levine, *The Ancient Synagogue*, pp.23, 115, 117, 128, 141; and idem, 'The Second Temple Synagogue', pp.13–14.

12   See Binder, *Temple Courts*, pp.229–33; and S. L. Guterman, *Religious Toleration and Persecution in Ancient Rome* (London: Aiglon, 1951), pp.75–158.

Sabbath observance, as well as the safe-passage of tithes and offerings from the synagogues to the Jerusalem Temple. Finally, it references the bestowal by the Jewish people of a monument of gratitude to the emperor. This was likely similar to the one seen earlier from the Jews of Berenice to Marcus Tittius (*AS* 132), with copies of it possibly erected within the Asian synagogues. In this case, the original was displayed in the imperial temple in Ancrya, a rather ironic placement given Jewish adherence to monotheism.

If the historical evidence clearly demonstrates that Jewish rituals and synagogues were given special rights and protections throughout most of the Greco-Roman period, what does it say with respect to the participation of Gentiles within these same? Here, we have already seen Josephus' claim regarding the city of Antioch in Syria, that the Jewish communities there were 'constantly attracting to their religious ceremonies multitudes of Greeks, and these they had in some measure incorporated with themselves' (*B.J.* 7.45 [*AS* 190]). This resonates with another, more generic, assertion Josephus makes elsewhere when he writes, 'Many of (the Greeks) have agreed to adopt our laws; of whom some have remained faithful, while others, lacking the necessary endurance, have again seceded' (*C. Ap.* 2.124). Somewhat earlier in the first century, Philo makes a similar observation when he states that Jewish customs 'attract and win the attention of all, of barbarians, of Greeks, of dwellers on the mainland and islands, of nations of the east and the west, of Europe and Asia, of the whole inhabited world from end to end' (*Mos.* 2.20).

Because Philo and Josephus are both writing apologetically, we might suspect these claims to be at least somewhat exaggerated. However, less sympathetic authors from this period paint a similar picture. For example, Seneca the Younger (4 BCE–65 CE) complains, 'the customs of this accursed race (the Jews) have gained such influence that they are now received throughout all the world. The vanquished have given their laws to their victors' (Seneca, *De Superstitione*, cited by Augustine, *Civ.* 6.11).[13] Likewise, Juvenal satirises a prototypical Roman citizen who 'reveres the Sabbath, worships nothing but the clouds' and goes on to 'practise and revere the Jewish law', including circumcision and 'idleness' on the Sabbath (*Sat.* 14.96–98).[14]

---

13 For commentary on this passage, see M. Stern, *Greek and Latin Authors on Jews and Judaism* (3 vols.; Jerusalem: Israel Academy of Sciences and Humanities, 1974–84), I, pp.431–2.

14 For additional non-Jewish references, see Schürer et al., *History*, III.1, pp.150–5; and Stern, *Greek and Latin Authors*, passim.

Most of these descriptions assume a gamut of participation by Gentiles, ranging from mild reverence to full-blown religious conversion. Josephus makes the opposite poles of this spectrum explicit. On the one side, he refers to a certain Fulvia as 'a woman of high rank who had become a Jewish proselyte (προσεληλυθυῖα)' (*A.J.* 18.82). Her level of commitment to Judaism would have corresponded to that of non-apostate ethnic Jews – likely coupled on the front-end with participation in a rite of initiation.[15] Conversely, Josephus refers to Nero's wife Poppea, who surely held concomitant loyalties to the Roman gods, as a θεοσεβής, a 'worshiper of God' (*A.J.* 20.195).

This same distinction appears in Acts, where Jewish proselytes appear both at Pentecost (presumably among some of the earliest Christian converts) and, in the case of Nicolaus of Antioch, even among the seven ordained 'servers of tables' (Acts 2.10; 6.5). While inclusion of these fully integrated Gentiles was not a source of controversy among the early Christians, this was certainly not the case for Gentiles who had not fully converted to Judaism prior to acceptance into the Christian community.[16] Acts identifies such persons either as a 'fearer of God' (φοβούμενος τὸν θεόν), as in the case of the Roman Centurion Cornelius (Acts 10.22), or, similarly to Josephus, as 'worshippers/worshippers of God' (σεβομένοι/ σεβομένοι τὸν θεόν), as with Lydia at Philippi (16.14 [*AS* 185]), Titius Justus at Corinth (18.7 [*AS* 91]) and unnamed Gentiles at Pisidian Antioch, Thessalonica and Athens (13.16, 26, 50 [*AS* 174]; 17.4 [*AS* 186], 17 [*AS* 90]).[17] This class of Gentile had some level of involvement with the local synagogue, in most cases as participants in the Sabbath synagogue services themselves.

Here it should also be noted that Josephus employs a phrase identical to Acts' most common usage when he explains to his Gentile readers the reason behind the Jerusalem Temple's great wealth: 'But no one need wonder that there was so much wealth in our Temple, for all the Jews throughout the habitable world, and σεβομένων τὸν θεόν (God-fearers), even those from Asia and Europe, had been contributing to it for a very long time' (*A.J.* 14.110). Thus it would appear that this term held a wide linguistic currency in the first century C.E.[18]

15   For a review of the evidence for Jewish proselytes in the Greco-Roman period, see P. Figueras, 'Epigraphic Evidence for Proselytism in Ancient Judaism', *Immanuel* 24/25 (1990), pp.194–206; and Levinskaya, *Acts*, pp.19–49.

16   As evidenced from the sharpness of the debate in Galatians and the controversies of Acts 11 and 15.

17   See also Acts 17.12 (*AS* 184) for a less explicit example of such God-fearers at Beroea.

18   See Binder, *Temple Courts*, pp.303–4.

While the early literary record clearly indicates the existence of both proselytes and God-fearers as participants within the early synagogues, the epigraphic evidence offers additional support for this construct. Of relevance here are a series of manumission inscriptions from the Bosporus Kingdom on the northern shores of the Black Sea. These attest to the practice of release ceremonies inside the synagogues of that region, a practice common in Greco-Roman temples at the time.

Of particular interest is an inscription from the city of Panticapaeum dating from the first century CE:

> ...I, (*unnamed woman*), release in the prayer hall (προσευχή) Elpias, my home-bred slave, so that he will be undisturbed and inviolable by all my heirs, except that he show devotion towards the prayer hall (προσευχή) under the guardianship of the congregation (συναγωγή) of the Jews, and reveres God. (*AS* 126)

The history of this inscription's interpretation is coloured by the fact that the stonecutter incorrectly carved the name of the manumitted slave, leaving the gender unclear. Reading the name as female has allowed some interpreters to emend further the phrase θεόν σέβων, 'reveres God' as θεό{ν}σεβῶν, 'God-fearers', meaning that the freed slave would be under the guardianship of the congregation of the Jews and 'God-fearers'. While this reading cannot absolutely be ruled out, it seems improbable. Not only does it involve a second emendation, but it omits one of two release requirements typically found in such inscriptions: that the released slave shows both devotion (προσκαρτέρησις) and deference (θωπέα) to the prayer hall. In the above inscription, the phrase θεόν σέβων would be a variant of the second condition.[19]

Although much of the debate regarding the existence of God-fearers in the Bosporus synagogues has revolved around the reading of this particular inscription, such a single-minded discussion overlooks the fact that such conditions would only be necessary for released Gentile slaves who would be maintaining an ongoing relationship with the local synagogue. To give another example from Panticapaeum, dating to 81 CE:

> In the reign of King Tiberius Julius Rhescuporis, friend of Caesar and friend of the Romans, pious, in the year 377, the twelfth of the month of Peritios, I Chreste, former wife of Drusus, release in the prayer hall

---

19   See Levinskya, *Acts*, pp.74–6, 232–4; Binder, *Temple Courts*, pp.385–6, 441, 444; and Levine, *The Ancient Synagogue*, pp.123–4.

(προσευχή), my home-bred slave Heraclas, free, once and for all, according to my vow, inviolable and undisturbed by all my heirs, and who may go wherever he desires, unhindered, as I have vowed, except that he show deference and devotion toward the prayer hall (προσευχή); both with the consent of my heirs Heracleides and Heliconias and with the joint guardianship of the congregation (συναγωγή) of the Jews. (*AS* 124)

The requirement that Heraclas show 'deference and devotion' towards the synagogue would be unnecessary if he were a Jew. On the other hand, it would serve as a natural safe-guard for the synagogue if he were a Gentile who had not become a full proselyte yet still maintained a relationship with the synagogue after his release.

The exact nature of that relationship (aside from the congregation serving as joint guardian) is unclear. It might be argued that Heraclas and others like him simply went on to become servants of the synagogue (rather than participate as 'worshippers of God'). However, it should be noted that such an economic relationship is never specifically defined in any of the extant manumission evidence. In addition, one type of relationship would not necessarily preclude the other. Indeed, one could easily envision the congregation desiring those in their employ to be one of the growing class of reverent Gentiles known as God-fearers.

To summarise this section, during the Greco-Roman period up through the first half of the first century CE, with a few major exceptions (the reigns of Antiochus Epiphanes and Caligula), the relationship between Jews and Gentiles in connection with the synagogues seems to have been cordial, at least on an official level. Greco-Roman rulers routinely bestowed upon the synagogues the same rights as those given to polytheistic temples, while simultaneously granting them numerous exemptions so that they might remain true to their religious observances. In addition, Gentiles sometimes served as patrons of the synagogues, with many more being attracted wholly or in part to Jewish practices and beliefs, including regular participation within the Sabbath synagogue services. In response to such benevolent and sympathetic actions, the Jews erected in their synagogues honorary plaques to such Gentiles and (at least in the Diaspora) welcomed them into their synagogue services.

As indicated in the introduction, the existence of such positive relationships does not mean that there were not tensions simmering beneath the surface. In fact, they did exist, and it would only take certain catalytic episodes to bring such tensions to a full boil, as we shall see in our next section.

3. Destructive Relationships between Gentiles and the Synagogues

In the preceding section, we noted in passing that the primary sources referencing the persecution of Jews and Jewish religious institutions involved Antiochus Epiphanes and the Gentiles of Delos in the second and first centuries BCE. During the next century and a half, underlying tensions between Jews and Gentiles would explode into religious pogroms and open warfare, leading to the destruction of many synagogues in the eastern reaches of the Roman empire where most Jews resided. While the inherent conflict between Jewish monotheism and Gentile polytheism was the ultimate source of the violence, the increasing level of incompetence and corruption of the Roman governors in the east served as the specific impetus. More and more, the Roman prefects and procurators sought to profit from their posts, often at the expense of the religious sensitivities of the Jews over whom they ruled.[20]

The prefect Flaccus serves as our opening example. As governor over Egypt in 38 CE, he presided over not only the desecration and destruction of many synagogues in Alexandria and its environs, but also the ghettoisation of the Jews in that city. Philo offers an eye-witness account:

> Assembling enormous hordes together, they attacked the prayer halls (προσευχαί), of which there are many in each section of the city. Some they smashed, some they rased to the ground, and others they set on fire and burned, giving no thought even to the adjacent houses in their madness and frenzied insanity...The prayer halls (προσευχαί) which they could not destroy either by fire or by demolition, because large numbers of Jews lived crowded together close by, they outraged in a different way, which involved the overthrow of our Laws and customs. They placed portraits of Gaius (Emperor Caligula) in all of them, and in the largest and most famous they also placed a bronze statue riding in a four-horse chariot. (Philo, *Legat.* 132, 134 [*AS* 140])

While Flaccus would eventually be arrested for these demonstrations, rival Greek and Jewish delegations from Alexandria soon went to Rome to petition Caligula with their grievances. Philo himself was leader of the latter delegation. Upon arriving in the capital, to his horror, he there

---

20   For a more in-depth analysis of the socio-religious tensions between Rome and the Jewish people in the first century CE, see L. L. Grabbe, *Judaism from Cyrus to Hadrian* (2 vols.; Minneapolis: Fortress, 1992), II, pp.409–18.

learned that the emperor had decided to transform the Jerusalem Temple into a temple for himself, much like Antiochus Epiphanes had done two centuries before. As preparations for this were being made, many synagogues around the empire were desecrated:

> Having conceived a violent enmity to them he took possession of the prayer halls (προσευχαί) in the other cities after beginning with those of Alexandria, by filling them with images and statues of himself in bodily form. For by permitting others to instal them he virtually did it himself. The Temple in the Holy City, which alone was left untouched being judged to have all rights of sanctuary, he proceeded to convert and transmogrify into a Temple of his own to bear the name of Gaius, 'the new Zeus made manifest'. (Philo, *Legat.* 346)

Josephus more specifically identifies the treatment given that year (40 CE) to a synagogue in the coastal city of Dora in southern Syria: 'certain young men of Dora, who set higher value on audacity than on holiness and were by nature recklessly bold, brought an image of Caesar into the synagogue (συναγωγή) of the Jews and set it up' (*A.J.* 19.300). King Agrippa I intervened to convince Caligula to reverse his earlier decision, which he did, albeit reluctantly. Within the year, he was assassinated by his own guards and Claudius was elevated. The new emperor subsequently restored the previous status quo, but not before the Jews of Alexandria staged a revenge riot for the pogroms of 38 CE, destroying the homes of many Greeks in that city.[21]

The relationship between the Jews and their Roman overlords continued to be strained over the next few decades, culminating with the eruption of the Jewish war in 66 CE. This epic clash between two nations and religious worldviews began with an incident that took place outside a synagogue in Caesarea Maritima:

> The ostensible pretext for war was out of proportion to the magnitude of the disasters to which it led. The Jews in Caesarea had a synagogue (συναγωγή) adjoining a plot of ground owned by a Greek of that city; this site they had frequently endeavoured to purchase, offering a price far exceeding its true value. The proprietor, disdaining their solicitations by way of insult further proceeded to build upon the site and erect workshops, leaving the Jews only a narrow and extremely awkward passage. Thereupon, some of the hot-headed youths proceeded to set upon the builders and attempted to interrupt operations. Florus having put a stop to their violence, the Jewish notables, with John, the tax collector, having no

21   See Binder, *Temple Courts*, pp.201–2.

other expedient, offered Florus eight talents of silver to procure the cessation of the work. Florus, with his eye only on the money, promised them every assistance, but, having secured his pay, at once quitted Caesarea for Sebaste, leaving a free field to sedition, as though he had sold the Jews a licence to fight the matter out. On the following day, which was a Sabbath, when the Jews assembled at the synagogue (συναγωγή), they found that one of the Caesarean mischief-makers had placed beside the entrance a pot, turned bottom upwards, upon which he was sacrificing birds. This spectacle of what they considered an outrage upon their laws and a desecration of the spot enraged the Jews beyond endurance. The steady-going and peacable members of the congregation were in favour of immediate recourse to the authorities; but the factious folk and the passionate youth were burning for a fight. The Caesarean party, on their side, stood prepared for action, for they had, by a con-certed plan, sent the man on to the mock sacrifice; and so they soon came to blows. Jucundus, the cavalry commander commissioned to intervene, came up, removed the pot and endeavoured to quell the riot, but was unable to cope with the violence of the Caesareans. The Jews, thereupon, snatched up their copy of the Law and withdrew to Narbata, a Jewish district sixty furlongs distant from Caesarea. Their leading men, twelve in number, with John at their head, waited upon Florus at Sebaste, bitterly complained of these proceedings and besought his assistance, delicately reminding him of the matter of the eight talents. Florus actually had them arrested and put in irons on the charge of having carried off the copy of the Law from Caesarea. (Josephus, *B.J.* 2.285-92 [*AS* 1])

Again, a corrupt governor, in this case Florus, was near the centre of the hostilities, which soon escalated into the tragic destructive conflict that followed over the next half-decade.

With war declared upon the Jewish people, Jews and their synagogues in the homeland and beyond became targets. Josephus enumerates a lengthy list of Hellenistic cities where Jews were massacred, including Ashkelon, Ptolemais, Tyre, Hippos, Gadara and Damascus (*B.J.* 2.477-80, 559-61). In the homeland, archaeological remains demonstrate evidence of destruction from this period at the synagogues uncovered at Gamla (*AS* 10), Masada (*AS* 28), Herodium (*AS* 11) and Qumran (*AS* 41). It was at this time, of course, that the Jerusalem Temple was also destroyed. Josephus describes the subsequent triumph in Rome as including parading displays of burning synagogues (*B.J.* 7.144 [*AS* 62]) followed by the spoils of the Jerusalem Temple.[22]

---

22   See Grabbe, *Judaism*, II, pp.445–61; and Schürer et al., *History*, I, pp.484–513.

In the first half of the next century, Jewish uprisings again occurred, first under Trajan in 115–117 CE and then under Hadrian in 132–135 CE.[23] While specific evidence of synagogue destruction during these conflicts can be found only at Herodium (*AS* 11), Modi'in (*AS* 29) and Kiryat Sefer (*AS* 35) during the latter Bar Kochba Revolt, there can be little doubt that other synagogues served as targets elsewhere throughout the war zones in both sets of conflicts.

Following this period, there would be a relative, though perhaps uneasy, peace between Rome and the Jewish synagogues, as Roman persecution shifted to the rapidly spreading new religion of Christianity, which served as the greater threat to polytheism and the rising Roman imperial cult.

4. *Conclusions*

In this study, we have explored primary evidence demonstrating both positive and negative relationships between Jews and Gentiles vis-à-vis the early synagogues. During the periods of Gentile tolerance, the synagogues prospered and served as potential places of interaction between Jews and Gentiles interested in Judaism, whether as a matter of moral and spiritual enlightenment or merely of civic and political inclusion. When the inherent tensions between monotheism and polytheism rose to the surface, however, violence ensued, demonstrating the great difficulty in maintaining two incompatible worldviews side-by-side.

Ironically, the decadent emperor Caligula saw precisely to the heart of the matter during his audience with Philo's embassy from Alexandria. When the Jewish delegation pointed out that their nation did indeed offer sacrifices on behalf of the Roman nation, the emperor replied, '"Grant", said he, "that all this is true, and that you did sacrifice; nevertheless you sacrificed to another god and not for my sake; and then what good did you do me? Moreover you did not sacrifice to me"' (Philo, *Legat.* 357). Philo then wrote, 'Immediately a profound shuddering came upon us the first moment that we heard this expression' (Philo, *Legat.* 357). The delegation shuddered because they knew that if the emperor insisted upon his own way, then their nation and their people were finished. Just as the character Tevye similarly realised near the end of *Fiddler on the Roof*, with such an edict, there was no 'on the other hand'. Religious accommodation could only go so far.

23   See Grabbe, *Judaism*, II, pp.595–605; and Schürer et al., *History*, I, pp.514–57.

And so, the early history of relationships between Gentiles and the synagogues serves as a microcosm of potential interactions between differing religions (or differing worldviews) down to our very day. As such, it remains a continuing source of insight in an increasingly pluriform world where tolerance and repression stand at opposite poles, with degrees of accommodation and tenets of self-identity being the variables of movement in between. Different eras and different religions will arrive at different solutions to these tensions, but the basic questions within this scheme will remain the same.

Chapter 8

Q AND THE GENTILES

Christopher M. Tuckett

In discussing the issue of 'Q and Gentiles', one or two preliminary points need to be mentioned first. In other contexts the assumptions made here could be debated and defended in detail: however, there is not the time or the space available to do so here. Thus in what follows, I am presuming the existence of a Q source used by Matthew and Luke as the best explanation of the agreements between these Gospels in the material which they did not derive form Mark; I am also presuming that this source had a relatively fixed written form, probably in Greek.[1] Further, I am presuming that there are sufficient characteristic, and at times distinctive, features of the Q material to justify thinking (in very broad terms) of this material as exhibiting some kind of 'theology', and/or reflecting a particular situation within early Christianity which led to (a) Q 'editor(s)' assembling and promoting the Q material. It is highly likely that the Q material, in the form that it was accessed by Matthew and Luke, is the outcome of what may have been a long and complex development in the history of the Jesus tradition. On the other hand, we may not be able to trace that development in terms of a specific history of the Q 'text' as a whole. The Q tradition may well have grown with the passing of time, but we cannot necessarily identify clear stages in the development of the document itself.[2] In what follows, therefore, I seek

---

1 For these general issues about Q's existence and nature, see C. M. Tuckett, *Q and the History of Early Christianity* (Edinburgh: T. & T. Clark, 1996), Chapters 1–3; and J. S. Kloppenborg, *Excavating Q: The History and Setting of the Sayings Gospel* (Minneapolis: Fortress, 2000), Chapter 2.

2 Hence contra e.g. the influential and seminal work of J. S. Kloppenborg, *The Formation of Q* (Philadelphia: Fortress, 1987), repeated in his *Excavating Q*, who identifies three clear stages or strata in Q (often referred to now as Q^1, Q^2, Q^3). See Tuckett, *Q and the History*, pp.69–73; and in more detail, C. M. Tuckett, 'On the Stratification of Q', *Semeia* 55 (1991), pp.213–22. Also P. Hoffmann,

to focus on 'Q' in its 'final' form (in line with many approaches to the Gospels themselves), insofar as that is accessible to us.[3]

The issue of how far Q shows a distinctive, or even clear, attitude to Gentiles, perhaps too whether Q presupposes a Gentile mission by Christians, has been debated many times.[4] Some have argued that Q presupposes and welcomes the Gentile mission;[5] others have claimed that Q rejected the idea of such a mission, or was unconcerned by the issue.[6] Others still have argued that Q presupposes the existence of a Gentile mission, but that the primary concern is to address the Jewish people and that it uses the fact of the success of a possible Gentile mission elsewhere as part of its message to other Jews to shame them.[7]

'Mutmassungen über Q. Zum Problem der literarischen Genese von Q', in A. Lindemann (ed.), *The Sayings Source Q and the Historical Jesus* (BETL 158; Leuven: Peeters, 2001), pp.255–88; and H. Fleddermann, *Q: A Reconstruction and Commentary* (Leuven: Peeters, 2005), pp.166–7.

3   See further Tuckett, *Q and the History*, pp.75–82. By 'final', I mean the form in which Q was accessed by Matthew and Luke. I am fully aware that the forms of Q available to Matthew and Luke may have been different. Indeed, this is in many respects highly probable: it is all but impossible to conceive that Matthew and Luke had access to the same handwritten copy of Q! On the other hand, the whole theory of the existence of Q is based on the agreements between Matthew and Luke being extensive enough to imply that they are due to dependence on a *common* source. Hence any possible differences between the versions of Q available to the two evangelists cannot be postulated as too extensive without undermining the theory of a common underlying source used by them.

4   For a summary of past studies of the issue, see U. Wegner, *Der Hauptmann von Kafarnaum (Mt 7,28a; 8,5–10,13 par Lk 7,1-10). Ein Beitrag zur Q-Forschung* (WUNT 2.14; Tübingen: Mohr, 1985), pp.305–27.

5   See, for example, T. W. Manson, *The Sayings of Jesus* (London: SCM, 1949), p.20; D. Lührmann, *Die Redaktion der Logienquelle* (WMANT 33; Neukirchen–Vluyn: Neukirchener, 1969), pp.58, 86–7; R. Laufen, *Die Doppelüberlieferungen der Logienquelle und des Markusevangeliums* (BBB 54; Bonn: Hanstein, 1980), pp.192–4, 237–43; and R. Uro, *Sheep among Wolves: A Study of the Mission Instructions of Q* (Helsinki: Suomalainen Tiedeakatemia, 1987), pp.210–23. Fledder-mann, *Q*, pp.164–7, is even stronger, and argues that Q is a 'gentile Christian gospel', whose author and original readers were themselves Gentile.

6   See, with varying emphases, O. H. Steck, *Israel und das gewaltsame Geschick der Propheten* (WMANT 23; Neukirchen–Vluyn: Neukirchener, 1967), pp.287–8; P. Hoffmann, *Studien zur Theologie der Logienquelle* (NTAbh 8; Münster: Aschen-dorff, 1972), pp.292–3; S. Schulz, *Q – Die Spruchquelle der Evangelisten* (Zurich: TVZ, 1972), pp.244–5, 410–12; and Wegner, *Hauptmann*, pp.327–34.

7   P. D. Meyer, 'The Gentile Mission in Q', *JBL* 89 (1970), pp.405–17; and A. D. Jacobson, *The First Gospel: An Introduction to Q* (Sonoma: Polebridge, 1992), pp.110, 256. This also seems to be the most recent view of Kloppenborg, who

The range of scholarly opinion on the subject is simply a reflection of the fact that the evidence from Q itself is ambiguous and inconclusive. Those who have argued for a positive attitude to Gentiles can point to a number of passages in Q in support. It is well known that Q contains a number of highly negative sayings threatening judgment against 'this generation', which in context seems to refer to the Jewish people (or at least part of the Jewish people); and quite often, this is coupled with a reference to Gentiles who by contrast are presented thoroughly positively and commended. Thus the Queen of the South and the Ninevites are held up as examples of people who responded positively to the wisdom of Solomon and the preaching of Jonah respectively, by contrast with 'this generation' which has failed to repent, even though 'something greater' than either Solomon or Jonah is present (Q 11.31-32).[8] Similarly, in the woes against the Galilean towns of Chorazin and Bethsaida in Q 10.13-14 (and the appended saying against Capernaum in v. 15), the cities of Tyre and Sidon are commended on the basis that they would have repented long ago if the same mighty works had been performed in them. In Q 13.28-29, those who come from the four corners of the earth (almost certainly Gentiles)[9] will sit down with the patriarchs in the eschatological kingdom and replace 'you'/the 'sons of the kingdom' (almost certainly the Jewish hearers). And the story of the healing of the centurion's servant in Q 7.1-10 holds up the Gentile centurion as an example of someone who has shown 'faith', a faith which exceeds

---

appears to have shifted ground slightly. In his earlier *Formation* (p.236) he argued that Q was actively involved in a Gentile mission; however, in his *Excavating Q* (p.256), he argues that the horizon of Q seems bound by Galilee and an entirely inner-Jewish perspective. This seems to be repeated in his most recent *Q, the Earliest Gospel: An Introduction to the Original Stories and Sayings of Jesus* (Louisville: Westminster John Knox, 2008), pp.68–9: 'Q presents us with a rural, Galilean Jewish gospel, not a gospel that imagines the extension of the mission of the Jesus movement to gentile areas and the cultic debates that this extension would provoke' (p.69). The story of the centurion is told in Q '...precisely because his confidence is so exceptional and because it puts to shame those who in Q's view ought to have confidence in Jesus' (p.68).

8   In accordance with what has become standard scholarly convention, I refer to passages in Q using the chapter and verse numbers in the Lucan parallel, prefixed by 'Q'. This is purely conventional and in no way presupposes that Luke's version is more original than Matthew's in instances where the two Gospels disagree with each other.

9   See Kloppenborg, *Excavating Q*, p.192, against, for example, Horsley who argues that Diaspora Jews are in mind: if that were the case, the saying would lose all its force.

anything that Q's Jesus has found elsewhere in Israel. On the basis of this sort of evidence, T. W. Manson drew the conclusion that Q 'shows a friendly attitude towards Gentiles'.[10]

Other possible texts which might also be relevant and contribute to this general 'Gentile-friendly' interpretation of Q would include the image of the 'harvest' used in Q 10.2: the image of the harvest is sometimes used to refer to the judgment of the Gentiles (cf. Joel 3.13-14; Isa. 27.11; Hos. 6.11), and hence the call to send labourers to the harvest may imply the existence of a Gentile mission.[11] The parable of the Great Supper in Q 14.16-24 can be taken as implying that, following the failure of the Jewish people to respond to Jesus, the mission will go out to Gentiles.[12] So too the end of the parable of the mustard seed in Q 13.18-19, with its note about the birds of the air coming and nesting in the branches of the great tree, which has been interpreted as a reference to the incoming of Gentiles into the kingdom.[13] Others too have seen a positive attitude to Gentiles as the other side of the coin of the polemic against 'this generation'. Thus D. Lührmann, for example, argues that all hope for Israel has now been surrendered and hence the mission has turned to non-Jews.[14] Fleddermann also appeals to the saying in Q 3.8 (denying any validity of an appeal to Abraham as an ancestor) as an example of Q's universalism; also the reference by Q's Jesus in the temptation narrative to monotheistic faith (Q 4.8) makes more sense if implicitly addressed to Gentiles; and the sayings in Q 14.5; 16.18 show Jesus reformulating and/or changing the Law in a way congruent with Gentile Christianity.[15]

Further possible texts which might be relevant to the topic here concern verses which appear in Matthew and Luke alone and which, it is argued by some, might have been in Q and omitted by one evangelist. Such a situation is of course theoretically quite possible, but it is very hard to be certain in individual cases whether such verses can be regarded as part of Q. In relation to the present topic, Mt. 10.5 has occasionally been ascribed to Q, suggesting a highly Jewish-centred

10   Manson, *Sayings*, p.20. Fleddermann, *Q*, p.166, is stronger: 'From start to finish, Q reads like a gentile Christian gospel'.

11   Cf. Lührmann, *Redaktion*, p.60.

12   Lührmann, *Redaktion*, p.87; and Uro, *Sheep*, pp.219–20.

13   See Manson, *Sayings*, p.123; Laufen, *Doppelüberlieferungen*, pp.192–3; Uro, *Sheep*, pp.218–19; and Fleddermann, *Q*, pp.164–5.

14   Lührmann, *Redaktion*, pp.47, 88; cf. too Kloppenborg, *Formation*, pp.148, 167, 236 (though see also above for perhaps a slight shift in Kloppenborg's views in his later writings).

15   Fleddermann, *Q*, p.164.

particularist mentality, but the evidence for this is weak and it has only very occasionally been suggested that the verse should be ascribed to Q.[16] The other verse which might be relevant here (and about which there is more uncertainty) is Lk. 10.2, particularly the last part of the verse with the command to those sent out on mission to 'eat whatever is put before you': this appears to imply that all food laws should be ignored and hence would appear to presuppose a fully fledged Gentile mission under-way. However, it is uncertain whether this part of the verse should be ascribed to Q or to Luke's redaction of Q.[17] Again, given the uncertainty of the situation one should probably not place any weight on the saying in the present context.[18]

On the other hand, others have pointed out that the evidence is rather less clear-cut than might appear at first sight. Gentiles are generally *not* present in Q's story world. Most of the Gentiles mentioned in the previous examples belong to the past (as in Q 11.31-32) or to the future (as in Q 10.13-15; 13.28-29).[19] The story of the centurion's servant in Q 7.1-10 does refer to a Gentile reacting positively to Jesus in Jesus' present, and being highly commended for doing so; nevertheless, there is nothing in the story to suggest that the centurion in Q is anything other than an exceptional case. Nothing indicates that the centurion stands at the head of a long line of other Gentiles who are responding positively to Q's Jesus or to later Q Christians.[20]

The argument appealing to the polemic against 'this generation' as implying an end to any realistic Israel mission, and hence a positive attitude to a Gentile mission, may also be unpersuasive in quite this form. The very fact that Jesus himself and his followers (in Q's narra-tive) are Jewish implies that 'this generation', the object of the polemic

16   For discussion (in relation to the claims of H. Schürmann and D. Catchpole), see Tuckett, *Q and the History*, p.398.

17   For the former, see, for example, Uro, *Sheep*, pp.68–9; for the latter, see Hoffmann, *Studien*, pp.276–81. Fuller discussion can be found in Tuckett, *Q and the History*, p.399.

18   One factor which might be important in the discussion of whether to ascribe the verse to Q would be whether the ideas presupposed here cohere with the rest of Q; but then one cannot use the verse itself as part of the evidence in determin-ing whether or not to ascribe it to Q without the argument becoming dangerously circular.

19   Cf. Hoffmann, *Studien*, p.293; and Wegner, *Hauptmann*, p.327.

20   Hoffmann, *Studien*, p.293. In this sense, Kloppenborg's insistence in his later writings – that the world of Q fits well in the context of Galilee where Gentiles do not really come into the picture at all and the presumed social/religious context is that of Judaism (see above) – fits this well.

of Q's Jesus, cannot be the nation of the Jewish people as a whole: it can at most be directed against *part* of the Jewish people. Further, there is a danger of taking the polemical language, with the threats about final judgment, too literally or woodenly. Part of the point of the polemic may be to paint the *possible* future in such negative and threatening terms precisely in order to try to alter other people's attitudes and to get them to change. The language need not imply that the speaker has given up all hope for his addressees.[21] Thus even the apparently stark prediction of the replacement of (the) Jews by Gentiles in the final kingdom (in Q 13.28-29) needs to be seen in its (probable) broader context in Q, viz. in Q 13.24-29, where the final saying is the climax of the appeal starting with the exhortation to strive to enter through the narrow door. The warning in the final saying is perhaps more to be read as a warning about what will happen *if* the hearers take no notice of the appeal which Q's Jesus is making. But the warning is implicitly a conditional one: if people respond positively, then the negative judgments, involving rejection and punishment, will presumably not take place. Similarly, although it is disputed, the final phrase of what may have been a unified section in Q ending in Q 13.35 may also strike a more positive note. There it is said that the audience will not see Jesus again until the End when they will say 'Blessed is he who comes in the name of the Lord' (citing Ps. 117.26 LXX). Rather than being a negative threat of judgment and rejection, the words of the psalm here are perhaps more appropriately interpreted as an acclamation of joyful praise, implying that the hearers have repented and are now welcoming (and presumably will be welcomed by) the returning Jesus. Thus the polemic in the whole passage is perhaps tempered by the ray of hope that is held out here for the listeners, *if* they will respond positively.[22]

Other pieces of evidence here may be rather indecisive in the present discussion. In the parable of the mustard seed, the birds coming and nesting in the branches of the great tree *may* represent Gentiles, but it in by no means certain; and in any case, the time reference is such that this, like 13.28-29, is a reference to an eschatological future, rather than to anything that is happening in the present (of Jesus or of Q). So too the imagery of the parable of the Great Supper is ambiguous. If one disregards the features in Matthew and Luke which are almost universally

---

21   For more details, see Tuckett, *Q and the History*, pp.196–207.

22   See Tuckett, *Q and the History*, p.205; D. C. Allison, *The Jesus Tradition in Q* (Harrisburg: Trinity Press International, 1997), pp.192–204. Contra, for example, Manson, *Sayings*, p.128; Schulz, *Q*, p.338; and D. Zeller, 'Jesus, Q und die Zukunft Israels', in Lindemann (ed.), *The Sayings Source Q*, pp.351–69 (356–8).

accepted as redactional, viz. the burning of 'the city of those murderers' in Mt. 22.7 and the double mission of the servants in Lk. 14.22-23, then there is no clear indication in the story that the first guests represent the Jews and that those summoned in from the streets are Gentiles. The two groups could just as easily represent Jewish leaders and (other) Jewish people, or 'pious' and 'sinners'. We could perhaps read a Jew/ Gentile distinction into the story if we knew of its presence in the wider context already, and in fact the wider context in Q may be one of warnings to Israel with accompanying threats that Gentiles may replace Jews in the Kingdom.[23] However, it is unclear if this is intended to imply anything positive about a current Gentile mission. The parable primarily functions as a warning to the listeners not to be like the first guests who refuse to respond. Thus, even if the second group of guests brought in to replace the original guests are thought of as Gentiles, the parable is primarily about those who are refusing to respond, rather than about their possible replacements. This interpretation would thus be in line with Meyer's theory that Q uses any possible Gentile mission as part of its plea to Israel to repent, but without necessarily engaging in such missionary activity directly (cf. n.7, above).

If then much of the possible evidence in favour of a Gentile mission being presupposed, and welcomed, by Q is ambiguous, can one go to the other extreme and say that Q opposed such a mission? Some have referred in this context to Q's attitude to the Jewish Law: in a number of Q passages, it appears that Q adopts a relatively 'conservative' attitude to the Jewish Law, and this would exclude the possibility of a positive attitude to any Gentile mission.[24]

It is certainly the case that Q does appear to adopt a relatively 'conservative' attitude to the Jewish Law. Sayings such as Q 11.42d ('these you ought to have practised, *without neglecting the others*'),[25] or Q 16.17,

---

23   Assuming, with most, that Luke's order may generally be closer to the original Q order than Matthew's: hence the parable in Luke 14.16-24 may in Q have followed closely after the warning of Q 13.28-29 and Q 13.34-35.

24   Schulz, *Q*, pp.401–2; and Wegner, *Hauptmann*, p.332.

25   That is, the final phrase in the saying about tithing: in the rest of the saying, Jesus appears to be questioning, potentially quite radically, the principle of tithing itself. But the final phrase ('these you ought to have practised, *without neglecting the others*'), which looks very much like a redactional addition to the saying, seems to backtrack and reassert the validity and obligation of the practice of tithing. See Hoffmann, *Studien*, p.170; and Tuckett, *Q and the History*, pp.409–10, with further references. The claim of Fleddermann, *Q*, p.556, that Q here implies that 'the weightier demands (of the Law) override the lesser demands', and that 'Q's hermeneutic distinguishes between the ritual demands and the moral demands' do not

asserting the abiding validity of even the last jot or tittle of the Law, do seem to imply that Q's Jesus (and hence presumably the Christians who preserved and assembled the Q material) does not question the validity of the Law. Other aspects of the issue are perhaps not so clear cut. For example, J. Kloppenborg has argued that Sabbath controversies are totally lacking in Q.[26] I have discussed this elsewhere, and suggested that perhaps the issue is less clear: Lk. 14.5 (//Mt. 12.11) may be a vestige of Q tradition involving a controversy about Sabbath.[27] Nevertheless, it is still the case even here that an attempt is made to produce a reasoned argument for permitting work on the Sabbath from within the presuppositions of (general) Law observance.[28] The argument is far removed from the polemical, and somewhat blunt, rhetorical questions found in, to take one example, Mk 3.4. Finally, a main feature of the detailed temptation narrative in Q (Q 4.1-13) is probably to show Jesus as primarily obedient to the Law in all that he does, and as such perhaps an example to his followers.[29] Thus it may well be the case that Q implies a rather more 'conservative' attitude to the Jewish Law than some other parts of the gospel tradition and/or the early church.[30]

Nevertheless, in relation to the issue of attitudes to Gentiles, and/or attitudes to a possible Gentile mission by early Christians, this may be

seem to be justified by the text: the final clause in Q 11.42 *affirms* the validity of *all* the demands of the Law equally, and clearly excludes the possibility of some demands being allowed to 'override' others.

26   J. S. Kloppenborg, 'The Sayings Gospel Q and the Quest of the Historical Jesus', *HTR* 89 (1996), pp.307-44 (332-4). From this Kloppenborg deduces that the Sabbath controversies of the Gospels cannot be traced back to Jesus himself, but that is another issue!

27   Tuckett, *Q and the History*, p.414, with further references. I have sought to discuss Kloppenborg's argument in more detail in C. M. Tuckett, 'Q and the Historical Jesus', in J. Schröter and R. Brucker (eds.), *Der historische Jesus. Tendenzen und Perspektiven der gegenwärtigen Forschung* (BZNW 114; Berlin: de Gruyter, 2002), pp.213-41 (including discussion of the issue of seeking to extrapolate back from Q to Jesus, especially in relation to silences).

28   Hence, *pace* Fleddermann, *Q*, p.166, this is a case of Jesus staying within the orbit of the Law and operating within its presuppositions.

29   For more detail, see C. M. Tuckett, 'The Temptation Narrative in Q', in F. Van Segbroek et al. (eds.), *The Four Gospels 1992: Festschrift Frans Neirynck* (Leuven: Peeters, 1992), pp.479-507.

30   *Pace* Fleddermann, *Q*, p.166. Q's Jesus does not then appear as a typical Gentile Christian, reformulating the Law and dispensing others from it (see above). As Fleddermann himself points out, in Q 16.17-18, Jesus affirms the validity of the whole Law in v. 17, while possibly radicalising and intensifying the demand expected of his followers even higher in v. 18 (Fleddermann, *Q*, p.791).

something of a red herring. One cannot simply equate a positive attitude to Gentiles with a critical attitude to the Law *and* vice versa, as if positive views about the validity of the Torah necessarily exclude any interest in, or positive attitude to, Gentiles. It is clear from the Pauline corpus of letters that important issues (of principle and praxis) were raised when the Christian mission spread out to Gentiles, with problems then raised about the requirements of the Law which Gentile converts to Christianity were expected to observe. Yet it is equally clear that in those debates, the issue is not simply one of a pro-Gentile, anti-Law 'Pauline' party versus an anti-Gentile, pro-Law 'Jewish Christian' party. For Paul and the Pauline mission, the key question was whether Gentile converts were expected to obey one specific command in the Law, the command about circumcision. But nothing in Paul suggests that Gentile Christians are free from all obligations in relation to the whole of the Jewish Law. Gentiles are still expected to obey some parts of the Law (e.g. the love command and parts of the Decalogue; cf. Rom. 13.8-10), even if it is notoriously difficult to identify precisely how and where Paul distinguished between the different parts of the Law. Further, there is no evidence to suggest that, in the 'judaising' debates in which Paul was involved, anyone ever objected to the principle of a Gentile mission *per se*. The point of dispute was the precise circumstances and/or conditions under which Gentiles could or should become Christians. Thus a reference to a somewhat 'conservative' attitude to the Law in Q by no means excludes a positive attitude to Gentiles and/or a Gentile mission: it might simply determine the conditions it was assumed should be adopted by Gentiles if they were to join the Christian community, presupposing a higher level of adherence to the requirements of the Law than some other Christian groups.

There is, however, one further part of the evidence from Q which has not often been explicitly brought into the discussion of Q and Gentiles, or Q and the Gentile mission, which may be relevant here. This is the presence in Q of slighting references to Gentiles in Mt. 5.47 and Q 12.30.[31] In both these texts, 'Gentiles' appear as the 'natural' group to

---

31   The reference to Gentiles in Q 12.30 occurs in both Matthew and Luke at this point and hence is as secure as anything for being the wording of Q. In Mt. 5.47, Luke's parallel (cf. Lk. 6.32-34) has 'sinners'. It is, however, widely agreed that Luke's version here is secondary, reflecting Luke's concern to tone down negative references to Gentiles; see Tuckett, *Q and the History*, p. 202, with further references. The Matthean reference to 'Gentiles' here is seen as reflecting the Q wording also by J. M. Robinson, P. Hoffmann and J. S. Kloppenborg (eds.), *The Critical Edition of Q* (Minneapolis: Fortress, 2000), p.70; and Fleddermann, *Q*, p.292.

mention when the writer wants to refer to people who are 'obviously' outside any in-group, and clearly distinguished from 'us'. In Mt. 5.47 it is a question of people who 'clearly' behave in a way that is regarded as second-rate in only reciprocating good to those from whom they expect to receive back similar favours in return. And in Q 12.30, it is a question of people getting their priorities wrong. In both cases, the tone is not overtly polemical: the teaching is addressed to those who are 'inside' the 'community' and does not constitute any violent invective against Gentiles themselves. Yet the very fact that the sayings are so *un*polemical seems to reveal a mentality in which 'Gentiles' are not included in 'our' community. They are not 'one of us'. There is a clear 'us/them' mentality and 'they' are apparently described as 'Gentiles', apparently without thinking or questioning.[32]

This makes it hard to conceive of Gentiles forming anything more than a tiny minority in the group of Christians responsible for Q. And it is correspondingly hard to believe that Q Christians were actively engaged in any positive mission to Gentiles. Nor is it easy to envisage a significant change in attitude to Gentiles in Q, as if Mt. 5.47 and Q 12.30 represented an early view which was subsequently changed as Q Christians became more open to Gentiles.[33] Otherwise, it is hard to see why these sayings were not edited or omitted by a later Q editor or redactor.[34]

The story in Q 7.1-10 within Q suggests that Q is aware of Gentiles who have responded positively to Jesus, and perhaps to the Christian preaching after Easter. But no more than an awareness is shown, and

---

32   For the generally negative tone of the reference here, see also M. Labahn, *Der Gekommene als Wieder kommender. Die Logienquelle als erzählte Geschichte* (Leipzig: Evangelische Verlagsanstalt, 2010), pp.435–7. Fleddermann, commenting on Mt. 5.47, seeks to explain such language in a supposedly 'gentile Christian gospel' (see above) by arguing that 'the author of Q strove for historical verisimilitude. For the Jesus of Q to be credible he must speak like a Palestinian Jew' (Fleddermann, *Q*, p.330). This, however, seems very forced and unconvincing.

33   Both verses are assigned by Kloppenborg to his early (Q[1]) stage in his stratigraphical model. However, see above for doubts about the validity of such a macro-theory for the interpretation of Q.

34   Such changes are probably there in Luke's version of the tradition. Thus Luke changes the 'Gentiles' of Mt. 5.47 to a more general 'sinners'; and in Q 12.30 he has 'worldly Gentiles', which may leave open the possibility of Christian Gentiles as well. See Tuckett, *Q and the History*, p.403. The presence of the sayings in Matthew remains difficult on any showing, though this is part of a wider problem of the co-existence within Matthew of strongly anti-Gentile (or anti-Gentile mission) sayings such as 10.5-6 and the thoroughly positive reference to Gentiles and a Gentile mission in 28.19-20.

Jesus' response of apparent wonder, possibly even surprise, at the centurion's 'faith' may imply that such a situation of Gentile response was more of an exception than any norm. The most likely situation thus seems to be one whereby Q may be aware of a Gentile mission by (some) Christians, but the Q Christians are not actively engaged in such a mission themselves.[35] Perhaps too this is simply a reflection in part of the geographical location of any possible Q 'community' (or at least of the group of Christians responsible for the collection and preservation of the Q material): they were simply not in a location where Gentiles were present in any significant numbers, and their horizon was primarily that of Jews and Judaism.[36] Any references to Gentiles' responding positively to Jesus, or Gentile participation in the blessings of the kingdom, are not so much a reflection of the missionary activity of Q Christians but are used as part of the appeal which Q Christians are making primarily to an audience that is primarily Jewish.

How Q Christians might have conceived of Gentiles actually participating in the Christian community and what conditions they might have had to observe (both to get 'in' and to stay in) is probably impossible to say. We know from the evidence of Paul that a key question was the issue of whether Gentiles should be circumcised or not. We have though already seen that, even among Pauline communities, Christians (including presumably Gentile Christians) were expected to observe and obey other parts of the Jewish Law as part of a *Christian* ethos. Notoriously, the whole Synoptic tradition is silent on the question of circumcision. And hence the Q tradition, as part of the wider Synoptic tradition, is silent too. In studies of Matthew, it is a standard conundrum to know whether Matthew might have expected any Gentile converts to Christianity to be circumcised,[37] but just as the silence of Matthew on the issue leaves the question unresolved, so too the silence of Q has the same effect.[38] Thus we simply do not know how Q might have regarded any 'Christian Gentiles', that is, whether it accepted that Gentiles could

---

35   Hence a view similar to Meyer and others noted in n.7.

36   See Kloppenborg, at least in his later writings, as noted in n.7 above.

37   I have discussed this in C. M. Tuckett, 'Matthew: The Social and Historical Context – Jewish Christian and/or Gentile?', in D. Senior (ed.), *The Gospel of Matthew at the Crossroads of Early Christianity* (BETL 243; Leuven: Peeters, 2011), pp.99–129 (126–7).

38   For Matthew it can be argued that the explicit command to take the mission to Gentiles, with a 'condition', or accompanying action, of baptism in the three-fold name explicitly mentioned (Mt. 28.19) implies that Christian baptism has replaced circumcision as the entry rite for possible new members of the community. But there is nothing comparable to Mt. 28.19 in Q.

remain Gentiles if they became Christians, and/or whether they were expected to adopt some specific requirements of Jewishness. If some requirements were expected, can we identify which ones they were? Did they involve circumcision, Sabbath observance, or other parts of the Torah? Perhaps Q allows us to see a relatively early stage in the development of Christian history, when many of these issues had not yet arisen. Q may reflect a Christian group still primarily set within a Jewish context, aware perhaps of possible positive responses by Gentiles to the Christian message but not in any significant numbers (and perhaps too not in its own immediate geographical context). Q Christians may still be addressing primarily non-Christian Jews and seeking to make them sympathetic to their cause.[39] As such they use a range of rhetorical strategies, including at times strong polemic with a somewhat threatening tone, warning of the future consequences of what might happen if others do not respond positively; and in that context, reference is sometimes made to Gentiles as potentially replacing Jews as the recipients of eschatological blessings. But perhaps the broader questions of how Gentiles would come into, and live within, the new Christian community, may not have come on to the mental radar screen of Q Christians with any seriousness.

---

39 'Convert' might be too strong a word to use in this context.

Chapter 9

PAUL'S ATTITUDES TO THE GENTILES

Sean F. Winter

1. *Introduction*

Paul is commonly referred to as the 'apostle to the Gentiles'. The title derives from those occasions in Paul's letters where he explicitly connects his experience of the risen Christ and apostolic vocation to the task of proclaiming the gospel of God's son to or among τὰ ἔθνη – the 'nations' or 'Gentiles'.[1] Scholarly discussion of Paul's 'attitude' to the Gentiles rightly focuses on the questions of how and why Paul came to understand his vocation in these terms and how Paul's self-under-standing as apostle to the Gentiles relates to his theological statements about Gentiles found in his letters, especially those to the churches in Galatia and Rome.[2]

The focus on Paul's apostleship and related theological questions does not tell the whole story, however. In the same letter in which Paul castigates the Jews who 'hindered us from speaking to the Gentiles that they may be saved' (1 Thess. 2.15-16), Paul can speak of 'the Gentiles

---

1   See Gal. 1.15-16; and Rom. 1.5; 15.16; cf. 1 Thess. 2.16; 1 Cor. 1.23; and Rom. 1.13; 15.18. Paul can speak of his apostleship without reference to the Gentile mission (see 1 Cor. 15.9-10), but in Gal. 1.16, Rom. 1.5 and Rom. 15.16 the connection between these is strongly established by the use of purpose clauses. Galatians 2.7-8 sets Paul's conviction about his divine appointment into the context of his narrative of seeking recognition from the Jerusalem leaders (cf. Gal. 1.1, 11-12, 17) and is the closest we get to Pauline usage of the phrase 'apostle to the Gentiles' (ὁ γὰρ ἐνεργήσας...εἰς ἀποστολὴν...εἰς τὰ ἔθνη).

2   In the present study the focus will be on those letters commonly agreed to have been written by Paul. There are interesting and important things that can be said about references to Gentiles in Ephesians (Eph. 2.11; 3.1, 6, 8; 4.17) that will not be considered here. See D. K. Darko, *No Longer Living as the Gentiles: Differentiation and Shared Ethical Values in Ephesians 4.17–6.9* (LNTS 375; London: T&T Clark International, 2008).

who do not know God' (1 Thess. 4.5).[3] Likewise in Galatians, after an account of a visit to Jerusalem in order to present his Gentile-focused gospel to the Jerusalem elders (Gal. 2.1-10), Paul speaks of his confrontation with Peter at Antioch in which he identifies with his fellow apostle as an 'Ιουδαῖος 'by nature' and, consequently, not a 'sinner from the Gentiles' (οὐκ ἐξ ἐθνῶν ἁμαρτωλός). In short, while Paul's attitude towards the Gentiles is in part conditioned by a set of convictions about what God has done for the world in Jesus Christ and Paul's role in that story, it is also shaped by Paul's ongoing Jewish identity and convictions. It is the task of this essay to trace some of the various modulations of Paul's epistolary voice on this topic, and to suggest some reasons for the changes in tone that we discover.[4]

2. *Terminology and Approach*[5]

Paul uses the term ἔθνος forty-five times in the undisputed letters.[6] All but two of these occurrences are in the plural form.[7] As such, Paul's usage simply reflects that of the Greek Bible and Hellenistic Jewish

3   The interpretative questions associated with 1 Thess. 2.14-16 cannot be discussed here. For a substantive analysis, see C. J. Schlueter, *Filling Up The Measure: Polemical Hyperbole in 1 Thessalonians 2.14-16* (JSNTSup 98; Sheffield: JSOT, 1994).

4   This means that the focus of the present study will be on the relevant data from Paul's authentic letters. Material related to the likely conceptual and historical background to Pauline thought can be found in the other essays in this volume. See also the essays in R. Feldmeier and U. Heckel (eds.), *Die Heiden: Juden, Christen und das Problem des Fremden* (WUNT 70; Tübingen: Mohr Siebeck, 1994), and discussion of primary texts in Donaldson, *Judaism and the Gentiles*.

5   For a detailed analysis of the linguistic data, see R. Dabelstein, *Die Beurteilung der 'Heiden' bei Paulus* (BBET 14; Frankfurt: Peter Lang, 1981); U. Heckel, 'Das Bild der Heiden und die Indentität der Christen bei Paulus', in Feldmeier and Heckel (eds.), *Die Heiden*, pp.269–96; J. M. Scott, *Paul and the Nations: The Old Testament and Jewish Background of Paul's Mission to the Nations with Special Reference to the Destination of Galatians* (WUNT 84; Tübingen: Mohr Siebeck, 1995), pp.57–134; and L. L. Sechrest, *A Former Jew: Paul and the Dialectics of Race* (LNTS 410; London: T&T Clark International, 2009), pp.54–109.

6   Rom. 1.5, 13; 2.14, 24; 3.29 (×2); 4.17-18 (×2); 9.24, 30; 10.19 (×2); 11.11-13 (×4), 25; 15.9-12 (×6), 16 (×2), 18, 27; 16.4, 26; 1 Cor. 1.23; 5.1; 12.2; 2 Cor. 11.26; Gal. 1.16; 2.2, 8-9 (×2), 12, 14-15 (×2); 3.8 (×2), 14; 1 Thess. 2.16; 4.5.

7   The exception is Paul's citation of Deut. 32.21 (LXX) in Rom. 10.19 where the singular form is found twice. A significant proportion of the plural references are found in Old Testament citations. See Scott, *Paul and the Nations*, p.121 and n.433.

literature of the period. In the vast majority of cases it is used to denote non-Israelites, either collectively or, more rarely, individually.[8] Even in those cases where Israel seems to be included within the 'nations', Paul's focus is on the salvation of non-Israelites.[9] Paul's use of related terms, Ἕλλην and ἀκροβυστία, reinforce this overall picture.[10] For Paul, the term 'Gentiles' presupposes the existence of Israel and its status as the nation with which God has established a covenant (Deut. 7.7-11). Paul's construal of ethnic identity is therefore framed in thoroughly Jewish terms.

However, any attempt to do justice to Paul's attitude towards the Gentiles must take in information beyond the linguistic data. We must survey not only Paul's explicitly stated convictions about the place of Gentiles within salvation history (the framework for most of the references discussed thus far, and the focus of the vast majority of scholarship), but also those places where Paul's argument presupposes or refers to the beliefs, practices and worldviews of non-Israelites in his own day. Scholarly discussion of these aspects tends to shift terminology at this point, preferring the language of 'paganism' (not a term Paul uses) when referring to cultic or ethical practices, 'Hellenism' when referring to cultural influence or, more narrowly, 'Roman/imperial' when considering social and political dimensions of Paul's thought.[11] It is the contention of the present study that these aspects overlap to a considerable degree, so that salvation history, Christology, ethics and politics can be

8   The two senses clearly overlap. As Scott notes, the latter sense comes to the fore when Paul addresses his audience as former Gentiles (Rom. 11.13; 1 Cor. 12.2). See Scott, *Paul and the Nations*, p.123. It can also be detected at 2 Cor. 11.26 (danger from some Gentiles) and Gal. 2.12 (Gentiles in the Antiochene church).

9   Scott, *Paul and the Nations*, p.133–80, sets out the case for viewing Paul's mission in terms of the Table of Nations tradition of Gen. 10–11 and Deut. 32. Although it is true that Paul sees the Abrahamic promise of Gen. 17.5 as directed to 'all of us' (Rom. 4.15-16), the exigence of Galatians suggests that Paul understands τὰ ἔθνη in Gal. 3.8 to refer to non-Israelites. See D.-A. Koch, *Die Schrift des Evangeliums: Untersuchungen zur Verwendung und zum Verständnis der Schrift bei Paulus* (BHT 69; Tübingen: Mohr Siebeck, 1986), p.123. In Rom. 11.25 Paul can use the term 'fullness of the nations' in distinction from 'part of Israel'.

10   For Ἕλλην, see Rom. 1.16; 2.9-10; 3.9; 10.12; 1 Cor. 1.22, 24; 10.32; 12.13; Gal. 2.3; 3.28. In every case it is used in explicit or implicit contrast to Ἰουδαῖος. It is paired with βάρβαρος in Rom. 1.14. For ἀκροβυστία as a term of ethnic distinction, see Rom. 2.25-27; 3.30; Gal. 2.7; 5.6; 6.15, with περιτομή as the contrasting term.

11   A notable exception is the recent study by L. T. Johnson, *Among the Gentiles: Greco-Roman Religion and Christianity* (AYBRL; New Haven: Yale University Press, 2009).

seen as a set of interrelated themes that help us to see the contours of Paul's attitude towards the Gentiles more clearly, albeit in less simplistic terms.

The questions to be explored fall into two categories. On the one hand there is a set of *descriptive* issues: On what basis does Paul envisage the necessity of Gentile inclusion into the covenant community, and what does their incorporation look like in practice? What is the nature of Paul's polemical statements about Gentile institutions, culture and practices? Is there discernible evidence of Gentile influence on Paul's theology and argumentation? On the other hand we are presented with a series of *explanatory* questions: How did Paul come to reach such views and why did he pursue his Gentile-focused vocation with such determination, even in the face of opposition? Together, these aspects help us to develop an overall understanding of the complex reality that lies behind the phrase 'apostle to the Gentiles'.

3. *Paul's Attitudes to Gentiles: A Descriptive Overview*

a. *Gentile Salvation*

Despite his categorisation of Gentiles as 'sinners' in Gal. 2.15, Paul goes on to explain, initially to Peter in Antioch and then to his Gentile audience in the Galatian churches, that 'a person is rectified not by works of the Law but through the faithfulness of Jesus Christ' (Gal. 2.16).[12] Implicit in the switch from 'Ιουδαῖοι (2.15) to ἄνθρωπος (2.16) is the idea that the familiar Jewish construction of ethnic identities no longer pertains straightforwardly in the light of the Christ event. Galatians 3.6-9 is a sustained exposition of this basic idea. Paul invites the Gentile Galatians (as well as, no doubt, the 'teachers' alluded to in Gal. 1.7; 4.17; 5.12; 6.12-13) to regard God's rectification of the Gentiles as something foreseen in Israel's Scripture (Gal. 3.8), enshrined in the Abrahamic promise (Gal. 3.8-9, 18) and secured by the faithful obedience of Christ Jesus in whom Gentiles can now share in the blessing of Abraham (Gal. 3.10-14, 26-29).

---

12   This translation betrays something of my own interpretative sympathies in the debates over the force and meaning of Paul's δικαιόω and πίστις language in this section. The debates cannot be rehearsed here, but for two distinctive treatments of Paul's formulation, see J. D. G. Dunn, *The Epistle to the Galatians* (BNTC; London: A. & C. Black, 1993), pp.13–141, and J. L. Martyn, *Galatians: A New Translation with Introduction and Commentary* (AB 33A; New York: Doubleday, 1997), pp.249–53.

Of course, a special emphasis throughout Galatians, and the argument of 2.15–5.1 in particular, is that all this is possible without the need for obedience to the Law, not least the command to circumcision. While there has been a strong tendency in earlier generations of scholarship, as well as more popular accounts of Paul's theology, to see this emphasis as the result of some inherent problem with the Law as the means to justification, the texts do not bear this out.[13] Paul's attitude to the Law is explicitly framed in eschatological/Christological terms. Because the law postdated the Abrahamic promise (Gal. 3.15-18), and predated the coming of the 'seed', who is Christ (Gal. 3.16, 19), its function can now be seen clearly as that of the παιδαγωγὸς ('instructor/disciplinarian') (Gal. 3.23–35) to whom those who are 'in Christ' are no longer subject. Gentiles are rectified apart from the Jewish Law not because the Law has failed, but because 'the fullness of time' has come (Gal. 4.4).

In contrast, Paul makes it clear that Gentiles are included within the covenant community, in fulfilment of the promise to Abraham, on the basis of the arrival of faith. As we have noted, Paul does not say that faith is necessary to deal with the inherent inadequacy of the Law in relation to the salvation of the Gentiles. Rather, faith has 'arrived' or has been 'revealed' (Gal. 3.23, 25).[14] For Paul and his Gentile audience, faith therefore becomes the key term for describing the objective work of God in Christ, which is in turn met by the subjective human response of 'believing' (Gal. 3.22). Gentiles become God's children in Jesus Christ and through faith (Gal. 3.26) and the result is that 'in Christ' the customary ethnic distinctions between 'Jew' and 'Greek' are relativised (Gal. 3.28).[15]

In writing to the churches in Rome, Paul provides an alternative rendition of the same themes, albeit now clearly directed towards addressing the conflictual situation in the Roman house churches – a different

13   This is the key insight of the New Perspective on Paul. See the essays in J. D. G. Dunn, *The New Persepctive on Paul* (Grand Rapids: Eerdmans, rev. edn, 2008) and the discussion of the shift from the old to the new paradigm in Donaldson, *Paul and the Gentiles*, pp.3–22.

14   The passive voice of the verb in the formula εἰς τὴν μέλλουσαν πίστιν ἀποκαλυφθῆναι in Gal. 3.23 suggests divine activity.

15   D. Boyarin has argued that Paul's formulation here is motivated by a 'Greek longing for universals' which erases all ethnic distinctions. See D. Boyarin, *A Radical Jew: Paul and the Politics of Identity* (Berkeley: University of California Press, 1994), p.228. For an effective rejoinder to this position, see J. M. G. Barclay, '"Neither Jew nor Greek": Multiculturalism and the New Perspective on Paul', in M. G. Brett (ed.), *Ethnicity and the Bible* (Leiden: Brill, 1996), pp.197–214.

situation to the Galatian crisis. Paul's aim in Romans is to 'reap some harvest…as I have among the rest of the Gentiles' (Rom. 1.13; cf. 15.14-29), a theme connected to the Gentile focus of Paul's apostolic ministry overall (Rom. 1.5; cf. 16.26).[16] Central to the letter's argument is the delineation of a specific account of the relation of Jew and Gentile in salvation history and, therefore, within the Roman house churches. The focus on Gentile inclusion on the basis of faith and apart from the Law is clearly set out in the opening chapters of the letter and reaches a climax in Rom. 3.21-31 in statements about the manifestation of the righteousness of God through the redemptive death of Christ, and the consequent ruling out of ethnic pride. Again Paul connects the theme of Gentile salvation to the Abrahamic promise (4.16-17).[17] Israel's God is therefore portrayed as taking no further account of the standard Jewish construal of ethnic differentiation. As the one who 'shows no partiality' (2.11), God can now be named as 'the God of the Gentiles also' (3.29).[18] However, in the use of the repeated phrase 'to the Jew first, and also to the Greek' (Rom. 1.16; 2.9-10) Paul anticipates the argument of Romans 9–11. Here it is made clear that although Gentiles are now to be counted among God's people (Rom. 9.24-26) and have attained 'righteousness through faith' (Rom. 9.30), God remains faithful to the covenant established with Israel. Even as Paul repeats his assertion from Galatians that 'there is no distinction between Jew and Greek' (Rom. 10.12; cf. Gal. 3.28) he proceeds to warn against Gentile arrogance by establishing a distinction between 'branches' (κλάδοι) and the 'wild olive shoot' (ἀγριέλαιος) which is 'grafted in' to the tree from which the branches have been

16   Thus Romans is written particularly with a Gentile audience in mind. See N. Elliott, *The Rhetoric of Romans: Argumentative Constraint and Strategy and Paul's Dialogue with Judaism* (JSNTSup 45; Sheffield: JSOT, 1990); S. K. Stowers, *A Rereading of Romans: Justice, Jews and Gentiles* (New Haven: Yale University Press, 1994); and A. A. Das, *Solving the Romans Debate* (Minneapolis: Fortress, 2007).

17   A number of the issues pertinent to the analysis of the relevant texts in Galatians also pertain to the study of Romans; specifically the issue of whose faith provides the grounds for Gentile justification. A particularly difficult aspect of Paul's argument in Romans is the reference to Gentiles who 'obey the law' in Rom. 2.14-15, on which see S. J. Gathercole, 'A Law Unto Themselves: The Gentiles in Romans 2.14-15 Revisited', *JSNT* 23 (2002), pp.27–49.

18   Paul's argument about divine impartiality, and thus about God's blessing of the Gentiles, is predicated on important Jewish monotheistic and covenantal premises about God's faithfulness to Israel (Rom. 3.1-4), identity as creator (Rom. 1.20-23) and 'unity' (Rom. 3.30).

broken off (Rom. 11.17-24). Gentile inclusion is, in Paul's argument in Romans, something real but preparatory in relation to the final 'full inclusion' of Israel (Rom. 11.11-12; cf. 11.1, 25-26).[19]

With a very clear focus on the nature, place, and origin of Paul's statements about Gentile 'salvation', T. L. Donaldson has provided a helpful taxonomy of the 'convictions' that lie behind Paul's statements in Galatians and Romans.[20] What his analysis makes clear is that there is no single explanatory factor that, when rightly understood, would lead inevitably to the position on Gentile inclusion that Paul holds. To explain Paul's attitude to the Gentiles by appealing to Paul's vocation to be an apostle to the Gentiles is 'simply to beg the question, to pass a tautology off as an answer'.[21] Similarly, Paul's beliefs about the 'oneness' of Israel's God (Rom. 3.30; 1 Cor. 8.4–6; Gal. 3.20), divine impartiality or God's righteousness (Rom. 1.17; 3.21) do not lead directly to the idea of Gentile salvation. The path to that idea must pass through a thicket of 'intervening assumptions concerning the equality of Jew and Gentile and the impossibility of righteousness through the law'.[22] Donaldson also argues that despite 'the undeniable centrality and significance of Paul's new convictions about Christ, convincing arguments prevent us from identifying any of them as the primary point where the salvation of the Gentiles enters into Paul's convictional structure'.[23]

It may be that the idea of Gentle salvation, while closely connected with Paul's discussion of salvation history, the place of the Law and the status of ethnic Israel, is related particularly to the apocalyptic structure of Paul's thought, with particular reference to the decisive importance of the Christ-event, understood as an apocalyptic event that has the whole

19   Donaldson helpfully notes that the issue in Rom. 9–11 is less to do with spatial logic, whereby believing Gentiles take up the covenantal space vacated by unbelieving Israel, and more about the temporal logic that views the Christ-event as inaugurating a time during which salvation is extended to the Gentiles. The result is a view of Paul's theology that is rightly critical of 'displacement' or 'replacement' readings and that highlights the ongoing significance of ethnic Israel for Paul. See Donaldson, *Paul and the Gentiles*, pp.215–48.

20   Donaldson, *Paul and the Gentiles*, pp.81–260. Donaldson's work is explicitly focused on the issue of Gentile 'salvation' (pp.47, 49) and is the best treatment of the data currently available. He is aware of the difference and relationship between Paul's convictions and the 'epistolary rhetoric' which are suggestive of different kinds of theological rationale (p.29).

21   Donaldson, *Paul and the Gentiles*, p.259.

22   Donaldson, *Paul and the Gentiles*, p.104, and the ensuing discussion at pp.107–86.

23   Donaldson, *Paul and the Gentiles*, p.212.

created order as its focus. Paul's Christology, in which Christ is raised from death not just as Israel's messiah but also as 'Lord' connects directly to the idea that Gentiles are called to 'the obedience of faith' (Rom. 1.4). Paul's account of Christ's defeat of the dominion of sin and death is cast in Adamic terms: Christ's 'act of righteousness leads to justification and life for all' (Rom. 5.18; cf. 1 Cor. 15.24-28). Paul's vision of the vindication of God's servant speaks of 'every knee' bowing and 'every tongue' confessing the Lordship of Christ (Phil. 2.9-11). When Paul writes to Gentile believers, then, he explicitly locates them within this cosmic drama. In Gal. 1.4 he addresses his Gentile audience as those who have been 'set free from the present evil age'. The idea that 'neither circumcision nor uncircumcision is anything' is, for Paul, the consequence of viewing the cross of Christ as that which constitutes a 'new creation' (Gal. 6.14-15). The Thessalonians are portrayed as those who, having 'turned to God from idols', are constituted by an identity shaped by apocalyptic convictions: 'to wait for his Son from heaven, whom he raised from the dead – Jesus, who rescues us from the wrath that is coming' (1 Thess. 1.10). Perhaps we get closest to the theological framework in which the motif of Gentile salvation takes its place in 2 Cor. 5.19: 'In Christ God was reconciling the world to himself'. The universal focus of Paul's understanding of the Christ-event provides the impetus for Paul's insistence that Gentiles are saved. Thus, although the issue of the justification of the Gentiles is the focus in only two of Paul's letters, the wider theological context that makes justification possible is present throughout the Pauline corpus.

However, Paul's outlook should not be understood as something that locates him beyond or outside of Judaism. It is clear that Paul, as a Jew, came to understand the universal scope of salvation as the fulfilment of God's covenant promises to Israel. Paul's recognition of Gentiles does not rely on a generic analysis of 'the human condition'. Even as Paul modifies traditional Jewish ethnic categories, he re-inscribes ethnicity into the 'new' identity that he is articulating.[24] Nor is the Pauline evidence best explained by the 'two-covenant' schema, in which Paul offers to Jews and Gentiles distinct but equally legitimate paths to salvation.[25]

---

24 This is the key insight of C. J. Hodge, *If Sons, Then Heirs: A Study of Kinship and Ethnicity Language in the Letters of Paul* (New York: Oxford University Press, 2007).

25 For a survey and critique of this view, see T. L. Donaldson, 'Jewish Christianity, Israel's Stumbling and the *Sonderweg* Reading of Paul', *JSNT* 29 (2006), pp.27–54.

It is clear that the ideas that allow Paul to extend salvation beyond the boundaries of ethnic Israel to the nations are deeply rooted in the traditions and Scriptures of 'Israel according to the flesh'.[26]

b. *Gentile Presence in Pauline Communities*

We have no exact information relating to the precise ethnic makeup of the Pauline churches. Paul's letters give a strong impression of a significant, and probably majority, Gentile audience in almost every case. Those included in the epistolary greetings almost always have Greek names (Rom. 16.31-36; 1 Cor. 16.15-20; Phil. 4.23-24) and in one case Paul can send greetings from 'the household of Caesar' (Phil. 4.22). Gentile identity is suggested not only by texts that speak clearly of the pre-Christian existence of his audience (Gal. 4.8-9; 1 Thess. 1.10; cf. the explicit statement in Eph. 2.11-12), but also by the study of those issues that seem to have arisen in the Pauline assemblies and to which the epistles respond. It may well be that that the presence of Gentiles in the Pauline communities resulted in local manifestations of belief and practice marked by characteristic features of Greco-Roman religion and society.[27] In 1 Corinthians it seems clear that Paul addresses a number of questions that have to do with the way the audience are to relate their Christian belief and practice with those familiar to them from their Gentile/Greco-Roman environment and their own Gentile identity.[28] For example, the material relating to the appropriateness of eating meat offered to idols (εἰδωλόθυτος, 1 Cor. 8; 10.14-30) deals with the common Gentile practice of purchasing meat that was made available for sale after it had been used in cultic settings and presupposes on-going social relationships between the Corinthian believers and Gentile unbelievers (1 Cor. 10.27).[29] A part of the epistolary situation of Philippians probably relates to the struggles that the Philippian believers had in re-negotiating their relationship with existing social, cultural and political realities in

26   For a recent account of the nature of Paul's universalism, see A. Sherwood, *Paul and the Restoration of Humanity in Light of Ancient Jewish Traditions* (AJEC 82; Leiden: Brill, 2013).

27   Johnson, *Among the Gentiles*, p.142.

28   See, for example, B. W. Winter, *After Paul Left Corinth: The Influence of Secular Ethics and Social Change* (Grand Rapids: Eerdmans, 2001).

29   Johnson argues that the Corinthians may have viewed participation in Gentile cultic meals as a form of participation in additional divine benefits (Johnson, *Among the Gentiles*, p.144). Cf. P. Borgen, '"Yes", "No", "How Far?": The Participation of Jews and Christians in Pagan Cults', in T. Engberg-Pedersen (ed.), *Paul in his Hellenistic Context* (SNTW; Edinburgh: T. & T. Clark, 1994), pp.30–59.

the colony.[30] Paul's language implies the likelihood that this involved significant levels of suffering for the Philippians (Phil. 1.27-30), an experience that also seems to be relate to the Thessalonian believers who suffered at the hand of their 'compatriots' (συμφυλέτης, 1 Thess. 2.14; cf. 1.6; 3.2-3). Although the setting of Galatians is primarily connected to the arrival of Jewish-Christian 'teachers' and their attempt to persuade the Gentile Galatians to judaise, it is possible that their message was well received, in part, as the result of local, non-Jewish practices and beliefs.[31] Even in Rome, where there seems to have been a significant Jewish component to the overall make up of the churches, Paul seems concerned to address the Gentiles in particular (Rom. 1.5, 13; 11.13; 15.15-19) and may be particularly concerned to tackle the problem of Gentile 'boasting'.[32] The situation that lies behind Paul's statements in Rom. 14.1–15.6 is best understood as the product of divergent attitudes towards traditional Jewish concerns relating to food laws and Sabbath observance, a difference of opinion exacerbated by the likelihood that, after the expulsion of Christian Jews from Rome in 49 CE, the Roman house churches were dominated by Gentile groups.[33]

It is, of course, a moot point as to whether the theology of Gentile salvation outlined above made Gentile majority Christian assemblies possible, or whether the theology developed in part to legitimate social practices and mission initiatives that were already in place. Scholarly opinion is divided, but the overall picture is clear: Paul's churches were communities in which Gentiles could and did discover and learn to live out a new kind of social existence that, to one degree or another, required forms of integration of their Christian and Gentile identities.

c. *Paul against the Gentiles*

For Gentile and Jewish believers, this new social identity raised challenges about aspects of their previous existence. In looking at Paul's response to some non-Jewish beliefs and practices we see clearly that his strong affirmation of Gentiles in the church does nothing to blunt the

---

30   See P. Oakes, *Philippians: From People to Letter* (SNTSMS 110; Cambridge: Cambridge University Press, 2001).

31   See S. Elliott, *Cutting Too Close for Comfort: Paul's Letter to the Galatians in its Anatolian Cultic Context* (JSNTSup 248; London: T&T Clark International, 2003).

32   See the references in n.16.

33   For a plausible account of the ethnic issues at stake in Rom. 14–15, the likely historical background and Paul's rhetorical response, see P. F. Esler, *Conflict and Identity in Romans: The Social Setting of Paul's Letter* (Minneapolis: Fortress, 2003).

sharpness of his polemic against what he perceives as 'ungodliness and wickedness' (ἀσέβεια καὶ ἀδικία, Rom. 1.18). At these points Paul the apostle to the Gentiles is not easily distinguishable from Paul the traditional Jew. Paul's critical attitude towards the Gentiles falls into at least three categories. First, there are texts that demonstrate a clear rejection of Gentile cultic practices, specifically their idolatrous nature. Gentile divinities are, for Paul, 'by nature not gods' (Gal. 4.8). For this reason the Corinthians are encouraged to 'flee from the worship of idols' who are subsequently characterised as 'demons and not God' (1 Cor. 10.14-20; cf. the same contrast in 1 Thess. 1.9-10).

Secondly, Paul's ethical teaching shows a marked hostility to certain beliefs and practices that would have been familiar to his Gentile audience.[34] While not every item in the Pauline vice lists (Rom. 1.29-31; 13.13; 1 Cor. 5.10-11; 6.9-10; 2 Cor. 12.20; Gal. 5.19-21; cf. Col. 3.5-8) is directly attributable to specifically Jewish ethical prohibitions, the form itself may well have come to Paul via the Hellenistic Jewish tradition and, in the focus on issues of sexual practice, reflect Jewish rather than non-Jewish Hellenistic values. When, in 1 Cor. 5.1, Paul states that 'there is sexual immorality among you, and of a kind not even found among the Gentiles', the point presupposes the fundamental Jewish critique of Gentile πορνεία. The point is reiterated in 1 Thessalonians, where Gentile idolatry and 'lustful passion' are connected. Above all, in Rom. 1.18-32 we find the critique of idolatry and of varieties of sexual practice combined in an extended indictment of Gentiles. The move from the failure to acknowledge the creator God (Rom. 1.18-23), to the consequent 'handing over' to sexual immorality (Rom. 1.24-27) and 'every kind of wickedness' (Rom. 1.28-32) finds its closest parallel in texts from the Wisdom of Solomon 13–14.

Finally, a growing body of scholarly opinion positions Paul in a place of direct opposition and resistance to the ideological claims and associated cultic practices of the Roman imperial system. It is difficult to have much certainty about the extent to which the apostle intentionally and explicitly sets his arguments in dialogue with the imperial context. There is little on the surface of the letters to suggest that he tackles such themes head on. However, Paul's choice of language (e.g. Lord, κυρίος; gospel, εὐαγγέλιον), articulation of key theological themes (e.g. eschatology, see 1 Thess. 5.3; Christology, see Phil. 2.9-11; soteriology, see

---

34   See the recent discussion by S. Ruden, *Paul among the People: The Apostle Reinterpreted and Reimagined in his Own Time* (New York: Pantheon, 2010). Cf. J. W. Thompson, *Moral Formation according to Paul: The Context and Coherence of Christian Ethics* (Grand Rapids: Baker Academic, 2011), pp.88–99.

Phil. 3.20-21), and social organisation (e.g. missionary strategy, redistribution of financial resources) can easily be seen to provide his churches with counter-imperial values and strategies.[35]

d. *Gentile Influence on Paul*

The final piece of our description relates to the ways in which Paul's own Jewish identity relates to the wider Hellenistic culture of his day.[36] Even as Paul is engaged in detailed interpretative work in relation to Israel's Scriptures, or developing his theology of Gentile inclusion, or castigating Gentile immoral practices, he is making use of rhetorical and epistolary conventions that he likely derived from a Hellenistic education; and all of it, of course, is written in Greek.[37] J. P. Sampley, in the introduction to a volume of essays exploring twenty-one separate points of contact between Paul's letters and the wider Greco-Roman culture makes the point well: 'how can it be surprizing that Paul, in his missionary efforts to "win some" of those "outside of the law"…had no choice but to employ categories, conceptions, perceptions, and inclinations that were familiar to non-Jewish audiences?'[38] Accompanying the scholarly rediscovery of Paul's fundamental Jewishness in post-World War II scholarship, an equivalent body of scholarship has emphasised his indebtedness to the conventions and categories of Hellenistic and Roman thought.[39] The key, as noted above, is to recognise that the two sources for Paul's ideas are not mutually exclusive.

---

35   The literature is extensive. See, for example, R. A. Horsley (ed.), *Paul and Empire: Religion and Power in Roman Imperial Society* (Harrisburg: Trinity Press International, 1997); idem (ed.), *Paul and Politics: Ekklesia, Israel, Imperium, Interpretation* (Harrisburg: Trinity Press International, 2000); J. D. Crossan and J. L. Reed, *In Search of Paul: How Jesus's Apostle Opposed Rome's Empire with God's Kingdom: A New Vision of Paul's Words and World* (New York: Harper-Collins, 2004); R. A. Horsley (ed.), *Paul and the Roman Imperial Order* (Harrisburg: Trinity Press International, 2004); D. C. Lopez, *Apostle to the Conquered: Reimagining Paul's Mission* (Minneapolis: Fortress, 2008); and B. W. Longenecker, *Remember the Poor: Paul, Poverty and the Greco-Roman World* (Grand Rapids: Eerdmans, 2010).

36   Hence the title of the important collection: T. Engberg-Pedersen (ed.), *Paul Beyond the Judaism/Hellenism Divide* (Louisville: Westminster John Knox, 2001).

37   See R. F. Hock, 'Paul and Greco-Roman Education', in J. P. Sampley (ed.), *Paul in the Greco-Roman World: A Handbook* (Harrisburg: Trinity Press International, 2003), pp.198–227.

38   J. P. Sampley, 'Introduction', in Sampley (ed.), *Paul in the Greco-Roman World*, pp.1–15 (1).

39   See, among others, A. J. Malherbe, *Paul and the Popular Philosophers* (Minneapolis: Fortress, 1989); T. Engberg-Pedersen, *Paul and the Stoics* (Edinburgh:

As an example we might consider the suggestion that Paul's letter to the church at Philippi makes substantive use of tropes and terminology relating to Greco-Roman traditions about friendship (φιλία). While the specific term does not appear in the letter (or any other for that matter), key words in Philippians are best understood as friendship *topoi*, for example: the call to be of 'one soul' (μιᾷ ψυχῇ, Phil. 1.27); the significance attributed to partnership (κοινωνία, Phil. 1.5, 7; 4.14-15); and the use of the phrase 'to think the same' (τὸ αὐτὸ φρονεῖν, Phil. 2.2; 4.2).[40]

While such aspects of Paul's thought do not obviously come into the category of his 'attitude to Gentiles', the point is that Paul does not see connections with Gentile culture, ideas, philosophy and education as inimical to his apostolic vocation. Rather, they are the means by which Paul pursues his calling in relation to the Gentile churches. In this, Paul reveals himself to be a Hellenistic Jew.[41]

4. Paul's Attitudes to Gentiles: An Explanatory Framework

Our descriptive account of Paul's attitudes to Gentiles has deliberately cast the net widely. This enables us to see that the issue cannot simply be reduced to the question of what Paul says about Gentile salvation, but relates to discussions of the ethnic makeup of the Pauline assemblies, Paul's own Jewish tradition and worldview, and his immersion in the wider Hellenistic culture of his day. Nevertheless, it is clear that Paul's particular take on the role of Gentiles in salvation history requires explanation. Once again, we are in the fortunate position of having a clear account of the major proposals as a result of the careful work of Donaldson, who outlines the main alternatives.[42] The question in what

---

T. & T. Clark, 2000); and idem, *Cosmology and Self in the Apostle Paul: The Material Spirit* (Oxford: Oxford University Press, 2010).

40   See J. T. Fitzgerald, 'Paul and Friendship', in Sampley (ed.), *Paul in the Greco-Roman World*, pp.319–43, and the detailed engagement with Philippians from this perspective in G. D. Fee, *Paul's Letter to the Philippians* (NICNT; Grand Rapids: Eerdmans, 1995); and S. E. Fowl, *Philippians* (THNTC; Grand Rapids: Eerdmans, 2005).

41   For an alternative view, see Barclay, *Jews in the Mediterranean Diaspora*, pp.381–95.

42   Donaldson, *Paul and the Gentiles*, pp.23–7, 263–307. Details of the scholars associated with the different proposals are fully documented there and need not be repeated here. See also the summary in T. L. Donaldson, 'Israelite, Convert, Apostle to the Gentiles: The Origin of Paul's Gentile Mission', in R. N. Longenecker (ed.), *The Road from Damascus: The Impact of Paul's Conversion on his Life, Thought, and Ministry* (MNTS; Grand Rapids: Eerdmans, 1997), pp.62–84.

follows is whether the broader view attempted here sheds any light on the adequacy of one or more of the main proposals. We can adopt Donaldson's overall schema and look at explanations that emphasise aspects of Paul's pre-call/conversion Jewish convictions, the call/conversion experience itself, and Paul's post call/conversion missionary practice and theological development.

We can begin with the idea that Paul, as a Pharisaic Jew prior to his 'Damascus' experience, already had some 'sympathy' for Gentiles that ultimately enabled the subsequent development of theological arguments in support of their inclusion. There are obvious problems with this view, especially when it is combined with the notion that Paul was somehow 'dissatisfied' with Jewish exclusion of Gentiles. There is no evidence for any such dissatisfaction with Jewish exclusivism that is not clearly a retrospective assessment made necessary by Paul's convictions about the universal scope of the Christ-event. The argument also fails to explain why Paul did not just engage in a programme of vigorous proselytising to secure as many Gentile adherents as possible.[43] However, thinking of it in terms of pre-Damascus 'sympathy' for Gentiles, or 'dissatisfaction' with Judaism is perhaps too limited a view. As a Hellenistic Jew Paul would himself have been the product of certain aspects of Gentile culture and thought, and so the notion that the newly revealed gospel might obviously speak into that culture and gain adherents from within it would not have been an impossible gap for the apostle Paul to leap. When combined with the strong possibility that the pre-Damascus Paul held to a thoroughly Israel-focussed conviction about the possibility that Gentiles would be saved, it comes as no surprise to know that Paul quickly comes to see his gospel in terms that make engagement with the Gentile world inevitable.[44]

Focusing on Paul's call/conversion experience itself, we might reaffirm the notion that the 'revelation of God's Son in me' should be understood in apocalyptic terms as the personal revelation of the truth of the Christ event as that which brings about a new creation (Gal. 1.12, 16, cf. 2.19-20; 6.14-15).[45] In this way, Paul's indication that the purpose of this revelation was 'so that I might proclaim him among the Gentiles', is an outworking of the way that Paul interprets his experience in terms of

43   Donaldson, *Paul and the Gentiles*, pp.264–5.

44   Donaldson's preference is for this kind of explanation, with an emphasis on the eschatological pilgrimage traditions; see Donaldson, *Paul and the Gentiles*, pp.273–92. See also Sherwood, *Paul*.

45   This reading of Gal. 1 is espoused with vigour in the recent commentary by M. C. de Boer, *Galatians: A Commentary* (NTL; Louisville: Westminster John Knox, 2011), pp.75–96.

a fundamentally *cosmic* drama of redemption. It is striking that the language of revelation is used by Paul to speak of the objective content of that event (Gal. 1.12), his subjective appropriation of it in relation to his apostolic call (Gal. 1.15-16), and his presentation of his gospel in Jerusalem (Gal. 2.2).

Finally, we can note that, while F. Watson's theory of a subsequent 'turn to the Gentiles' following on from a period of unsuccessful mission to the Jews is unsustainable, there is some mileage in positing the idea that Paul's convictions took more definite shape as the result of his experience in a mixed Jew-Gentile community of Christian believers.[46] Here the primary candidate is the church at Antioch of which Paul seems to initially have been a member (Acts 11.25–26) and then delegate (Acts 13.1-2).[47] Paul's account of the Antioch incident in Gal. 2.11-21 contains the earliest articulation of the notion of the justification of the Gentiles that we possess. There is good reason to suppose that the theological convictions stated in 2.15-16 were developed precisely as a way of legitimating the existing practice of table-fellowship across the Jew/Gentile divide. While Paul may have joined the Antioch church already convinced that God's saving work in Jesus Christ encompassed Gentiles, the experience of life in that community and the tensions that it generated could only have strengthened those convictions.

5. *Conclusions: Apostle to the Gentiles*

So, just as Paul holds various attitudes to the Gentiles that depend, in turn, on the interplay between his Hellenistic Jewish background, Christian convictions and the issues faced by one who felt 'under daily pressure' because of concerns about the largely Gentile communities of believers for which he had responsibility, so too these attitudes are to be explained by a combination of factors relating to Paul's background, beliefs and experience.

T. L. Donaldson has noted that the defining question for most Second Temple Jews with regard to Gentiles related to the extent to which Jews might, or might not, accommodate themselves to the wider, non-Jewish

---

46   See F. Watson, *Paul, Judaism and the Gentiles: Beyond the New Perspective* (Grand Rapids: Eerdmans, rev. and exp. edn, 2007), and the critique in Donaldson, *Paul and the Gentiles*, pp.269–72.

47   For the significance of Antioch for developing views on the place of Gentiles, see J. D. G. Dunn, *Christianity in the Making.* II. *Beginning from Jerusalem* (Grand Rapids: Eerdmans, 2009), pp.292–321.

world. The question of whether, and how, Gentiles might come to share in the promises and inheritance of Israel was less obviously a matter for concern.[48] Paul, in bringing the latter question to the front and centre of the early Christian movement, quite obviously strikes a new and distinctive note. But, as we have seen, questions about how Gentile believers are then to live in relation to what, from our perspective, we might call the non-Christian world, remained live issues for Paul and his churches. Paul's varied attitudes to the Gentiles are the result of his desire to answer both questions in the light of his belief that God has raised Israel's messiah from the dead, and established him as Lord of all.

48   Donaldson, *Judaism and the Gentiles*, p.3.

Chapter 10

FISHING THE OTHER SIDE:
THE GENTILE MISSION IN MARK'S GOSPEL

Ian J. Elmer

There is an interesting scene in the humorous Australian film *Crocodile Dundee* (1986) where the central character, Michael J. 'Crocodile' Dundee (Paul Hogan), speaks about his religious faith. In answer to a question from the American journalist, Sue Charlton (Linda Kozlowski), about his fear of dying after an earlier brush with a huge crocodile, Mick Dundee replies; 'Nah. I read the Bible once. You know God and Jesus and all them apostles? They were all fishermen, just like me. Yeah, straight to heaven for Mick Dundee. Yep, me and God, we'd be mates.'

   Crocodile Dundee has a point. Our earliest Gospel, Mark, testifies that the first disciples were all fishers and much of Jesus' early ministry appears to have been exercised among the fisherfolk who plied their trade on the Sea of Galilee. In this Gospel, the evangelist relates that the first disciples whom Jesus called were four fishers, Simon (Peter), his brother Andrew, and the sons of Zebedee, James and John (1.16-20). Three of these four disciples, Peter, James and John, would become part of Jesus' most intimate inner circle (5.13; 9.2; 10.38; 13.3), and all four would be commissioned as 'apostles' (3.13-19), an event which is apparently prefigured in Jesus' promise to make them 'fishers of people' (1.17). Accordingly, it would seem that the term 'fishers of people' (ἁλιεῖς ἀνθρώπων) serves to predict how these first disciples, having left their nets and boats (1.18, 20), would 'come after' (δεῦτε ὀπίσω) Jesus (1.17) as heralds of the imminent reign of God.[1] R. H. Gundry opines that the call to the disciples to become 'fishers' of people stresses 'Jesus' power to make the fishers capable of catching human beings, a far more

---

1   R. H. Gundry, *Mark: A Commentary on his Apology for the Cross* (Grand Rapids: Eerdmans, 1993), p.67. A similar comment is made by V. Taylor, *The Gospel according to St. Mark: The Greek Text with Introduction, Notes, and Indexes* (London: Macmillan, 2nd edn, 1966), p.169.

difficult task than catching fish'.[2] Gundry assumes that the idea inherent in the title 'fishers of people' was that these apostles would 'lure' people into the Jesus movement. As we read further into Mark's Gospel we discover that the term 'fishers of people' is far from a simple figure of speech.

For one, we should note that the disciples never appear to take up the role of evangelists or teachers. The term seems more likely related to their call to 'come after' Jesus who spends the bulk of his ministry around the shores and amongst the fishing villages circling the Sea of Galilee. Moreover, we quickly come to realise that the 'catch' envisaged by the evangelist as the object of the Jesus' mission includes Gentiles on 'the other side of the sea' (4.35; 5.1; 6.45; cf. 3.8; 7.31), and that this appears to be a source of some tension between Jesus and his 'fishers'.[3]

Just as the fisher's cast nets to a varied array of fish, so too the mission in Mark draws in Jews and Gentiles alike.[4] What Jesus does for Jews, he also does for Gentiles; as Jesus exorcises among the Jews (1.21-28), so he also exorcises among the Gentiles (5.1-20); as Jews believe, so do Gentiles (5.18-20; 7.29-30); as a crowd of Jews see a feeding miracle (6.30-44), so the Gentiles see a similar revelation (8.1-13).[5]

These obvious parallels have led some scholars to postulate the view that Mark is advocating two separate missions, one to Jews and one to Gentiles.[6] Others, however, see an inherent tension between these episodes

---

2   Gundry, *Mark*, p.67. Similarly, J. Mánek, 'Fishers of Men', *NovT* 2 (1957), pp.138–41; W. T. Shiner, *Follow Me! Disciples in Markan Rhetoric* (SBLDS 145; Atlanta: Scholars Press, 1995), pp. 175–6.

3   The most significant recent study on the Gentile Mission in Mark comes from K. R. Iverson, *Gentiles in the Gospel of Mark: 'Even the Dogs under the Table Eat the Children's Crumbs'* (LNTS 339; London: T&T Clark International, 2007). See also W. M. Swartley, *Mark, the Way for All Nations* (Scottdale: Herald, 1979). Numerous articles have been written on aspects of the Gentile mission in Mark. Of particular value are J. Anthonysamy, 'The Gospel of Mark and the Universal Mission', *Bible Bhashyam* 6 (1980), pp.81–91; J. D. M. Derrett, 'Crumbs in Mark', *Downside Review* 102 (1984), pp.12–21; E. A. LaVerdiere, 'Do You Still Not Understand?', *Emmanuel* 96 (1990), pp.382–9; idem, 'Jesus among the Gentiles', *Emmanuel* 96 (1990), pp.338–45; D. Senior, 'The Eucharist in Mark: Mission, Reconciliation, Hope', *BTB* 12 (1982), pp.67–72; and E. K. Wefald, 'The Separate Gentile Mission in Mark: A Narrative Explanation of Markan Geography, the Two Feeding Accounts and Exorcisms', *JSNT* 18 (1996), pp.3–26.

4   A similar observation is made by E. A. LaVerdiere, *The Beginning of the Gospel: Introducing the Gospel according to Mark* (Collegeville: Liturgical, 1999), p.19.

5   Iverson, *Gentiles in the Gospel of Mark*, pp.122–3.

6   Most notably Wefald, 'The Separate Gentile Mission in Mark'.

as 'the shift in Mark from a Jewish past to a Gentile future is navigated with considerable resistance, both amongst Jews (2.1–3.6, 12.1-9) and toward Gentiles (7.24-31)'.[7] It is my contention that in Mark's Gospel, those called to be 'fishers of people' function not so much as agents for the harvest of converts, but more as opponents or, at least, foils against whom Jesus must struggle to bring about his vision of the kingdom, which will include Gentiles 'on the other side of the sea'.

The purpose of the present study is to examine, not just Mark's presentation of the advent of the Gentile mission, but also Mark's use of the disciples as characters in this drama. To this end I will begin by exploring how Mark prepares for the Gentile mission by the employment of the enigmatic figure of speech 'fishers of people' to describe those whom the Markan Jesus calls to 'come after him' as he embarks upon his mission (1.17).

1. *Fishers of People*

The use of the term 'fishers of people' at Mk 1.17 (on which depends Mt. 4.19, but only indirectly Lk. 5.10) has in the past been understood as a self-evident metaphor, standing for those who are called to be 'disciples and heralds of the Kingdom of God' as, for example, V. Taylor suggested in his 1966 commentary on Mark.[8] C. Smith, responding directly to Taylor, asks whether other figures of speech might have sufficed for the dual purpose of identifying those so designated as 'disciples' and 'heralds'.[9] Smith makes the point that Taylor does not explore the peculiar nature of the metaphor 'fishers of people', especially when the actual terms 'disciples' and 'heralds' could have been used. In fact Mark does not use either of these other possible terms at this juncture. Similarly, there is a later call story in Mark (2.13-14), that of

---

7   C. C. Black, *Mark: Images of an Apostolic Interpreter* (SPNT; Edinburgh: T. & T. Clark, 2001), p.232. See also Senior, 'The Eucharist in Mark', p.69. Senior suggests that the two feeding stories in particular may point to tensions concerning table fellowship and the Eucharist in early Christianity vis-à-vis the inclusion of Gentiles. Similarly, M. D. Hooker, *The Gospel according to St. Mark* (Peabody: Hendrickson, 1993), p.292.

8   Taylor, *Gospel according to St Mark*, p.169.

9   C. W. F. Smith, 'Fishers of Men: Footnotes on a Gospel Figure', *HTR* 52 (1959), pp.187–203 (187). See also J. R. Donahue and D. J. Harrington, *The Gospel of Mark* (SP 2; Collegeville: Liturgical, 2002), p.74; and B. Byrne, *A Costly Freedom: A Theological Reading of Mark's Gospel* (Strathfield: St Paul's, 2008), pp.42–3.

Levi the tax collector, where the term 'fisher' is not applied. So Mark must have something specific in mind in using the term here at the outset of his Gospel.

Most commentators draw attention to the fact that the metaphor 'fishers of people' has a biblical background, which might provide some clue to the nature of the disciples' new calling or, since they are already fishers, to a new type of fishing and a new catch.[10] The aforementioned Levi is not called as a 'fisher'. It would fit less tidily his prior profession as a tax collector; but that does not mean that Levi is called to a different vocation or role, or that the word 'fishers' can be applied only to those who fished before they were called.

The image of fisherfolk spreading their nets to capture a huge haul of those destined to be saved from the final judgment echoes the eschatological visions of a restored Israel in Ezekiel. In Ezekiel (47.9-11), fisherfolk ply their trade along a bountiful stream that flows from the Temple out into the desert bringing fecundity and new life to the whole land of Israel (47.13-20), turning the salt water of the Dead Sea fresh and the barren wilderness into a green orchard. Similarly, Jeremiah (16.16) speaks of 'sending many fishers' as agents of the regathering of Israel for a new Exodus (cf. Hab. 1.14). The latter reference, which is the closest in wording to Mark's passage, finds a ready parallel with the Exodus theme apparent in Mark's opening sequences of Jesus' journeys into and out of the wilderness.[11] But Mark makes far less use of these prophetic and eschatological allusions than the other Synoptists.

Unlike Mark, Matthew (4.12-23) makes the prophetic connection clearer when he relates that Jesus chose to relocate his mission to the seaside fishing village of Capernaum in fulfilment of the prophecy of Isaiah (8.23–9.1), who foretold that new life would come from the ancestral lands of 'Zebulun' and 'Naphtali' that abutted the Sea of Galilee.[12] So, when Matthew opens his story of Jesus with a relocation to Capernaum he, unlike his source in Mk 1.16-20, explicitly presents Jesus' actions as

10 See, for example, Byrne, *A Costly Freedom*, p.43; Gundry, *Mark*, p.67; Shiner, *Follow Me!*, p.176; and J. Marcus, *Mark 1–8: A New Translation with Introduction and Commentary* (AB 27; New York: Doubleday, 2000), pp.184–5.

11 Marcus, *Mark 1–8*, p.184. Similarly, S. W. Henderson, *Christology and Discipleship in the Gospel of Mark* (SNTSMS 135; Cambridge: Cambridge University Press, 2006), pp.33–4.

12 See the discussion of differences between Mark and Matthew in their use and appropriation of eschatological themes from the Old Testament in R. E. Watts, *Isaiah's New Exodus in Mark* (Grand Rapids: Baker Books, rev. edn, 2000), pp.55–77. Similarly, Henderson, *Christology and Discipleship*, pp.59-62.

a conscious fulfilment of the prophecy of Isaiah (8.23–9.1) that, from the lands of 'Zebulun' and 'Naphtali', light would dawn on all 'people who sit in darkness, overshadowed by death'. The actions of the Matthean Jesus are such as to bring people living in darkness to a light which is also new life. The later Matthean parable (Mt. 13.47-50) of the dragnet presents a similar scenario.

The Lucan story of the call of Peter and the fisherfolk is different in many respects, with the disciples responding to a miraculous catch of fish rather than a pre-emptive call from Jesus (Lk. 5.1-11). But it follows a similar line to that of the Matthean version. In Matthew and Luke, the fishing motif is used in the manner in which most scholars assume Mark also uses it, as indicative of apostles as fishers who would 'lure' converts into the Jesus movement much as they had the fishes of the sea.

However, none of the more detailed allusions to the prophetic texts appears in Mark. Indeed, without the explicit reference to Isaiah, the figure of the 'fishers of people' as it stands in Mark is inappropriate if the mission of the disciples is considered one of rescuing people or bringing them to salvation. As Smith points out, the metaphor of 'fishers' lacks the eminent suitability of the more widely used biblical metaphors of the shepherd seeking the strayed sheep or the jilted husband seeking out an unfaithful wife.[13]

Of course, it could simply be, as our hero Dundee assumes, that the first four disciples were fishers and, as a result, the play on words is merely a convenient happenstance.[14] Were it not that fishing was a very common occupation in Capernaum we might be more inclined to say that the occupation of the first four disciples arose from the terms of their call rather than to say that the term arose from their occupation.[15] So, for example, Robinson suggests that the call of the disciples to be 'fishers of people' is a 'deliberate play on their occupation' intended to demonstrate the nature of their call to commit themselves to the 'welfare of others'.[16]

It may certainly be true that the metaphor is meant to draw parallels between the disciples' former occupation and their new vocation, but in what sense does fishing serve the 'welfare of others'? Fishing may provide for the welfare of the fisherfolk, but scarcely for the fish. For them the arrival of the fisherfolk portends only death and a decrease in

13   Smith, 'Fishers of Men', p.189.
14   Donahue and Harrington, *The Gospel of Mark*, p.74.
15   Smith, 'Fishers of Men', p.194.
16   G. Robinson, *A Change of Mind and Heart: The Good News according to Mark* (Revesby: Parish Ministry Publications, 1994), p.69.

their numbers. Something of this is already present in the prophetic appeal to fishing imagery, which is primarily an ominous one, threatening in tone and content.[17]

To those examples already mentioned, I also draw attention to Amos 4.2, where the women of Israel are threatened with a judgment which finds apt expression in fishing language: 'Behold, the days are coming upon you, when they shall take you away with hooks, even the last of you with fishhooks'. In Hab. 1.14-15 the Chaldeans are agents of judgment and appear as fishermen with a net and the people they pursue as fish. The term is used most clearly in Jer. 16.16-18 where it stands in close relation to the Gospel figure, 'Behold, I am sending for many fishers, says the Lord, and they shall catch them…(and) many hunters to hunt them down…(for) their guilt cannot escape my view'.

In these images there is an implicit sense of judgment and finality that bespeaks more the terror of God's final reckoning than a bucolic image of happy fishers upon the shore of the sea catching converts.[18] This rather negative tone would seem to contradict later, more positive images of the role of the disciples as agents of healing and forgiveness (Mk 3.13-19; 6.7-13, 30). The possibility that Jesus or some primitive Christian preacher used this well-known figure of the eschatological fishers in an entirely new sense seems remote – especially in this case, where a pre-existing negative image is radically transformed into a supposed positive one. Obviously Mark has something else in mind.

All commentators have been impressed with the apparent abruptness of Jesus' initial call to his disciples, the lack of preparation for it, the immediate response of the disciples without question or qualification as though to an inescapable imperative, involving a complete severance with their former way of life. But it is noteworthy that Jesus does not call his disciples to be his assistants in the work of teaching; we never see them in that capacity. Within the parameters of Mark's story, the call of the disciples to be 'fishers' was a summons to an eschatological task, which would virtually preclude learning and teaching in the ordinary sense.

The fishing imagery employed here along with all the pre-existing eschatological connotations is probably intended to be 'multilayered'.[19] With the coming of Jesus and the proclamation of the good news, there

---

17   M. E. Boring, *Mark: A Commentary* (NTL; Louisville: Westminster John Knox, 2006), p.59. Similarly, A. Y. Collins, *Mark: A Commentary* (Hermeneia; Minneapolis: Fortress, 2007), p.159; Henderson, *Christology and Discipleship*, pp.40–1; and Marcus, *Mark 1–8*, p.184.

18   Smith, 'Fishers of Men', p.190.

19   Boring, *Mark*, p.59.

are those who will be condemned and those who will be saved. Collins rightly points out that the use of the fishing metaphor in Mk 1.17 'must be interpreted in the light of the summary of Jesus' proclamation (of the coming kingdom and the need to repent) in vv.14-15'.[20] I would add to this observation the further proposal that we can only fully comprehend the ambiguity of the metaphor 'fishers of people' in terms, not just of this summary statement in Mk 1.14-15, but in Mark's story as a whole.

Jesus' use of the term 'fishers of people' at this early juncture in the plot serves to signal a radical reconsideration of what his messianic mission is all about and to whom it is addressed.[21] To return again to the subject of this chapter, we note that just as Mark's Jesus can speak of new wine bursting forth from old wine skins (2.22), the movement inaugurated by him in the company of his 'fishers' spills out of Judaism into the Gentile world. In Mark's description of Jesus' mission, Gentile communities (3.8; 5.1, 20; 7.31; 8.27) and customs (10.2-12) figure prominently in the narrative.[22] This focus on Gentiles prompts the question: For whom is the coming of kingdom 'good news', Jews or Gentiles?

2. *The Missionary Journeys of Jesus*

Recent scholarship has stressed the fact that Mark's Gospel must be read as 'story', even a 'hero story' rather than history or biography in the modern sense. As such, Mark's Gospel functions both for the edification and the entertainment of its original readers.[23] Rhoads, Dewey and Michie

---

20   Collins, *Mark*, p.160.

21   So too, Smith, 'Fishers of Men', p.195. Smith makes the point that Jesus' proclamation of the good news and his call to repentance in 1.14-15 marks the transition from the message of John to the story of Jesus. Hence, the 'appearance of the term "fishers of men"' may cause us to reread the previous verses and to ask whether an immediately arriving Kingdom of God is necessarily *good* news – for instance to those who prefer their own will and their own institutions to God's will and His Kingdom' (p.195). See also Boring, *Mark*, p.51; Collins, *Mark*, pp.90–1; and B. M. F. van Iersel, *Reading Mark* (Edinburgh: T. & T. Clark, 1989), pp.20–1.

22   Black, *Mark*, p.231. See the significant study on characterisation in Mark presented by E. S. Malbon, *Mark's Jesus: Characterization as Narrative Christology* (Waco: Baylor University Press, 2009). With specific reference to the Gentiles, both individually and as a group, as central characters in Mark's Gospel, see Iverson, *Gentiles in the Gospel of Mark*, pp.2–3.

23   C. Bryan, *A Preface to Mark: Notes on the Gospel in its Literary and Cultural Settings* (Oxford: Oxford University Press, 1993), pp.58–61.

have observed that when 'we enter the story of the Gospel of Mark, we enter a world of conflict and suspense, a world of surprising reversals and strange ironies, a world of riddle and hidden meanings, a world of subversive actions and political intrigues'.[24]

At the outset of Mark's Gospel, Jesus emerges as a hero and a worker of wonders. Like Hercules and other classical heroes, Mark's Jesus embarks upon a great journey that sees him tasked with trials equivalent to those faced by Hercules or, probably more relevantly, Jonah and the heroes of the Deuteronomic history, Moses, Elijah and Elisha.[25] In the early chapters of Mark, the hero Jesus heals the sick and casts out demons. From ch. 4 onwards, however, the action intensifies with Jesus calming 'the sea' (4.35-41) and pitting himself against a wild man (5.1-20), delivering the demoniac from not one demon, but a whole 'legion' of demons (5.9) and, finally, taking on death itself, curing an incurable haemorrhage and raising Jairus' daughter (5.21-43).

In assuming these Herculean tasks, Mark's Jesus and his would-be disciples traverse a landscape that is, on the one hand, recognisable with identifiable names, such as Galilee, Judaea, Tyre, and Sidon, and on the other hand, incomprehensible, in that such place names seem misaligned or inaccurately placed side by side. It may be that the evangelist lacked an intimate knowledge of regional geography. But it is more likely that such inaccuracies serve to create an appropriate narrative world that functions as a vehicle for Mark's story.[26] This brings us again to where we began, Jesus' call to Peter, Andrew, James and John to become 'fishers of people', which prefaces Jesus' initial journeys.

Back in 1957 J. Mánek suggested that we should look for an explanation of the call for disciples to be 'fishers' in the background of 'old cosmological myths' in which the waters represent chaos, an enemy to

24   D. M. Rhoads, J. Dewey, and D. Michie, *Mark as Story: An Introduction to the Narrative of a Gospel* (Minneapolis: Fortress, 2nd edn, 1999), p.1.

25   See discussion of parallels between Mark and other 'hero' stories in biblical and non-biblical sources in E. Best, *Mark: The Gospel as Story* (Edinburgh: T. & T. Clark, 1983), pp.140–5; and Bryan, *A Preface to Mark*, pp.50–3. While direct quotations and direct dependence upon the Old Testament are far from abundant in Mark, the evangelist clearly draws upon Old Testament materials, such as the Psalms and the so-called suffering servant songs in Isaiah, to construct his image of Jesus. See R. E. Watts, 'Mark', in G. K. Beale and D. A. Carson (eds.), *Commentary on the New Testament Use of the Old Testament* (Grand Rapids: Baker Academic, 2007), pp.111–249.

26   E. S. Malbon, *Narrative Space and Mythic Meaning in Mark* (Sheffield: JSOT, 1991), pp.1–3; and D. M. Rhoads, *Reading Mark, Engaging the Gospel* (Minneapolis: Fortress, 2004), pp.167–73.

be subdued and which may be equated with the pit of the underworld.[27] But on the immediate level of this story, 'the sea' and the motif of 'fishers' by the sea referred to here is the Sea of Galilee and those who fished its waters or traversed its waves.

Soon after his story of the call of the fishers, Mark summarises Jesus' early ministry by telling of a particular event by 'the sea', where crowds 'from Galilee followed, and also from Judea' (3.7). In addition to these Jewish groups, Mark expands Jesus' following to include people from 'Idumea, from beyond the Jordan, and from the neighborhood of Tyre and Sidon' (3.8).[28] The picture Mark presents is not only one of Jews being lured to Jesus, although their homelands are listed first, but also of people coming to him from the Gentile areas to the east and to the north of Galilee. Most scholars see in this passage a foreshadowing of those Gentiles who would later come to believe in Jesus without necessarily converting first to Judaism, of whom Mark presents several exemplars: the Gerasene demoniac (5.1-20); the Syrophoenician woman (7.24-30); and the deaf man from the district of Tyre (7.31-37).[29]

In Mark, however, Jesus is not content to wait for Gentiles to come to him, but crosses the sea to encounter them in their homelands; not once, but a total of six times. For our purposes it is noteworthy that three of these crossings of the sea depict or, as we shall see presently, anticipate movement from Jewish into Gentile territory (4.35-41; 6.45-53; 8.13-22). Three are narrated in summary fashion (5.21; 6.32-34; 8.10) and three frame larger stories – the calming of the storm (4.35-41), Jesus walking on water (6.45-53), and a discussion about loaves following a miraculous feeding (8.14-22).[30] All three of the more detailed stories of sea journeys (4.35-41; 6.45-53; 8.14-22), as opposed to the single-verse transitional passages (5.21; 6.32-34; 8.10), involve movement from west to east, from Jewish territory into Gentile territory, a movement, moreover, that appears problematic in each case. All three crossings follow a typical pattern. The disciples and/or Jesus endeavour to cross the sea, an event or

---

27   Mánek, 'Fishers of Men', p.140. Similarly, Rhoads, *Reading Mark*, p.169.

28   Marcus, *Mark 1–8*, p.259. Marcus makes the point that the evangelist is probably responsible for the additional localities from 'Judea' onwards. He also draws attention to the fact that in this passage, it is the crowds who 'follow' Jesus, not the disciples. See also Gundry, *Mark*, p.162.

29   Black, *Mark*, p.232.

30   Iverson, *Gentiles in the Gospel of Mark*, p.87; Malbon, *Narrative Space*, pp.76–9; Rhoads, *Reading Mark*, pp.111–14; and Wefald, 'The Separate Gentile Mission in Mark', pp.9–13.

conversation transpires, and each time the disciples fail to comprehend the proceedings.[31]

To explore the problematic nature of theses sea voyages, we must first recall Mánek's observation that on a deeper level the references to the sea crossings must refer to the archetypical primal sea, the remnant of which is found in all great bodies of water traversed by those who go 'down to the sea in ships' and who were destined to see 'the deeds of the Lord, his wondrous works in the deep' (Ps. 107.23-24). Indeed, it is precisely these lines and other similar verses that hold the key to interpreting the particular stories of Jesus calming the sea (4.35-41) or walking on the waters (8.45-52). It is the disciples in the boat who will see and marvel at 'the Lord's wondrous works in the deep' (Ps. 107.24; cf. Mk 8.51).

With specific reference to the first of these sea stories, the calming of the storm (4.35-41), there is an attempt by Mark to evoke echoes of a similar story in the book of Jonah (1.4-6), where the hapless prophet is cast into the sea to appease what his shipmates perceive as an angry deity. In Mark Jesus is (like Jonah) sleeping in the prow of the boat, which seems incredible. How could he sleep through a violent storm? Ability to sleep during trouble was often a sign of faith in God (Pss. 3.5; 4.8), and the Greeks also praised philosophers who demonstrated consistency with their teaching by maintaining a serene attitude during a storm (e.g. Diogenes Laertius, *Phil. Bioi* 1.86; 2.71; 9.11, 68).[32] But the most likely explanation is that Mark wants to evoke the Jonah story; and, therefore, the motif of Jesus sleeping is a 'literary necessity'.[33] Matthew (or more accurately the Q tradition) will draw even clearer connections between Jesus and Jonah (Mt. 12.39-41; 16.4; Lk. 11.29-32).

In later Synoptic tradition, Jonah's memory is recalled for his spending three days in apparent death in the belly of primordial sea monster Leviathan, which served to make him a 'sign' of Jesus' death and resurrection (Mt. 12.38-42; 16.4; cf. Lk. 11.29-32). Unlike Jonah, however, Jesus is not cast into the sea, but rebukes the wind and the waters are becalmed instantly (Mk 4.39). Curiously, like the motif of Jesus sleeping in the prow of the boat, calming the storm does not appear to have been absolutely necessary because he criticises the disciples for not having faith (4.40). Apparently Jesus expected them to have taken charge of the

---

31 Malbon, *Narrative Space*, p.78.

32 Collins, *Mark*, pp.260–2.

33 O. L. Cope, *Matthew: A Scribe Trained for the Kingdom of Heaven* (CBQMS 5; Washington: Catholic Biblical Association of America, 1989), pp.96–8.

storm themselves, or that they should have trusted that nothing would happen to them while he was around.[34] The other, probably more relevant, connection to the Jonah story for Mark is the implied parallels between the missions of Jonah and Jesus, both of whom are called to preach to the Gentiles. Unlike Jonah, Jesus is not fleeing from his mission but fulfilling it, and again unlike Jonah, Jesus is not subject to the forces of the natural world or to those of the supernatural world.[35]

Immediately following the turbulent crossing of the sea (4.35-41), Mark's Jesus encounters the demoniac 'on the other side of the sea (in) the territory of the Gerasenes' (5.1), so initiating the first of four sorties Jesus will make into Gentile lands. Mark makes it clear that Jesus is in Gentile territory by reference to 'a great herd of swine' (5.11). Given that Jews neither keep pigs nor consume pork, this is a conscious signal to the audience that Jesus and his disciples are on the non-Jewish, eastern shore of the sea.[36]

To pursue this line of enquiry further, the literary design of the early sequence of events in Mark, beginning with the rough sea crossing (4.31-41) and ending with the cure of Jairus' daughter (5.21-43), reveals a thematic progression that showcases Jesus' power and authority over various natural and supernatural phenomena. Iverson observes that this sequence serves to demonstrate that no power, natural or supernatural, can thwart Jesus' mission – a mission that culminates in Jesus' first foray into Gentile territory.[37] Jesus and his disciples will make two further voyages 'to the other side', to Gentile Bethsaida (6.45-52; 8.13). Malbon argues that in mythic terms, Jesus' crossing of the Sea of Galilee presents him as mediating between the traditional oppositions of the familiar and the strange; and in geo-political terms, between the Jewish homelands and foreign lands of the Gentiles.[38]

For Mark, Jesus' crossing of the Sea of Galilee, travelling north beyond the borders of Galilee or touring the eastern regions of the

---

34 Rhoads, Dewey, and Michie, *Mark as Story*, pp.90, 93.

35 LaVerdiere, *Beginning of the Gospel*, pp.127–8. See the discussion of the ambiguous portrayal of the disciples in this sequence of events in Henderson, *Christology and Discipleship*, pp.10–15, 62–70. Henderson raises an interesting possibility that this first section of Mark explores the disciples' fear and resistance to Jesus' mission, which forces them beyond common Jewish messianic expectations, not just in terms of Christology, but also in terms of the breadth of Jesus' pastoral outreach (pp.13–15).

36 Wefald, 'The Separate Gentile Mission in Mark', p.10.

37 Iverson, *Gentiles in the Gospel of Mark*, p.24.

38 Malbon, *Narrative Space*, pp.76–9, 100; and Rhoads, *Reading Mark*, pp.164–5.

Decapolis, is tantamount to crossing boundaries – not just political, but also ethnic and religious.[39] This motif is further highlighted in ch. 7 when some Pharisees and scribes who take issue at Jesus' disciples eating with 'unclean hands' in contravention of the tradition of the elders (7.5). Jesus' responds by attacking the scribes and Pharisees claiming that they have elevated tradition above the commandment of God, keeping the tradition but breaking the commandment. In Mk 7.14-23 Jesus denies that what is eaten defiles a person and the narrator concludes, 'Thus he declared all foods clean' (7.19). In Matthew's version of the same incident, there is no mention of Jesus declaring 'all foods clean'. Instead Matthew returns to the issue which introduced the discussion and has Jesus conclude 'but to eat with unwashed hands does not defile a person' (Mt. 15.20). Matthew is careful to avoid even the inference of what Mark makes explicit. Jesus abandons the dietary laws and thereby breaks down the barriers preventing wider commerce with Gentiles. After this significant development, the disciples can now complete their trip to Bethsaida and beyond.

From Bethsaida, Jesus goes with his disciples to Caesarea Philippi (8.27), a pagan site of worship in Gentile territory, is transfigured (9.2-8), and passes back through Galilee (9.30) to Capernaum (9.33) in the Jewish homeland. In between these two crossings, Jesus and his disciples make a long and circuitous land journey to Tyre (7.24), Sidon (7.31), and 'into the district of the Decapolis' (7.31), all known to be Gentile cities and regions. The reader is further alerted that Jesus is on Gentile territory, for the woman he encounters there was a 'Greek', a Syrophoenician by birth (7.26), who admits she is not one of the children (a Jew), but is a dog (a Gentile) (7.27-28).[40]

This series of events is marked out by parallel feeding stories: one is to the Jews (symbolised by the feeding of the five thousand on Jewish territory in Mk 6.34-44), and the other is to the Gentiles (symbolised by the feeding of the four thousand on Gentile territory in Mk 8.1-10).[41]

---

39   Malbon, *Narrative Space*, pp.17, 38–40.

40   Iverson, *Gentiles in the Gospel of Mark*, pp.15–19; Malbon, *Narrative Space*, pp.27–38; and Rhoads, Dewey, and Michie, *Mark as Story*, pp.69–70. Interestingly, Matthew retains much of this material, but transforms the woman into a 'Canaanite' (Mt. 15.21) and deletes the tour of the Decapolis region and the healing of the Gentile deaf man that precedes Mark's story of the Syrophoenician woman (Mt. 15.29-31; cf. Mk 7.31-37). Matthew thereby effectively plays down Jesus' commerce with the Gentiles, having the Canaanite woman come to him on the border of Jewish territory (15.22) and locating the second feeding story on the Jewish side of the sea (15.29).

41   Wefald, 'The Separate Gentile Mission in Mark', pp.16–20.

These two feedings act as 'bookends' to Jesus' third journey into Gentile territory, just as a similar set of parallel stories about the healing of a blind man – one, a Gentile at Bethsaida (8.22-26); the other, a Jewish man Bartimaeus (10.46-52) – frames Jesus' final journey to Jerusalem, including a fourth detour into Gentile territory round Caesarea Philippi (8.27–9.29).[42]

Mark's story presents Jesus as preaching and healing on both sides of the ethnic and religious divide. Jesus heals Jews (e.g. 5.1-43) and crosses the notional land and topographical sea boundaries to heal Gentiles (7.24-37; 8.22-26), just as he feeds a crowd of five thousand Jews and a similar crowd of four thousand Gentiles with a miraculous bounty on opposing sides of the sea. Wefald argues that this penchant for paralleling Jesus' activity on different sides of the cultural and spiritual divide suggests that Mark wants to present Jesus as launching two independent missions.[43] While this seems a fair assessment of the evidence, I would suggest a point of difference with Wefald. I would argue that Mark is not presenting Jesus as initiating two independent missions, but, rather, heralding the advent of the Gentile mission and the reckoning that this would entail for Israel.[44] This is particularly noticeable in the six Marcan references to Jesus' performing exorcisms (1.21-28, 32-34, 39; 3.11-12; 5.1-20; 7.24-30 and 9.14-29), whereby the second set of three stories occurs on Gentile territory. To begin with, Wefald is correct when he points out,

> The first exorcism reference describes the first act of Jesus' ministry in Jewish lands (after the calling of the disciples). The fourth reference describes the first act of Jesus' ministry that occurs in heathen territory. The result of the first exorcism referred to is that Jesus' fame spreads throughout that region of Galilee (1.28). The result of the fourth exorcism (of the Gerasene demoniac) is that Jesus' fame is spread throughout the region of the Decapolis (5.20).[45]

Wefald is incorrect in assuming, however, that these exorcism stories are mere parallels. The progression from exorcising demons on Jewish territory to doing so on Gentile territory describes rather a shift in Jesus' missionary efforts from the Jewish homeland to Gentile territory. Wefald fails to consider adequately the fact that throughout this sequence of events, we find Mark's Jesus making further and progressively longer

---

42   Iverson, *Gentiles in the Gospel of Mark*, pp.84-6.
43   Wefald, 'The Separate Gentile Mission in Mark', pp.16–20.
44   A similar point is made by Iverson, *Gentiles in the Gospel of Mark*, p.123.
45   Wefald, 'The Separate Gentile Mission in Mark', p.13.

journeys into Gentile territory.[46] This remarkable turn of events is marked by a significant episode that sees Jesus return to his home territory only to be rejected by his kin and country.

After Jesus' trials at sea and on land in the early chapters of the story, and between the second aborted crossing of the sea to Gentile territory (6.45-52) and the third successful trip to Bethsaida (8.13), Jesus returns to Nazareth (6.1-6). In Nazareth, Jesus' former neighbours and his nearest kin are unable to comprehend the transformation that Jesus has undergone. They ask incredulously, 'What is this wisdom that has been given to him that he even does miracles?' (6.2). He remains for them 'Mary's son', the 'carpenter', whose brothers and sisters still reside in the village (6.3). Such was their lack of faith, Jesus could 'work no miracles' among them, except to 'heal a few sick people' (6.5). Jesus leaves Nazareth saddened and amazed by the lack of faith shown by his family and former neighbours, although we should not wonder why. After all, on an earlier occasion his mother Mary and his brothers had sought 'to take charge of him' and carry him home because they thought that he 'was out of his mind' (Mk 3.20-21). As Jesus later laments, 'Only in his hometown and among his relatives in his own house is a prophet without honour' (6.4).

The irony is obvious. In the story of Jesus' return to Nazareth, the lack of faith exhibited by his former neighbours and his relatives (and only Mark explicitly includes Jesus' relatives here) stands in stark contrast to the more positive reception the former demoniac experienced when he followed Jesus' command: 'Go home to your family and announce to them all that the Lord in his pity has done for you' (5.19).[47] Similarly, the failure of the residents of Nazareth to secure any significant miracles from Jesus stands in contrast to the later stories of the Syrophoenician woman (7.24-30) and the Gentile deaf man in the Decapolis (7.31-37). Jesus heals the daughter of the Syrophoenician woman because of her

---

46   Iverson, *Gentiles in the Gospel of Mark*, pp.121–3. Iverson observes that 'the plotting of the narrative across 7.24–10.52 underscores the significance of the Gentile mission and dispels any notion of exclusivity on the part of the Jews... Mark highlights the Gentile mission not only by the order of events but also by their relative duration... The first Gentile journey (5.1-20) is relatively brief, while the third and fourth journeys (7.24–8.9; 8.22–9.29) are more involved and require increasing narrative space' (p.123).

47   It is notable that the Gerasene demoniac is the first character in the Gospel who seeks to 'be with' Jesus (Mk 5.18), which clearly echoes Jesus' earlier call to the four fishers to 'follow' him and must be understood as a request to become Jesus' disciple. While this plea is rejected, later in the Gospel a Gentile crowd is exhorted to 'take up their cross and follow' alongside Jesus' disciples (8.34-38).

faith and her knowledge of the Scriptures (7.29), and the healing of the deaf man brings forth expressions of 'astonishment' and exclamations that Jesus 'has done all things well' (7.37).

Jesus' increasing openness to Gentiles is paralleled by the Gentiles' growing receptiveness to Jesus' message. By contrast to the gathering opposition to Jesus in the Jewish homeland, it is a Gentile crowd who are the first to identify Jesus as the fulfilment of messianic expectations (7.37). And it is they who are willing to follow him through the wilderness, with obvious allusions to Exodus, despite limited provisions and at risk to their life and limb (8.2-3). The allusion to Exodus is further highlighted by the motif of the miraculous feeding, which takes its cue with obvious irony from the preceding story of the Syrophoenician woman's comment that 'even the dogs under the table eat the children's crumbs' (7.28).[48] The fruit of the Gentile mission is consistently one of receptive faith and astonishment, whereas the fruit of Jesus' encounters with his own family and neighbours is negativity, incredulity, and even open hostility.

In effect, Mark appears to be juxtaposing the success of the Gentile mission over against the failure of the Jewish mission. The Gentiles prove far more receptive to Jesus' message than Jesus' family and former neighbours in Galilee, who now stand judged by their failure. This reading would function as an adequate explication of the sense of Jesus' call to his disciples to be 'fishers of people' with all the inherent sense of a final judgment.

3. *Disciples, Fishers and Gentiles*

We began this study by noting that there were problems with reading Jesus' call to the first disciples to be 'fishers of people' as a self-evident metaphor. Read against the background of earlier biblical allusions to fishers who would be agents of the final judgment, the term as it is applied to Jesus' disciples seems ambiguous. We have explored the link between the call of the disciples as 'fishers' to the motif of the sea in Mark's Gospel as the boundary marking the advancement of the mission from Jewish territory into the Gentile lands 'on the other side'. What we have yet to address are the implications of the disciples' role in Mark's telling of his story of sea voyages and missionary expeditions into foreign lands.

---

48   Iverson, *Gentiles in the Gospel of Mark*, pp.185–6.

Mark's ambiguous treatment of the disciples is well documented.[49] To summarise, we note that while the disciples are the ones called, taught and commissioned by Jesus, it is not always clear that Mark wants to hold the disciples up as exemplars of the Christian mission. In Mark, those called to be Jesus' companions and fellow missionaries (3.14) can only partially comprehend Jesus' messianic vocation (8.29), and they confuse their vocation as his disciples with social status and elitism (8.31-33; 9.33; 10.13-16, 23-24, 35-37). The more positive examples of discipleship in Mark are typically displayed by characters living on society's margins. These include the leper (1.40-45), the paralytic (2.1-12), the deaf (7.31-37), the blind (8.22-26; 10.46-52), the widow (12.41-44), tax collectors and sinners (2.15) and, as demonstrated above, we find a similar pattern to Jesus' interactions with Gentiles and Gentile communities (3.8; 5.1, 20; 7.31; 8.27).

With specific reference to the role of the disciples in the Gentile mission, we find a comparable ambivalence. Although called to be 'fishers' plying the waters for a catch of converts on both sides of the sea, the disciples show themselves to be resistant to any activity in the Gentile territory.[50] Nowhere is this made more explicit than in the two feeding stories (7.24-37; 8.22-26), both of which involve the disciples (who are instructed to distribute the loaves to the crowds; cf. 6.41; 8.6) – but to varying effect. The two incidents employ the motif of loaves and fishes and therefore have Eucharistic overtones, a fact made explicit by the Fourth Evangelist who appropriates the first story as a narrative introduction to Jesus' Eucharistic discourse on the 'bread of life' (Jn 6.22-59).[51] Elsewhere in the New Testament, fish play an important 'Eucharistic' role in the Easter story. In Luke's Gospel the risen Jesus consumes a piece of fish to prove his identity (Lk. 24.41-42), which echoes the earlier story of the two disciples on the road to Emmaus who only recognise the risen Jesus in the breaking of the bread (Lk. 24.30-31).

---

49   See discussion in Rhoads, Dewey, and Michie, *Mark as Story*, pp.122–9. The disciples have been the subject of many articles, dissertations and monographs. Of particular note are Henderson, *Christology and Discipleship*; E. Best, *Following Jesus: Discipleship in the Gospel of Mark* (JSNTSup 1; Sheffield: JSOT, 1981); idem, *Disciples and Discipleship: Studies in the Gospel according to Mark* (Edinburgh: T. & T. Clark, 1986); C. C. Black, *The Disciples according to Mark: Markan Redaction in Current Debate* (JSNTSup 27; Sheffield: JSOT, 1989); J. D. Kingsbury, *Conflict in Mark: Jesus, Authorities, Disciples* (Minneapolis: Fortress, 1989); and E. S. Malbon, *In the Company of Jesus: Characters in Mark's Gospel* (Louisville: Westminster John Knox, 2000).

50   Donahue and Harrington, *The Gospel of Mark*, p.246.

51   Senior, 'The Eucharist in Mark', pp.68–9.

The Johannine Jesus similarly serves 'fish and bread' for an Easter breakfast on the banks of the Sea of Galilee, and 'none of his disciples dared ask, 'Who are you?' (for) they knew it was the Lord' (Jn 21.12).

In Mark, the feeding of the five thousand (6.30-44) is also implicitly linked to the question of Jesus' identity with the subsequent story of Jesus walking on water (6.45-52; cf. Mt. 14.22-32; Jn 6.15-21). Mark explains in an editorial aside that the disciples were frightened of the spectre of Jesus crossing the waves because 'they had not understood the meaning of the loaves; their hearts were hardened' (6.52), an observation which is not found in either Matthew's or John's versions of the story. The message here seems to be that the disciples were unable to recognise Jesus' true identity despite the miracle of the loaves and fish.[52]

An even more pointed indictment comes after the second feeding story, which occurs in the Gentile area of the Decapolis. When Jesus directs them to feed the crowd, the disciples question their ability to do so in this wilderness on the other side of the sea (Mk 8.4). I would argue that the disciples' question is to be understood in part as, 'How can we feed these people – these Gentiles who are not part of the people of God – with bread here in the desert?' After all, the disciples never questioned Jesus about how one could feed the Jews in the first feeding of 6.30-44, but in fact they volunteered to go and buy bread for that Jewish crowd, something which they do not volunteer in the second feeding of 8.1-10.

The motif of misunderstanding and misapprehension is continued in the subsequent pericope detailing the crossing of the sea to Bethsaida. The disciples misunderstand Jesus' reference to the 'leaven' of the Pharisees (8.15); they presume he is speaking about the sparse provisions ('only one loaf', 8.14) they had brought with them in the boat. Jesus' reply to the disciples is strongly stated – their lack of perception is explicitly connected with the two previous feeding stories:

> Jesus said to them, 'Why do you discuss the fact that you have no bread? Do you not yet perceive or understand? Are your hearts hardened? Having eyes do you not see, and having ears do you not hear? And do you not remember? When I broke the five loaves for five thousand, how many baskets full of broken pieces did you take up?' And they said to him, 'seven'. And he said to them, 'Do you not yet understand?' (8.17-21).

We see a similar pattern of resistance on the part of the disciples to crossing the sea into Gentile lands. In the crossing described in 4.35-41 the disciples are frightened of perishing. Jesus questions their lack of

---

52 Henderson, *Christology and Discipleship*, p.215.

faith and the disciples are filled with awe on the way to the encounter with the Gentile Gerasene demoniac. Jesus and his disciples then make two further voyages across the sea to Gentile Bethsaida. The first (6.45-52) is aborted because of the disciple's fear, misunderstanding and apprehension (6.48, 51-52), while the second (8.13) is successful but only after Jesus rejects the ethnic particularity of his Jewish co-religionists (7.1-23). He then actively turns to Gentiles, making a fourth journey into Gentile territory via a crossing of the sea from west to east, feeding four thousand Gentiles in the wilderness (8.1-10) with no lingering fears of being polluted by close contact and commerce with them (Mk 7.24-30; cf. 7.18-23).

D. Rhoads astutely points out that while 'Jesus crosses many culturally established boundaries internal to Israel...the external geographical and social boundaries separating Israel from the Gentiles is the boundary against which all internal boundaries are hedges'.[53] Following the internal logic of Mark's plot it seems clear enough that once Jesus has abrogated the Jewish dietary prescription (7.17-23), the way lies open to a fuller engagement with Gentiles. In Mark the new community of the followers of Jesus includes Gentiles who do and will respond to the gospel in faith (7.24-30; 11.17; 12.1-12; 13.9; 14.10), while many Jews will be excluded for unbelief (4.12; 6.1-6; 7.1-23; 11.12-19; 12.9; 15.11-15). But, there is an implicit irony in Mark's presentation of the disciples' reaction to this significant development.

Called to be 'fishers of people', to be agents of the coming kingdom, the disciples prove reluctant to cross the sea in search of easy quarry. In what seems to be a crucial passage of stories in Mk 6.34–8.10, between the two feeding episodes, we see a dramatic transformation of Jesus' ministry and a possible concomitant transformation in the attitude of the disciples towards that mission – they are being dragged reluctantly towards the Gentile lands on the other side of the sea (cf. 6.45).[54]

As the Gospel reaches its climax, the disciples stand in an ambiguous situation. During Jesus' final, fateful clash with the religious authorities in Jerusalem, Jesus is betrayed by one disciple, Judas (14.12), denied by another, Peter (14.66-71), and forsaken by the rest (14.50). Only the women remain to share his suffering (15.40-41), anoint his body (16.1), and accordingly are the 'first' to be commissioned to proclaim the resurrection (16.7). The disciples are called to 'return' to Galilee and, we

53   Rhoads, *Reading Mark*, p.87.
54   Malbon, *Narrative Space*, pp.28–9; and Wefald, 'The Separate Gentile Mission in Mark', pp.11–12.

must assume, take up their role as 'fishers' and heralds of the final judg-ment.[55] But, ironically, the disciples are both harbingers of judgment and recipients of the same indictment.

The rather surprising failure on the disciples' part and the strange ambiguous ending to Mark's story that leaves only a hint of their redemption, should force us to reconsider afresh their original call to be 'fishers of people'. Our Aussie hero Mick Dundee is probably correct in one respect: the disciples' call to be 'fishers of people' has something to do with the final judgment. The term 'fishers of people' does have eschatological overtones. But, unlike Matthew (4.12-23), Mark does not explicitly link the call story to Isaiah's messianic prophecies focused upon the lands around Sea of Galilee (Isa. 8.23–9.1). Unlike Luke (5.1-11), Mark does not explain the response of the disciples to Jesus' call in terms of their awe at seeing the miraculous catch of fish. Indeed, the term 'fishers of people' does not admit easy explanation in terms of disciple-ship. They are never seen in the roles of teacher or evangelist. The task of the disciples as 'fishers of people' is a future eschatological one that is never fully realised within the story itself and only implied ambiguously in the conclusion. From a literary point of view, these companions of Jesus function as foils for Mark's presentation of Jesus' mission to herald the imminent kingdom and the ingathering of all people, and especially those citizens of the Gentile nations on 'the other side of sea'.

---

55   See Rhoads, Dewey and Michie, *Mark as Story*, p.141, who conclude correctly that the final call of Jesus for his disciples to return to Galilee, which brings Mark's narrative to a close, 'points to the follower's hopes for Jesus' return away from Jerusalem toward Galilee and the Gentile nations'.

Chapter 11

THE ATTITUDE TO GENTILES IN THE GOSPEL OF MATTHEW

David C. Sim

1. *Introduction*

The unanimous testimony of the Church Fathers was that the Gospel of Matthew was written by a Jew, the disciple of Jesus, for a Jewish readership. In the first third of the second century Papias reported that Matthew's Gospel was originally written in Hebrew (or Aramaic), which presumes that the intended readers were Jews, and then later translated into Greek (Eusebius, *Hist. eccl.* 3.39.15-16). Some fifty years later Irenaeus maintained that Matthew composed a Gospel for the Hebrews in their own language, while Peter and Paul were preaching in Rome (*Haer.* 3.1.1), and this became the unquestioned position of the Christian Church until the rise of critical biblical scholarship. In the modern day, the identification of the evangelist with the disciple Matthew has completely fallen from favour, and almost all Matthean scholars now contend that the author of the Gospel was an anonymous Christian of the late first century.[1]

Yet scholars have not completely overridden the witness of the Church Fathers. That Matthew was a Christian of Jewish origin who wrote for a predominantly Jewish readership continues to find acceptance in

---

1   The one major exception in recent times is R. H. Gundry, who has argued that the testimony of Papias can be trusted and that the disciple of Jesus did indeed compose the Gospel that bears his name. See R. H. Gundry, *Matthew: A Commentary on his Handbook for a Mixed Church under Persecution* (Grand Rapids: Eerdmans, 2nd edn, 1994), pp.609–22; and more recently, idem, 'The Apostolically Johannine pre-Papian Tradition Concerning the Gospels of Mark and Matthew', in R. H. Gundry, *The Old Is Better: New Testament Essays in Support of Traditional Interpretations* (WUNT 178; Tübingen: Mohr Siebeck, 2005), pp.49–73. For a critique of Gundry's arguments, see D. C. Sim, 'The Gospel of Matthew, John the Elder and the Papias Tradition: A Response to R. H. Gundry', *HTS* 63 (2007), pp.283–99.

Matthean scholarship. There was, however, a period from the 1940s to the 1980s when even these points were challenged by some scholars. The notion that the evangelist was a Gentile who wrote for a largely Gentile community was first proposed in a short article by K. W. Clark,[2] and it was given a good deal of impetus in the works of the early German redaction critics in the following decade or so.[3] A small group of scholars upheld this view through the 1960s to the early 1980s,[4] but it has had no serious advocate in the past three decades. The thoroughly Jewish nature of Matthew is now virtually unchallenged,[5] and most scholars would argue that he composed his work for a largely Christian Jewish community which also probably contained some Gentiles and perhaps even a growing Gentile membership.

The purpose of this study is to evaluate this Jewish evangelist's attitude towards the Gentiles. It has long been held that Matthew has a universalistic stance and a largely positive view of the Gentile world. The major evidence in favour of this thesis derives from the Gospel itself and can be summarised as follows.[6] The opening sentence of the Gospel

---

2   K. W. Clark, 'The Gentile Bias in Matthew', *JBL* 66 (1947), pp.165–72.

3   See in particular W. Trilling, *Das Wahre Israel: Studien zur Theologie des Matthäusevangeliums* (ETS 7; Munich: Kösel, 1959, 3rd edn, 1964); and G. Strecker, *Der Weg der Gerechtigkeit: Untersuchung zur Theologie des Matthäus* (FRLANT 82; Göttingen: Vandenhoeck & Ruprecht, 1962; 3rd edn, 1971). Further references to these works in the present study will be to the third editions.

4   See the list of scholars in W. D. Davies and D. C. Allison, *A Critical and Exegetical Commentary on the Gospel according to Saint Matthew* (ICC; 3 vols.; Edinburgh: T. & T. Clark, 1988–97), I, pp.10–11.

5   On the Jewishness of Matthew, see the definitive study by A. J. Saldarini, *Matthew's Christian-Jewish Community* (CSHJ; Chicago: University of Chicago Press, 1994), esp. pp.194–206. Cf. too the more recent statement in A. Runesson, 'Judging Gentiles in the Gospel of Matthew: Between "Othering" and Inclusion', in D. M. Gurtner, J. Willitts and R. Burridge (eds.), *Jesus, Matthew's Gospel and Early Christianity: Studies in Memory of Graham N. Stanton* (LNTS 435; London: T&T Clark International, 2011), pp.133–51. However, C. M. Tuckett has re-opened this whole question in a recent study by emphasising the difficulty of defining central terms such as 'Jew', 'Gentile', 'Christian', 'Jewish Christian' and so on, and concluding that Matthew's Jewishness is questionable for a number of reasons. See Tuckett, 'Matthew: The Social and Historical Context'.

6   See the detailed summary in D. Senior, 'Between Two Worlds: Gentiles and Jewish Christians in Matthew's Gospel', *CBQ* 61 (1999), pp.1–23 (14–16). Cf. too B. Byrne, 'The Messiah in Whose Name "the Gentiles Will Hope" (Matt 12:21): Gentile Inclusion as an Essential Element of Matthew's Christology', *ABR* 50 (2002), pp.55–73. The most detailed examination Matthew's universalism and pro-Gentile stance is G. Tisera, *Universalism in the Gospel of Matthew* (EUS 482; Frankfurt: Peter Lang, 1993).

describes Jesus not merely as the son of David but as the son of Abraham, the father of all nations. In the genealogy that follows (1.2-16), four Gentile women (Tamar, Rahab, Ruth and the wife of Uriah) are mentioned among the ancestors of Jesus. The birth narrative continues this positive portrayal of the Gentiles by recounting how the Gentile magi travelled to Bethlehem to find and worship the infant Jesus (2.1-12). In the ministry of Jesus there are positive encounters with Gentiles. At Capernaum the Matthean Jesus heals the servant of a Roman Centurion and praises the soldier's great faith as superior to that of anyone in Israel. He further relates that the Gentiles will participate in the messianic banquet (8.5-13) at the expense of the Jews. Later in the narrative he heals the daughter of a Canaanite woman and also praises her great faith (15.21-28). In two formula quotations (4.15-16; 12.18-21), the evangelist emphasises that Jesus is the light to the Gentiles and that in his name the Gentiles will hope. As Jesus dies on the cross, the Gentile Centurion and the other guards at the foot of the cross confess Jesus to be the Son of God (27.54), and at the very end of the Gospel the risen Christ commands the disciples to evangelise all the nations (28.16-20). When this and other evidence is taken into account, it is impossible to escape the conclusion that Matthew had a very positive attitude toward the Gentile peoples.

But, as is often the case, appearances can be deceptive. I have argued in a number of previous studies that this view, though widespread in the field, is rather simplistic on a range of important points and simply wrong on others.[7] It also tends to overlook or at least marginalise some pieces of crucial evidence. In the current study limitations of space preclude a full discussion of all the relevant issues, so it will focus on a few key themes. It will begin not with the usual evidence cited in favour of Matthew's pro-Gentile stance, but with the material that is often neglected, the Gospel's anti-Gentile passages. These texts provide solid and consistent information concerning the evangelist's attitude towards the Gentile world and demonstrate that his view was largely negative. The analysis of these texts will then be followed by an examination of the Gentiles who appear in the Gospel narrative. The discussion here will show that Matthew is hardly consistent in his depiction of his Gentile characters; some are portrayed positively while most are painted in rather unfavourable terms. The Gentiles who are acceptable to the

---

7   See in particular D. C. Sim, 'The Gospel of Matthew and the Gentiles', *JSNT* 57 (1995), pp.19–48; and idem, *The Gospel of Matthew and Christian Judaism: The History and Social Setting of the Matthean Community* (SNTW; Edinburgh: T. & T. Clark, 1998), pp.215–56.

evangelist are those who have belief or faith in Jesus and who have also made a commitment to Judaism. In line with his anti-Gentile perspective, Matthew does not approve of Gentiles who remain Gentiles, even if they accept Jesus; they have to leave the Gentile world and convert to the Jewish tradition if their allegiance to Jesus is to be acceptable. Finally, there will be a brief discussion of the numbers and status of any Gentiles in the evangelist's community. Here it will be argued that Gentile numbers were comparatively small, and that any Gentile converts were by definition both proselytes and believers in Jesus.

2. Anti-Gentile Statements in Matthew

Any discussion of Matthew's attitude towards the Gentiles must take into account a number of texts that portray the Gentiles in a rather negative light. No fewer than four of these appear in the Sermon on the Mount (chs. 5–7), the definitive Gospel discourse which details how followers of Jesus are to act and how they ought to relate to outsiders, while the fifth is found in the so-called ecclesiastical discourse in ch. 18. Two of these pericopes derive from Q and the other three are unparalleled. Let us discuss these texts briefly.[8]

The first Q text is Mt. 5.46-47 (//Lk. 6.32-33). This logion, which deals with love of enemies, is perhaps the least critical of the Gentiles. It reads: 'For if you love those who love you, what reward have you? Do not even the tax-collectors and the Gentiles (οἱ ἐθνικοί) do the same?' The parallel in Luke refers twice to 'sinners' (οἱ ἁμαρτωλοί), a favourite Lucan term, and it is generally agreed that Matthew represents the Q original while Luke has twice substituted a favourite word. This tradition contains a comparatively mild criticism of the Gentile world. The evangelist compares the behaviour of his community with the behaviour of tax-collectors and Gentiles, and by urging his readers to exceed the standards of these two groups there is an implicit critique of them in view of the inherent contrast. The second Q passage appears in Mt. 6.31-32 (//Lk. 12.29-30). Matthew's version states, 'Therefore do not be anxious saying "What shall we eat" or "What shall we drink", or "What shall we wear?", for the Gentiles (or nations; τὰ ἔθνη) seek all these things and your heavenly Father knows you need them all'. The Lucan counterpart also contains τὰ ἔθνη, so it is clear the word appeared in Q. Matthew has

---

8 I have discussed these texts in detail in a number of previous publications; see, for example, Sim, 'Matthew and the Gentiles', pp.25–30, and *Matthew and Christian Judaism*, pp.227–9, 237–9.

again taken over a tradition that views the Gentiles in a negative light because it encourages the followers of Jesus not to model themselves on Gentile practice. The third text for consideration is the unique material in Mt. 6.7-8, which appears just prior to Matthew's version of the Lord's Prayer in 6.9-13. This text reads: 'And in praying, do not heap up empty phrases as the Gentiles (οἱ ἐθνικοί) do...do not be like them, for your heavenly Father knows what you need before you ask him'. There is here a further criticism of a Gentile practice, and again the evangelist warns his readers not to imitate this aspect of Gentile life.

The Sermon's fourth anti-Gentile passage is found in 7.6. In this unparalleled tradition, the Matthean Jesus states, 'Do not give dogs what is holy; and do not throw your pearls before swine, lest they trample them under foot and turn to attack you'. While the language here is metaphorical and there is no specific mention of Gentiles, it is clear that non-Jews are the targets of this pericope. The pearls represent the kingdom (cf. 13.45-46), and what is holy may have the same meaning,[9] but our interest lies with the identity of the dogs and the swine which are to be denied these things. The pig was considered unclean in Jewish law (Lev. 11.7; Deut. 14.8) and dogs were generally detested by Jews; to be compared to a dog was an insult of the highest order (cf. 1 Sam. 17.43; 24.14; 2 Sam. 9.8; 16.9; 2 Kgs 8.13). There can be no doubt that in Matthew this reference to the dogs applies to Gentiles. Not only is this suggested by the fact that this was a known derogatory Jewish term for Gentiles in the ancient world,[10] but it is confirmed in the story of the Canaanite woman where Jesus specifically refers to the Gentiles in such terms (15.26). It is also probable that the reference to the pig applies to Gentiles, since we find this meaning of the term in contemporary Judaism as well.[11] Once we have identified the imagery in this text, its meaning for Matthew becomes clear. The members of the evangelist's community are not to take their precious message of the kingdom to the unclean Gentile world.

We may now turn to the text that appears in Mt. 18.15-17. This passage specifies the procedure when one community member has a grievance against another member, and it doubtless reflects the practice of Matthew's church. At first the wronged individual is to discuss the

9 Davies and Allison, *Matthew*, I, p.676; and D. A. Hagner, *Matthew* (2 vols.; WBC 33A, 33B; Dallas: Word, 1993–95), I, p.171.

10 See the discussion of the relevant texts in H. L. Strack and P. Billerbeck, *Kommentar zum Neuen Testament aus Talmud und Midrasch* (4 vols.; Munich: Beck, 3rd edn, 1951–56), I, pp.722–6.

11 Strack and Billerbeck, *Kommentar*, I, pp.448–50.

matter with the offender alone in an effort to settle the matter. If this fails, then he or she is to try again but this time in the presence of two or three witnesses according to Jewish Law (cf. Deut. 19.15). If this action fails to resolve the dispute, then it is to be brought before the whole church (ἐκκλησία). And if the wrongdoer does not heed the will of the church, then he or she is to be treated as a tax-collector and a Gentile (ἐθνικός). Since this action by the church must be taken as a punishment, there is widespread agreement that it involves the practice of avoiding or shunning the offender. This amounts effectively to an act of official excommunication.[12] If this interpretation is correct, then it relates not simply that Gentiles are considered outsiders by the evangelist's community, which agrees with the sentiments expressed in the Sermon on the Mount, but also that Matthew's group largely avoided contact with its Gentile neighbours.[13]

Full weight must be given to these five anti-Gentile passages. Not only do they relate that the members of the evangelist's community opposed the practices of the Gentile world, but they also testify that they tried to avoid contact with their Gentile neighbours and were wary of conducting a mission among them.[14] It is interesting to note how those scholars who affirm the evangelist's generally positive view of the Gentiles respond to these texts. There are three major ways of dealing with them.

The first is simply to ignore them. In his full-scale study of Matthew's universalism and pro-Gentile perspective, G. Tisera hardly mentions these five passages. A glance at the index of cited texts reveals that Mt. 6.7-8; 7.6 and 18.17 are never referred to at all, while Mt. 5.47 and 6.32 receive one mention each, though neither reference discusses the Gentiles.[15] Clearly this approach, which does not even acknowledge the problem, is hardly satisfactory.

---

12   So most scholars, including Davies and Allison, *Matthew*, II, p.368; Hagner, *Matthew*, II, p.532; and R. T. France, *The Gospel of Matthew* (NICNT; Grand Rapids: Eerdmans, 2007), p.694.

13   So correctly G. N. Stanton, *A Gospel for a New People: Studies in Matthew* (Edinburgh: T. & T. Clark, 1992), pp.160–1. Cf. too Saldarini, *Matthew's Christian-Jewish Community*, pp.76–7, 79.

14   For similar views, though with differing emphases at certain points, see Runesson, 'Judging Gentiles', pp.143–4; idem, 'Rethinking Early Jewish–Christian Relations: Matthean Community History as Pharisaic Intragroup Conflict', *JBL* 127 (2008), pp.95–132 (104–6); and B. Repschinski, 'Matthew and Luke', in D. C. Sim and B. Repschinski (eds.), *Matthew and his Christian Contemporaries* (LNTS 333; London: T&T Clark International, 2008), pp.50–65 (51–7).

15   Tisera, *Universalism*, pp.379–83.

The second method of dealing with these texts is to argue that some or even all of them are not anti-Gentile at all. For example, in his analysis of Mt. 7.6, R. H. Gundry maintains that for Jews 'Gentiles' means non-Jews and that such people were referred to as pigs and dogs by some Jews. But then he suggests that for followers of Jesus the term 'Gentiles' means non-disciples rather than non-Jews, and it carries this sense in 5.47; 6.7, 32; 18.17, in which case the references to dogs and pigs here also refer to those who are not disciples.[16] There is, in short, no anti-Gentile perspective in any of these texts. It should be noted in response that Gundry produces no evidence whatsoever for this view, and it is not surprising that most scholars have not adopted it. A variation on this position is proposed by A.-J. Levine who contends that οἱ ἐθνικοί does not refer to Gentiles as a corporate group, but to 'pagans' who have rejected the Christian message.[17] But such a narrow definition of the term is hardly warranted by the text.

We come now to the third approach, which is the one most favoured in Matthean scholarship. This manner of interpreting these texts acknowledges rather than denies their anti-Gentile sentiments, but its advocates contend that they do not reflect the viewpoint of the evangelist. There are a number of variations to this approach. One is to draw a sharp distinction between the tradition Matthew inherited and his own redactional work. This was the ploy of Trilling and Strecker, who both argued that the evangelist was a conservative preserver of his sources: Matthew inherited and largely retained a Jewish Christian source which was critical of the Gentiles, but he added new material that reflected his own more universal perspective.[18] A similar view is found in more recent studies. D. Senior tries to dismiss the importance of these texts by describing them as a block as 'stereotypical and stock judgments',[19] while J. Nolland identifies them throughout his commentary as 'Jewish negative stereotypical images'.[20] A third variation merely notes that such anti-Gentile material points to the Jewishness of the evangelist and his

---

16   Gundry, *Matthew*, p.123; cf. too pp.99, 103–4, 368.

17   A.-J. Levine, *The Social and Ethnic Dimensions of Matthean Salvation History: 'Go Nowhere among the Gentiles' (Matt. 10.5b)* (SBEC 14; Lewiston: Edwin Mellen, 1988), pp.31–7.

18   Trilling, *Wahre Israel*, p.192; and Strecker, *Weg*, p.35.

19   Senior, 'Between Two Worlds', p.11. See too W. Carter, 'Matthew and the Gentiles: Individual Conversion and/or Systemic Transformation?', *JSNT* 26 (2004), pp.259–82 (280).

20   J. Nolland, *The Gospel of Matthew* (NIGTC; Grand Rapids: Eerdmans, 2005), pp.270, 313, 747–8. Nolland's discussion of Mt. 6.7 does not use this expression but he makes the same point; *Matthew*, p.284.

intended readers, and basically leaves the matter there.[21] All of these positions work on the same assumption. They all assume that Matthew inherited from his (Jewish Christian) sources negative and stereotypical depictions of Gentiles which he simply reproduced in his Gospel, even though they ran quite contrary to his own positive attitude towards the Gentiles.

This suggested solution to the problem simply does not work. Matthew was no slave to his sources. He was a creative author and redactor who was free to use his sources in any manner he wished.[22] When he opted to follow his source material exactly or closely, it must be assumed that he was either largely or completely in agreement with it. Conversely, when he felt the necessity to revise his sources by omitting sections or by significantly modifying passages, then we must presume that he did so because he disagreed with his source at those points and altered the material to a more agreeable form that coincided with his own point of view. We can trace from Matthew's use of Mark (and to a lesser extent his treatment of Q, whose original text is not certain) how he employed these editorial principles of retention, omission and redaction. This means that we cannot so easily divorce these anti-Gentile passages in the Gospel from the viewpoint of the evangelist. Had these negative Jewish stereotypes conflicted with Matthew's attitude towards the Gentiles, we would expect him to have omitted or seriously edited them. The fact that he did not indicates that he accepted the negative view of the Gentile world contained in these traditions. The common complaint that I (and others) have assigned too much weight to these passages[23] can and should be dismissed. A single anti-Gentile statement in the Gospel can be attributed to some carelessness on the part of the evangelist, but the inclusion of five such traditions necessitates that these pericopes be given a considerable amount of weight when reconstructing the evangelist's view of the Gentile world.

These anti-Gentiles passages in Matthew testify that the members of his Christian Jewish community saw the Gentile world as a foreign place, held its religious practices in some contempt, and minimised their

21   So Hagner, *Matthew*, I, p.135, II, p.532; France, *Matthew*, pp.227, 694; and D. J. Harrington, *The Gospel of Matthew* (SP 1; Collegeville: Liturgical, 1991), pp.89, 269. We may also place Davies and Allison, *Matthew*, I, pp.559, 589, in this general category, though their discussion is perhaps more nuanced.

22   See Stanton, *Gospel for a New People*, pp.41–2.

23   So, for example, France, *Matthew*, p.694 n.16; and E. M. Wainwright, *Shall We Look for Another? A Feminist Rereading of the Matthean Jesus* (TBLS; Maryknoll: Orbis, 1998), p.44.

contact with their Gentile neighbours. Gentiles provide the members of Matthew's group with examples of how they should *not* behave.[24] It might be argued that this stance can be explained by the Jewish nature of the evangelist's group. They simply propagated the common contemporary Jewish view that the 'pagan' world should be treated with suspicion and contempt.[25] While there is probably some truth in this,[26] the complete answer may be more complex. There is good evidence in the Gospel that the Matthean community had undergone persecution at the hands of the Gentiles. I have argued this point in some detail in earlier studies,[27] so all that is required here is a summary of that discussion.

The mission discourse testifies that (Matthean) missionaries will be dragged before governors and kings to bear testimony before them and to the Gentiles (10.18), which is a clear reference to Gentile persecution.[28] Matthew's addition of καὶ τοῖς ἔθνεσιν in this verse (cf. Mk 13.9) makes the further point that these Gentile officials conduct their persecution on behalf of the whole Gentile world. This is reinforced in 10.22, where Matthew follows Mark in commenting that missionaries will be hated by all. More evidence is found in the apocalyptic discourse. In 24.9 reference is made to tribulation, martyrdom and hatred by all the nations for the sake of Jesus' name. A comparison with the Marcan parallel (Mk 13.9) reveals that Matthew has inserted the references to tribulation and death, and expanded Mark's 'hated by all' to 'hated by all the nations (πάντων τῶν ἐθνῶν)'. These redactional alterations point to a particularly violent persecution at the hands of the Gentiles. Can we pinpoint this persecution?

If we place the evangelist and his community in Antioch, as most scholars do, then we need look no further than the extremely violent persecutions of the Antiochene Jews by the Gentile population both during and after the Jewish revolt against Rome (Josephus, *B.J.* 7.46-62). According to Malalas (*Chron.* 10.45), the victorious Titus confirmed the anti-Jewish sentiment by donating some of the spoils of war to the

---

24   Runesson, 'Judging Gentiles', p.143.

25   So K. Tagawa, 'People and Community in the Gospel of Matthew', *NTS* 16 (1970), pp.149–62 (153).

26   Of course, there have been attempts to protect Matthew from the charge of 'ethnic bigotry', but these are largely apologetic. See, for example, Levine, *Social and Ethnic Dimensions*, pp.32–6.

27   Sim, 'Matthew and the Gentiles', pp.35–9; and idem, *Matthew and Christian Judaism*, pp.231–6.

28   See D. R. A. Hare, *The Theme of Jewish Persecution of Christians in the Gospel according to St. Matthew* (SNTSMS 6; Cambridge: Cambridge University Press, 1967), pp.106–8.

citizens of Antioch, building a theatre on the site of a Jewish synagogue which bore the inscription 'From the Jewish spoils' and which contained a statue of Vespasian.[29] It can safely be assumed that the evangelist's Christian Jewish community did not escape this violence. While it was involved in its own internal Jewish conflict with local scribes and Pharisees, it still remained fundamentally Jewish and would have been targeted as such by the rampaging Gentile mobs. In the aftermath of these events, Matthew's group no doubt harboured the same resentment of their Gentile neighbours as the other Jews of Antioch, and would have shared the same fear and trepidation that further outbreaks of violence could occur suddenly and without provocation. We can well understand such a group viewing itself as hated by all the nations, and taking practical steps to avoid the Gentile world.

3. *Attitudes to Gentiles in Matthew's Story of Jesus*

We may move now to the subject of the Gentiles in Matthew's narrative. As with the other Synoptic Gospels, Gentiles populate Matthew's story of Jesus, and it is instructive to examine how the evangelist depicts these non-Jewish characters. Given that the Gospel narrative is set in Roman-occupied Galilee and Judea, it is not surprising that most of the Gentiles in Matthew are Roman. We shall therefore begin our analysis by attending to the Roman characters in the evangelist's story. In order to contextualise this discussion, it is necessary first to ascertain Matthew's attitude towards the Roman empire as a military, economic, political and religious power. Studies of this theme have unequivocally concluded that Matthew stood completely at odds with the Roman empire.[30] The evangelist disputed Rome's imperial claims and opposed Roman arrogance, oppressive power and exploitation, as well as its idolatrous imperial theology. Like the author of the book of Revelation, Matthew saw Rome working in the service of Satan against the purposes of God (cf. Mt. 4.1-11), and he looked forward to the ultimate defeat and

---

29   G. Downey, *A History of Antioch in Syria from Seleucus to the Arab Conquest* (Princeton: Princeton University Press, 1961), pp.206–7.

30   The most prominent scholar in this area of Matthean studies is W. Carter, who has produced a number of significant publications. For his most detailed statement, see W. Carter, *Matthew and Empire: Initial Explorations* (Harrisburg: Trinity Press International, 2001). Cf. too the collection of essays in Riches and Sim (eds.), *Matthew in its Roman Imperial Context*.

punishment of Rome at the eschaton (24.27-31).[31] Bearing all this in mind, how does Matthew depict the Roman characters in his story?

The major study of this theme is that of D. J. Weaver,[32] who argues that there is no consistency in the evangelist's portrayal of the Romans in his narrative. While she contends that Pilate (Mt. 27.1-2, 11-54, 57-66; 28.11-15) and the Roman soldiers who guard the tomb of Jesus (27.62-66; 28.2-4, 11-15) are cast in a very poor light, the Centurion of Capernaum (8.5-13), Pilate's wife (27.19), and the soldiers who crucify Jesus and acknowledge that he is the Son of God (27.27-54) can be said to be positive characters.[33] I have no problem with Weaver's analysis of Pilate, his wife, and the guard at the tomb, but I would not follow her discussion of the soldiers at the foot of the cross, and I would modify her conclusions regarding the Centurion of Capernaum. Let us examine these texts in turn.

In terms of the soldiers who execute Jesus and then acknowledge his divine sonship, Weaver follows the scholarly consensus that these Roman executioners make a Christian confession of faith following the apocalyptic signs at Jesus' death. They are therefore depicted as Gentile converts who foreshadow the conversion of other Gentiles once the mission to all nations is introduced after the resurrection. I have argued previously that this is a serious misreading of the evangelist's intentions.[34] Matthew takes pains to portray these soldiers in the most negative of terms. They torture and mock the messiah prior to crucifying him, and they only come to realise the true nature of Jesus after they react in fear to the apocalyptic events that accompany his death. The scene is not one of Gentile or Roman conversion, but is in reality a proleptic enactment of the judgment. The murderers of the messiah come to understand who Jesus is and they acknowledge his status as the Son of God as a cry of defeat in the face of divine power. In this way they foreshadow the fate of Rome at the universal judgment.

---

31   See D. C. Sim, 'Rome in Matthew's Eschatology', in Riches and Sim (eds.), *Matthew in its Roman Imperial Context*, pp.91–106 (94–100); and W. Carter, 'Are There Imperial Texts in the Class? Intertextual Eagles and Matthean Eschatology as "Lights Out" Time for Imperial Rome (Matthew 24.27-31)', *JBL* 122 (2003), pp.467–87.

32   D. J. Weaver, '"Thus You Will Know Them By Their Fruits": The Roman Characters of The Gospel of Matthew', in Riches and Sim (eds.), *Matthew in its Roman Imperial Context*, pp.107–27.

33   Weaver, 'Roman Characters', pp.114–24.

34   D. C. Sim, 'The "Confession" of the Soldiers in Matthew 27.54', *HeyJ* 34 (1993), pp.401–24; and idem, 'Rome in Matthew's Eschatology', pp.100–105. In agreement is Runesson, 'Judging Gentiles', p.144.

The case of the Centurion of Capernaum is different. There is no question that this Roman is depicted in positive terms. Jesus acknowledges his great faith as exceeding that of anyone in Israel, but there is a serious question mark over the meaning of this affirmation in the context of the Gospel. In the view of most scholars, the Matthean Jesus prophesies the influx of Gentiles at the eschaton who, like the Centurion, are saved because of their great faith. Yet, despite the popularity of this interpretation, it is nowhere near as soundly based as its proponents would have us believe. A full discussion of all the pertinent issues is not possible here, but a few comments are in order. First, there is no certainty that those who share in the eschatological feast with the patriarchs are Gentiles. D. C. Allison has argued, in my view convincingly, that those who come from the east and the west to share in the messianic banquet are Diaspora Jews, who are contrasted with the excluded sons of the kingdom from the land of Israel; the eschatological fate of the Gentiles is not in view here at all.[35]

The second point that can be raised is that the normative interpretation of this passage does not make much sense within its immediate context in the Gospel. In the Sermon on the Mount (chs. 5–7), Jesus takes pains to instruct his listeners that the Torah remains operative in the current age and that followers of Jesus are expected to observe all of its demands. This is made perfectly clear in 5.17-19.[36] The eschatological penalty for not obeying the Mosaic Law finds expression towards the end of the Great Sermon, at 7.21-23. Here Jesus refers to himself in his role as the end-time judge and explicitly states that not all who call him 'Lord, Lord' will enter the Kingdom of Heaven. Despite their confession of faith, these people are excluded because they are workers of lawlessness (οἱ ἐργαζόμενοι τὴν ἀνομίαν) – in other words, they have not obeyed the Torah, which is required for salvation in addition to having faith in Jesus.

The Sermon is followed immediately in chs. 8 and 9 by a series of miracle stories, but only the first two are relevant for our purposes. In the first narrative (8.1-4) a Jewish leper approaches Jesus, addressing him as Lord, and asks to be healed. Jesus duly heals him, and then instructs him

---

35   D. C. Allison, 'Who Will Come from East and West? Observations on Matt 8.11-12//Luke 13.28-29', *IBS* 11 (1989), pp.158–70. Cf. too Davies and Allison, *Matthew*, II, pp.25–30.

36   For discussion of these texts, see Sim, *Matthew and Christian Judaism*, pp.124–7; and B. Repschinski, *Nicht aufzulösen, sondern zu erfüllen: Das jüdische Gesetz in der synoptischen Jesuserzählungen* (FzB 120; Würzburg: Echter, 2009), pp.81–9.

to show himself to the priest and to offer the gift that Moses commanded (Lev. 14.1-32). This pericope thus reinforces the point made earlier in the Sermon. Faith in Jesus and the confession of Jesus as Lord must be supplemented by strict observance of the Mosaic Law. The next passage is the healing of the Centurion's servant. The Gentile soldier shows faith in Jesus by addressing him as Lord (twice) and by asking him to heal his servant, and Jesus as the merciful messiah complies with his request. But the faith of this Gentile, while sufficient to ensure the healing of his servant, is insufficient for his acceptance into the end-time kingdom; his entry into the kingdom depends as well on his obedience to the Torah, and there are no indications in the passage that this occurs.[37] The immediate context does not therefore support the majority interpretation of this passage. It works only on the basis that the Jesus who demands both confession of his Lordship and observance of the Torah in 7.21-23 and 8.1-5 now teaches a few verses later that faith and confession alone are sufficient for salvation and that Torah-observance is no longer necessary. That would be a rather major and inexplicable shift, and it is unlikely that this was Matthew's intention. This evidence supports the view of Allison that those who enjoy the eschatological rewards in 8.11-12 are Diaspora Jews rather than Gentiles. The evangelist of course accepts that Gentiles are capable of faith in Jesus, but he is just as adamant that faith alone does not guarantee salvation at the eschaton.

We may now turn our attention to other Gentile characters in the Matthean narrative. It is instructive to begin with the story of the Canaanite woman, since this episode is often connected to the Centurion narrative as a further example of enormous Gentile faith and Gentile inclusion. But as with the Centurion, faith alone and the confession of Jesus as Lord is not sufficient – observance of the Torah is necessary as well. Does this particular story contain this theme? In a wholesale reinterpretation of the traditional understanding of this story, G. S. Jackson has argued in a very detailed study that Matthew's emphasis here is less on the miracle as the response to faith and more on the Canaanite's woman's journey towards proselytism.[38] In this narrative she becomes a member of Jesus' circle (or Matthew's group) by undergoing the ritual of conversion to Judaism; her obedience to the Law, though not specifically mentioned in the text, is implicit. Although Jackson does not make the connection between this text and Mt. 7.21-23 in her discussion, the

---

37   I would thus disagree with Repschinski, 'Matthew and Luke', p.55, who claims that the Centurion '...becomes a convert to Judaism by his faith in Jesus'.

38   G. S. Jackson, *'Have Mercy on Me': The Story of the Canaanite Woman in Matthew 15.21-28* (JSNTSup 228; London: Sheffield Academic, 2002).

Canaanite woman fulfils the criteria for entry into the kingdom as defined in that earlier passage. She addresses Jesus as Lord on no fewer than three occasions and she has joined the Jewish people by observing the Law.

The subject of proselytism is also paramount when examining the women in Jesus' genealogy. The first point to note in this regard is that it is not absolutely certain that the four women were ethnically Gentile. Certainly Rahab was a Canaanite (Josh. 2.2), as too was Tamar (Gen. 38.11), and Ruth was a Moabite (Ruth 1.22), but the ethnic status of Uriah's wife (Bathsheba) is less certain. While it is tempting to identify her as a Hittite like her husband, there is reason for caution on this point.[39] But even if we accept her Gentile status, it is by no means clear that Matthew was interested simply in their Gentile origins and that he wished to affirm that the ancestry of Jesus betrays an openness to the non-Jewish world.[40] In later Judaism and certainly by the time of Matthew, the three certain Gentile women were viewed as proselytes to Judaism. Ruth had always been viewed as such, and Tamar and Rahab came to be seen in these terms as well.[41] In this respect they serve as precursors to the Canaanite woman who appears later in Matthew's story. Thus, if these women are mentioned in the genealogy because they serve as protoypes or role models for Gentile women in Matthew's community, then they suggest that such converts had fully abandoned their pagan ways and fully embraced Judaism and the Torah.[42]

Let us now consider briefly the magi, who are usually said to represent the believing Gentile world and prefigure the inclusion of Gentiles in the Matthean community. Yet, as I have argued in a detailed study, Matthew never spells out concretely that the magi are Gentiles, and we cannot take for granted, as almost all scholars do, their non-Jewish ethnicity. There were Jewish magi in antiquity and the evangelist may have intended those in his narrative to be understood as Jews.[43] I would

---

39   See J. B. Hood, *The Messiah, his Brothers, and the Nations (Matthew 1.1-17)* (LNTS 441; London: T&T Clark International, 2011), pp.107–8.

40   This is the view of Byrne, 'Gentile Inclusion', p.60. Cf. the similar view in France, *Matthew*, p.37.

41   See the detailed discussion in M. D. Johnson, *The Purpose of the Biblical Genealogies with Special Reference to the Genealogies of Jesus* (SNTSMS 8; Cambridge: Cambridge University Press, 2nd edn, 1988), pp.159–70. Cf. too Jackson, *Canaanite Woman*, pp.94–9.

42   So correctly Saldarini, *Matthew's Christian-Jewish Community*, p.69.

43   D. C. Sim, 'The Magi: Gentiles or Jews?', *HTS* 55 (1999), pp.980–1000. For a brief critique, see Byrne, 'Gentile Inclusion', pp.60–2.

not overstate the case and claim baldly that they were not Gentiles, but there is sufficient evidence to question that identification, and because of this one of the main pillars in the consensus view begins to look decidedly shaky.

While the above discussion does not pretend to have discussed all the relevant evidence and texts in relation to Matthew's depiction of his Gentile characters, the major elements have been dealt in sufficient detail. Despite the common view that Gentiles dominate Matthew's Gospel, they are in many ways peripheral to the overall narrative.[44] This correlates with the place of the Gentile world in relation to Matthew's community. Most Gentiles are depicted negatively, although the evangelist does make the point that individual Gentiles are capable of great faith in Jesus. Yet he spells out in a variety of ways how Gentile outsiders can become acceptable and how they can join the community established by Jesus. Faith in Jesus is not sufficient in itself but must be matched by a prior conversion to Judaism. As 7.21-23 makes explicit, one has to observe the Torah in addition to having faith if entry to the kingdom is to be attained. The Centurion of Capernaum is on the way but not yet there, while the Canaanite woman, following the example of the women in Jesus' genealogy, is represented as the model Gentile convert.

4. *The Gentiles in Matthew's Community*

It is commonly thought that the Matthean community was engaged in a concerted mission to the Gentiles, or at least was beginning to do so.[45] I have argued previously that the Gospel evidence is much less clear on this issue than is often supposed, and that if we take seriously the persecution of the Matthean community by Gentiles then such a mission appears far less plausible.[46] Despite some derisive comments about this

---

44   So correctly Saldarini, *Matthew's Christian-Jewish Community*, pp.68–9; cf. too Repschinski, 'Matthew and Luke', pp.56–7. For a critique of this stance, see Senior, 'Between Two Worlds', p.13.

45   For an earlier statement of this view, see S. Brown, 'The Matthean Community and the Gentile Mission', *NovT* 22 (1980), pp.193–221. A more recent proponent of this view is P. Foster, *Community, Law and Mission in Matthew's Gospel* (WUNT 2.177; Tübingen; Mohr Siebeck, 2004), pp.218–52.

46   See Sim, *Matthew and Christian Judaism*, pp.236–47; idem, 'Matthew and the Gentiles', pp.39–44. Cf. too Saldarini, *Matthew's Christian-Jewish Community*, p.69.

hypothesis,[47] I am yet to be convinced that it is incorrect. The major text that points to such a mission is the Great Commission at the conclusion of the Gospel, where the risen Christ commands the disciples to evangelise all the nations (28.19). The usual interpretation of this command is that Matthew presents it because it applies to the missionary practice of his own community, which included an outreach to Gentiles. This view is of course possible, but it is not the only or even the most likely explanation of the evangelist's intentions in this passage. A much more probable interpretation is that Matthew has inserted this demand of the risen Jesus, not to confirm or legitimate his own community's missionary activity, but as part of his anti-Pauline polemic. The risen Christ charges the disciples with the responsibility of overseeing both the Jewish and the Gentiles missions, and this effectively undercuts Paul's claim that he was commissioned by the risen Jesus to lead the Gentile mission quite independently of the disciples (cf. Gal. 1.11-17).[48] To say that the Matthean community had no concerted mission to the Gentiles does not exclude the possibility that there were members of Gentile origin in his Christian group, but it does perhaps suggest that their numbers were comparatively small.[49]

This brings us to the question of the requirements for membership for those Gentiles who formed part of Matthew's Christian Jewish community. On the basis of our previous discussion, it must be concluded that Gentile converts were expected to observe completely the Mosaic Law as a necessary part of their Christian commitment. In other words, Gentile outsiders had to become Jews in order to become followers of Jesus the Christ. This is fully in accord with the demand to observe the Torah fully in 5.17-19 and with the eschatological rejection of Law-free Christians in 7.21-23 (cf. 13.36-43). Of course this is a highly controversial topic in Matthean studies, and other scholars contend that following the Law was not necessary for Gentile Christians. These exegetes point to the Great Commission at the end of the Gospel where the risen Jesus overturns his earlier view to restrict the mission to the Jews (10.5b-6; 15.24) and now expands it to include the Gentiles as well as the people

47   According to Senior, 'Between Two Worlds', p.11, this view 'borders on the preposterous'.

48   D. C. Sim, 'Matthew, Paul and the Origin and Nature of the Gentile Mission: The Great Commission in Matthew 28:16-20 as an Anti-Pauline Tradition', *HTS* 64 (2008), pp.377–92.

49   In agreement with Saldarini, *Matthew's Christian-Jewish Community*, p.157; and J. A. Overman, *Matthew's Gospel and Formative Judaism: The Social World of the Matthean Community* (Minneapolis: Fortress, 1990), p.157.

of Israel. The entry rite into the Christian community mentioned here is baptism rather than circumcision. It is inferred from this that in the post-Easter period baptism has replaced circumcision, in which case it follows that Gentile Christians are exempt from at least the ritual demands of the Torah.[50]

Such a conclusion, however, is by no means necessary. The risen Christ also commands the disciples to teach all the nations, both Jew and Gentile, all that he has commanded. This clearly refers to his teachings in the Gospel narrative and, as noted above, Jesus demands of his followers complete obedience to the Mosaic Law. There is no need to mention circumcision for (male) Gentile converts because it is presumed. The reason why the risen Christ specifically refers to baptism is not because it replaces circumcision, but because it is an entirely new rite not previously mentioned in the narrative. Therefore, the position of Matthew regarding Gentile converts was that they needed first to become Jewish proselytes before they could become true followers of the messiah.[51]

5. *Conclusions*

This brief evaluation of Matthew's attitude towards the Gentiles demonstrates that the evangelist was less positive about non-Jews than most scholars claim. There are a number of significant anti-Gentile statements in the Gospel that cannot be dismissed from consideration. They are in fact important pieces of evidence that reveal that the evangelist and his Christian Jewish community held the Gentile world in some contempt and attempted to distance themselves from their Gentile neighbours. The Matthean community may have suffered persecution at the hands of the Gentiles at the time of the Jewish war. In terms of the Gospel narrative Gentiles do not feature prominently, and most are depicted in negative terms. Matthew accepted that Gentiles could become Christians or followers of Jesus, but their faith in Jesus as the messiah and Lord

---

50   So Davies and Allison, *Matthew*, III, p.685; J. Riches, *Conflicting Mythologies: Identity Formation in the Gospels of Mark and Matthew* (SNTW; Edinburgh: T. & T. Clark, 2000), pp.216–22; and M. Konradt, *Israel, Kirche und der Völker im Matthäusevangeliums* (WUNT 215; Tübingen: Mohr Siebeck, 2007), pp.343–4.

51   So Sim, *Matthew and Christian Judaism*, pp.247–54; idem, 'Matthew, Paul and the Origin and Nature of the Gentile Mission', pp.383–8; Repschinski, 'Matthew and Luke', pp.78–9; and Runesson, 'Judging Gentiles', pp.146, 150. This position is implied rather than explicitly stated by Senior, 'Between Two Worlds', p.23, and Nolland, *Matthew*, p.1270.

needed to be supplemented by the act of conversion to Judaism. As a number of texts specify, one needs both to observe the Mosaic Law and have faith in Jesus if one is to enter the kingdom of heaven. The Canaanite woman fulfils these requirements and in this respect follows the lead of the female Gentile converts in the genealogy, while the Centurion of Capernaum does not. If there were people of Gentile origin in the Matthean community, and it can be assumed that there were some, then they must be considered as proselytes. They were Gentiles who believed that Jesus was the promised messiah and who took seriously his claim that the Torah must be followed in its entirety. Such proselytes, who had forsaken their Gentile origins, social networks and religious convictions, would have been perfectly acceptable to Matthew.

Chapter 12

'TO THE ENDS OF THE EARTH':
ATTITUDES TO GENTILES IN LUKE–ACTS

Elizabeth V. Dowling

Early in the Gospel of Luke, Simeon identifies Jesus as 'a light for revelation to the Gentiles and for glory to your people Israel' (Lk. 2.32).[1] In the final verses of this Gospel, the risen Jesus directs his disciples to proclaim to all nations (24.47), and in Acts 1.8, the eleven are commissioned as Jesus' witnesses 'in Jerusalem, in all Judea and Samaria, and to the ends of the earth'.[2] It is clear that Luke's vision of salvation encompasses Gentiles as well as Jews and the mission to the Gentiles is the main focus of the book of Acts.

Within this inclusive overall vision, however, it is interesting to find that Jesus' interaction with Gentiles is given far less focus in the Gospel of Luke than it is in the Gospel of Mark. Two pericopes which are key to Mark's portrayal of the Gentiles (Mk 7.24-30; 8.1-10) are missing from Luke's Gospel. At the same time, Samaritans take centre stage in a number of Lucan pericopes, though Samaritans are mentioned in only one Matthean passage (Mt. 10.5) and are not mentioned at all in the Gospel of Mark.[3] The more significant Samaritan presence is therefore a Lucan emphasis. It would appear that Luke deliberately modifies his sources to downplay the Gentile presence within his Gospel and to highlight the influence of the Samaritans.[4] It is not until the book of Acts that the Lucan focus shifts to the Gentiles.

An obvious issue is to consider why Luke has portrayed the Gentile and Samaritan presence in his Gospel in this way. After a brief comment on Luke's audience, this study will explore the portrayal of Gentiles and

---

1   Biblical translations are from the NRSV unless otherwise indicated.

2   Along with the majority of scholars, I consider Luke–Acts to be a two-volume work from the same author.

3   Repschinski, 'Matthew and Luke', p.60.

4   I am assuming here that Luke has used both Mark and Q as sources for his Gospel.

then Samaritans in the Gospel of Luke. This will lead into an examination of the portrayal of the Samaritan and Gentile mission in the book of Acts. This study will argue that Luke portrays the Samaritans as an intermediary position between the Jews and Gentiles, and that the story of the healing of the Samaritan leper (17.11-19) replaces the Markan Syrophoenician woman story (Mk 7.24-30) as a story of boundary-crossing. Furthermore, in Acts the mission moves out first to the Samaritans, then to God-fearers before including other Gentiles, so that God-fearers can likewise be considered to have an intermediary role in Luke's presentation. This study will also consider why Luke chooses to present Samaritans and Gentiles in this fashion, suggesting that the Lucan motif of the restoration of Israel facilitating the drawing in of the Gentiles is an influential factor.

While a minority of scholars argues that Luke's audience is predominantly Jewish,[5] most argue that it consists mainly of Gentiles.[6] An alternative position is presented by P. F. Esler, who argues that Luke's audience is a mixture of Jewish and Gentile, although he holds that the Gentiles in the community are 'God-fearers' who attended the synagogue. For Esler, Luke portrays nearly all of the Gentile converts in Acts as God-fearers rather than pagan idolators prior to their conversion because this reflects the composition of his own community. Since this portrait of the Gentiles differs in places from Paul's depiction (e.g. 1 Thess 1.9), it would seem that Luke's portrayal is influenced by the circumstances of his community rather than by historical accuracy.[7]

1. *Gentiles and the Gospel of Luke*

As noted at the beginning of this study, the first reference to Gentiles in the Gospel of Luke occurs during the infancy narrative when Simeon proclaims Jesus as God's salvation to the Gentiles and Israel (2.29-32). While Jew and Gentile are both portrayed as recipients of this salvation, the mention of the Gentiles first highlights the inclusion of the Gentiles

5   So, for example, M. Salmon, 'Insider or Outsider? Luke's Relationship with Judaism', in J. B. Tyson (ed.), *Luke–Acts and the Jewish People: Eight Critical Perspectives* (Minneapolis: Augsburg, 1988), pp.76–82.

6   So, for example, L. T. Johnson, *The Gospel of Luke* (SP 3; Collegeville: Liturgical, 1991), p.3; and J. A. Fitzmyer, *The Gospel according to Luke* (AB 28, 28A; 2 vols.; New York: Doubleday, 1981–85), I, pp.57–9.

7   P. F. Esler, *Community and Gospel in Luke–Acts: The Social and Political Motivations of Lukan Theology* (SNTSMS 57; Cambridge: Cambridge University Press, 1987), pp.31–45.

as a special Lucan theme. In the following chapter, Luke adapts his Marcan source, which cites verses from the prophet Isaiah, to include extra verses. In particular, Luke adds 'and all flesh shall see the salvation of God' (Lk. 3.6), which is from Isaiah (Isa. 40.5 LXX) but not included in Mark. As with Simeon's earlier proclamation, Luke is emphasising that salvation extends beyond the Jews.

A key text in regard to Gentiles occurs when Jesus goes to the synagogue in his home town, Nazareth (4.16-30). Again, Luke adapts his Marcan source (Mk 6.1-6), moving the Nazareth visit to the start of Jesus' ministry and providing content for his teaching which is not provided in Mark.[8] These Lucan changes highlight the significance of this text for understanding and interpreting Jesus' ministry. The Lucan Jesus proclaims good news to the poor and release to those who are bound (4.18-19). The ensuing Gospel narrative shows how Jesus fulfils what is announced at this beginning of his ministry. The 'poor' does not only refer to the physically destitute. It can also refer to those who are considered outside the dictates of honourable behaviour (e.g. Zacchaeus in 19.1-10). The release proclaimed by Jesus incorporates physical healing, forgiveness of sins and inclusion.[9] This augurs well for the inclusion of Gentiles.

For the purposes of this study, the words of Jesus after the initial proclamation of 4.18-19 are of particular significance. Here Jesus reminds the people in the synagogue in Nazareth that the prophets Elijah and Elisha ministered to people outside of Israel who were in need (4.25-27; cf. 1 Kgs 17.8-24; 2 Kgs 5.1-19). For Fitzmyer, 'vv. 25-27 provide a justification from the OT for the Christian mission to the Gentiles'.[10] The portrayal in this pericope of Jesus as a prophet (4.24), in line with Elijah and Elisha, suggests that Jesus will also minister to Gentiles as well as Jews. The mission to the Gentiles in Acts, therefore, has its origins in the actions of Jesus. The release proclaimed by Jesus in 4.18 is not only for Jews but also for Gentiles. The inclusion of those on the outside extends to the Gentiles. This understanding is supported by the eclectic nature of the great multitude that comes to hear Jesus and be healed in 6.17-19.

---

8 For the different view that Luke does not use Mark's version, see M. F. Bird, *Jesus and the Origin of the Gentile Mission* (LNTS 331; London: T&T Clark International, 2007), p.65.

9 For more detail on the significance of Jesus' words in 4.18-19, see E. V. Dowling, *Taking Away the Pound: Women, Theology and the Parable of the Pounds in the Gospel of Luke* (LNTS 324; London: T&T Clark International, 2007), pp.102–5; and J. B. Green, *The Theology of the Gospel of Luke* (Cambridge: Cambridge University Press, 1995), pp.78–84.

10 Fitzmyer, *Luke*, I, p.537.

The crowd is described as from 'all Judea, Jerusalem, and the coast of Tyre and Sidon' (6.17). Since Tyre and Sidon are Gentile cities,[11] it is reasonable to assume that the crowd would be a mixture of Jews and Gentiles. Hence, in this summary statement, Jesus is portrayed as ministering to Gentiles as well as Jews, just as the prophets Elijah and Elisha did before him.

A more detailed example of Jesus responding to the healing request of a Gentile is presented in the healing of the Centurion's slave (7.1-10). While it is possible a Centurion (ἑκατοντάρχης) could be Jewish,[12] other elements of this pericope lead to the understanding that this Centurion is a Gentile. In particular, Jesus contrasts the faith of the Centurion with the faith in Israel (7.9). He is also distinguished from Jews by the remarks of the Jewish delegation to Jesus (7.5). That he loves Jews and built the synagogue for them would indicate that he is a Gentile and possibly a God-fearer.[13] It is the faith of the Centurion that enables him, along with his slave, to benefit from God's salvation, embodied in Jesus. This narrative about Jesus and a Gentile Centurion also points ahead to the encounter between Peter and a Gentile Centurion, Cornelius, in Acts 10, which forms a central element in the mission to the Gentiles in Acts.

A key element which distinguishes the Lucan healing of a Centurion's slave from its Matthean equivalent (Mt. 8.5-13), however, is that the Centurion does not meet Jesus face-to-face in Luke. Rather, he sends some Jewish elders to Jesus on his behalf (7.3). This Gentile ministry of Jesus therefore occurs at a distance. While the Centurion is portrayed positively as faith-filled, Luke has removed the direct dealing of Jesus and this Gentile from his narrative.

In the story of the healing of the Gerasene demoniac,[14] Legion (8.26-39; cf. Mk 5.1-20), Jesus encounters Gentiles once again. Most of the features of Luke's story come from his Marcan source. While the healed man is not explicitly described as a Gentile, there is enough information in the pericope to indicate its Gentile flavour. M. Bird claims that 'the story is one of an unclean man (Gentile), in an unclean place (Gentile territory), in an unclean area (tombs), near unclean animals (pigs), in an

---

11   See Bird, *Gentile Mission*, pp.61, 63.

12   Bird, *Gentile Mission*, pp.118–21.

13   Johnson, *Luke*, p.117. While Stenschke considers the Centurion a Gentile, he does not think he is a God-fearer. See C. W. Stenschke, *Luke's Portrait of Gentiles Prior to their Coming to Faith* (WUNT 2.108; Tübingen: Mohr Siebeck, 1999), p.104.

14   Textual difficulties make it uncertain where the story is specifically located. See Fitzmyer, *Luke*, I, pp.736–7, for a discussion of the issues.

unclean state (demonized)'.[15] Once again, a Gentile benefits from Jesus' ministry. The Gerasenes ask Jesus to depart because they are afraid (8.37), so not all Gentiles are portrayed in a positive light. In Mark, the healed man proclaims about Jesus in the Decapolis (Mk 5.20). On the other hand, in Luke the man proclaims throughout the city (Lk. 8.39).[16] The Marcan version suggests that the proclamation is spreading among the Gentiles of the Decapolis, but the proclamation in Luke is not as widespread. So, while there is direct contact between Jesus and the healed man, in the Lucan version the extent of the man's Gentile ministry is decreased.

The Gentile theme emerges again in some of the pronouncements and sayings of the Lucan Jesus. His words of condemnation against Chorazin,[17] Bethsaida and Capernaum (10.13-15; cf. Mt. 11.20-24) portray him as continuing in the tradition of prophetic condemnation of unfaithful Israelite locations. It is Jesus' unfavourable comparison of these cities with Tyre and Sidon, however, which is most pertinent to this study. The Phoenician towns, Tyre and Sidon, are condemned in the prophetic literature (e.g. Isa. 23.1-18; Ezek. 26–28),[18] but Jesus announces that it will be more bearable for them at the time of judgment than for those Jewish towns. People from the Gentile towns of Tyre and Sidon have previously been portrayed as coming to Jesus and being healed (6.17). The pronouncement in 10.13-15 continues this Lucan motif. Gentiles can experience salvation if they respond appropriately to Jesus, the agent of God's salvation. Gentiles appear again in the sayings of Jesus concerning the people of Nineveh and the Queen of the South (11.29-32). The Ninevites who listened to Jonah and repented and the Queen of the South who listened to Solomon will rise at the judgment and condemn this 'evil generation'. Once again, Gentiles are portrayed positively.[19]

Gentiles also feature in several of Jesus' sayings as he gets closer to and then teaches in Jerusalem. The third passion prediction in Luke, as in Mark, declares that Jesus will be handed over to the Gentiles who will mock, spit upon, flog and kill him (Lk. 18.32-33; Mk 10.32-34) with

15   Bird, *Gentile Mission*, p.110. While Bird is referring here to the Marcan version, his comment is also applicable to the Lucan story.

16   See Repschinski, 'Matthew and Luke', p.58.

17   For locating Chorazin as a Galilean town, see Fitzmyer, *Luke*, II, p.853.

18   Bird, *Gentile Mission*, p.63.

19   There may also be references to the situation of Gentiles in three parables (13.18-19; 13.20-21 and 14.15-24). For discussion of these elements, see B. E. Reid, *Parables for Preachers: Year C* (Collegeville: Liturgical, 2000), pp.295–300; and Johnson, *Luke*, p.232.

Luke including that this fulfils what the prophets have written (18.31). According to Repschinski, 'It appears that the Gentiles have become part of the plan of salvation laid out in scripture, recognized by Jesus and explained to his disciples on the road to Emmaus'.[20] In foretelling the destruction of Jerusalem, Jesus asserts that it will be the Gentiles who will be the destroyers (21.24), a detail not in the Marcan version. At the Lucan last supper, Jesus states 'the kings of the Gentiles lord it over them' (22.25). A similar statement appears in Mark, although in a different setting (Mk 10.42). The Lucan passion account describes Pilate sentencing Jesus to death (23.24-25) and other Roman involvement (23.36-37, 47), in line with Jesus' earlier words.

The final reference in the Gospel of Luke that pertains to this study is the risen Jesus' instruction to the disciples that 'repentance and forgiveness of sins' be proclaimed 'to all nations' (24.46-47). These words bring to a climax the Gentile theme in the Gospel of Luke. From the beginning, there are indications that Jesus will bring light to Gentiles as well as Jews (2.32). His words and his healings show openness to Gentiles. At the conclusion of the Gospel, Jesus authorises a mission to 'all nations', thus including Gentile lands. For Luke, then, the mission to Gentiles is based in the actions and words of Jesus.

It is curious, therefore, that two Marcan stories with clear significance for the mission to the Gentiles have not been included in the Lucan Gospel. The first of these is the story of the Syrophoenician woman (Mk 7.24-30; cf. Mt. 15.21-28). Within the story, barriers of religion, ethnicity, gender and demonisation are traversed as the Gentile woman obtains healing for her daughter. Moreover, the woman matches, if not betters, Jesus in her response (Mk 7.27-28). The symbolic imagery of Gentiles being nourished by the bread of the Jews affirms the inclusion of the Gentiles into the early communities of believers. While Matthew also includes a version of this story, Luke does not. This may be because it is part of the so-called great omission, or because a woman bettering Jesus in a verbal challenge does not fit Luke's characterisation of women.[21] It will be argued below, however, that Luke's story of the Samaritan leper serves a similar purpose in regard to crossing the boundaries of religion and impurity. The whole story of Lk. 17.11-19 points to the boundaries that are being crossed in Jesus' proclamation of the good news. Like the Syrophoenician woman, the Samaritan leper

20   Repschinski, 'Matthew and Luke', p.58.
21   For discussion of Luke's characterisation of women, see Dowling, *Taking Away the Pound*, pp.119–85.

finds himself at the feet of Jesus (Mk 7.25; Lk. 17.16). In a sense, Luke replaces the Marcan boundary-crossing story of the Syrophoenician woman with one involving a Samaritan.[22]

Another key Marcan story with Gentile overtones to be omitted in Luke is the second feeding story (Mk 8.1-10). With Gentile boundaries crossed in the Syrophoenician woman story, the way is opened in the Marcan Gospel for a feeding story with Eucharistic overtones to take place in Gentile territory.[23] The combined effect of these two Marcan stories is highly significant for the Gentile mission in Mark, yet to suit his own purposes Luke chooses not to include them. The overall result of Luke's adaptation of his sources is that, within the Gospel of Luke, Gentiles are clearly announced as being included in salvation and Jesus ministers to some Gentiles, but, at the same time, his interactions with Gentiles are far more limited and given less focus.

2. *Samaritans and the Gospel of Luke*

Before exploring the portrayal of Samaritans in the Gospel of Luke, it is important to consider the debated issue of whether or not Samaritans are regarded as Gentiles. Some class Samaritans as non-Jews and implicitly include them with the Gentiles.[24] J. Jervell challenges this thinking, arguing that Luke considers the Samaritans to be Jews. He writes, 'If Luke regards the Samaritans as Gentiles, why has he singled out a particular group of Gentiles? There is no support in the text for understanding the Samaritans as Gentiles or the missionary activity in Samaria as a transition to a purely Gentile mission'.[25] For Jervell, the Samaritans are 'Jews who have gone astray'.[26]

Words of the Lucan Jesus concerning the Samaritan leper in Lk. 17.18, however, might challenge Jervell's understanding here. Jesus refers to

22   For a discussion of other Marcan healings in Gentile territory which are not included in the Lucan Gospel (Mk 7.31-37; 8.22-26; and 9.14-29), see Iverson, *Gentiles*, pp.57–125.

23   For a strong argument that this feeding story takes place in Gentile territory, see Iverson, *Gentiles*, pp.67–9.

24   See, for instance, Stenschke, *Luke's Portrait*, pp.111–12.

25   J. Jervell, 'The Lost Sheep of the House of Israel: The Understanding of the Samaritans in Luke–Acts', in J. Jervell, *Luke and the People of God: A New Look at Luke–Acts* (Minneapolis: Augsburg, 1972), pp.113–32 (117).

26   Jervell, 'Lost Sheep', p.124. For Samaritans as part of Israel, see also A. Weissenrieder, *Images of Illness in the Gospel of Luke: Insights of Ancient Medical Texts* (WUNT 2.164; Tübingen: Mohr Siebeck, 2003), p.206.

the Samaritan as a foreigner (ἀλλογενής). While this is the only occurrence of this word in the New Testament, the term appeared in the inscription on the Temple barrier between the Court of the Gentiles and the space for Jews only, forbidding entrance of any foreigner.[27] The use of ἀλλογενής by Jesus in 17.18 would suggest that Luke is making a definite distinction between Samaritans and Jews.[28] At the same time, since Samaritans and Jews shared a common heritage, Samaritans may not be as 'foreign' to the Jews as others. In a sense, Samaritans form an intermediate position between Jews and Gentiles.[29] As we shall see below, the healing of the Samaritan leper (17.11-19) becomes an important example of crossing boundaries.

At the beginning of the Lucan Jesus' journey to Jerusalem, Samaritan villagers reject him. Despite this, Jesus prevents any attempt by James and John at retribution (9.51-56). This is the first reference to Samaritans in the Gospel of Luke. The mission of the seventy (10.1-12)[30] follows soon after and it is likely that the mission includes Samaria among its destinations.[31] The instructions by Jesus imply that the disciples may encounter some hostility on their mission and the direction to eat what is set before them raises the question about the fulfilment of Jewish purity laws in relation to the food they receive.[32] This may point ahead also to the issue in Acts 10 about unclean foods.

Further on in Luke 10, a Samaritan features in the teaching of Jesus (10.25-37), continuing the Samaritan presence in the Lucan Gospel. Both

27   See D. Hamm, 'What the Samaritan Leper Sees: The Narrative Christology of Luke 17:11-19', *CBQ* 56 (1994), pp.273–87 (284); and J. H. Moulton and G. Milligan, *The Vocabulary of the Greek Testament: Illustrated from the Papyri and Other Non-Literary Sources* (London: Hodder & Stoughton, 1930), p.23.

28   For second-century BCE accusations that the Samaritans were 'foreigners', see M. Kartveit, *The Origin of the Samaritans* (VTSup 128; Leiden: Brill, 2009), p.360. Against this understanding, A. Weissenrieder argues that 'one who is different' is the best translation for ἀλλογενής in 17.18. She claims this leper is different because he is the one who comes to faith. See Weissenrieder, *Images of Illness*, pp.203–9.

29   For an argument that Luke portrays Samaritans as neither fully Jews nor fully Gentiles, see V. J. Samkutty, *The Samaritan Mission in Acts* (LNTS 328; London: T&T Clark International, 2006), pp.196–7.

30   It is debatable as to whether the number here is seventy or seventy-two. For a discussion of the textual evidence, see B. M. Metzger, *A Textual Commentary on the Greek New Testament* (Stuttgart: Deutsche Bibelgesellschaft, 2nd edn, 1994), p.126.

31   See D. Ravens, *Luke and the Restoration of Israel* (JSNTSup 119; Sheffield: Sheffield Academic, 1995), p.82.

32   See the discussions in Repschinski, 'Matthew and Luke', pp.60–1; and Johnson, *Luke*, p.170.

this and the later pericope featuring a Samaritan (17.11-19) present a far more favourable portrait of Samaritans than that of their initial rejection of Jesus (9.52-53). Jesus tells the Parable of the Good Samaritan (10.25-37) in response to the questions of a lawyer whose motive is to test Jesus (10.25). The parable challenges the thinking of the lawyer and, more broadly, Jesus' Jewish audience. While a Jewish priest and Levite each see the wounded man but fail to help him (10.30-32), perhaps because of concerns about ritual impurity,[33] a Samaritan pours out his oil and wine to heal the man's wounds and provides money to cover his expenses (10.33-35).[34]

A key aspect of the Samaritan's characterisation is that when he sees the wounded man he is moved with compassion (10.33). The Greek verb used here, σπλαγχνίζομαι, appears only two other times in the Gospel of Luke – to describe Jesus' response when he sees the widow of Nain (7.13) and, in another parable, to describe the father's response when he sees his returning son (15.20). The father images God's welcome of the lost (cf. 15.1-32). Hence, the Samaritan models the compassion of God as embodied in Jesus. Moreover, Jesus tells his Jewish audience to act as the Samaritan does (10.37).

In this uniquely Lucan parable, the Samaritan is clearly distinguished from and contrasted with the Jewish characters, the priest and Levite.[35] The outsider is the one to be emulated. As discussed previously, a Samaritan could perhaps be considered not fully Jew or Gentile, but rather someone in-between these categories. Luke highlights here that it is the response of a person rather than their label of 'Jew', 'Samaritan', or 'Gentile' which is of ultimate importance (cf. 10.13-15).

As mentioned earlier, a Samaritan features in another Lucan story, that of the healing of the ten lepers (17.11-19). The geographical setting of the story is the region between Samaria and Galilee (17.11).[36] Comparing this with 13.22, as Jesus heads towards Jerusalem, D. Hamm claims that this setting 'suggests that Jesus' entourage has made no progress southward whatsoever. Clearly, then, Luke's references to Samaritans and

---

33   For a discussion of the dilemma which the prospect of ritual impurity would raise for the priest, in particular, see K. Bailey, *Poet and Peasant and through Peasant Eyes: A Literary-Cultural Approach to the Parables of Luke. Combined Edition* (Grand Rapids: Eerdmans, 1983), pp.43–7.

34   For oil and wine being used for healing purposes, see Reid, *Parables*, p.115.

35   Repschinski, 'Matthew and Luke', p.62 n.39 claims that 'the Samaritans in the Gospel are portrayed as a foil to show up Jewish deficiencies'.

36   Weissenrieder concludes that the area between Samaria and Galilee in which Jesus is travelling is the Jezreel Valley. See Weissenrieder, *Images of Illness*, pp.187–92.

Samaria are made for reasons other than tracing itinerary.'[37] This story takes place in a border region. Such a setting symbolically points to and opens up other boundaries which are to be crossed in the course of the narrative.

The approach of ten lepers, albeit keeping their distance, towards Jesus (17.12) and the subsequent healing of the lepers by Jesus overcomes the boundary of separation which the Torah prescribes for those with leprosy (Lev. 13.46). The later identification of one of the lepers as a Samaritan (17.16) introduces another barrier into the social context, that of the problematic historical relationship between Jews and Samaritans. While the identity of the other nine lepers is not specified, Jesus' words of approval about a 'foreigner' (17.18) suggest some, if not all, of the other nine are Jews. It would appear that the barrier between Samaritans and Jews has been broken down by the needs of living with leprosy.[38] Jesus' healing ministry also traverses this divide between Jews and Samaritans. The gender of the nine is not specified, leaving open the possibility that gender boundaries have also been crossed by the lepers.

A key element of the story is the return and praise of God by the one leper, identified later as a Samaritan (17.15-16).[39] That this Samaritan praises God with a loud voice ($\phi\omega\nu\hat{\eta}\varsigma$ $\mu\epsilon\gamma\acute{\alpha}\lambda\eta\varsigma$, 17.15)[40] and falls at the feet of Jesus (17.16) indicates that he recognises God's action and presence in Jesus.[41] Similarly, in 13.10-13 when Jesus in the synagogue lays his hands on the woman who is bent over and she is healed, she praises God, recognising God's action in Jesus.

As D. Hamm and J. Green both note, the healed Samaritan praising God at the feet of Jesus overcomes the divide of correct place of worship among Samaritans and Jews.[42] Across the divide of whether to worship in Jerusalem or on Mount Gerizim, this Samaritan, just as the woman in the

37   Hamm, 'Samaritan Leper', p.276.

38   Weissenrieder argues instead that Jews and Samaritans co-existed in the Jezreel Valley. See Weissenrieder, *Images of Illness*, p.192.

39   Again, the response of the Jews in the story is compared unfavourably to that of a Samaritan. See n.35 above.

40   The same words ($\phi\omega\nu\acute{\eta}$ $\mu\epsilon\gamma\acute{\alpha}\lambda\eta$) are used on five other occasions in the Gospel of Luke (4.33; 8.28; 19.37; 23.23, 46). In particular, the last instance occurs when Jesus, from the cross, cries out with a loud voice in a final expression of trust. See B. E. Reid, *Choosing the Better Part? Women in the Gospel of Luke* (Collegeville: Liturgical, 1996), p.72.

41   Repschinski ('Matthew and Luke', p.62) states that the leper 'knows that the place to give glory to God is at the feet of Jesus'.

42   See Hamm, 'Samaritan Leper', p.284; and J. B. Green, *The Gospel of Luke* (NICNT; Grand Rapids: Eerdmans, 1997), p.621.

synagogue had done earlier, recognises Jesus as the locus of God's action. Within the Gospel of Luke, then, both a Jew and a Samaritan worship God's presence in Jesus.

As outlined earlier, differing views within the scholarship perceive Samaritans as either errant Jews or Gentiles and, in a sense, the status of Samaritans is a border position between that of Jews and Gentiles. The coming to faith of the Samaritan leper and his endorsement by Jesus bridges the distance between Jews and Gentiles. Green states, 'Luke has narrated this episode in a way that seems deliberately to challenge notions of the privileged position of the Jewish people within the redemptive economy of God'.[43] The story highlights that Jesus' ministry crosses boundaries and is thus an important stage in the outward movement of the good news to the Gentiles which is narrated in Acts. Just as the story of the Syrophoenician woman in the Gospel of Mark functions as a story of boundary-crossing in the Marcan narrative, the Samaritan leper story functions as a story of boundary-crossing in the Lucan narrative, traversing the divide between Jews and Gentiles.

We can see then that the Samaritan presence in the Gospel of Luke is significant. In two key pericopes, Samaritans are the models to be followed. A pivotal Gentile boundary-crossing story in the Marcan Gospel is omitted by Luke, who instead includes a boundary-crossing story featuring a Samaritan. There seems to be a definite intention by Luke to have a Samaritan presence in the Gospel which replaces some of the Marcan focus on Gentiles. Having explored the portrayal of Gentiles and Samaritans in the Lucan Gospel, it is important now to consider the situation in the second volume of the Lucan narrative. Does the book of Acts give any indication as to why Luke might present the Samaritans and Gentiles in this way?

3. *Samaritans and Gentiles in the Book of Acts*[44]

The end of the Gospel of Luke leads directly into the beginning of the book of Acts. While the group whom Jesus addresses at the end of the Gospel is wider than the eleven (Lk. 24.33-49), the focus is clearly on the eleven or reformed twelve again at the start of Acts (Acts 1.13, 21-26). Jesus' commission to them, 'you will be my witnesses in Jerusalem, in all Judea and Samaria, and to the ends of the earth' (1.8), has

---

43   Green, *Gospel of Luke*, p.620.

44   Biblical references in this section will be to the book of Acts unless otherwise specified.

overtones of the commission of the Servant of God in Isaiah: 'It is too light a thing that you should be my servant to raise up the tribes of Jacob and to restore the survivors of Israel; I will give you as a light to the nations, that my salvation may reach to the end of the earth' (Isa. 49.6; cf. Acts 13.47).

This allusion to Isa. 49.6 gives crucial insight into Luke's theological purpose here. For Luke, the twelve apostles, as the commissioned witnesses, will restore the twelve tribes of Israel and facilitate God's salvation, reaching out to include the Gentiles, in fact 'to the ends of the earth'. If Luke understands the Samaritans to be the descendants of the northern tribes, as D. Ravens argues, then they become a vital element in Luke's schema. The restoration of Israel requires Samaritans to be included.[45] He states, 'Without the return of the Samaritans there could be no restored Israel and without an Israel in the process of restoration there would be nothing for the Gentiles to enter'.[46] This accounts for the importance given to Samaritans in the Lucan Gospel as a forerunner to the Samaritan mission in Acts. The coming to faith of the Samaritans is an essential part of the restoration of Israel.

Acts 1.8 summarises the way that the narrative in Acts will unfold. The witness will begin in Jerusalem before extending to all Judea and Samaria and beyond, as far as Rome. In this way, the mission to Samaria appears as an important intermediate step before the mission to the Gentiles. Before the beginning of the mission to Samaria is narrated, however, a further indication of the prominence given by Luke to Samaritans is presented within the speech of Stephen (Acts 7). Stephen reports that Israel's ancestors were buried in a tomb in Shechem, a tomb bought by Abraham (7.15-16). This appears to be a conflation of aspects of two burial legends (Gen. 23.1-20; 33.19). The resultant version announced by Stephen links Israel's ancestors to Samaritan soil and thus 'seems to continue the Lukan narrative's inclusion of the Samaritans among the favored people of God'.[47]

Within Acts, the preaching in Samaria begins with Philip proclaiming the word there after fleeing persecution in Jerusalem. His proclamation is embraced by the Samaritans (8.4-8), though it is the later presence of Peter and John, two of the twelve, which gives authority to the mission in

---

45   Ravens, *Restoration of Israel*, pp.96–108; see also Samkutty, *Samaritan Mission*, p.209.

46   Ravens, *Restoration of Israel*, p.106.

47   F. S. Spencer, *Acts* (Sheffield: Sheffield Academic, 1997), p.73. See also Samkutty, *Samaritan Mission*, p.68.

Samaria. When Peter and John pray for the people of Samaria and lay their hands on them, the people receive the Holy Spirit (8.14-17). Peter and John continue to proclaim the good news in many Samaritan villages, with the imperfect tense of εὐηγγελίζοντο indicating the repeated nature of their action (8.25). With this Samaritan mission, 'the dividing wall of hostility between Samaritans and Jews has been officially broken down'.[48]

Philip's missionary activity continues with his baptism of the Ethiopian eunuch (8.26-40).[49] The eunuch is introduced as a court official of the queen of the Ethiopians. That he is in charge of her treasury indicates that he has an important position within the court (8.27). Whether the eunuch is a Jew or Gentile is a debated issue. We learn that the eunuch is reading the prophet Isaiah on his return home from a pilgrimage to Jerusalem (8.27-28). This suggests that he is either a Jew or a God-fearer who is familiar with the Jewish Scriptures. It is his piety which is clearly identified and not his religious background, however.

If the eunuch is a Gentile, then he is the first Gentile convert portrayed in Acts rather than the centurion, Cornelius, whose conversion by Peter is described in Acts 10.[50] Regarding the beginning of the Gentile mission in Acts, Johnson queries whether Luke intends for the reader to understand the conversion of the eunuch as the beginning of the Gentile mission. He concludes that the detailed description of the Cornelius story and its consequence (Acts 10–15) indicates that Luke is representing this as 'a fundamentally new step', while the eunuch story is 'part of the "ingathering of the scattered people" of Israel'.[51] Thus, while the text does not specify the faith of the Ethiopian eunuch, the overall development of the narrative in Acts suggests that Luke intends the reader to understand him as symbolic of the remnant to be gathered in by God

48 Spencer, *Acts*, p.86.

49 Samkutty argues that 6.3; 8.4-13, 26-40; and 21.8-9 indicate that Luke had access to a series of stories concerning Philip. See Samkutty, *Samaritan Mission*, p.27.

50 L. Schottroff suggests this may be the case. See L. Schottroff, *Lydia's Impatient Sisters: A Feminist Social History of Early Christianity* (Louisville: Westminster John Knox, 1995), p.13. Repschinski also argues the eunuch is a Gentile but claims that the Gentile mission in Acts begins at 10.1 rather than here. See Repschinski, 'Matthew and Luke', p.62. Regarding the eunuch, Spencer states that 'ethnically, he appears to occupy some border position between Jew and Gentile'. See Spencer, *Acts*, p.91.

51 L. T. Johnson, *The Acts of the Apostles* (SP 5; Collegeville: Liturgical, 1992), p.159.

(cf. Isa. 11.11).[52] This is further evidence that Israel is being restored, leaving the way open for the mission to the Gentiles, beginning with the conversion of Cornelius.

This is an important point. As we have seen earlier, the Lucan Gospel portrays Jesus as ministering to Gentiles and Samaritans. It is in the book of Acts, however, that the formal mission of the early Church to the Gentiles is portrayed. The emphasis given to the Cornelius story in Acts indicates that the earlier mission to the Samaritans and the conversion of the Ethiopian should be considered as part of an essential overture to the mission to the Gentiles. With Israel's restoration, the apostles are indeed bearing witness in 'Samaria, and to the ends of the earth' (1.8).

Unlike the Ethiopian, Cornelius is specifically identified as a God-fearer and a Gentile (10.2, 22, 28) and the extended narrative repeatedly makes reference to the fact that Peter is with Gentiles when he stays with Cornelius (10.28, 45; 11.2-3, 18). Thus, there is no ambiguity in regard to the religious background of Cornelius and his household and friends. That the Holy Spirit is poured out on the Gentiles as well as the circumcised (10.44-45) authenticates this mission to the Gentiles.

The setting of the Cornelius story in Caesarea (10.1) is significant here. Caesarea, a port city, was geographically situated in Samaria. It was built under Herod the Great to honour the Roman emperor and was thus Roman space. Hence, the Gentile, Cornelius, lives in a Gentile city in Samaria.[53] That the mission to the Gentiles begins within the area of Samaria is a further example that the apostles are bearing witness to 'Samaria, and to the ends of the earth' (1.8). Significantly, Samaria is again shown to be an important stage in the movement to the Gentiles.

Additional to the conversion of the Gentiles in this pericope is Peter's declaration that no person or food should be declared unclean (10.28). Luke emphasises that it is the Spirit who gives Peter this insight (10.19-20), leading him to offer hospitality to his three visitors (10.23) and later to stay with converted Gentiles (10.48). Peter understands that God has approved table-fellowship between Jew and Gentile.[54] For Esler, the importance of the Cornelius episode within Luke's overall narrative should not be underestimated. The episode is important for legitimating

---

52   Johnson, *Acts*, p.158.

53   V. Lawson, 'Tabitha of Joppa: Disciple, Prophet and Biblical Prototype for Contemporary Religious Life', in R. M. Chennattu and M. L. Coloe (eds.), *Transcending Boundaries: Contemporary Readings of the New Testament* (Biblioteca di Scienze Religiose 187; Rome: Libreria Ateneo Salesiano, 2005), pp.281–92 (288).

54   Esler, *Community and Gospel*, p.94.

table-fellowship between Jews and Gentiles, not just the inclusion of Gentiles within communities of believers. For a Lucan community composed of Gentiles and Jews, as Esler suggests, Luke is opening the way for Eucharistic meals to be shared by all believers.[55]

The subsequent question addressed to Peter by the believers in Jerusalem in 11.1-3 indicates that it is Peter's eating with Gentiles rather than his conversion of them which is contentious.[56] The tension between this understanding of table-fellowship and that of some of the believers from Judea leads eventually to the so-called Jerusalem council (15.1-35) where it is debated as to whether Gentile believers need to become Jews.[57]

In the meantime, Paul and Barnabas are commissioned to preach in various regions (13.1-4), beginning their preaching in the synagogues (13.5, 14, 43) but also preaching to Gentiles (13.48). The words of 13.47 have overtones once again of Isa. 49.6 and consequently also of Acts 1.8. This mission to the Gentiles is fulfilling the commission to the Gentiles given by the risen Jesus to the apostles (1.8). The three versions of the conversion of Saul/Paul each include an account of God's authorisation and sending of Paul to the Gentiles (9.15; 22.21; 26.17-18). Furthermore, at the council at Jerusalem God's actions in the work of Peter and Paul are emphasised (15.7-8, 12). Peter's announcement that God had chosen him to be the one who would bring the good news to the Gentiles (15.7) confirms that Luke intends Peter's conversion of Cornelius to be the beginning of the Gentile mission. Luke is clearly making the point that the mission of the early Church to the Gentiles, initiated by Peter and carried on by Paul in particular, is God's work and God's initiative. Comparisons with information in the Pauline letters (e.g. Gal. 1–2) suggest that there may be doubts about the historical accuracy of the Lukan description in Acts 15. Luke's priority is theological rather than historical.[58]

The essential criterion for a believer is faith, so that Gentiles as well as Jews can experience salvation (15.7-11). James' words at the council, drawing on Amos 9.11-12 (LXX), suggest that the house of David will

55   Esler, *Community and Gospel*, pp.96–7.

56   See Repschinski, 'Matthew and Luke', p.63; also Esler, *Community and Gospel*, p.93.

57   Esler argues that it is the issue of table-fellowship between Jew and Gentile in the Eucharistic meals that is behind the teaching of 15.1. See Esler, *Community and Gospel*, p.98.

58   See the discussions in Esler, *Community and Gospel*, pp.97–9; and Johnson, *Acts*, pp.269–70.

be restored and will draw in all others of faith, including Gentiles (15.14-18).[59] Once again, the restoration of Israel is an important motif, vital to the inclusion of the Gentiles. James then makes a key pronouncement that Gentile believers should not be burdened and only be required to observe four prohibitions which would enable them to be in communion with the Jewish believers (15.19-21).[60] As a result of this decision, the mission of Paul and others to the Gentiles flourishes and constitutes the majority of the remainder of the book of Acts.

The Antioch community rejoice when they learn of the decisions of the council (15.30-31), reinforcing that the four prohibitions announced by James are not to be considered burdensome. Given that these decisions are very likely not historical (cf. Gal. 2.1-14), a key matter is why Luke would include these prohibitions within his narrative. Esler's understanding of the mixed Jewish and Gentile composition of Luke's community is an important factor in addressing this issue. It would seem that Luke here is addressing and legitimising the practice of table-fellowship between Gentiles and Jews within his own community. According to Esler, 'The fourfold prohibition quoted by Luke in Acts 15 probably represents the core of a compromise agreement reached between Jewish Christians and Gentile Christians'.[61] Hence, the composition and nature of Luke's community impacts on the way he shapes his narrative.

This is also reinforced by the portrayal of the Gentile converts in Acts. As discussed earlier, Cornelius is specifically labelled a God-fearer (10.2, 22). In Antioch of Pisidia, Paul addresses Jews and God-fearers in the synagogue (13.16, 26, 43). According to Acts, Paul's common practice is to preach in the synagogue in each place (13.5, 14; 14.1; 17.1-2, 10, 17; 18.4, 19; 19.8). The Gentiles who hear his teaching in the synagogues can therefore be considered God-fearers (14.1; 17.4, 12, 17; 18.4).[62] That most of the Gentile converts are specifically identified as being God-fearers further supports Esler's theory that Luke shapes the story to address the circumstances of his own community, a mixture of Jews and Gentiles who are mainly God-fearers.[63]

---

59   Johnson, *Acts*, p.271.
60   Johnson, *Acts*, pp.272-3.
61   Esler, *Community and Gospel*, p.106.
62   Titius Justus is described as a God-fearer who lives next to the synagogue (18.7). Though his conversion is not explicitly narrated, he may be included in the description of the many Corinthians who hear Paul and are converted (18.8).
63   Esler, *Community and Gospel*, pp.42-4.

In Philippi, Paul and his companions go on a Sabbath to a house of prayer (προσευχή) which is outside the city gate (16.13). Drawing on the writings of Philo and Josephus, as well as inscriptional material, I. Richter Reimer argues convincingly that this προσευχή can be understood as a synagogue.[64] Thus, in Philippi, Paul continues his usual practice of teaching in synagogues. Lydia's identification as a worshipper of God (16.14) also continues the portrayal of Gentile converts as being God-fearers.[65] Lydia prevails upon Paul and his companions to stay at her house (16.15), suggesting that this is another example where Jews and Gentiles will share table-fellowship.[66]

While Gentiles who are converted in Acts are often portrayed as God-fearers before their conversion, not every Gentile convert is portrayed in this way. No faith background of the jailer is presented (16.25-34), for instance, so that we cannot assume that he and his household were God-fearers before their meeting with Paul. In Athens, Paul preaches in the public arena and attracts some who become believers. These include Dionysius, the Areopagite, a woman named Damaris and others (17.34) who are not first portrayed as God-fearers. A general statement also indicates that many Jewish and Gentile residents of Ephesus come to believe (19.17-20). Paul's final announcement in the book of Acts is directed to the leading Jews in Rome: 'Let it be known to you then that this salvation of God has been sent to the Gentiles; they will listen' (28.28). This brings the mission to the Gentiles to a climax. The proclaimed message has indeed reached 'the ends of the earth' (cf. 1.8). Furthermore, it is clear that Luke–Acts ends on a hopeful note and that the hope is triggered by the response of the Gentiles.

Within the book of Acts it is apparent that the mission to the Gentiles develops in stages. After the church in Jerusalem is persecuted and scattered throughout Judea and Samaria (8.1), the mission to Samaria is described. This becomes an intermediate step before the mission to the Gentiles, which begins within Samaria (in Caesarea) and with the conversion of a God-fearer. The first Gentile converts are God-fearers before other Gentile converts are included. In a sense, the God-fearers, like the Samaritans, could also be said to form an intermediate position between Jews and other Gentiles.

---

64 I. Richter Reimer, *Women in the Acts of the Apostles: A Feminist Liberation Perspective* (Minneapolis: Fortress, 1995), pp.85–2.

65 See the detailed discussion in Richter Reimer, *Women*, pp.93–8, which can be used to counter Johnson's claim that it is impossible to determine whether she is a Gentile or a Jew (Johnson, *Acts*, p.293).

66 Esler, *Community and Gospel*, p.41.

4. *Conclusions*

From the beginning of his Gospel, Luke highlights salvation as open to both Jews and Gentiles. Faith is the essential criterion for benefitting from God's salvation. Luke, however, puts limits on the level of interaction between Jesus and the Gentiles in comparison with his sources, especially Mark. Instead, Luke introduces interaction between Jesus and Samaritans into his Gospel. In particular, the healing of the Samaritan leper (17.11-19) serves as a boundary-crossing narrative, functioning in a similar manner to the Marcan Syrophoenician woman story (Mk 7.24-30), which is omitted by Luke. In Luke's second volume, the good news is proclaimed to Jews, Samaritans, God-fearers and, ultimately, other Gentiles. This progression of the mission to the Gentiles fulfils the proclamation to preach 'in Jerusalem, in all Judea and Samaria, and to the ends of the earth' (Acts 1.8).

The Lucan motif of the restoration of Israel enabling the drawing-in of all peoples may be a decisive factor in why Luke chooses to portray the mission to the Gentiles in this way. Since the inclusion of the Samaritans is a key element within the restoration of Israel, Luke emphasises the Samaritans and their inclusion in both the Gospel and Acts before he describes the official mission to the Gentiles. This also explains the limited interaction between Jesus and Gentiles. The Lucan Jesus is open to Gentiles and his final words pronounce that the Gentiles are to be included in the proclamation of the good news, but this proclamation only takes place in Acts after the formal mission to the Samaritans.

Like the Samaritans, God-fearers form an intermediate position between Jews and pagan idolators in Acts. Again, this would seem to be a Lucan construction to suit his own purposes. He may have been influenced by a significant God-fearer presence in his own mixed community of Jews and Gentiles. Issues of table fellowship within his own community are likely to have also shaped his writing. The fact that Luke develops his narrative over two volumes rather than one is another element which influences his treatment. He can allow his theology to continue to evolve in the mission of the early Church. The final product is a uniquely Lucan portrayal of Gentiles.

Chapter 13

GENTILES IN THE GOSPEL OF JOHN:
NARRATIVE POSSIBILITIES – JOHN 12.12-43

Mary L. Coloe

The Gospel of John poses a particular problem when considering the
early Christian missionary movement beyond the world of Judaism and
into the world of the Gentiles. The problem in the Gospel of John is that
Jesus is never seen outside the borders of first-century Palestine; he
travels in Galilee, in Samaria and in Judea but there is no journey to
the Decapolis or to Tyre and Sidon as we find in the Synoptic Gospels.[1]
J. A. T. Robinson argued very strongly that in John there is no presence
of a Gentile mission. He states, 'The remarkable fact is that there is not a
single reference to "the Gentiles" in the entire book. The Fourth Gospel,
with the Johannine Epistles, is the only major work in the New Testament in which the term τὰ ἔθνη never occurs.'[2]

The only two pericopes that some scholars consider represent the
future Gentile mission of the church are the cure of the royal official at
Cana (4.46-54),[3] and the coming of 'some Greeks' to Jesus' disciples and
their request to see Jesus (12.20). In the present study, I will focus on the
second episode using narrative-critical methods, to examine if these
'Greeks' could be Gentiles and, if so, what significance this might have

1   For a listing of the numerous Synoptic references to non-Jews, see J. A. T.
Robinson, 'The Destination and Purpose of St John's Gospel', *NTS* 6 (1959–60),
pp.117–31 (119).
2   Robinson, 'Destination', p.124.
3   The structural context of Jn 4.46-54, which concludes the 'Cana to Cana'
section, suggests, though not necessarily demands, that the royal official is a Gentile.
A very thorough discussion of this section can be found in F. J. Moloney, 'From
Cana to Cana (John 2:1–4:54) and the Fourth Evangelist's Concept of Correct (and
Incorrect) Faith', *Salesianum* 40 (1978), pp.817–43. Robinson argues that the
official, called a βασιλικός, 'was in all likelihood a Herodian'; see Robinson, 'Destination', p.120.

in the Gospel narrative. In the light of these considerations, the present study will then conclude with a discussion of the Johannine community and the claims made that this community included both Jews and Gentiles.

1. *The Greeks (John 12.20)*

The first question to be considered in discussing Jn 12.20 is the identity of these Ἕλληνες. Are they Greek-speaking Jews from the Diaspora who have come up to the feast, or are they Gentiles, who in some way have been attracted to Judaism?[4] Robinson states categorically that they are not Gentiles, and that the only certainty that can be deduced is that they spoke Greek rather than Aramaic.[5] Robinson's position on the identity of the Ἕλληνες is part of a wider discussion of the purpose of the Gospel, which he considers is written to convince Jewish believers in Judea to remain faithful under pressure from the synagogue, and also to make an appeal to Jews in the Diaspora.[6] In Robinson's view, the Gospel emerges from 'the heart of southern Palestinian Judaism',[7] and he proposes an early dating for the Gospel.[8] Others have disputed the

---

4   As part of Robinson's argument that the term Ἕλληνες must refer to Jews, is the fact that they have come up to Jerusalem to worship at the feast ('Destination', p.120). Against this Cohen discusses seven ways a Gentile can show affection or attraction to Judaism, with only the seventh being a full conversion. See S. J. D. Cohen, 'Crossing the Boundary and Becoming a Jew', *HTR* 82 (1989), pp.13–33. See also P. F. Stuehrenberg, 'Proselyte', in *ABD*, V, pp.503–5.

5   Robinson, 'Destination', p.121. Among Johannine scholars, the majority view is that the term Ἕλληνες does mean a non-Jew, whether a proselyte or a God-Fearer. According to Dodd, 'they stand for the great world at large, primarily the Hellenistic world which is his (the evangelist's) own mission field'. See C. H. Dodd, *The Interpretation of the Fourth Gospel* (Cambridge: Cambridge University Press, 1953), p.371. For a listing of other scholars who take this position, see H. B. Kossen, 'Who Were the Greeks of John XII.20?', in J. N. Sevenster (ed.), *Studies in John Presented to Dr. J. N. Sevenster on the Occasion of his Seventieth Birthday* (NovTSup 24, Leiden: Brill, 1970), pp.97–110 (97, esp. nn.1–4).

6   Robinson, 'Destination', p.131.

7   Robinson, 'Destination', p.124.

8   Robinson argues for four stages in the development of the Johannine Gospel and Epistles: Stage 1, shaping the Gospel in dialogue with Palestinian Judaism (30–50 CE); Stage 2, a first edition of the Gospel in Ephesus (50–55 CE); Stage 3, the Epistles (60–65 CE); Stage 4, a final edition of the Gospel with Prologue and Epilogue (65 CE+). See J. A. T. Robinson, *The Priority of John* (London: SCM, 1985), p.67 n.150.

details of all Robinson's claims and so the present study will not directly contest his view.[9] Rather, I will look at the broader narrative context of 12.20 to see if it may shed light on the identity and significance of the term Ἕλληνες at this point in the Gospel.

a. *Narrative Context*

The statement about some Greeks coming to see Jesus occurs in a long section describing Jesus' entry into Jerusalem and various responses to this event (12.12-43). Following this is a brief conclusion to the first part of the Gospel (vv. 44-50). I divide this passage into three sections using the explanatory comments by the narrator to indicate the conclusion of each section:

Section 1.	The entry into Jerusalem – the crowd and Jesus' response (vv. 12-14) (narrator's explanation vv. 15-18)
Section 2.	Various responses – the Pharisees, the Greeks, Jesus, the Father, the crowd (vv. 19-32) (narrator's explanation v. 33)
Section 3.	Concluding reactions – the crowd and Jesus' response (vv. 34-36) (narrator's explanation vv. 37-43)

b. *Section 1. The Entry into Jerusalem: vv. 12-18*

The Johannine account of Jesus' entry into Jerusalem is noticeably different to the Synoptic accounts. In the Synoptics, Jesus initiates the event by sending disciples to procure a donkey for him to ride into Jerusalem (Mk 11.1; Mt. 21.2; Lk. 19.30). The crowd then respond to Jesus' actions by spreading cloaks on the road, waving branches and shouting acclamations. This sequence is reversed in John. The crowd, motivated by the raising of Lazarus (12.9), takes branches and goes out to meet Jesus, crying 'Hosanna! Blessed is he who comes in the name of the Lord, even the King of Israel' (12.13). It is in response to the crowds that Jesus finds a young donkey and sits on it. The narrator then offers two explanations about this event: first, in terms of what is written in the Scriptures, which, according to the narrator, the disciples did not understand or remember until after Jesus was glorified (12.16); second, the crowd have acted as they did because of the sign of Lazarus (12.18).

---

9 See the cogent arguments of Kossen, 'Who Were the Greeks?', pp.97–110; and J. Beutler, 'Greeks come to see Jesus (John 12:20f)', *Bib* 71 (1990), pp.333–47 (342–3).

To understand the meaning of this event, I propose examining the explanations given by the narrator,[10] through the Scripture citation, 'Fear not, daughter of Zion; behold your king is coming, sitting on an ass's colt' (v. 15). This citation, drawing on both Zephaniah and Zechariah, repeats the title 'king' from the crowd's acclamations. On the lips of the crowd, the title 'king' expresses Jewish nationalist hopes such as at the time of David or the Maccabees.[11] The crowd cites Ps. 118.26, 'Blessed is he who comes in the name of the Lord', and then adds their own acclamation calling Jesus 'the king of Israel'. Jesus' action, in response to this, when interpreted through the narrator's Scripture citation, corrects the crowd's limited nationalistic perceptions.[12]

The first part of the Scripture citation, 'Fear not, daughter of Zion', follows closely the MT of Zeph. 3.16 – 'Fear not, O Zion'.[13] The reason

10   In this ancient text, unlike some modern narratives, I am assuming the narrator speaks reliably on behalf of the author. The narrator's explanatory comments therefore offer the reader a clue to interpreting the events. In his analysis of narrative techniques, Moloney states: 'What the narrator communicates directly to the reader through commentary is a reliable representation of the overall point of view of the omniscient author'. See F. J. Moloney, 'Who Is the Reader in/of the Fourth Gospel?', *ABR* 40 (1992), pp.20–33 (23).

11   The Fourth Gospel describes the palm branches, naming them τὰ βαΐα τῶν φοινίκων. These are the palm branches used when Simon arrives triumphantly in Jerusalem following his victory over the 'yoke of the Gentiles' in 1 Macc. 13.41. According to Schuchard, the 'palm was for the Jews a symbol which, at least from the time of the Maccabees, stood for the nation and functioned as an expression of their hope for an imminent national liberation (see 1 Macc. 13.51; 2 Macc 10.7; cf. *Test. Naph.* 5.4; Rev 7.9)'. See B. G. Schuchard, *Scripture within Scripture: The Interrelationship of Form and Function in the Explicit Old Testament Citations in the Gospel of John* (SBLDS 133; Atlanta: Scholars Press, 1992), p.77. This allusion gives added meaning to the crowd's hailing Jesus as 'king'.

12   Note the use of the adversative conjunction δέ: '*But* Jesus found a young donkey and sat upon it' (v. 14).

13   The expression 'daughter of Zion' occurs just above in Zeph. 3.14. In a detailed discussion of this citation, Schuchard (*Scripture within Scripture*, pp.74–84) argues that the allusion is to Isa. 44.2. His argument is based on the fact that the acclamation of the crowd, 'the king of Israel' (βασιλεὺς τοῦ Ἰσραήλ), is found only once in the Greek version of the Scriptures in Isa. 44.6, but in my opinion, the words 'Fear not', in close association with 'daughter of Zion' in Zech. 3.14, 16, are more compelling. Also, the phrase βασιλεὺς Ἰσραὴλ is found in Zeph. 3.15 (LXX). See also the discussion in R. Sheridan, *Retelling Scripture: 'The Jews' and the Scriptural Citations in John 1.19–12.15* (BIS 110; Leiden: Brill, 2012), pp.226–7. Menken considers both Isa. 40.9 and Zech. 3.16 as likely sources for John's citation. See M. J. J. Menken, *Old Testament Quotations in the Fourth Gospel: Studies in Textual Form* (CBET 15; Kampen Kok Pharos, 1996), pp.83–4.

why Zion/Jerusalem is not to fear is because 'The king of Israel, the LORD, is in your midst (Zeph. 3.15).[14] In Zephaniah the coming of the king is to have implications well beyond Israel's nationalistic hopes: 'For my decision is to gather nations' (Gr. ἐθνῶν; Heb. גוים; Zeph. 3.8), then the speech of all the people will be changed 'that all of them may call on the name of the Lord and serve him with one accord' (Zeph. 3.9). As Brown comments, the crowd 'should not be acclaiming him as an earthly king, but as the manifestation of the Lord their God', who has come to gather all the nations.[15]

The second part of the Scripture citation – 'behold your king is coming, sitting on a donkey's colt' – continues the universalist outlook of Zephaniah by adding a citation from Zechariah: 'Behold your king comes to you; (triumphant and victorious is he, humble and riding on a donkey) on a colt, the foal of a donkey' (Zech. 9.9).[16] By omitting part of the quotation, the Gospel refrains from interpreting the action as a gesture of humility. Once again the context in Zechariah is most significant, for this king will 'command peace to the nations (ἐθνῶν); his dominion shall be from sea to sea, and from the river to the ends of the earth' (Zech. 9.10). While the crowd acclaimed Jesus with the title, 'king of Israel', Jesus' actions, understood through the Scripture citations, correct this title; Jesus comes into Jerusalem for the gathering of all the nations, not simply for the children of Israel.

c. *Section 2. Various responses: vv. 19-33*

The crowd's acclamations and Jesus' corrective response cause various reactions. The Pharisees declare their helplessness and say, 'Look, the world has gone after him' (v. 19). In confirmation of these words, some Greeks approach Philip saying, 'Sir, we wish to see Jesus' (12.22). Jesus'

14   This title 'the king of Israel', from Zeph. 3.15 may lie behind the Johannine addition to the psalm acclamation in 12.13. See R. E. Brown, *The Gospel according to John* (AB 29, 29A; 2 vols.; New York: Doubleday, 1966, 1970), I, p.458 n.15.

15   Brown, *The Gospel according to John*, I, p.462. In the later prophetic literature, as part of Israel's eschatological hopes, many nations were to be gathered to Jerusalem to worship the God of Israel (Isa. 55.5; 60.5-6; Zech. 2.11; 8.21-23; 14.16; Zeph. 3.9; Mic. 7.12). The Temple was to become 'a house of prayer for all nations' (LXX πᾶσιν τοῖς ἔθνεσιν in Isa. 56.7). See D. L. Christensen, 'Nations', in *ABD*, IV, pp.1037–47 (1044–5).

16   There is no argument from scholars about the source of this citation from Zechariah. See Schuchard, *Scripture within Scripture*, pp.73–84; and Menken, *Old Testament Quotations*, pp.88–95. Both also consider the description in 1 Kgs 1, where Solomon sits upon David's own mule, as the sign that he is David's heir.

response to the request of the Greeks is to declare 'The hour has come for the Son of Man to be glorified' (12.23). His response concludes with an invocation: 'Father glorify your name' (v. 28). The Father's voice is then heard: 'I have glorified it, and I will glorify it again' (v. 28). On hearing this, some in the crowd think this is simply thunder, while others think it is an angel (v. 29). Jesus explains to the crowd that the voice they heard was for their sake and then continues in vv. 31-32: 'Now is the judgment of this world, now shall the ruler of this world be cast out; and I, when I am lifted up from the earth, will draw all ($\pi \acute{\alpha} \nu \tau \alpha / s$) men/things to myself'.[17] The narrator then concludes this dense theological exchange with his explanation: 'He said this to show by what death he was to die' (v. 33).

The perspective in this section continues the shift from the limited, nationalist hopes of the crowd to a cosmological judgment that the 'ruler of this world' will now be vanquished, and linked to this 'now' is the declaration that the 'hour', spoken of throughout the Gospel,[18] has arrived. The shift in perspective to a cosmological victory is triggered by the arrival of 'some Greeks'. Their arrival on the scene brings the first part of the Gospel, the 'Book of Signs', to its conclusion and announces the movement into the 'Book of Glory'. Who are these Greeks whose arrival is so portentous that it draws into the narrative for the first time the heavenly voice of the Father?

The context of the narrative strongly suggests that these Greeks are Gentiles. As shown above, the Scripture citations from Zephaniah and Zechariah have in view the final eschatological judgment of God on the nations, and the establishing of God's reign over all. The Pharisees' comment, 'Look, the world has gone after him' (v. 19), recognises that Jesus' arrival in Jerusalem has world-wide implications. While there is no direct scriptural quotation,[19] a passage that reflects the action of the Johannine scene is from Zechariah 8:

---

17   There is disagreement in the manuscript tradition as to whether the term should be $\pi \acute{\alpha} \nu \tau \alpha$ ('all things') or $\pi \acute{\alpha} \nu \tau \alpha s$ ('all people'). $\mathfrak{P}^{66}$ and $\aleph$ are strong witnesses to $\pi \acute{\alpha} \nu \tau \alpha$ and the cosmic dimension of Jesus' mission has just been announced, making 'all things' a credible reading; it is also possible that the final sigma was added by a copyist who found $\pi \acute{\alpha} \nu \tau \alpha$ ambiguous. See the comments in Metzger, *Textual Commentary*, p.202.

18   Jn 2.4; 4.21, 23; 5.25, 28; 7.30; 8.20.

19   But note that the final part of Zech. 8.23, 'God is with you', corresponds with Zeph. 3.15, 17, 'the Lord is in your midst', which formed part of the preceding Scripture citation in Jn 12.15, as discussed above.

Many peoples and strong nations (λαοὶ πολλοὶ καὶ ἔθνη πολλὰ) shall come to seek the Lord of hosts in Jerusalem, and to entreat the favour of the Lord. Thus says the Lord of hosts. In those days ten men from nations of every language shall take hold of a Jew, grasping his garment and saying, 'Let us go with you, for we have heard that God is with you'. (Zech. 8.22-23)

As Jn 12.15 is a clear citation of Zechariah 9, there is a strong likelihood that the above passage, at the end of Zechariah 8, could be in mind. Zechariah 8 combines a number of oracles of end-time salvation. These oracles include the following themes, all of which are relevant to the Johannine passage: the gathering of Israel in Jerusalem (Zech. 8.8); the repetition of the phrase, 'Fear not' (8.13, 15); the image of sowing and fruitfulness (8.12), which will be developed in Jesus' image of the seed that must die in order to bear fruit (12.24); and the gathering of the nations to Jerusalem (8.20-23). In addition to these themes, there is the depiction in 8.23 of Gentiles coming to a Jew seeking the 'God who is with you'. This is what happens in John. Greeks come to Philip seeking Jesus. Coming immediately after the Pharisees' comment that 'the world has gone after him', these Greeks are representative of that world, confirming the prophetic character of the Pharisees' comment.[20]

With the coming of the Greeks/Gentiles, Jesus' immediate response is to recognise that 'the hour has come for the Son of Man to be glorified' (12.23).[21] Several times in the narrative so far, the reader has been told that the 'hour' has not yet come (2.4; 7.30; 8.20). That this 'hour' involves his death is made clear in the brief parable of the seed that must die in order to bear fruit (12.24), but in John this death is also the 'hour' of his exaltation (12.32), his glorification, as the divine voice testifies, (12.28), and the defeat of 'the ruler of this world' (12.31).

20   Similarly, Brown, *The Gospel according to John*, I, pp.463–4; F. J. Moloney, *John* (SP 4; Collegeville: Liturgical, 1998), p.351.

21   With the exception of 5.27 and 9.35, the Son of Man title has always been used with the cross in view (3.13, 14; 6.27, 53, 62; 8.28), and even 5.27 and 9.35 are linked to the cross through the themes of judgment and revelation. Moloney writes, 'the Son of Man revealed God to men [*sic*] and brought judgement to men through his presence, as a man, among them. The high point of this revelation and judgement took place on the Cross.' See F. J. Moloney, *The Johannine Son of Man* (BSR 14; Rome: Libreria Ateneo Salesiano, 1978), p.213. See also his recent work on this title 'Son of Man' and its relation to Jesus' death in F. J. Moloney, 'The Johannine Son of Man Revisited', in G. van Belle, J. G. van der Watt, and P. Maritz (eds.), *Theology and Christology in the Fourth Gospel* (BETL 184; Leuven: Peeters, 2005), pp.177–202 (202).

The coming of the Greeks, representative of 'the world' in the words of the Pharisees, sets into motion the ultimate cosmic victory of God. The cosmic dimension of the coming struggle is indicated by the breaking into this world of the Father's voice (12.28). What appears to be a struggle between Jesus and the Jewish authorities is in fact the final eschatological struggle between God and Satanic powers. Jewish thinking at this time considered that the world was under the dominion of a power of evil, named as Satan, the devil, Belial and here, the 'ruler of this world'.[22] Conventional Jewish eschatology expected that the kingdom of evil would one day be overcome by the power of God, through a saviour-figure who would engage in a final and decisive cosmic battle and whose victory would inaugurate the reign of God in peace and a full flourishing of life.[23] Jesus' announcement indicates that the time of this final battle has now arrived.

As a consequence of the defeat of the 'ruler of this world' through the lifting-up of Jesus in his 'hour', 'all people/things – πάντα/ς' will be drawn to him (12.32). Jesus' statement continues the universal perspective that has been running through this entire passage through the use of the previous scriptural citations and allusions. Jesus' death is not only for the people of Israel; it is for all. The coming of the Greeks/Gentiles in 12.20 proleptically testifies to the fruitfulness of the 'hour'. The seed will fall into the ground, and when it dies, it will bear much fruit. The explanatory comment by the narrator brings this section to closure by signalling that the term 'lifted up' indicates, with artistic irony, that the 'hour' is both the crucifixion and the exaltation of Jesus.[24]

---

22   On Jewish understanding of the cosmic power of evil in the first century, see L. T. Stuckenbruck, '"Protect them from the Evil One" (John 17:15): Light from the Dead Sea Scrolls', in M. L. Coloe and T. Thatcher (eds.), *John, Qumran, and the Dead Sea Scrolls: Sixty Years of Discovery and Debate* (EJL 32; Atlanta: SBL, 2011), pp.139–60 (145–59).

23   A helpful discussion of the 'Cosmic Battle' theme in relation to John's Gospel can be found in J. L. Kovacs, '"Now shall the ruler of this world be driven out": Jesus' Death as Cosmic Battle in John 12:20-36', *JBL* 114 (1995), pp.227–47.

24   Space does not permit further development of the major Johannine theme of 'lifting up' to mean both death and exaltation, and the associated theme of glorification. Kovaks argues that these themes are part of the Johannine portrayal of Jesus' 'kingship' and his enthronement as king through the defeat of the 'the ruler of this world'. She writes: 'For the evangelist, the glorification of 12:23 involves more that Jesus' return to the "glory" he had before (John 17:5); the cross is not merely the metaphorical jumping off point for Jesus' reascent to his heavenly Father. It is the locus of a cosmic battle, in which Jesus achieves a decisive victory over Satan.' See Kovacs, 'Now shall the ruler of this world be driven out', pp.244–7 (246).

d. *Section 3. Concluding Reactions: vv. 34-43*

The passage so far has depicted two contrasting responses to Jesus. In the first section, the crowd fails to understand Jesus' messianic identity and role. They are limited by their nationalistic hopes. By contrast, the second section depicts some Greeks who come wishing to see Jesus. The third section opens with a typical misunderstanding by the crowd (12.34). They understand Jesus' statement about being lifted up from the earth as something akin to an ascension. This puzzles them. The comment from the crowd that the Christ, the messiah, is to remain forever, reveals that with the raising of Lazarus they had believed that the messianic age had arrived, for the resurrection of the dead had become part of Jewish thinking by the first century, at least for some. In his study of Judaism in the first century, Schürer states: 'In this glorious future kingdom not only the dispersed members of the nation, but also all *deceased Israelites* are to participate. They will come forth from their graves to enjoy, with those of their fellow-countrymen who are then living, the happiness of the Messiah's kingdom.'[25] In Jewish writing contemporary with the New Testament we find evidence of a first-century theology linking the resurrection of the dead with the coming of the messiah: 'And it shall come to pass after these things, when the time of the advent of the messiah is fulfilled, that he shall return in glory. Then all who have fallen asleep in hope of him shall rise again' (*2 Bar.* 30.1-2).[26] But in these Jewish perceptions of the messiah, there was no thought that this figure would then return to the heavens.

The resurrection of Lazarus has led some of the people to consider that Jesus might be the messiah, but if Jesus is to be lifted up from the earth, that is, return to the heavens, then that would disqualify him from being the messiah, since they '*have heard*, from the Law, that the Christ remains forever' (12.34). Their words are in sharp contrast with the words of the Gentiles in Zechariah 8. In Zechariah's oracle, the Gentiles *have heard* that 'God is with you' (8.23), while the Jews in John, because of their Law, are blind and fail to see the presence of the Christ in their midst.

---

25   E. Schürer, *A History of the Jewish People in the Time of Jesus Christ, Second Division* (4 vols.; Edinburgh: T. & T. Clark, 1890), II, pp.174–5.

26   *2 Baruch* is a compilation of independent writings belonging to various dates between 50 and 90 CE. For a discussion of this complex text in its multiple versions, see R. H. Charles, 'II Baruch: The Syriac Apocalypse of Baruch', in R. H. Charles (ed.), *Pseudepigrapha of the Old Testament* (2 vols.; Bellingham: Logos Research Systems, 2004), II, pp.470–527.

Jesus then sums up the struggle depicted in this passage between himself and the crowd. From the opening scene, when they hail him as the king of Israel, their understanding has been limited by nationalistic hopes. Neither his actions nor his words have been able to change their perception. Using the image of 'walking in the light' or 'walking in the darkness', Jesus makes a final appeal to them to believe, and so to become children of the light (vv. 35-36).[27]

Jesus' words are followed by the narrator's comment (12.37-41), which brings this long passage to a close and sums up the theological insight that this passage has revealed and passes a commentary on the entire public ministry of Jesus. The narrator cites two passages from Isaiah (53.1 and 6.10) which continue the contrast between belief and unbelief, blindness and sight. These narrative comments reflect the perplexity of the Johannine community as they try to make sense of the fact that Jesus, and the later Gospel message, was unacceptable to many within Judaism, while the community's post-Easter mission to Gentiles was successful. How could this be possible? The narrator's answer is that this was to fulfil the Scriptures.

The first citation in 12.38 is an exact citation of Isa. 53.1 (LXX), part of the fourth Servant Song, which begins: 'Behold my servant shall prosper, he shall be lifted up and glorified (ὑψωθήσεται καὶ δοξασθήσεται, Isa. 52.13). This one verse has in close proximity two themes found in Jn 12.19-33, namely exaltation and glorification. The Song continues with the rejection of the servant (Isa. 53.3), his death and burial (Isa. 53.8-9) and yet the Servant will see his offspring and from the anguish of his soul (τῆς ψυχῆς αὐτοῦ, Isa. 53.11) he will see the light (φῶς), and his suffering will benefit many (πολλοῖς, 53.11; πολλῶν, 53.12). These words and themes are echoed in John 12. Like the Servant, Jesus is rejected (12.37); his soul (ἡ ψυχή μου) is troubled (12.27); he speaks of himself as the light (τὸ φῶς, v. 35) and in his lifting up in death he will draw all (πάντα) to himself (v. 31). The citation of Isa. 53.1 and the correspondence between the fate of the Servant and Jesus identify that Jesus fulfils the role of the Servant who is chosen and endowed with God's spirit (Isa. 42.1).

---

27 The images of walking in darkness and walking in the light may be an allusion to Isa. 50.10 where these same phrases occur at the close of the third Servant Song. This possibility is strengthened by the fact that following Jesus' words the narrator cites Isa. 53.1, which is part of the fourth Servant Song. For more on the influence of the Servant Songs on Jn 12.20, see Kossen, 'Who Were the Greeks?', pp.103–4; and Beutler, 'Greeks come to see Jesus (John 12:20f)', pp.341–2.

The exact citation of the LXX version of Isa. 53.1 offers a significant insight into the evangelist's consistent universalist theme across this entire episode. In its context, Isa. 53.1 is directly related to the preceding verse: 'so he shall startle many nations (ἔθνη πολλὰ); kings shall shut their mouths because of him; those (οἷς) who have not been told concerning him – they shall see, Those who had not heard – they shall understand. Who has believed what we have heard' (53.1).

The original MT of Isa. 52.15 text uses the relative pronoun *esher* in its neuter sense and so reads: '*That* (*esher*) which was not been told them they shall see', and '*that* (*esher*) which they have not heard they shall understand'. The LXX translates this pronoun in a personal sense using the masculine plural pronoun οἷς. So the LXX version speaks of 'Those (οἷς) *who* have not yet come to knowledge of the Servant will see, and *those who* have not yet heard (about him) will hear'.[28] The LXX reading, in conjunction with the use of nations (ἔθνη, Isa. 52.15a),[29] indicates the Servant's broader mission to the Gentiles, which is consistent with the mission indicated in earlier Servant songs. The first Servant Song commissions the Servant to establish 'judgment upon the earth' (ἐπὶ τῆς γῆς κρίσιν) and then describes the 'nations (ἔθνη) awaiting his name' (Isa. 42.4).[30]

Added to the citation from the fourth Servant Song in Jn 12.38 is a second citation from Isaiah offering the narrator's judgment on why Israel could not believe. While the quotation obviously draws on Isa. 6.10, the Johannine wording does not agree exactly with either the LXX or the MT text. A question then follows: Is the evangelist citing here from memory in a free manner or is he deliberately altering the text for his own purpose? Most scholars attribute the text to the evangelist's redaction of Isaiah.[31]

The structure of the LXX shows reverse parallelism, while John shows synthetic parallelism:

28   Beutler, 'Greeks come to see Jesus (John 12:20f)', p.342 (emphasis mine).

29   The term ἔθνη is used to speak of Gentiles, as distinct from the λαός, the people of God. See G. Bertram, 'ἔθνος, ἐθνικός', in *TNDT*, II, pp.364–9.

30   Where the MT speaks of the islands or coastlands awaiting his Law, the LXX has translated this as the nations (ἔθνη) awaiting his name – possibly influenced by what follows in Isa. 42.6-8, which speak of the Servant being a light to the nations (εἰς φῶς ἐθνῶν, 42.6).

31   Menken, *Old Testament Quotations*, p.121; see also p.100 n.7 on pesher exegesis and p.106 n.26; Schuchard, *Scripture within Scripture*, pp.98–106; and C. H. Williams, 'Isaiah in John's Gospel', in S. Moyise and M. J. J. Menken (eds.), *Isaiah in the New Testament* (NTSI; London: T&T Clark International, 2005), pp.101–16 (109–15).

Isaiah 6.10 LXX	*John 12.40*

A Make the heart of this people fat,
B and dull their ears,
C and shut their eyes;
C' lest they see with their eyes,
B' and hear with their ears,
C' and understand with their hearts,
    and turn and be healed.
	A He has blinded their eyes
	B and hardened their heart,
	
	A' lest they see with their eyes,
	
	B' and understand with their heart
	    and turn – and I would heal them.

In leaving out the reference to hearing with their ears, the Gospel emphasises the importance of correct sight, or seeing the signs and recognising the glory of God now revealed in Jesus. By redacting the Isaian passage in this way, the evangelist has scriptural confirmation that the Jews in the Gospel narrative have been blinded, and are therefore unable to perceive the signs correctly. The Scriptures of Israel thus confirm that in some way the rejection of Jesus by the Jews and the successful mission to the Gentiles is part of the mysterious plan of God. Unlike Paul, John does not offer further explanation of this divine action and how it might be resolved in the future, but he does offer a glimmer of hope in the final comment by the narrator: 'Nevertheless many, even of the authorities, believed in him...' (v. 42). The added comment that they feared to confess this lest they be put out of the synagogue (v. 42) is a further indication that this passage is the evangelist's theological reflection on the later community's experience.[32]

2. *The Johannine Community and the Gentiles*

Having examined a significant text in the Fourth Gospel that provides narrative clues supporting a future mission to the Gentiles, I will now turn to the possible historical development of the Johannine community and its inclusion of Gentiles. At the outset, we must note the difficulty of having any historical certainty due to the lack of clear archaeological evidence that can identify the location(s) of this community. J. L. Martyn

---

32   For a recent appraisal of the texts which speak of being put 'out of the synagogue' (9.22; 12.42; 16.2) and their relation to the 12th Benediction as proposed by J. L. Martyn, see Joel Marcus, '*Birkat Ha-Minim* Revisited', *NTS* 55 (2009), pp.523–51. In a more nuanced manner, Marcus supports Martyn's hypothesis that the use of the term ἀποσυνάγωγος reflects a 'decision by "the Jews" (9.22) or "the Pharisees" (12.42) to put out of the synagogue and the Jewish community in general anyone who confesses Jesus as the Messiah, and it is easy to see the self-curse of Birkat Ha-Minim as a weapon for enforcing such an edict' (p.533).

likened the Gospel narrative to an archaeological 'tell' and all reconstruction of the Johannine community and theories about their missionary outreach at present can only be based on this sole 'tell' and the skill
of the interpreter.[33]

In the mid-70s, a number of Johannine scholars attempted to reconstruct the history of the development of Johannine theology, the
community and the Gospel.[34] Among these hypotheses, the work of R. E.
Brown has gained the widest acceptance.[35] Since his work considered not
only the development of the Gospel's theology but also the community's
social makeup I will focus on his reconstruction, giving particular
attention to his theory about the Gentiles within the community. Brown
postulates four phases in the development of the community.[36]

Phase 1 (mid-50s to late 80s). In or near Palestine, an originating
group of Jews, including disciples of John the Baptist, accept Jesus
within traditional Jewish concepts as a Davidic messiah. To this group
was added a second group of Jews and Samaritans who understood Jesus
in terms of a 'prophet like Moses', rather than as a Davidic figure.[37] The
addition of this group led to a high, pre-existence Christology resulting in
conflict with other Jews and eventually those believers openly confessing
faith in Jesus were expelled from the community (9.22; 12.42; 16.2).

---

33   J. L. Martyn, *The Gospel of John in Christian History: Essays for Interpreters* (New York: Paulist, 1979), p.90.

34   G. Richter, 'Präsentische und futurische Eschatologie im 4. Evangelium', in
P. Fiedler and D. Zeller (eds.), *Gegenwart und kommendes Reich: Schülergabe
Anton Vögtle zum 65. Geburtstag* (Stuttgart: Verlag Katholisches Bibelwerk, 1975);
W. Langbrandtner, *Weltferner Gott oder Gott der Liebe: Die Ketzerstreit in der
johanneischen Kirche* (BBET 6; Frankfurt: Lang, 1977), pp.373–404; M.-É.
Boismard and A. Lamouille (eds.), *L'Évangile de Jean* (Synopse des quatre
évangiles en français 3; Paris: Cerf, 1977); O. Cullmann, *The Johannine Circle: Its
Place in Judaism among the Disciples of Jesus and in Early Christianity. A Study in
the Origin of the Gospel of John* (London: SCM, 1976); and Martyn, *The Gospel of
John in Christian History*.

35   R. E. Brown, *The Community of the Beloved Disciple: The Life, Loves, and
Hates of an Individual Church in New Testament Times* (New York: Paulist, 1979).
In an appendix (pp.171–82), Brown provides a brief summary of earlier reconstruc-
tions of the community by Martyn, Richter, Cullmann, Boismard, and Langbrandt-
ner. See also the summary by Moloney in R. E. Brown, *An Introduction to the
Gospel of John: Edited, Updated, Introduced and Concluded by F. J. Moloney*
(ABRL; New York: Doubleday, 2003), pp.70–5.

36   Brown's early hypothesis about the development of the Gospel and the
Johannine community was only slightly modified in a later work, which was edited
and published posthumously, *An Introduction to the Gospel of John*, pp.64–89.

37   Brown, *An Introduction to the Gospel of John*, p.68.

Phase 2 (during the 90s). By this time the group may have moved into the Diaspora and here they began to make Gentile converts.[38] During this time, the final form of the Gospel was produced. The Christological debates with Judaism led to some within the Johannine community breaking away.

Phase 3 (c. 100). By the end of the first century, those in the break-away group were placing such emphasis on the divinity of Jesus they were losing sight of his humanity. The main group continued to empha-sise the humanity of Jesus and this group is responsible for the Johannine Epistles and the strong condemnation against the breakaway group.

Phase 4 (the second century). The main group is assimilated into the broader Apostolic Church, while the breakaway group, who may have had greater numbers, moved into Docetism and Gnosticism.

During the first pre-Gospel phase, Brown suggests that the originating group of believers was joined by Samaritans and also by a group of Jews with anti-Temple views that led to the formation of a higher, pre-existence Christology. This higher Christology caused tension and finally rupture with the Jewish synagogue. Brown suggests that 'it was particu-larly when the Johannine Christians of Jewish descent were rejected by Judaism and no longer thought of themselves as "Jews" that they received numbers of Gentiles into the community'.[39] He points to the explanations of Jewish terms such as 'Rabbi' and 'messiah' as evidence that there were non-Jews within the community. He also sees evidence for Gentiles within the community in the events narrated in John 12 with the coming of the Greeks and use of Scripture (12.37-40) to understand why Jesus was rejected by the Jews. He cites Gospel passages that insist that the true child of God is not determined by ethnic origins such as birth, since entry into the kingdom requires being begotten by God (1.12; 3.3, 5). John's Gospel therefore reformulates what it means to be one of 'the children of Israel': 'The real Israel consists of those who receive the revelation of Jesus (1.37, 47) and so Jesus is the 'king of Israel' (1.49; 12.13).[40] I would also consider that the statement, 'I am the true vine' (15.1), is part of this polemic to reconfigure Israel in terms of Jesus and his followers since the vine was an ancient symbol of Israel.[41]

---

38   On this point Brown takes the opposite position to that of Martyn, who considers that there was no 'knowledge of the mission to the Gentiles', or at least the community was not involved in such a mission. See Martyn, *The Gospel of John in Christian History*, p.101.

39   Brown, *The Community of the Beloved Disciple*, p.55.

40   Brown, *The Community of the Beloved Disciple*, p.48.

41   'The vineyard of the Lord of hosts is the house of Israel' (Isa. 5.7).

3. *Conclusions*

The episode in Jn 12.20, describing the coming of 'some Greeks' when read within it narrative context (12.12-43) offers, what I consider, compelling evidence that the Johannine community was engaged in a mission to the Gentiles. While the clues are subtle, it must be noted that writing towards the end of the first century the evangelist is dealing with two historical periods. One is the time of Jesus, where there is little evidence that he was involved in a Gentile mission, and the other is the later time of the early Christian community, which quite obviously had been involved in such a mission since the time of Paul. The evangelist has negotiated this by turning to the ancient prophecies that in the final days Gentiles would be included within Israel's worshipping community. The Scripture citations, drawing on Zephaniah and Zechariah, evoke the eschatological theme of the gathering of the nations. The Pharisees are the first to recognise this in their ironic statement, 'Look the world has gone after him' (12.19). Confirming this statement, some Greeks then approach Philip desiring to see Jesus. In response to the desire of the Greeks, Jesus recognises that his 'hour' has come. This 'hour' will be both his death and glorification, and through the events of this 'hour', the eschatological promises will be realised. The final citations from Isaiah comment on why Jesus (and the gospel) was not received within Judaism and yet was received in the post-Easter mission to the Gentiles. The Fourth Gospel therefore remains within the parameters demanded by the life and ministry of the historical Jesus, while at the same time it proleptically speaks of the future fruitfulness (12.25) of the Gentile mission in the time of the later community.

Chapter 14

GREEKS IN COLOSSAE:
SHIFTING ALLEGIANCES IN THE LETTER
TO THE COLOSSIANS AND ITS CONTEXT

Alan Cadwallader

1. *Introduction*

It has been a long-standing commitment of Pauline scholarship to explore the apostle's efforts to theologise and ecclesialise the place of Gentiles within the Jesus groups that were his special or at least epistolary concern. Historical analysis has used this as a substantial, if refracted, foundation for a further exploration of the passage of the Jesus movement from its Jewish matrix to Gentile dominance.[1] Whether this 'parting of the ways' became a reality at the end of the first century or only reached sociological precision in the fourth century, that there was a defining shift is axiomatic. The present study argues that a distinct indication of that shift is already discernible in the letter to the Colossians. It will provide evidence that such a shift has already pushed the Jewish presence and ideological influence in the Jesus households/groups in Colossae to the periphery, that recent epigraphical discoveries from Colossae make a significant contribution to the search for an explanation for this situation, and that a major theological commitment and its linguistic construction in Paul's authentic letters actually facilitates the rationalisation of such a sociological and historical development even as it is substantially reconfigured.

In the course of my argument it will become clear that I consider that the letter to the Colossians could not possibly be written by Paul or a close associate since, *inter alia*, the conceptualisation of Greeks and Jews in the letter marks a radical modification of a fundamental Pauline

---

1   See, for example J. D. G. Dunn, *The Partings of the Ways between Christianity and Judaism and their Significance for the Character of Christianity* (London: SCM, 1991); and Wilson, *Related Strangers*.

tenet. Authorship is not a major focus, however. It must also be acknowledged that this study of the Colossian Jesus groups in the context of the
wider Colossian society makes no claim for general application across
the early churches in the Mediterranean. Colossae may be, in the last
three decades of the first century, merely a harbinger or an exception
compared to other Pauline groups of Jesus followers in other cities. That
there was a great diversity between such groups, in expressions of Jewish
community and in the relations between the two, has become a substantial qualification on the fixed categories often imposed upon the
complexities of Jewish and Christian identities and interactions in the
first century and beyond.[2] What can be asserted, however, is that the passage from Jewish dominance and even presence amongst the followers
of Jesus to the prevalence of Gentile membership and control is already
in evidence in Colossae in the final decades of the first century. Further,
the language of 'Gentile' as a description by which the Jesus groups in
Colossae understood themselves has already lost all meaning beyond a
post-Paul nod of acknowledgment towards Pauline tradition (Col. 1.27;
cf. Rom. 16.25).[3]

In the authentic letters, Paul frequently addresses the problem of the
Gentiles for a Jewish-spawned religious movement. The problem had
many facets – from eating practices to the hierarchy of authority in
governance, even if (and possibly because) many Gentiles who became
Jesus-followers had been mediated by an established connection with

---

2   So J. M. Lieu, '"The Parting of the Ways": Theological Construct or
Historical Reality?', *JSNT* 56 (1994), pp.101–19; and J. Neusner, 'Explaining the
Great Schism: History versus Theology', *Religion* 28 (1998), pp.139–58. Cf. R.
Stark, *The Rise of Christianity: A Sociologist Reconsiders History* (Princeton:
Princeton University Press, 1996), pp.49–71.

3   Space prevents any exploration of the vexed question of any Jewish presence
at Colossae. The assumption of Jews in Colossae is derived from a general reference
in Josephus (*A.J.* 12.149-53) and particular evidence for Jews in Laodiceia and
Hierapolis (Cicero, *Flac.* 28.68) sealed by supposed Jewish practices mentioned
in the letter itself (Col. 2.16-17). On the artefactual evidence for Jews in Laodiceia
and Hierapolis, see W. Ameling, *Inscriptiones Judaicae Orientis II: Kleinasien*
(Tübingen: Mohr Siebeck, 2004), pp.398–440, 443–7; E. Miranda, 'La communità
giudaica di Hierapolis di Frigia', *EA* 31 (1999), pp.109–56; and C. Şimşek,
Laodikeia (Laodikeia ad Lycum) (Istanbul: Ege Yayınları, 2007), pp.148–9. The
only *specific* evidence of Jews in Colossae comes from the twelfth century: the
Metropolitan Nicetas of Chonai (the successor name to Colossae) refused to readmit
Jews after the disruption of a Turkish threat to the city. See Michael Choniates,
Encomium 88; text in P. Lampros, Μιχαὴλ Ακομινατοῦ τοῦ Χωνιατοῦ τὰ σωζόμενα
(2 vols.; Groningen: Bouma, 1968), I, p.53.

Judaism.[4] Paul was often content to use traditional biblical language in this context. And so, in Romans 9 for example, the Jewish vision of Israel and the 'nations/Gentiles' (ἔθνη) is taken up, undergirded by manifold scriptural citations, in his efforts to negotiate a theo-historical pattern by which Gentiles, already present, can be included amongst Jesus' followers without the sacrifice of Jewish identity and privilege.[5] The language clearly reflects a summary Jewish perspective on the ethnic and religious divisions in God's world. 'Gentiles' makes no distinction amongst the various ethnic groups encompassed by the Roman empire. They are 'an undifferentiated mass' defined solely by what J. Neusner calls an 'antonymic relationship' of Israel to non-Israel.[6] It is, as C. Stanley observes, a Judeocentric viewpoint, one which modern scholarship on the Pauline letters often uncritically reiterates.[7]

However, when it comes to Paul's own summary of the composite demography of the groups he is addressing, he modifies the language of the categories. He writes of 'Jew and *Greek* (ἕλλην)'. The summary dichotomy, 'Jews and Gentiles', does not occur in Paul. Many regard 'Gentile' and 'Greek' as synonymous,[8] so that for translation purposes and conceptual analysis there is a constant slippage between the two terms. This has obscured the question of how and why Paul initiates such an apparent slippage, given that there is no clear ancestor to such a conjunction. Rather, Paul's Jewish contemporaries seem to retain an ethnic specificity for the term 'Greek' in relation to 'Jew'.[9]

For my purposes, it is not a prime concern whether there is any substantial difference between 'Jews and Gentiles' and 'Jews and Greeks' in Paul's writings.[10] It may be a concession by Paul that many of his

---

4   So Stark, *Rise of Christianity*; and W. S. Campbell, *Paul and the Creation of Christian Identity* (London: T&T Clark International, 2008).

5   See Campbell, *Paul and Christian Identity*, pp.55–6; and A. H. Cadwallader, 'Anniversary Overlap: Or What Happens when St Paul Meets the Universal Declaration of Human Rights', in P. Babie and N. Rochow (eds.), *Freedom of Religion under Bills of Rights* (Adelaide: University of Adelaide Press, 2012), pp.51–62.

6   J. Neusner, 'The Doctrine of Israel', in J. Neusner and A. Avery-Peck (eds.), *The Blackwell Companion to Judaism* (Oxford: Blackwell, 2000), pp.230–46 (234).

7   C. Stanley, '"Neither Jew nor Greek": Ethnic Conflict in Graeco-Roman Society', *JSNT* 64 (1996), pp.101–24 (105).

8   See, for example, Johnson, *Among the Gentiles*, p.357; and Campbell, *Paul and Christian Identity*, pp.12–13.

9   So, for example, Josephus, *A.J.* 12.263; 13.378; 18.373-74.

10   For the view that they are synonymous, see W. Gutbrod, ''Ισραήλ', in *TDNT*, III, pp.369–91 (381). The contrary view is presented by Stanley, 'Neither Jew nor Greek'.

addressees would not identify themselves as 'Gentiles'. This, after all, is a Jewish designation. Even allowing for Jewish proselyte drift into the Jesus movement, such a self-designation would at best be only secondary – a religious fiction accepted for the sake of belonging. However, as I will argue, that Paul adopts 'Greek' in the dichotomous summation assists in justifying and extending subsequent moves in emphasis.

What is important here is the order: Jew and Greek. Paul remains totally consistent in his Jewish belief in the priority of the Jews, across a range of letters.[11] This is not only played out in his extended argumentation such as we receive in Romans 9–11. It is meticulously observed in his summative formulae related to the pattern of salvation and to community identity. Indeed, in every combination of 'Jew' and 'Greek' in Paul's writings, this is the order (Rom. 1.16; 2.9, 10; 3.9; 10.12; 1 Cor. 1.22, 23, 24; 10.32; 12.13; Gal. 3.28; cf. similarly Rom. 3.29; 1 Cor. 9.20-21; Gal. 2.15). Its influence can be traced throughout the Acts of the Apostles both as a remembrance of Paul's mission and as Luke's own (inherited) theological perception (e.g. Acts 2.10; 13.46; 14.1; 18.4; 19.10, 17; 20.21; cf. 13.5; 14.26; 16.1; 17.2; 18.6; 28.28). It may even have had broader currency (Mt. 10.5-6; 15.24). As M. Gese emphasises, tying it to the priorities of salvation-history, 'Paul always places Jew before Greek'.[12] This theological commitment is so fundamental to Paul's gospel (Rom. 10.12) that it finds its way into his syntactical ordering (and expansion?) of this foundation in 1 Cor. 12.13 and Gal. 3.28. One can reasonably assert that for Paul the ethnic distinction and the priority of one over the other in the dispensation of God is more fundamental than gender difference.

This is what makes the code in Col. 3.11 so confronting in its reversal: 'where there is no longer *Greek and Jew*, circumcised and uncircumcised, barbarian, Scythian, slave, free; but Christ is all and in all'. Now it is the Greek who occupies the privileged position. This order occurs

11   The argument of D. Campbell notwithstanding; see D. Campbell, *The Deliverance of God: An Apocalyptic Re-reading of Justification in Paul* (Grand Rapids: Eerdmans, 2009), pp.552–4. His blending of Greek and Gentile into 'pagan' becomes a consequence of an unwarranted shift of πρῶτον into an adverb of emphasis in Rom. 1.16. Further, he introduces a category ('pagan') that belongs more properly to ecclesial debates of later centuries, even as it sucks in strictly religious language (ἀσεβής as in Rom. 4.5) to subsume both Greek and Gentile.

12   M. Gese, *Das Vermächtnis des Apostels: Die Rezeption der paulinischen Theologie im Epheserbrief* (Tübingen: Mohr Siebeck 1997), p.113 n.16. He argues that Ephesians narrows Pauline language to the Septuagint – that of Israel and the nations. He notes, without explanation, the reverse order in Colossians but by implication this is not authentic Paul.

only here in the New Testament.[13] Most commentators do not see the significance of the transposition, even if they notice it at all.[14] They are distracted into the problematic additions – Scythian (and) barbarian.[15] Some blithely turn the order in Colossians back to its Pauline template.[16] M. Barth and H. Blanke claim that 'It is questionable that the order has some deeper meaning',[17] thereby dismissing Paul's Jewish perspective on the world and on God's salvific work. It is certainly questionable that the 'Gentile' demography of the Colossian Jesus groups or the prevalence of Hellenistic culture would justify the shift from what was a fundamental commitment of Paul's theology.[18] The order in 1 Cor. 12.13 remains secure and Luke's renowned commitment to the Gentiles did not disturb the formula in his second volume. Some disposed to the authenticity of Colossians as Paul's letter or to its close proximity to Paul's authority see in this verse nothing other than a literary modulation on a theme, arguing that Colossians demonstrates that the formula was not fixed for Paul, not necessarily designed to address any particular situation.[19] The weight of evidence in Paul that is constant in its primacy of 'Jew' contradicts this apologetic, which obscures the extraordinary adjustment in Paul's theology. The conjunction of Jew and Greek *may* have been a Jewish ellipsis for the whole world (though the evidence is weak), but the world, for the writer and addressees of the letter, has begun to shift

13   The reference to 'Gentiles' and 'Jews' in Acts 14.5 is not parallel – this is a construction of opposition to Paul's witness.

14   P. Pokorný notices the change but extracts no significance from it. See P. Pokorný, *Colossians: A Commentary* (Peabody: Hendrickson, 1991), pp.169–70.

15   The full formulation is not the focus here. However, given the evidence in the inscription detailed below, there is now external support for W. T. Wilson's speculation that the 'roster' is a clue to the ethnic diversity of Colossae; see W. T. Wilson, *The Hope of Glory: Education and Exhortation in the Epistle to the Colossians* (Leiden: Brill, 1997), p.83.

16   See, for example, Johnson, *Among the Gentiles*, p.357 n.18.

17   M. Barth and H. Blanke, *Colossians* (AB 34B; New York: Doubleday, 1994), p.415.

18   Contra P. O'Brien, who dismisses it as 'simply a reminder of the pervasiveness of Hellenistic culture in the Mediterranean basin'; see P. O'Brien, *Colossians, Philemon* (WBC 44; Waco: Word, 1982), p.224; cf. E. Lohse, *Colossians and Philemon* (Hermeneia; Philadelphia: Fortress, 1971), p.143. Hellenistic culture was ubiquitousfor Paul in his entire mission and not confined to Colossians, and yet nowhere else does this flag of Hellenistic pervasiveness enter into Paul's schematics.

19   J. D. G. Dunn, *The Epistles to the Colossians and to Philemon* (NIGTC; Grand Rapids: Eerdmans, 1996), p.223; and A. T. Lincoln and A. J. M. Wedderburn, *The Theology of the Later Pauline Letters* (NTT; Cambridge: Cambridge University Press, 1993), pp.10, 13.

fundamentally. It is now Greek and Jew, not Jew and Greek,[20] and is on its way in subsequent centuries to becoming Christian and Greek and thence to Christian and pagan.[21]

In the remainder of this study I offer an explanation for this momentous change in the order that opens the code of Col. 3.11.

2. *The Presentation of Hellenic Credentials at Colossae*

The most conclusive evidence to date that Colossae well survived the 61 CE earthquake that hit the Lycus Valley[22] comes from a recently published inscription that honours a certain Korumbos for the repair of the baths at Colossae.[23] The Colossian demos and a list of probably thirty subscribers[24] delivered this honorific bomos. The public honour functioned to assert Colossae's continued nominal independence as a polis (under Rome's oversight and control)[25] with the economic resources to draw upon for its well-being. The lithographic style and the Greek naming pattern indicate a date of the late first to early second century.

This inscription from Colossae, given its date, becomes vital for the insights that it can provide into the values and backgrounds of Colossian citizens, roughly at the time when the letter to the Colossians was written. Those values include social and familial stability, euergetism and Hellenic display. For the sake of reference, I give here only the list

20   There is little attempt in the history of transmission to revert the word order of 'Greek and Jew' to the Pauline template – the isolated exception is minuscule 17, plus some Armenian manuscripts. This lack of assimilation reflects the later 'Gentile' triumph in Christianity.

21   See M. Kahlos, *Debate and Dialogue: Christian and Pagan Cultures c. 360–430* (Aldershot: Ashgate, 2007), p.26.

22   Tacitus, *Ann.* 14.27.

23   For a thorough critique of the assertion that Colossae was irreparably damaged, see A. H. Cadwallader, 'Refuting an Axiom of Scholarship on Colossae: Fresh Insights from New and Old Inscriptions', in A. H. Cadwallader and M. Trainor (eds.), *Colossae in Space and Time: Linking with an Ancient City* (Göttingen: Vandenhoeck & Ruprecht, 2011), pp.151–79.

24   The inscription is severely damaged in the middle section of the list of names but it certainly included further subscribers in the same pattern as the top and bottom sections of the shaft.

25   P. Harland has noted the continued vibrancy of the Greek poleis in the east even under the early Principate; see P. Harland, 'The Declining Polis? Religious Rivalries in Ancient Civic Context', in L. E. Vaage (ed.), *Religious Rivalries in the Early Roman Empire and the Rise of Christianity* (Waterloo: Wilfred Laurier University Press, 2006), pp.21–49.

of extant subscribers (lines 6 to 35 of the inscription) allowing without argument the reconstruction of some names and letters as laid out in detail in the *editio princeps*:[26]

Τρύφων •Β̄ Διοδώ[ρου – –]
Μηνογᾶς •Δ• τοῦ Ν[– – –]
Διόδοτος •Γ• τοῦ Δ[– – –]
[6-7 letters]Τρυφωνᾶ τ[– – – –]
[6-7 letters]νιου τοῦ Διο[– – – –   ]

Lines 11-18 severely damaged

[10-11 letters το]υ̣ Ζωσίμου̣[ος   – –]
[11-12 letters] •Β• τοῦ 'Ακρι[– – – –]
Θεόδωρος Δημητρίου •Β• Θεοδ[ώρου]
Δημᾶς 'Απολλωνίου τ[οῦ – – –]
⊛Μηνᾶς Κτησᾶ •Γ• το̣[ῦ – – – –   ]
Θεόδωρος •Β• Λικιννν[ίου]
'Ηρακλέων •Β• 'Ανωτ[– – – –]
'Ηρακλέων 'Ηρακλείδου 'Η[ρακλέων]ος
῎Ατταλος Τρυφωνιώνο[υ – – – –   ]
Θεόδωρος •Β• τοῦ Δημητρίου[5-6 letters]νει^α
'Αλέξανδρος 'Ηρακλείδου[– 6-7 letters –]ου
'Απολλώνιος Β 'Αττάλου τοῦ Σκ[επα]ρνᾶ
Εὐτύχης Ζωσίμου 'Αντιμήδου
  Τρύφων• Μενάνδρου •Γ• Μιννίωνος
    Τυδείδης Ζωσίμου
  Δημήτριος 'Απολλωνίου Μωκεᾶ
Κτησᾶς 'Ηρακλίδου•'Ιουλίδος

The extant list displays careful attention to the genealogical pedigree of each subscriber. It delivers 66 extant names in whole or part. The list probably contained more than 100 names originally. The patronymics stretch back for up to five generations (as for Menogas and Tryphon son of Menandros), a pattern also found on the coins of Colossae in the second century.[27] This genealogical concern is more than the usual Greek display of three generations (male, father and grandfather),[28] although ten

26   A. H. Cadwallader, 'Honouring the Repairer of the Baths: A New Inscription from Kolossai', *Antichthon* 42 (2012), pp.150–83. The rosette before the name Menas in line 23 may indicate a recently deceased subscriber.

27   H. von Aulock, *Münzen und Städte Phrygiens* (2 vols.; Tübingen: Wasmuth, 1980, 1987), II, nos.566–78 (pp.91–2); nos.588–9 (p.93).

28   See E. Matthews, 'names, personal, Greek', in S. Hornblower and A. Spawforth (eds.), *Oxford Classical Dictionary* (Oxford: Oxford University Press, 3rd edn, 1996), pp.1022–4 (1022–3).

names appear to follow this onomastic pattern. The extension of one's genealogy is not unique to Colossae, since it is found in many cities throughout Asia Minor.[29]

At one level, the genealogical succession underscores a desire to demonstrate (if not assert) the stability of family connection, based upon the Greek model.[30] Stability and permanence are values of intensified importance in the aftermath of a major disaster. In part the name list engaged the symbolics of the restoration of the baths. Baths in Asia Minor had begun to blend with the gymnasium as a united or combined architectural complex during this period.[31] The damage to the baths-gymnasium is likely also to have damaged the epigraphic lists of ephebes and their families, crucial in the public display of social integration and status in a polis. The subscribers were thereby participating, through the inscribed list on the pedestal, in the restoration of a key function of the baths-gymnasium – namely the indication of Colossian citizens, now taking responsibility not only for the repair of the baths, but in main-taining the honours that speak of a functioning city.[32] Though this can only be surmised, at the very least the onomastic list mirrors the main-tenance of societal stability that ephebic lists conveyed.

The extensive patronymics indicate that an overtly Greek mode of genealogical display is in operation. This 'Greekness' is reflected in the names of the subscribers themselves. Of the eighteen extant names of subscribers, sixteen are manifestly Greek: Tryphon, Theodoros and so on. The remaining two names, Menogas and Menas, clearly owe their origin to the Anatolian deity Mên.[33] However, theophoric derivatives from Mên were already well-established as Greek names. On this basis

29   See, for example, *IK* 57.126 (from Pisidia), *CIG* 2843 (from Aphrodisias), *TAM* II.309 (from Xanthus).

30   Cf. K. Hopkins, *Death and Renewal* (Cambridge: Cambridge University Press, 1983), p.112.

31   F. Yegül, *Baths and Bathing in Classical Antiquity* (New York: MIT, 1992), p.250; and A. Zuiderhoek, *The Politics of Munificence in the Roman Empire: Citizens, Elites and Benefactors in Asia Minor* (Cambridge: Cambridge University Press, 2009), p.83. Cf. H. Pleket, 'The Infrastructure of Sport in the Cities of the Greek World', *Scienze dell'Antichità* 10 (2000), pp.627–44 (634–5). On the impact of Roman models on the transformation of Greek civic structures, see E. Thomas, *Monumentality and the Roman Empire: Architecture in the Antonine Age* (Oxford: Oxford University Press, 2007), p.222.

32   See Pausanias, *Desc.* 10.4.1 for his view of the key characteristics of a functioning πόλις.

33   For the ubiquity, but not exclusivity, of this god in Asia Minor, see E. Lane, *Corpus Monumentorum Religionis Dei Menis* (3 vols.; Leiden: Brill, 1971–76).

T. Drew-Bear and C. M. Thomas claim that Mênogas is a Greek hypocoristic name.[34] While a caveat might be placed over the complete validity
of this assertion – the specific name Mênogas is not known with any
frequency outside Asia Minor – the general acceptability in Greek (or
Greek-aligning) families for such μην- theonyms certainly is.[35]

Some of these Greek names are almost assertively Greek. There are
theonyms (Apollonios, Eutuches, Diodotos, Theodoros) including the
hypocoristic Demas (a contraction of Demetrios) and herophoric names
that include legendary heroes (Herakleon) and famous leaders (Alexan-
dros, Attalos and possibly Ktesas).[36] Tudeides is especially significant.
The unusual name tracks a lineage back to Homer, as one of the Achaean
leaders loyal to Odysseus.[37] But it is also a name that can track an etymology indigenous to Asia Minor. In Lycian, it means 'son of Tudeus',[38]
the very accent given to the name in Homer. There may be secondary
(local) support behind its choice.

This emphasis on Greek names continues in the patronymics (Herak-
leides, Demetrios, Zosimos, Diodoros, Antimedes). However, it is not
uniform. There is, in the genealogical lines of the subscribers, evidence
of family members bearing non-Greek names. Thracian names (Skeparnas,
and probably Môkeas) are present. There may be a specific indication of
a Scythian name, albeit here occurring in a fragmentary state (Anôt-) as
well as one that may have a Phrygian affinity (Minnion).[39] Interestingly,

---

34   T. Drew-Bear, C. M. Thomas and M. Yıldızturan, *Phrygian Votive Steles*
(Ankara: Ministry of Culture, 1999), p.387.

35   Note G. H. R. Horsley, *The Greek and Latin Inscriptions in the Burdur
Archaeological Museum* (RECAM V) (London: British Institute at Ankara, 2007),
p.287b.

36   Ktêsias was a famous Carian historian, a contemporary of Xenophon. The
name, for this reason, is not precluded from being epichoric.

37   Homer, *Od.* 3.181; *Il.* 5.1. The imitation of Homer is attested throughout Asia
Minor; see G. H. R. Horsley, 'Homer in Pisidia: Aspects of the History of Greek
Education in a Remote Roman Province', *Antichthon* 34 (2000), pp.46–81.

38   S. Colvin, 'Names in Hellenistic and Roman Lycia', in S. Colvin (ed.), *The
Greco-Roman East: Politics, Culture, Society* (Cambridge: Cambridge University
Press, 2004), pp.44–84 (56).

39   L. Zgusta, *Kleinasiatische Personennamen* (Prague: Czechoslovakian
Academy, 1964), pp.318, 512. Cf. L. Robert, *Noms indigènes dans L'Asie-Mineure
Gréco-romaine* (repr.; Amsterdam: Hakkert, 1991 [1963]), p.226. The name pre-
dominates in the Carian region; see F. Marchand, 'The Philippeis of *IG* VII 2433', in
R. W. V. Catling and F. Marchand (eds.), *Onomatologos: Studies in Greek Personal
Names Presented to Elaine Matthews* (Oxford: Oxbow, 2010), pp.332–43 (337–8).
The name may be homonymic for the Phrygian, Munnion, especially if the phonemic

there is only one Roman name: Likinnios, a gentilicium that here, stand-ing alone, almost certainly indicates the servile origins of one grand-father. One name might be metronymic – Ioulis – though it may also function like a demotic, tying the bearer to the island of Keos. It is to be expected, there is no Jewish name.[40] One would more confidently expect a Persian name, but none is extant. Neither the poverty nor absence of Roman (or Jewish or Persian) names is conclusive, however, of ethnic, legal or marital ties, especially given that other Colossian inscriptions do attest Latin names, sometimes with the Roman citizenry formula (*BCH* 11.10; *MAMA* VI.39).

The genealogies, for all their modeling on the Greek form, appear to have no concern at allowing non-Greek patronymics to be noticed in their family line, or even a servile connection and, in possibly one case, a metronym. At the same time, there is a discernible move away from the epichoric names of past generations to Greek names in the present. The usual Greek onomastic pattern is to confer a grandfather's name on the grandson, but not if the grandfather's name was not Greek. A 'reduced' multiple ethnic identity is perfectly possible without compromising a dominant or public self-ascription to Greek identity,[41] just as multiple citizenships could be held without qualifying one's *patris* or home city. If there are ethnic backgrounds matching the ethnic origins of the names in these Colossian families, then there has been a very deliberate move to a Greek appearance. The Colossian office of interpreters and translators supports the presence of multiple ethno-linguistic backgrounds.[42] But the epigraphic language at Colossae is predominantly Greek. The dominant commitment is 'Greekness', with a growing Hellenic display in naming practices which coheres with other Greek values – stability in family and social structures, euergetism, civic landmarks and, of course, the Greek language.

These brief observations concur with the results *and* the chronological pattern of a more extensive survey made by S. Colvin in his study of Lycian and Greek names. He found a four-fold propensity in name

---

quality of 'u' is proximate to the Greek *iota*. Such influences of pronunciation are likely attested in other Colossian inscriptions (e.g. *MAMA* VI.44).

40   Cf. the third-century CE ephebic list from Memphis, where one Semitic name is included; see M. N. Tod, 'An Ephebic Inscription from Memphis', *Journal of Egyptian Archaeology* 37 (1951), pp.86–99 (98).

41   So Esler, *Conflict and Identity*, p.57.

42   See A. H. Cadwallader, 'A New Inscription [read: Two New Inscriptions]: A Correction and a Confirmed Sighting from Colossae', *EA* 40 (2007), pp.109–18 (113–14).

choice. First, there were Greek theophoric names, no doubt assisted by the adaptation of Greek gods to pre-existing indigenous deities.[43] Secondly, names with mythical-historical resonances in the region, especially those that had attracted some sort of Greek valorisation, were available. Third, were the 'herophoric names' of Macedonian colonisation and its aftermath and, fourth, names with phonetic similarity to epichoric names.[44] All these characteristics can be paralleled in the Colossian inscription. Furthermore, Colvin found a decline in the frequency of occurrence of indigenous names the closer one came to the early imperial period, although a willingness to retain an identifiable indigenous connection remains in evidence.[45] The Colossian inscription of itself is a small sample to compare with Colvin's regional sweep and may, in the end, follow more closely the Carian picture where indigenous names had almost disappeared from public and private inscriptions by the first century CE.

However, when one recognises the Phrygian names of women conjoined with males with Greek names in Colossian or Colossian-related text and epigraphy, then one suspects that the incentive for the presentation of 'Greekness' as a means to political and economic advancement and social status is operating more strongly for males than for women.[46] Here the public/private aspect of gender relationships surfaces. Thus in an honorific dedication to the emperor Trajan by a local woman named Apphia, her father and probably grandfather (the stone, when recorded in the 1880s, was damaged) were both bearers of Greek names: Herakleos and Dioskourides/Dioskouridos-.[47] In a funerary inscription from Balboura, a woman with a similar Phrygian name, Arphias, is married to a local man, Hermas, but is also carefully named as from Colossae (a citizen?), daughter of a man named Tryphon (the name ubiquitous in the baths inscription above).[48] Such a conjunction of a woman bearing a Phrygian name in a family or household with two men with Greek names

---

43   The same propensity is found in Caria; see I.-J. A. Lajara, *The Carian Language* (Leiden: Brill, 2007), pp.331–2.

44   Colvin, 'Names in Lycia', pp.57–67.

45   Colvin, 'Names in Lycia', p.69.

46   Cf. the lack of 'homogenous onomastic content' in the list of women's names deemed to be from Laodiceia; see P. Ö. Aytaçlar and E. Akıncı, 'A List of Female Names from Laodicea', *EA* 39 (2006), pp.113–16.

47   *BCH* 11.354 = *IGR* iv.868 as amended by L. Robert, in J. des Gagniers et al. (eds.), *Laodicée du Lycos: le Nymphée, Campagnes 1961–1963* (Quebec: L'Université Laval, 1969), pp.278–9.

48   *CIG* 3.4380k3 = *RECAM* 3.1.26; 3.4.11.

is precisely what we find in the opening of Paul's letter to Philemon (vv. 1-2). Indeed, if, as appears likely, the move to Greek names is designed for political and economic advantage and/or social status, then the distinction of males of a household bearing Greek names whilst the females retain an epichoric name, may itself be corroborative of the motivation, given the paucity of women in public life.[49] M. Olender's critical insight is pertinent here, that since male and female roles are not equivalent in the ancient world, words and gestures, and for that matter, names, cannot be expected to align symmetrically.[50] Of course, the evidence for Colossae is limited and would need to be correlated across Phrygia. Nevertheless, it is suggestive of a line of further research.

One final observation from Colvin is pertinent. He writes, 'a Greek inscription on a monument can have had no value except to someone who appreciated the *Greekness itself* of the text'.[51] Overall, then, this inscription underscores the high value placed on things 'Greek' in first-century Colossae, even though indigenous self-consciousness (Scythian and 'barbarian') may have continued in family and private life. It is the Hellenic sensibility that delivers a section of Colossae's citizens a confirmation of their influence in the Colossian polity. Moreover, it is clear that they have every expectation that such a value would be shared by those intended to view the pedestal and inscription.

49   This is not to deny the presence and independent authority of elite women in public life; see R. A. Kearsley, 'Women and Public Life in Imperial Asia Minor: Hellenistic Tradition and Augustan Ideology', in G. R. Tsetskhladze (ed.), *Ancient West and East* (Leiden: Brill, 2005), pp.98–121.

50   M. Olender, 'Aspects of Baubo: Ancient Texts and Contexts', in D. M. Halperin, J. J. Winkler and F. I. Zeitlin (eds.), *Before Sexuality: The Construction of Erotic Experience in the Ancient Greek World* (Princeton: Princeton University Press, 1990), pp.83–113 (103). Olender was applying the principle to the interpretation of obscenity, but the methodological caution is generally pertinent; so Horsley's brief aside of similar import in G. H. R. Horsley (ed.), *New Documents Illustrating Early Christianity*, II (North Ryde: Ancient History Documentary Research Centre, 1982), p.103. A. Davies shows the application in part to women's names: distinctions according to gender are a primary concern in naming. See A. Davies, 'Greek Personal Names and Linguistic Continuity', in S. Hornblower and E. Matthews (eds.), *Greek Personal Names: Their Value as Evidence* (Oxford: British Academy, 2000), pp.15–39 (20–21). Here I would argue that the distinctions of gender operate not only within Greek onomastics but also in application to non-Greek names.

51   Colvin, 'Names in Lycia', p.70 (his emphasis).

3. *The Hellenic Negotiation under Imperial Rome*

The chronology of this shift in naming behaviour is significant. G. Horsley notes, 'The indigenous embrace of Hellenism becomes widely evident epigraphically only in the early Imperial centuries'.[52] Even allowing for the mimetic cultivation of the 'epigraphic habit' in the Augustan era,[53] one still has to account for the adoption of an Hellenic stance. Certainly, in the post-Alexandrian cultivation of Hellenism, the dominant cultural expression was as protected as it was broadcast.[54] However, with the advent of the Roman supremacy, the dominant centre had changed.[55] It brought with it a shake-down of Greek restriction on matters Greek, not for the reduction of Hellenistic commitment but, rather, for its democratisation, given that Rome had taken the position previously occupied by the Greek elite. As Horace satirically distilled the result: *Graecia capta ferum victorem cepit* ('Greece the captive, took her savage victor captive').[56] With the restrictions on Roman citizenship so clear in the early principate, the next best option, especially to maintain or advance position in urban life in Asia Minor, was to display one's Hellenistic credentials. Encouragement came from the top. The Augustan revolution did not dispense with Greek culture but gave it a decidedly Roman vision, as a means of accenting, through a 'Classicistic Revival', the highest civilisation (now secure under Rome). There were many aspects to this program: a disdain for Asian expressions, a concern over gender roles and above all the incorporation of Greek culture under, and as a demonstration of, Roman commitment.[57] Of course, the intricacies of the

---

52   Horsley, *Greek and Latin Inscriptions*, p.2b.

53   See generally, R. MacMullen, 'The Epigraphic Habit in the Roman Empire', *AJP* 103 (1996), pp.233–46.

54   See Athenaeus, *Deipn.* 624d; cf. 632a. Cf. too Euripides, *Tro.* 764: 'Greeks from barbarians finding evil ways'; and Plato, *Menex.* 245d: 'We are pure Greeks here (Athens), not semi-barbarians'. See also Polybius, *Hist.* 1.67.7, and Heliodorus, *Aeth.* 9.24.

55   This is the fundamental problem with C. Stanley's evidence (see n.7, above) cited to explain Paul's use of 'Greek' rather than 'Gentile' in his summary formulations. He sees 'Greek' as ethnically specific, built on the antagonisms between Jew and Greek under *republican* Rome. Not only does this fail to attend to the dramatic change in imperial politics that comes with the Augustan accent on 'Greekness', but it also fails to allow that race and ethnicity are undergoing significant reconstruction in the early imperial period. See D. K. Buell and C. J. Hodge, 'The Politics of Interpretation: The Rhetoric of Race and Ethnicity in Paul', *JBL* 123 (2004), pp.235–51.

56   Horace, *Ep.* 2.1.156.

57   Note A. J. S. Spawforth, *Greece and the Augustan Cultural Revolution* (Cambridge: Cambridge University Press, 2011).

spectrum between embrace and (usually passive) resistance were played out in the east, but the modeling and display of a Hellenic sensibility under a Roman imprimatur is clear from the late first century BCE to beyond the first century CE.[58] Accordingly, ethnicity undergoes considerable innovative (self-)construction.

Names and epigraphical practice were but two of the tactics deployed to adjust to the realities of this shift in political realities. The advent of Roman imperial rule in Asia Minor had the curious result of extending Greek identification in those places that, prior to Rome's control of Asia Minor, had operated as Greek *poleis*. Indigenous or earlier settled groups might have had to find different ways of relating to the Greek elite under Seleucid rule but the advent of Rome made the old divisions more permeable. Rome held the ultimate authority and power in those cities, but status, at least for the early period of the imperium, became defined broadly, as it was more accessible in Greek terms.[59] The increase of Hellenistic identification in the early Roman principate turns out to be a key element in the transition and remodeling of Asian cities into Roman conformity.[60] The transition, however, actually required or at least received a more pervasive Hellenistic expression as a precursor or preparation, ironic because it actually testified to the erosion of Greek elite dominance.

4. *Naming Practices and Greek Identity*

For those without such substance, the easy means to identify with 'Greekness' and its values in a pre-existing Greek polis lay in the adoption of a Greek name. Throughout the Mediterranean are examples of members of native or non-Greek constituencies taking hold of names more identified with Greek onomastics.[61] The obvious choice was to go

58   See G. Woolf, 'Becoming Roman, Staying Greek: Culture, Identity and the Civilizing Process in the Roman East', *PCPS* 40 (1994), pp.116–43.

59   See the distinction between Roman and Greek civic status articulated by S. Dmitriev, *City Government in Hellenistic and Roman Asia Minor* (Oxford: Oxford University Press, 2005), pp.138–39.

60   C. Ratté, 'The Urban Development of Aphrodisias in the Late Hellenistic and Early Imperial Periods', in C. Bern, L. Vandeput and M. Waelkens (eds.), *Patris und Imperium: Kulturelle und Politische Identität in den Stadten in den römischen Provinzen Kleinasiens in der frühen Kaiserzeit* (Leuven: Peeters, 2002), pp.5–32 (7).

61   The significant exception is in Rome itself where the move is *away* from Greek names (because of its association with servility). See T. Frank, 'Race Mixture in the Roman Empire', *AHR* 21 (1916), pp.689–708 (691).

for a homonym, that is, a name in Greek that sounded similar to the epi-choric name, though the adoption of a second and Greek name was not restricted to homonyms.[62] Egyptians are known to have practised it,[63] as identified long ago by A. Deissmann.[64] T. J. Smith finds such homonymic practice amongst the local population at Balboura south of Colossae, where both Phrygian and Pisidian names were given a homophonic Greek equivalent.[65]

Jews appear to have been as much part of this practice as other non-Greek populations.[66] G. Mussies saw 'Ιάσων in Rom. 16.21 as a homonymic substitute for 'Ιησοῦς.[67] Closer to Colossae are examples found at Hierapolis and at Aphrodisias.[68] M. Williams argues that the explanation for such onomastic practice is simple – it was assimilationist behaviour designed to advance prospects and facilitate connections in the dominant culture.[69] All these examples come from the Roman imperial period. They are strongly in evidence in the New Testament.[70] And this is, I have argued elsewhere, precisely how Col. 4.11, 'Jesus also called Justus', is to be interpreted.[71]

---

62   See G. H. R. Horsley, *New Documents Illustrating Early Christianity*, I (North Ryde: Ancient History Documentary Research Centre, 1981), pp.89–96; and M. H. Williams, 'The Use of Alternative Names by Diaspora Jews in Graeco-Roman Antiquity', *JSJ* 38 (2007), pp.307–27 (324–7).

63   P.Berol. 7080B.

64   A. Deissmann, *Bible Studies* (Edinburgh: T. & T. Clark, 1909), p.315.

65   T. J. Smith, 'Votive Reliefs from Balboura and its Environs', *AS* 47 (1997), pp.3–47 (35 and n.18).

66   For example, 'Ιώνιος for Jonas, at Sepphoris, *CIJ* 1.362 = *JIWE* II.60.

67   In Horsley, *New Documents*, I, p.93. See also G. Mussies, 'Jewish Personal Names in Some Non-literary Sources', in J. W. van Henten and P. W. van der Horst (eds.), *Studies in Early Jewish Epigraphy* (Leiden: Brill, 1994), pp.242–76 (273). Identical is Josephus, *A.J.* 12.239. See N. G. Cohen, 'The Names of the Translators in the Letter of Aristeas: A Study in the Dynamics of Cultural Transition', *JSJ* 15 (1984), pp.32–64 (46–48).

68   'Jason the Jew': Miranda, 'La comunità giudaica', p.117 no.3 = *IJO* II.190; at Aphrodisias, the same homonym: *MAMA* VIII.488, *IJO* II.14B.

69   Williams, 'The Use of Alternative Names', pp.313, 318; see also I. M. Gafni, *Land, Center and Diaspora: Jewish Constructs in Late Antiquity* (Sheffield: Sheffield Academic, 1997), pp.49–50.

70   See R. Bauckham, *Gospel Women: Studies of the Named Women in the Gospels* (London: Continuum, 2002), pp.182–5.

71   A. H. Cadwallader, '"What's in a Name": The Tenacity of a Tradition of Interpretation', *Lutheran Theological Journal* 39 (Festschrift for Victor Pfitzner edited by P. Lockwood) (2005), pp.218–39.

5. *Marginalising the Jew in Colossians*

And yet, this level of assimilation, its 'unremarkability' in the wider context of Diasporan Jewry's negotiation of the Mediterranean world,[72] is *not* what is achieved in the letter to the Colossians, even though a homonym is recorded. Jesus, who is called Justus *is marked out*, along with Mark (qualified by his tie to Barnabas) and perhaps Aristarchos[73] as οἱ οὖντες ἐκ περιτομῆς οὖτοι μόνοι συνεργοὶ εἰς τὴν βασιλείαν τοῦ θεοῦ, οὕτινες ἐγενήθησάν μοι παρηγορία (NRSV: 'These are the only ones of the circumcision among my co-workers for the kingdom of God', Col. 4.11). The obvious intent of the phrasing is to present Jewish companions of Paul as now in a minority (note μόνοι), and a decided one at that (two, at most four).

The debate over the Pauline authenticity of the letter bedevils the interpretation here. Those favouring Paul's authorship read the phrase as a small sample of a wider number of Jews in the Pauline mission, thence to argue that the Colossians letter and its references to Jewish practices and influence reflects Jewish opposition from the 'Colossian synagogue'.[74] Even M. MacDonald, who favours pseudonymous authorship, interprets the meaning as if it is authentic, pointing to Paul's other Jewish co-workers such as Prisca and Aquila (Rom. 16.3) and using the phrase ἐκ περιτομῆς in Colossians to delimit the unqualified use of the same phrase in Gal. 2.12 (cf. Tit. 1.10).

However, two considerations are key to its interpretation here. First, this is the only time in a Pauline greetings list that anyone is identified by reference to an ethnicity/cultural mark. Secondly, J. Bassler has demonstrated the methodological necessity in allowing the semantics of a word or phrase in a Deutero-Pauline writing to be different from its use in the authentic letters.[75] Accordingly, the use of the phrase ἐκ περιτομῆς in Galatians may not necessarily have the same connotation in Colossians.

---

72   Cf. S. Honigman, 'Abraham in Egypt: Hebrew and Jewish-Aramaic Names in Egypt and Judaea in Hellenistic and Early Roman Times', *ZPE* 146 (2004), pp.279–97.

73   It is altogether possible that Aristarchos is separated from the others by the description ὁ συναιχμάλωτός μου (καί). M. MacDonald allows this, though without explanation. See M. MacDonald, *Colossians and Ephesians* (SP 17; Collegeville: Liturgical Press, 2000), p.181. Dunn sees Aristarchos as distinguished on other grounds by collation with Acts 20.4. See Dunn, *Colossians*, p.278.

74   Dunn, *Colossians*, p.278.

75   J. M. Bassler, 'The Enigmatic Sign: 2 Thessalonians 1.5', *CBQ* 46 (1984), pp.496–510.

The NRSV concurs, reading 'the circumcision faction' in Galatians, indicating a party allegiance, whereas it uses simply 'of the circumcision' in Colossians, turning the phrase into a synecdoche or metonymy for a distinct people (cf. Eph. 2.11). In Colossians, the intent is not to brand a party of opposition within the Jesus groups[76] but rather to indicate that the followers of Jesus who are Jews, even those aligned with Paul of Tarsus, are now noticeable precisely because they are a minority in the Church, at least in Colossae and its vicinity. The anchor of identity, the point to which and against which early Jesus followers in Colossae were to be measured, has shifted. No longer are Jews, with their distinguishing mark of circumcision, the point of reference (whether or not one adopted that mark), so much so that when Jews are mentioned, they can now be referred to by the mark that no longer has any hold or bearing on the life of the majority. For the majority, circumcision becomes a bare metaphor, with no physiological contention (so Col. 2.11, 13). It is no longer the primary concern of Jesus followers, at least at Colossae. The effective environment that is now shaping and directing the life of the Jesus groups in Colossae, and I would say of whatever Jewish communities were present as well, is now the Hellenistic-come-Graeco-Roman society and culture, whether that be in a conflictual or consensual stance or a pragmatic circumstantial negotiation.[77]

6. *Conclusions*

The letter to the Colossians provides one of the earliest indications that the place of the Jew in the reckoning of groups of Jesus followers is diminishing. It may be localised at this point in time but the change has begun, both demographically and conceptually. The Korumbos inscription alerts us to at least one of the key influences upon that shift – the wider society and culture in Colossae and beyond is now reconfiguring itself in relation to Rome by a widespread accent on Hellenic display. And, as T. L. Donaldson observes, 'religious groups cannot be understood apart from the cities in which they are embedded...'[78] This societal

---

76   And thereby use Mark and Jesus as the welcome exceptions to opponents (MacDonald, *Colossians, Ephesians*, p.181).

77   See R. A. Atkins, *Egalitarian Community: Ethnography and Exegesis* (Tuscaloosa: University of Alabama Press, 1991), p.27.

78   T. L. Donaldson, 'Introduction', in T. L. Donaldson (ed.), *Religious Rivalries and the Struggle for Success in Caesarea Maritima* (Waterloo: Wilfred Laurier University Press, 2000), pp.1–8 (3).

reconfiguration is reflected in Col. 3.11 and 4.11, which indicate that the (aspirant) Greek perspective and commitment in the Jesus groups at Colossae is rising at the expense of the Jewish – and the text is likely to be subsequent to ethnic and cultural allegiance.[79] A thorough analysis of the Jewish-flavoured references in Col. 2.16-17 must await another opportunity. However, enough has been established to yield a *prima facie* contention that their inclusion is part of the rhetorical and strategic manoeuvres of the writer to assist a community to define itself.

I have suggested that this wider society and culture in Colossae was characterised by a growing and diversifying Hellenic ethos, fired by the impact of the Roman imperium in Asia and that this, not the presence of Jews or Jewish-Christians, has become, in the history of the Jesus groups at Colossae, the main point of reference for the construction of its life and a major realignment of the direction of the Pauline tradition. The irony is that Paul himself was not unaffected by the Augustan revolution that continued through the first century and that his own shift from 'Jew and Gentile' to 'Jew and Greek' probably owes its impulse, obliquely, to this context and finds its meaningful exchange there. But it is also this larger context that explains the confronting change from 'Jew and Greek' to 'Greek and Jew' and the portrayal of Jew and Jewish practices as a peripheral oddity, with 'Gentile' no longer a key element in the self-identity of Jesus followers at Colossae. There is, as Lincoln and Wedderburn admit, a shift to 'a more pronouncedly *Greek* point of view',[80] albeit a Greek point of view cultivated under the auspices of Rome.

---

79   See Esler, *Conflict and Identity*, pp.56–8, 62; cf. J. M. Lieu, *Christian Identity in the Jewish and Graeco-Roman World* (Oxford: Oxford University Press, 2004), pp.34–7.
80   Lincoln and Wedderburn, *Later Pauline Letters*, p.13 (my emphasis).

Chapter 15

'YOU SHALL NOT GIVE WHAT IS HOLY TO THE DOGS' (*DIDACHE* 9.5): THE ATTITUDE OF THE *DIDACHE* TO THE GENTILES

Jonathan A. Draper

1. *Introduction*

After ten years of seminars at the SBL on the subject, the *Didache* remains, perhaps, one of the most contested fields of study for the reconstruction of early Christian origins. While most scholars of the *Didache* today take it as an early Jewish Christian or Christian Jewish text, those outside the field are wary of using it in the reconstruction of Christian origins. In the massive collection of his studies on *Jews, Christians and Jewish Christians in Antiquity* published in 2010, James Carleton-Paget[1] makes only one reference to the *Didache* and that in the context of Harnack's declaration in his *Dogmengeschichte* that it would be wrong to describe it as Jewish Christian because this term can only apply to those Christians, 'who really maintained in their whole extent, or to some degree, the national and political forms of Judaism and the observance of the Mosaic law in its literal sense, as essential to Christianity, at least to the Christianity of born Jews, or who, though rejecting these forms, nevertheless assumed a prerogative of the Jewish people even in Christianity'.[2] It might, therefore, seem premature to try to delineate the attitude of the *Didache* towards the Gentiles, when its Jewishness is not accepted by all, but I do not wish to rehearse old arguments here but move the discussion on.[3] The only assumption I will begin my discussion

---

1   J. Carleton-Paget, *Jews, Christians and Jewish Christians in Antiquity* (WUNT 251; Tübingen: Mohr Siebeck, 2010), p.304.

2   A. von Harnack, *The History of Dogma* (2 vols.; London: Williams & Norgate, 1894), I, p.289.

3   For my position on this, see J. A. Draper, 'The Holy Vine of David Made Known to the Gentiles through God's Servant Jesus: "Christian Judaism" in the *Didache*', in M. Jackson-MacCabe (ed.), *Jewish Christianity Reconsidered: Rethinking Ancient Groups and Texts* (Minneapolis: Fortress, 2007), pp.257–83.

with is that the whole text served as a manual for a particular community at a particular time, however and whenever its various sections originated. I will begin with *Didache* 9.5, a text which has not attracted much comment.

2. *You Shall Not Give the Holy to the Dogs*

The text itself in the Jerusalem manuscript (H54) runs as follows:

μηδεὶς δὲ φαγέτω	But let no one eat
μηδὲ πιέτω	and let no one drink
ἀπὸ τῆς εὐχαριστίας ὑμῶν	from your Eucharist
ἀλλ' οἱ βαπτισθέντες	But those who have been baptised
εἰς ὄνομα κυρίου	in the name of the Lord
καὶ γὰρ περὶ τούτου εἴρηκεν ὁ κύριος	For also concerning this the Lord has said
Μὴ δῶτε τὸ ἅγιον τοῖς κυσί	*You shall not give what is holy to the dogs.*

In his important study of the meal ritual in the *Didache*, J. Schwiebert has noted correctly that 'The implication of this saying is that the food was somehow (at least in a symbolic sense) a sacred meal, akin to a sacrifice',[4] although I am not sure what 'sacred in a symbolic sense' might mean, and that 'This usage assumes a sacrificial understanding of the meal as food dedicated to the deity and consumed by the community'.[5] Schwiebert, correctly in my opinion, cites the parallels in the practice of the *Community Rule* from Qumran, though he does not note

4   J. Schwiebert, *Knowledge and the Coming Kingdom: The Didache's Meal Ritual and its Place in Early Christianity* (LNTS 373; London: T&T Clark International, 2008), p.159.

5   Schwiebert, *Knowledge and the Coming Kingdom*, p.159. Schwiebert's lack of precision about 'food dedicated to the deity' follows a tradition in North American scholarship. J. W. Riggs, 'The Sacred Food of *Didache* 9–10 and Second-Century Ecclesiologies', in C. N. Jefford (ed.), *The Didache in Context: Essays on its Text, History, and Transmission* (NovTSup 77; Leiden: Brill, 1995), pp.256–84, argues that this text, which he dates to the late second-century redaction, 'reveals a transition from table-sharing towards divine food' as opposed to the hypothetical 'open commensality' of Jesus posited by the Jesus Seminar of the Westar Institute, which is revealed in the 'simple Christian variation of a Jewish thanksgiving prayer' in *Did.* 9; see Riggs, 'Sacred Food', p.265. In my estimation, this text is precisely about Jewish table-sharing and its consequences for purity in a mixed community of Jews and Gentiles and has nothing to do with 'divine food' in a sacramental sense.

that the instructions concerning the purity of the community's meal come from the context of instruction for initiation there as it does in *Did.* 9.5. He also does not raise the question of the identity of the 'dogs'. Do the 'dogs' refer to all those outside the community, Jews and Gentiles alike, or do they refer to a limited group, namely Gentiles and not Jews? I will come back to this later.

In a fine study written as a contribution to ecumenism between Roman Catholics and Protestants, W. Rordorf[6] points to this text as establishing that the *sanctorum communio* was regarded by a number of very early texts as a communion of holy *people* established by baptism and the forgiveness of sins rather than a communion of holy *elements*.[7] However, he overlooks the fact that, while clearly baptism brings people into a state of holiness, there is no mention of forgiveness of sins in the baptismal instructions of *Didache* 7, and that repentance and confession of trespasses is not related to the *creation* of holiness but to the *maintenance* of holiness *after* baptism (10.6; 14.1). Lustration in ritually pure water brings those living in a state of impurity (in the understanding of the community) into a state of purity. The meal is holy because those sharing the table are living in a state of purity which has to be constantly maintained in the initiation of new members and in the discipline of existing members. This is where the parallel with the Qumran texts raised by Schwiebert is most telling.

1QS is applying to its members the rule concerning *tohoroth*, the pure things reserved to the priests in Leviticus, since the community regards itself as a priestly Temple community.[8] The meal of the community is described in the language of the Temple and its sacrifices as *kodesh*, which is translated as τὸ ἅγιον in the Septuagint, the food which is reserved for the priests. Access to the holy Temple food is only permitted to those in a state of purity, so the question as to who is allowed to eat or drink that which is holy defines their state of purity. To eat what is holy in a state of impurity (*tumah*) is to risk the anger and punishment of the holy God. The result is that the purity of food and drink become the boundary marker and guarantor between insiders and outsiders for both Qumran and the community of the *Didache*. Those outside are in a state

---

6 W. Rordorf, '*Ta hagia tois hagiois*', *Irénikon* 72 (1999), pp.346–64.

7 Rordorf argues that the ambiguous phrase should be left ambiguous!

8 See B. Gärtner, *The Temple and the Community in Qumran and the New Testament: A Comparative Study in the Temple Symbolism of the Qumran Texts and the New Testament* (SNTSMS 1; Cambridge: Cambridge University Press, 1965); and H. Harrington, *The Purity Texts* (CQS 5; London: T&T Clark International, 2004), pp.7–44.

of impurity which prohibits them from sharing in the pure meal of the community. The uninitiated in Qumran are excluded from this purity until they have been purified over a two-year period of separation and instruction, after which they are immersed and admitted to the pure meal (first year) and drink (second year) of the community.[9] An additional aspect of this period of 'quarantine' is that their material goods are impounded before being finally merged with the common property of the community when they are admitted to full membership. This has economic aspects in terms of the sustainability of the community, of course, but it is motivated more by the need to preserve the purity of the community.

Since the pioneering work of J. Milgrom[10], the central principle of Torah is the sanctity of life found in blood, from which humans must abstain, although as a concession they may kill and eat animals:

> Since impurity and holiness…are semantic opposites, and since the quintessence and source of holiness is God, it behoves Israel to control the occurrence of impurity lest it impinge on the realm of the holy God. The forces pitted against each other in the cosmic struggle are no longer the benevolent and demonic deities who populate the mythologies of Israel's neighbours, but the forces of life and death set loose by man himself through his obedience to or defiance of God's commandments.[11]

Furthermore, this holiness of God is associated with God's moral attributes, so that both ritual and moral purity is required. Recent studies have tended to emphasise the separation between ritual and moral purity.[12] Nevertheless, Milgrom's suggestion that the opposition of life and death at the heart of the ritual purity system of Israel is linked also to an ethics of life and death rooted in the life of God is certainly suggestive for our purposes.

Purity in ancient Israel and also in Second Temple traditions is understood as 'necessary for the activation of holiness' supremely centred from the Temple and the land of covenant outward, and its opposite, impurity,

---

9   This may be why the *Didache* at this point mentions food first and drink second in reverse order to the Eucharistic prayers in 9.1-4, although it could also plausibly reflect a later redaction.

10   J. Milgrom, *Leviticus: A New Translation with Introduction and Commentary* (AB 3, 3A, 3B; 3 vols.; New York: Doubleday, 1991–2001), especially his first volume. His theory is succinctly summarised in J. Milgrom, 'Rationale for Cultic Law: The Case of Impurity', *Semeia* 45 (1989), pp.103–9.

11   Milgrom, 'Rationale', p.106.

12   J. Klawans, *Impurity and Sin in Ancient Judaism* (New York: Oxford University Press, 2000); and Hayes, *Gentile Impurities*.

'can impinge on God's realm and bring destruction on the community'.[13] Impurity could come from two different sources, ritual and moral. Ritual impurity ultimately derives from the exigencies associated with natural causes and is not considered to be morally reprehensible, indeed it is often unavoidable: death in the family, sexual intercourse, menstruation, and skin disease. Although there is some ambiguity at times whether sin might be involved, the norm would be that ritual impurity is only sin if it is deliberately ignored or contracted in a careless or inappropriate manner. It could be removed easily by ritual purification, often involving bathing or washing. Moral impurity on the other hand requires repentance and sacrifice. Ritual impurity is contagious and can isolate the whole community from contact with a holy God, so that its removal by purification or cutting off an obdurate offender is necessary. The test case for ritual purity or impurity is linked to fitness or otherwise for consumption of holy food from the Temple sacrifices.

The implication of this is that the saying, 'You shall not give the holy thing to the dogs' in *Did.* 9.5 should be understood with reference to Temple food reserved for the priests in the first instance, which is then extended to the whole eschatological community understood as the Temple. This is found also in the Qumran community understanding of itself as a Temple of men 'not made with human hands' (4QFlor) and in Paul (1 Cor. 3.16-17). This is why members can give thanks that God has made his holy Name dwell in their hearts (*Did.* 10.1) when they eat this meal together. The community constitutes a spiritual Temple. *Didache* 10.1-2 reads:

Μετὰ δὲ τὸ ἐμπλησθῆσαι οὕτως εὐχαριστήσατε Εὐχαριστοῦμεν σοι, πάτερ ἅγιε, ὑπὲρ τοῦ ἁγίου ὀνόματος σου, οὗ κατεσκήνωσας ἐν ταῖς καρδίαις ἡμῶν, καὶ ὑπὲρ τῆς γνώσεως καὶ πίστεως καὶ ἀθανασίας ἡμῖν διὰ Ἰησοῦ τοῦ παιδός σου. σοι ἡ δόξα εἰς τοὺς αἰῶνας

And after you have had enough, give thanks as follows: We give thanks, Holy Father, for your holy Name which you have caused to dwell in our hearts, and for the knowledge and faith and immortality that you have made known to us through Jesus your servant; to you be the glory forever.

It would be unthinkable that God's holy Name should dwell in anything which was not in a state of ritual purity. Therefore it is unthinkable that an unbaptised person should be admitted to the meal of the community

---

13   Harrington, *Purity Texts*, p.10.

of the *Didache*. Purification is achieved in this case through washing the ritually impure person in ritually cleansing water while the Name of the Lord is vocalised over the person (note the problem with the contradiction between 7.1-2 and 9.5).[14] *Didache* 7.2-4 requires washing in 'living water'(ἐν ὕδατι ζῶντι), which is the equivalent of the *mayim khayim* that are required to remove ritual impurity, as in Lev. 15.13; 'When the person with a discharge is cleansed of his or her discharge, s/he shall count seven days for his or her cleansing; s/he shall wash his or her clothes and bathe his or her body in running water (*mayim khayim*), and s/he shall be clean'.[15] In the eschatological age, *mayim khayim* shall flow out from the Temple to purify the land polluted by idolatry (Zech. 14.8). In other words, the connection between the baptism and Eucharist created by 7.2-4 and 9.5 is that community meals (*tohoroth*) are eaten in ritual purity created and maintained by ritual immersion in purificatory water (*mayim khayim*). This is why the kinds of water are more important than anything else and the grades of water are carefully specified: running water if at all possible at the one end, and water poured over the head separating the source of the water from the source of the impurity on the other, thus creating a ritually purified body.

It appears to me that the citation attributed to 'the Lord' may be a conscious reference to Jesus' teaching as mediated by Matthew, but it could equally be a reference to the Lord YHWH and his instructions in the Torah. This is because, whether the saying originates in *Didache* or in Matthew, its primary reference is to the principle of *tohoroth*. Leviticus 22.10-11 reads, 'No lay person shall eat of the sacred donations. No bound or hired servant of the priest shall eat of the *kodesh*/sacred donations, but if a priest acquires anyone by purchase, the person may eat of them; and those that are born in his house may eat of his food'. Leviticus 22.1-9 provides instruction to the priests concerning eating holy food from the Temple, while 22.10-16 provides instruction concerning non-priests and holy food – who may and who may not eat it. The key term *zar* in the saying is somewhat ambivalent and has led to a variety of translations and interpretations. According to Milgrom, however, it does not refer to a lay person in contrast to the priest but rather to an outsider (which is in any case semantically more appropriate): 'But according to the content of vv. 10-13, the definition of *zar* is more restricted [than "layperson"] to one who is neither a servant nor a family member or a

---

14   J. A. Draper, 'Ritual Process and Ritual Symbol in *Didache* 7–10', *VC* 54 (2000), pp.1–38.

15   I have used gender-inclusive language because I believe that the rule would apply to all those who are required to wash in this way to remove ritual impurity.

priest – that is, an outsider'.[16] While some Rabbis argue that not even this *kodesh* of the priests could be rendered unclean by contact with Gentiles, since they cannot convey impurity (*b. Nid.* 34a), nevertheless Gentiles do come to be regarded as impure as those suffering from *zab* (*t. Zab* 2.1; *b. Shab.* 17b; *b. Avod Zar.* 46b etc.), which would mean that they do convey uncleanness. It is also true that many texts prohibit eating with Gentiles on account of idolatry (*t. Avod Zar.* 4.6 and *Sifre Num.* 131). This saying in Leviticus is used as a proof-text oriented towards the Gentiles in the LXX (καὶ πᾶς ἀλλογενὴς οὐ φάγεται ἅγια), while the Targum Neofiti interprets *toshab* as a reference to the resident alien and provides the addition, 'the Gentile also shall not eat what is holy'. Milgrom[17] sees this as a misunderstanding of what is a hendiadys to refer to two separate categories. However, for our purposes the confusion patently reflects a widespread usage of the text to prohibit Gentiles from eating ritually pure food. Since the *Didache* community viewed itself as a holy community and a living Temple, the principle would prohibit the admission of Gentiles to the meal without ritual purification. In the context of an initiation ritual in early Christianity it could be applied more specifically, as in the LXX and *Tg. Neofiti*, to Gentiles.

The reference to dogs in the text of the *Didache* obviously depicts them as a quintessential source of defilement of the holy Temple food. Interestingly, the Qumran community was so anxious about the desecration of its *tohorah* or holy meal, that animal bones left over from meals were buried in clay pots to prevent dogs from eating them.[18] There is evidence from elsewhere also that Gentiles were insultingly referred to as 'dogs' with respect to their impurity. One need only refer to Mt. 15.26-27 and its source in Mk 7.27-28. While Matthew's Gospel has often been cited as the source of *Did.* 9.5, this is unlikely in my opinion. *Didache* 9.5 uses τὸ ἅγιον literally, while Mt. 7.6 uses it metaphorically in connection with 'pearls before swine'. What is more significant for our study is that Matthew apparently knows the connection between the saying and admission to the community. It is located between an injuction not to judge others (when they are unclean? a feeling of superiority over the Gentiles?) in 7.1-5, and the urgent instructions to knock and enter through the door (7.7-8), to trust that God will indeed give good things when people ask (7.9-11), the positive form of the Golden Rule (7.12), which is the summary of the Torah found also at the beginning of the Two Ways in the *Didache*, and then the instruction to enter through the

16   Milgrom, *Leviticus*, II, p.1861; cf. Deut. 25.5.
17   Milgrom, *Leviticus*, II, p.1861.
18   Harrington, *The Purity Texts*, p.23.

narrow gate which leads to life rather than through the gate and broad way that leads to destruction (7.13-14). The parallels with the Two Ways in *Didache* are obvious, in my opinion. So, whichever of the two texts comes first and whatever their relationship, they both acknowledge the origin of the saying in ritual initiation and consider those outside the community to be ritually unclean. The connection of the desecration of the holy meal by dogs with trampling of pearls by pigs in Matthew intensifies the warning of danger of impurity with the addition of a second impure animal. It is possible that Matthew has re-oriented what was originally an instruction on the holy meal to the Two Ways as holy teaching (pearls [of wisdom]) which would be defiled by inappropriately instructing Gentiles who are not yet ready for it.

The reference of the passage to ritual purity and to Gentiles as dogs has not escaped the close attention of the redactor of the *Apostolic Constitutions* VII.9.5, the only witness to this passage besides the Jerusalem Manuscript (H54), a text which Schwiebert[19] insightfully places at 'the end of a trajectory' of the Eucharistic prayer in the *Didache*. The much altered version in the *Apostolic Constitutions* removes all traces of the specific theology and practice of the community with regard to baptism and Eucharist. The text which is honoured, preserved and collected because of its antiquity and widespread use at some stage to the knowledge of the redactor is made to conform with the theology and practice of the stabilising Catholic Church. The recommendation to become 'perfect' by taking on the yoke of the Lord is removed, as is the requirement to keep as much of the Torah and *Kashrut* as possible, as too is the requirement to attend to grades of water – the Eucharistic prayer is re-oriented to the saving death of Christ and his resurrection; the elements are designated the body and blood of Jesus Christ, and the eschatological urgency is ameliorated (omitting, for instance, 'Let the Lord [Coptic; H54 "grace"] come and let this world pass away' in 10.6). In this context our logion has also received attention from the canonist:[20]

> Let no one eat of these things that is not initiated; but only those who have been baptised into the death of (Christ).[21] But if any one that is not initiated conceal himself, and partake of the same, he eats eternal judgment; because, being not of the faith of Christ, he has partaken of such

19   Schwiebert, *Knowledge and the Coming Kingdom*, pp.239–47.
20   The translation is that provided by P. Schaff, *The Teaching of the Twelve Apostles* (New York: Funk & Wagnalls, 1885). Where I have altered his translation, I have put it in parentheses.
21   Schaff has 'Lord'.

things as it is not (right)[22] for him to partake of, to his own punishment.
But if any one is a partaker through ignorance, instruct him quickly, and
initiate him, that he may not go out and despise you.

It can be seen immediately that the canonist in the *Apostolic Constitutions* does not consider the exclusion rule in *Didache* to be 'innocent' but
turns it from a matter of ritual purity through washing as the requirement
for sharing in the pure meal into a matter of whether a person has been
initiated or not. Eating without initiation will attract judgment on the
person and s/he should be at once instructed and initiated if possible to
avoid bringing the community into disrepute. The concern of the *Didache*
that the purity of the community and its meal would be jeopardised by
the admission of a ritually impure person is entirely erased.

To summarise: the first aspect of the attitude of the *Didache* community towards Gentile outsiders is that they are ritually impure and convey
impurity. To share in the meal they must be ritually cleansed by fasting
and washing in running water or other kinds of specified water and practice appropriate to ritual purity (7.1-4), so not to jeopardise the pure meal
of the community as it waits in a state of holiness for ingathering into the
eschatological kingdom (τὴν ἀγιασθεῖσαν, *Did.* 10.5 [H54], but absent
from Coptic and *Apostolic Constitutions*). Members of the *Didache*
community must also keep as much of the Torah as possible, especially
with regard to food, but as a non-negotiable minimum must abstain
strictly from food which has been offered to idols (6.2-3). With this as
their base line, I think it legitimate to assume that those excluded would
be Gentiles. Whatever else they may be accused of, the 'hypocrites'[23]
of *Didache* 8 are not accused of impurity. Fasting before baptism is
required for the same reason that the *Manual of Discipline* requires a
drastic two-year exclusion of initiands from sharing their meal fully,
namely to maintain the ritual purity of the community meal. Aseneth, in
ch. 10 of the first-century Jewish romance, *Joseph and Aseneth*, likewise
fasts for a week in sackcloth and ashes followed by washing to remove
the impurity of food offered to idols from her lips. She symbolically
throws away the unclean *eidolothuton* to the unclean 'strange' dogs
outside (10.13).

22   Schaff has 'lawful'.
23   The 'hypocrites' seemingly refer to Pharisees or proto-Rabbinic communities. For the less likely view that they include all Jews, see H. van de Sandt and
D. Flusser, *The Didache: Its Jewish Sources and its Place in Early Judaism and
Christianity* (CRINT, III.5; Assen: Van Gorcum, 2002), pp.291–6.

It also stands in alignment with what is revealed in other sources from the Second Temple period, in which the impurity of Gentiles was widely accepted but also contested since there is no prohibition against eating with Gentiles in the Torah. J. Klawans[24] and C. Hayes[25] deny that Gentiles were considered unclean or that idolatry rendered them unclean. Hayes maintains that

> In *Sifra Perek Zavim* 1.1, the rabbis assert that by biblical law Gentiles are exempt from levitical impurity, and neither contract nor convey ritual defilement through physical states. According to a rabbinic decree, however, Gentiles were deemed to convey defilement to Israelites like a *zav*, which is to say by their urine and spittle. The date of this decree cannot be determined...[26]

However, it is clear from texts coming from first century CE that Gentiles were popularly considered to be unclean and convey uncleanness, and that there was a widespread suspicion that Gentiles could not be trusted in the preparation of food because of idolatry.[27]

I am not convinced that this *Didache* community would have baptised fellow Jews who were living in a state of ritual purity. This is not mere speculation: there is no record of the first disciples being baptised and it is only in the context of the baptism of John, which is for moral impurity in Israel, rather than in the ministry of Jesus that one might suspect that this community baptised fellow Jews. At what stage did this happen and in which communities? In *De Baptismo Liber* 12 Tertullian knows of people who make just such an argument against the requirement for Jews to be baptised:

> Now there is a standing rule that without baptism no man can obtain salvation. It derives in particular from that (well known) pronouncement of our Lord, who says, *Except a man be born of water he cannot have life.* Hence arise certain persons' over-precise or even audacious discussions as to how, in view of that standing rule, the apostles can have obtained salvation, when we observe that none of them except Paul were baptised in our Lord: in fact, since Paul is the only one from among them who has put on the baptism of Christ, either we have the case pre-judged (they say)

24   Klawans, 'Notions of Gentile Impurity'.
25   C. Hayes, 'Intermarriage and Impurity in Ancient Jewish Sources', *HTR* 92 (1999), pp.3–36.
26   Hayes, 'Intermarriage', p.35.
27   See J. D. Rosenblum, 'Food and Identity in Early Rabbinic Identity' (unpublished Paper given at the SBL Section *Meals in the Greco-Roman World Group*, San Francisco, 19–22 November 2011).

concerning those others' peril who are without Christ's baptism, so that
the standing rule may be safe: or else, if salvation is appointed even for
these unbaptised, the general rule is repealed.[28]

Whoever these people may have been, it seems from his argument that
they are Jewish Christians, Christian Jews or hostile Jews, since he
identifies them not with the apostles but with 'enemies of the faith,
doctors of the law, and Pharisees'. It is at least a possibility that still in
the second and third centuries CE some communities of Christian Jews
did not regard it as necessary for Jewish members to be baptised but only
Gentiles, because they were not ritually impure. This contrasts with
Paul's practice because Paul regarded baptism not as purification from
ritual impurity but rather as baptism into Jesus' death and resurrection –
maybe removal of *moral* impurity/sin too – which united the believer
with him as Lord. It is significant that there is no reference to Jesus'
death and resurrection anywhere in the *Didache*.

3. *Teaching of the Lord to the Gentiles*

However, despite this reservation with regard to the ritual purity and
participation of outsiders to their meals, and hence to the general life of
their community – and I am suggesting that these would have been
Gentiles – the community does seem to have been very positive towards
their admission, in fact to have had an orientation towards a mission to
Gentiles. In its final form the unabridged text calls itself in its *incipit*,
'Teaching of the Lord through the twelve apostles to the Gentiles (τοῖς
ἔθνεσιν)'. This has, again, caused a considerable amount of controversy
as to whether it is an insertion or original, but the consensus appears to
be that it was attached at least as early as the insertion of the Q material
into the beginning of the Two Ways teaching in 1.3-6. If that is so, then
it is significant that the form of Q evidenced here has, 'For what credit is
it if you love those who love you? Do not even the Gentiles (τὰ ἔθνη) do
the same?' Besides the Q material, the teaching of the Two Ways is
largely a collection of lists of virtues and vices derived from or
expanding from the second table of the Ten Commandments, together
with material related to requirements known as the Noachide commandments which were binding on all human beings through the covenant

---

28   Trans. E. Evans, 1964. The online text, available at http://www.tertullian.org/
articles/evans_bapt/evans_bapt_text_trans.htm, was accessed on 11 November 2011.

with Noah.[29] Instruction in this teaching is made a requirement for admission to baptism. Acceptance of the full Torah, 'the whole yoke of the Lord' including circumcision, is 'to be perfect', but is only recommended and not required (6.2-3). Again, this relates to the position in Mt. 5.17-20 where the Torah is affirmed as lasting forever without any subtraction; in fact, 'greater righteousness' is required, but Jesus nevertheless proclaims that his 'yoke' is easy and its 'burden is light' (Mt. 11.29-30). For Gentiles this would be the case, since the yoke of obedience does not require circumcision and observation of the 'special laws' since they are not obligated to Torah obedience by God's covenant with Israel. For Jews the Torah would continue its applicability and would not be seen as a burden but as a privilege (τέλειος; being 'perfect' in *Did.* 6.2; cf. Mt. 5.48). The *Didache* community in its final form, then, is positively oriented towards Gentile admission and sees itself as the 'teaching of the Lord entrusted to the twelve apostles', but does not see any contradiction between their admission without circumcision and continuing observation of the 'special laws' by Jewish members viewed as 'perfection'. It may be that Jewish members of this community would not allow their children to marry those who were not 'perfect' unless they were circumcised and adopted Torah. There is no way of knowing now, but it would be the logic of the situation. Again, whichever came first and whatever their relationship, the text of the *Didache* lines up broadly with the position of Matthew's Sermon on the Mount in Matthew 5–7, instructions on the 'yoke' in Mt. 11.28-30 and the so-called Great Commission of 28.16-20.

4. Koinonia *as a Purity Community*

The only point at which the Two Ways of the *Didache* moves into actual positive delineation of the community's life is in ch. 4. This teaching forms a coherent unit, including the instructions on slaves and children.[30]

29   J. A. Draper, 'Vice Catalogues as Oral-Mnemonic Cues: A Comparative Study of the Two Ways Tradition in the *Didache* and Parallels from the Perspective of Oral Tradition', in T. Thatcher (ed.), *Jesus, the Voice, and the Text* (Waco, TX: Baylor University Press, 2008), pp.111–35.

30   J. A. Draper, 'The Moral Economy of the *Didache*', *HTS* 67 (2011), Art. #907, 10 pages, DOI: 10.4102/hts.v67i1.907, and 'Children and Slaves in the Community of the *Didache* and the Two Ways Tradition' (unpublished paper presented to the International Meeting of the SBL at Kings College, London, August 2011).

Besides honouring the teacher and the teaching (as mediating together the presence of God, 'wherever the Lord's nature is preached, there the Lord is', 4.1), it views the community as a holy community (4.2). This has two immediate consequences: first, judgment must be done inside the community under the auspices of Torah (akin to voluntary adoption of *Sharia* law by Muslims in modern Western societies). The instructions are a modified form of Lev. 19.17, which played a big role in the later Rabbinic judicial process, the *hatra'ah*.[31] The same approach is found in *Didache* 15. Members of the community are all required to participate in judgment of particular cases which may be brought against someone. Secondly, individual property is also somehow communal property because control is necessary for the sake of purity. If the *Didache* reflects a holiness community concerned with purity, then trading, sharing and so on would require a *koinonia* of property of some kind. Otherwise how could members keep *strictly* from food offered to idols with the attendant impurity, and how would the community know that the other rules of food purity required by Torah were kept? Poor or destitute members of the community required support to ensure the preservation of a holiness community, which would have financial implications in terms of bodily and material purity. This was off-set against the 'spiritual wealth' which they brought to the table (4.8). It sounds to me as if the poor would likely be Jewish members of the community while the well-off refers to prosperous Gentiles who join the community and benefit from their 'spiritual wealth'.

The requirement that new members 'call nothing their own' but rather share (συγκοινωνήσεις) everything with other members had consequences for members of the οἶκος and its economy. It would have big repercussions for family and especially the adult children of the converts who did not convert; the *Didache* requires the head of the household to compel the conversion of their male and female children by using their *potestor* (4.9). It would have big repercussions also for converts with slaves, since they would be compelled to undergo baptism and join such a purity community also. But if they were baptised and no member could call anything their own, then slaves, as property, ceased to be 'owned' and could regard themselves as free. That question would certainly arise if the convert decided to become 'perfect' and get circumcised along

---

31   H. van de Sandt, 'Two Windows on a Developing Jewish-Christian Reproof Practice: Matt 18:15-17 and *Did.* 15:3', in H. van de Sandt (ed.), *Matthew and the Didache: Two Documents from the Same Jewish-Christian Milieu?* (Assen: Van Gorcum, 2005), pp.173–92; and J. A. Draper, 'Pure Sacrifice in *Didache* 14 as Christian Halakah', *Neot* 42 (2008), pp.223–52.

with his slaves! Again, the *Didache* community requires a compromise under which slaves remain slaves but have a certain new status since they now both 'fear the same God' and are 'called by the Spirit'.

5. *First Fruits Outside* Eretz Yisrael

One of the unexpected and interesting aspects of the *Didache* is that it requires its members to contribute first fruits, not only of the field but also of the processed produce thereof.[32] These things are required of Jews in *Eretz Yisrael* but not required of them outside the land of covenant and not of Gentiles at all. Yet *Didache* 13 requires contributions of community members for the support of the prophets and teachers and finally the poor. There is evidence that Diaspora Jews did make payments of tithes and other financial requirements of Torah, even though they might technically have held themselves exempt. These were sent corporately by synagogues to support the Temple system in Jerusalem before the destruction. But first fruits are never mentioned in connection with the obligations of Diaspora Jews, as far as I can ascertain. Consequently, they would be available for Torah-observant Jews, who already contributed to the Temple through the various taxes, to pay into a 'separatist' community such as the Christian one. They could also require it of Gentiles as a condition of membership and in this way support the alternative economic arrangements of the Christian community alongside Jews, who could participate without jeopardising their membership of 'all Israel'.[33]

6. *Comparison with* Gerim

One of the things which is also interesting and significant is the similarity of these 'purity' regulations for converts to the Christian Jewish community and the rules provided by the minor Rabbinic tractate

32   J. A. Draper, 'First-Fruits and the Support of Prophets, Teachers, and the Poor in *Didache* 13 in Relation to New Testament Parallels', in A. Gregory and C. Tuckett (eds.), *Trajectories through the New Testament and the Apostolic Fathers* (Oxford: Oxford University Press, 2005), pp.223–43.

33   For this expression as an over-arching self-designation for Jewish people, see P. Tomson, '"Jews" in the Gospel of John as Compared with the Palestinian Talmud, the Synoptics and Some New Testament Apocrypha', in R. Bieringer, D. Pollefeyt and F. Vandecateele-Vanneuville (eds.), *Anti-Judaism and the Fourth Gospel: Papers of the Leuven Colloquium, 2000* (Assen: Van Gorcum, 2001), pp.301–40.

Gerim. Of course, there is no knowing the exact date of the material in this writing, nor how it might relate to arrangements for Gentile converts to Pharisaic/proto-Rabbinic communities in the first century CE. Its origin is probably as a late collection of Rabbinic traditions in the Gaonic period, but its provisions may reflect much earlier practice. Even the existence of Jewish proselytising is disputed. However, its existence is not necessary for the purposes of the present study. What is important is that if Gentiles in the Diaspora did convert, how would they be received and what would be required of them?

Gerim	*Didache*
No immediate acceptance of Gentiles, but first interrogation and instruction (I.1-2)	Preliminary instruction (1–6; 7.1)
Water immersion up to navel and teaching (I.3)	Water immersion (7.2-3)
Admission conditional on economy of Torah	
Gleanings, forgotten sheaves, corner of the field and tithes (*ma'aser*) (I.3)	First fruits required (13)
Women to observe purity regulations (*niddah*) and Sabbath lamp kindling (I.3)	
Debate over relation of bathing to circumcision. Circumcision required, but seemingly some bathe without circumcision (I.6)	Circumcision not required, nor full acceptance of Torah's 'special laws' but 'as much as possible' (6.2-3)
Genuine religious conversion required (I.7)	
Person administering must be same sex (I.8)	Strict abstention from food offered to idols (6.3) and as much attention to *kashrut* as possible (6.2)
No food or drink to be brought in on admission unless certified by a *haber* to ensure its purity (I.9)	
No usury paid by Jews after admission (I.10)	No requirement of those baptised to take on 'the whole yoke of the Lord' (6.2), but expectation that they will finally (16.2)
Debate over circumcision of those already circumcised (II.1-3)	
Problem of slaves at baptism, regulated to enable proselytes to keep their slaves (II.4)	Problem of slaves: masters be just and not provoke; slaves to submit as to God in fear and trembling and 'fear the same God' (4.10-11)
Circumcision, immersion and Temple sacrifice required (last suspended after 70 CE) (II.5)	Only immersion required (6–7)

Difference between *ger toshab* (who 'lives in the midst of the Jewish community', avoids idolatry and keeps *kashrut*, presumably made pure by immersion) and *ger zedek* (who keeps the whole Torah, presumably including circumcision) (III.1)	Difference between the 'perfect' convert and those who 'do as much as they can' of Torah (6.2)
Ger toshab can still render others unclean and may not marry a Jew (III.2-3)	Converts, 'perfect' or not, can eat with others in a state of ritual purity after baptism (9.5)
Proselytes are bound by incest rules of Torah (III.5-6)	*Porneia* is frequently prohibited in 1–5
	Judgment is by whole community including converts and seemingly by
At the death of a proselyte his property is 'ownerless' if his children converted with him and slaves are freed. Jews can seize his fields or 'draw' minor slaves and livestock; wives can claim *ketuboth* (III.8-13)	the Torah (4.2-4) All property is understood as belonging in some sense to all in the community and members required to share both material and spiritual resources (4.5-8)
Jews to act justly to proselytes and not insult them (IV.1-2)	
God loves proselytes and titles applied to Israel can be claimed also by them, especially for the sake of Abraham (IV.3)	Admissions related to Jesus as Davidic messiah of eschatological kingdom rather than Abraham (9–10)
Special care to be taken with proselytes from the Diaspora	

It is remarkable that the arrangements and the problems faced by Christian communities attested by the *Didache* and the Jewish community(ies) of whatever date or occasion which produced *Gerim* overlap to such a degree. My argument would be that a Torah-faithful community of any kind which admitted Gentiles would be bound to respond in a similar way to that evidenced by these texts if they were to stay bound to Israel. The difference between the two is the belief in the eschatological significance of Jesus as the messiah of David, who had initiated the process of ingathering faithful Israel and righteous Gentiles, as this Christian Jewish community believed.

7. *Conclusions*

This analysis has at least created space to recognise continuing Christian Jewish communities in the first century CE, attempting to stay faithful to the Torah and to the requirements of faithfulness to Israel in the messianic age, while opening their community to Gentiles attracted to their community and their Jewish lifestyle. This community was active in at least the first two centuries CE and perhaps died out in the third or fourth. It is clearly associated in some way with Matthew's community in its thinking and practice, although there are also discernible differences which may be the result of a continuing evolution of the community(ies). Matthew's Gospel was considered acceptable by the emerging Catholic Christianity and indeed it is taken up as one of its normative texts in due course. The *Didache* was regarded with more suspicion, although not rejected entirely, according to Eusebius (*Hist. eccl.* 3.25), who records that it continued to be used for catechesis. It did not survive in its current form except by accident. If our analysis is correct, this is hardly surprising.

JEWS, CHRISTIANS AND GENTILES:
OBSERVATIONS AND SOME CONCLUDING REMARKS

David C. Sim

It hardly needs saying that both of the great religions of Judaism and Christianity were to a large extent shaped and defined by their attitudes towards, and their interactions with, one another. The so-called parting(s) of the ways, the separation of the Christian tradition from the religion of Judaism, has dominated modern scholarship and produced a wealth of literature. As might be expected from such a complicated subject, no consensus has emerged. While some scholars date the definitive break between Judaism and Christianity to some point in the first century of the Common Era, others argue that we can only speak of different and separate religions in the fourth century. Needless to say, there are many who would plumb for a date or period in between these two extremes. An integral part of this process of separation, though often overlooked by many scholars, is the attitude(s) of each to the Gentile or 'pagan' world, especially in terms of the full inclusion of such people in these religious traditions. Both accepted Gentiles as full converts, but there were significant differences in the mode of conversion as well as the status of such converts, although the very early Christian tradition itself was by no means uniform on this issue. It is well known that Judaism remained fundamentally Jewish in ancient times, resisting stridently any accommodation to foreign traditions such as Hellenism, and has continued in this vein to the modern era, while the Christian tradition began as a movement or sect within Judaism and ultimately became a Gentile religion that to this day still defines itself as a religion over and against Judaism. Therefore, the attitudes towards Gentiles and their inclusion in or exclusion from both Judaism and Christianity is thus integrally related to the 'parting(s) of the ways' and the nature and ethnic make-up of both religions in the modern day.

The collections of essays in this volume has demonstrated that at the turn of the eras the interactions between Jews and Gentiles on the one hand, and between Christians and Gentiles on the other, were multi-faceted and complex. This is not unexpected, given the inevitable and widespread engagement between Jews, Christians and Gentiles in the ancient world, and the importance of Gentile inclusion or exclusion in both of these religious traditions. Nor is it unexpected that different authors and/or texts in each religion had divergent attitudes to the Gentile world. All Jews and Christians reacted to their own religious, historical, and social conditions, and these circumstances are reflected in the positions they took in relation to the Gentile world.

In terms of ancient Judaism, we meet a tradition that re-invented itself in response to changing circumstances. Beginning as a tribal and ethnically enclosed religion, Judaism saw the necessity to redefine itself in the post-Exilic era in direct response to the challenge posed by Hellenism. Judaism became more of a religion of lifestyle, characterised by observance of the ancient Mosaic laws, rather than by birth and racial identity. This development was momentous. In this new scheme of things, conversion to Judaism became a reality, and there is ample evidence to suggest that some Gentiles took the opportunity to convert. Some of these conversions may have been involuntary, which may have been the case when the Jews were in a position of power during the Hasmonean period, but most were probably voluntary in later times during Roman rule when the Jews were in no position or saw no necessity to coerce people against their will. During this time, Judaism proved attractive to other Gentiles who are referred to as God-fearers or God-worshippers. These were Gentiles who were attracted to Judaism, and participated in the synagogue and observed many of the Jewish laws. Josephus, Philo, the Rabbinic literature, the inscriptional evidence from contemporary synagogues and the Aphrodisias inscription, testify to the existence and importance of these Gentile sympathisers.

As D. Binder points out, the Jewish synagogue stands as an important symbol of Jewish/Gentile relations. The Ptolomies in Egypt contributed towards the construction of synagogues, and synagogues were given special privileges by Romans. They were especially important places for God-fearers, a fact confirmed also in Acts. Cordial interactions between the Jews and their Gentile neighbours often meant some protection for or contribution to the local synagogue. But when relations soured it was often the synagogue that bore the brunt of Gentile antagonism or violence. Unfortunately, this pattern of violence against synagogues by anti-Jewish elements has endured for the last two thousand years.

While it is true that Gentiles were allowed to enter the synagogue and participate in its rites, the same did not hold true of ancient Judaism's most sacred site, the Temple in Jerusalem. The rules governing Gentile access and participation in fact provide important evidence that even with the relaxation of the boundaries between Jew and Gentile, the fundamental distinction between the two remained firmly intact. In his essay, J. McLaren points out that the Jewish Temple, which remained the heart and soul of Judaism until its destruction by the Romans in 70 CE, still restricted Gentile access to the inner sanctums of the Temple complex. In fact, the renovations of Herod the Great, while permitting Gentiles to enter the general Temple area, effectively excluded them from the Temple cult by virtue of a sign that debarred their admission to the inner courts. The denial of access to the inner Temple areas was matched by the preclusion of Gentile participation in the Temple cult. The role of the Temple as a place of sacrifice only by Jews and only to their God remained non-negotiable, and sacrifice was not permitted for those outside the covenant community.

It is perhaps pertinent at this juncture to make the point that this distinction between Jew and Gentile was not completely removed even when Gentiles made the ultimate commitment and converted to Judaism. Despite the theory of complete equality between native-born Jew and proselytes espoused by Philo, Josephus and some Rabbinic texts, the reality was probably very different. We know from Acts, the Aphrodisias inscription and the Rabbinic material that converts were defined as 'the proselyte', which immediately identifies their Gentile origins and their secondary status by comparison with those born to Jewish parents. This is confirmed by the fact that proselytes are always listed below native-born Israelites (Jews) in listings that rank the most important groups in the eyes of God, as is evidenced in Acts, the Dead Sea Scrolls and certain Rabbinic statements.

The above material represents of course only one side of the coin – those Gentiles who were sympathetic to Judaism, who became either God-fearers or proselytes. On the other side of the coin we find many texts which provide a wholly negative view of the Gentiles, texts which predict and look forward to their ultimate destruction at the end of time. These documents of course were written by Jews who had experienced terrible atrocities or oppression at the hands of Gentile perpetrators. As M. Theophilos makes clear in his chapter on the apocalyptic literature, the Gentiles will face eternal and terrible punishments because of their crimes against the Jews. Most of these texts were written in the aftermath of the crises initiated by Antiochus Epiphanes or by the destruction of Jerusalem and its Temple by the Romans in 70 CE. Under these circumstances, it is perfectly understandable that the oppressed Jewish people hoped that God would punish the Gentiles at the end of the age. In his discussion of the Qumran literature, J. Collins points out that the 'kittim', who appear in a number of texts and who were ultimately identified with the Romans, were also earmarked for eschatological destruction.

It is well to remember, however, that not all Jews reacted to Gentile hostility in this manner. For two of the best-known Jews of the first century, Philo and Josephus, eschatological fantasies were far removed from their writings. Although, as D. Runia argues in his chapter, Philo may not have been overly interested in the Gentile world, at least some of his voluminous writings in many ways were composed in response to it, in so far as they serve the apologetic purpose of presenting the superiority of the Jewish tradition over other peoples and cultures, including Greek culture in which he was so thoroughly immersed. For his part, Josephus, as maintained by J. McLaren, had no special interest in Gentiles as such. They of course figure prominently in his *Jewish War* and are rarely depicted favourably, but in his apologetic discourse against the critic Apion Josephus openly defends his religious and cultural heritage against its Gentile opponents. Despite both being involved in major crises, in the case of Philo the attempt by the emperor Gaius to erect a statue of himself in the Jewish Temple, and in the case of Josephus the catastrophe of the Jewish war and the destruction of Jerusalem and its Temple, neither writer resorts to an apocalyptic solution. Instead, they make use of apologetics to defend and promote the Jewish way of life and to denigrate in their own ways the traditions of other peoples.

The literature and institutions of ancient Judaism thus reveal that Jewish attitudes towards the Gentile interactions were largely dominated by a number of factors. First, there was the need to preserve the cultural and religious heritage of the Jewish people. The Jews viewed their own religious tradition as superior to the religions of the Gentile world, which they perceived as idolatrous and grossly immoral. Yet this negative perception of Gentile society did not result in the complete exclusion of Gentiles, as had been the case in the pre-Exilic period. It did, however, entail that those sympathetic to Judaism were encouraged to participate but only on the fringes, while the process of conversion was such that it erased the idolatrous and immoral Gentile nature of converts and forged for them a new Jewish identity that followed the ancient laws of Moses and enabled integration with the Jewish community. Secondly, there was the necessity to defend the Jewish tradition against Gentile critics. The apologetic works of Philo and Josephus are especially prominent here. Thirdly, a common attitude to the Gentile world was that non-Jews, though enjoying power and prosperity in the present, would meet a gruesome end at the *eschaton*. This view was widespread throughout apocalyptic circles, including the Qumran community, and can be directly related to the oppression of the Jewish people by foreign powers or to serious acts of violence towards the Jews by their Gentile neighbours.

When we turn to the early Christian literature, we find that the issues that dominate Christian/Gentile relationships are mostly different. The most common subject is that of the Gentile mission. While there is still an ongoing debate as to whether ancient Judaism was a missionary religion, actively seeking converts as opposed to accepting those who approached the Jews with the desire to convert, the evidence strongly suggests that there was no real attempt on the part of the Jews to conduct missions to the Gentiles – sympathisers and converts were welcome but were never sought out and recruited. The early Christian tradition shows the opposite tendency. The mission to the Gentiles began very early on, though there is little agreement in the texts concerning who initiated it, who was in charge of it, and the conditions by which Gentiles became Christians.

In his analysis of Q, C. Tuckett notes that scholars are divided over whether or not the tradents of this source were open to the Gentile world and advocated a Gentile mission. Given the absence of a definitive text, such ambiguity in the evidence is perhaps to be expected. Tuckett himself argues that the community that transmitted Q was basically Jewish and, while aware of Gentile Christians, was not actively recruiting them. The situation is rather different of course in the letters of Paul, where the question of the Gentile mission is a dominant theme throughout the Pauline corpus. Paul traces the beginning of the Gentile mission not back to the historical Jesus but to his own encounter with the risen Christ who commissioned him to be the apostle to the Gentiles. S. Winter demonstrates that, while the Jewish Paul had little truck with many common Gentile practices, especially moral practices, he nonetheless was firmly of the view that God had planned from the beginning for the salvation of the Gentiles. This salvation was made possible through Christ and not through the Law, and Paul believed that he himself had been called to play a major part in this process.

The Gospels that follow Paul chronologically and purport to provide a narrative of the mission of Jesus reveal a diverse range of options in terms of their attitudes towards the Gentiles and their views about the Gentile mission. As noted in the Preface, this volume unfortunately was unable to include a chapter on the historical Jesus and the Gentiles, but whatever his attitude actually was, the Gospels demonstrate that the early Christian tradition portrayed it in startlingly different ways.

If we begin with the Gospel of Mark, I. Elmer argues that the Marcan Jesus is actively engaged in a Gentile mission alongside his mission to the Jews, and this mission to non-Jews causes significant problems between Jesus and his disciples. Gentiles are accepted as long as they demonstrate the requisite faith in Jesus; the ritual requirements of the Torah are dispensed with as no longer relevant (cf. Mk 7.19). There is here a tacit agreement with Paul, although it needs to be said as well that Mark disagrees with the apostle by tracing the Gentile mission back to Jesus himself. The evangelist's generally positive view of the Gentile world probably reflects that he and the majority of his community members were of Gentile background.

The situation could not be more different in Matthew's Gospel. In this Christian Jewish text, Matthew limits the historical mission of Jesus to the Jewish people (15.24; cf. 10.5-6) and it is only after the resurrection that the risen Christ instructs the disciples to take the Christian message to Jew and Gentile alike (28.16-20). There is an agreement with Paul against Mark that the Gentile mission is post-Easter, but Matthew contradicts the claim of Paul that he was commissioned to lead the Gentile mission by having the risen Lord charge the disciples with this task. While the Jewish Matthew agrees further with the Jewish Paul in criticising Gentile society, as his anti-Gentile statements make clear, he and the apostle part company over the means by which Gentiles can transform themselves and be acceptable to God. For Paul, justification comes through faith alone and not by works of the Law, while the evangelist emphasises the continuing validity of the Torah within the Christian community (5.17-19), and that faith in Christ alone is not sufficient for salvation (7.22-23). In his analysis of this Gospel, D. Sim concludes that in this traditionally Jewish community full membership involved conversion to Judaism in addition to acceptance of Jesus as messiah and Lord.

Luke–Acts provides yet another view of the Gentiles in the early Christian literature. As E. Dowling shows in her chapter, in the Gospel Luke plays down the interactions between Jesus and Gentiles but introduces a new theme whereby Jesus engages with Samaritans; the Gentile mission proper is held over until the book of Acts. While it is not immediately apparent when this mission begins due to the ambiguity of the relevant texts, what is clear is that the second half of Acts focuses almost exclusively on Paul's successful mission to the Gentiles. In terms of the conditions of conversion, the Lucan account of the apostolic decree in Acts 15 dictates that Gentiles were bound only by rules that made it possible for Jews and Gentiles to eat together and share the Eucharist. This may reflect the practice of the evangelist's community which perhaps comprised a mixture of Jews and former God-fearers.

Finally, the Gospel of John contains another account of Jesus' interaction with Gentiles. Although Gentiles do not figure as prominently in John as in the other Gospels, M. Coloe's narrative reading of Jn 12.12-43 demonstrates that the story of the 'Greeks' approaching Jesus shows an openness to the Gentile world and probably indicates that the Johannine community was engaged in a Gentile mission, which was justified as fulfilling the Scriptures. Coloe follows the work of R. E. Brown, which reconstructs the history of the Johannine community from its Jewish beginnings in Palestine, its conflict with other Jewish groups, and its ultimate move to the Diaspora where it began to make Gentile converts. Despite its Jewish origins, the Johannine community had seemingly at some point in its history left Judaism proper and no longer observed the Torah (cf. Jn 1.17-18; 5.18). If this were the case, then Gentile converts would not have been expected to observe the Law, but would have been expected to embrace the distinctive Christology that the Gospel manifests.

The early Christian document known as the *Didache* raises different issues, in particular the practicalities of a Jewish Christian group opening its doors to Gentile converts. J. Draper suggests that the community responsible for this text emphasises the necessity of ritual purity by baptism for those who partake of the communal meal. In customary Jewish fashion, Gentiles, who are referred to as 'dogs', are considered ritually impure and require baptism to rectify this. In contrast to the Pauline tradition, Jewish converts perhaps were not baptised because they were not as inherently impure as Gentiles. But, as Draper, suggests, the *Didache* is well-disposed towards the Gentiles and exceptions were made in terms of Gentile observance of the whole Torah. Circumcision was not required, but Gentile converts were expected to keep as much of the Law as possible, especially the dietary restrictions to maintain ritual purity. The *Didache* is an interesting text in that it deals directly with the practical issues of how Jewish Christians and Gentile Christians can live and worship together. While it is difficult to ascertain whether this text reflects the practices of a real community or simply presents the ideal on how such communities should function, it became less and less useful in the Christian community as the Church moved beyond its Jewish heritage and became predominantly Gentile in character.

This brings us to the relevance of A. Cadwallader's chapter on the Christian community in Colossae. We see here a reversal of the Pauline phrase 'Jew and Greek', which points to the diminishing importance of Jews in the Christian tradition (at least at Colossae) and the importance of being Greek. Cadwallader explains the shift in perspective in Col. 3.11 by reference to inscriptional and other evidence that demonstrates that in the period in which the epistle was written there was a growing tendency in Colossae and its environs to emphasise one's 'Greekness', particularly by the adoption of a Greek name. Assessing other evidence within the letter itself, Cadwallader shows that the importance and numbers of Jews in Christianity was diminishing. Although Cadwallader focuses mainly on Colossae, this was the reality of the Christian Church in the early second century.

In subsequent centuries, the Gentile Christians would continue to interact with the Jewish world, with whom they remained in competition until the 'Christianisation' of the empire in the fourth century, but also with the 'pagan' world of non-Christian Gentiles. The initial contrasts between Jew and Gentile, and later Christian and Gentile, would be replaced by the contrast of Christian and 'pagan'. From the second century onwards, the question of Christian attitudes to Gentiles became less relevant, while the Christian attitude towards 'pagans' assumed major importance. It was also during this time that Christianity began to take on some of the characteristics of Judaism – the need to promote the superiority of the Christian tradition and lifestyle, the need to denigrate the idolatry and immorality of the non-Christian Gentile world, and the need expressed in apologetic literature to defend Christianity against Jewish and 'pagan' opponents. The place of Gentiles in the Christian Church and the terms of the Gentile mission that so dominated the early Christian literature had long receded into obscurity.

BIBLIOGRAPHY

Abegg, M. G., 'Messianic Hope and 4Q285: A Reassessment', *JBL* 113 (1994), pp.81–91.

Albertz, R., 'Are Foreign Rulers Allowed to Enter and Sacrifice in the Jerusalem Temple?', in R. Albertz and J. Wöhrle (eds.), *Between Cooperation and Hostility: Multiple Identities in Ancient Judaism and the Interaction with Foreign Powers* (JAJSup 11; Göttingen: Vandenhoeck & Ruprecht, 2013), pp.115–33.

Allison, D. C., *The Jesus Tradition in Q* (Harrisburg: Trinity Press International, 1997).

———. 'Who Will Come from East and West? Observations on Matt 8.11-12//Luke 13.28-29', *IBS* 11 (1989), pp.158–70.

Ameling, W., *Inscriptiones Judaicae Orientis II: Kleinasien* (Tübingen: Mohr Siebeck, 2004).

Anthonysamy, J., 'The Gospel of Mark and the Universal Mission', *Bible Bhashyam* 6 (1980), pp.81–91.

Atkins, R. A., *Egalitarian Community: Ethnography and Exegesis* (Tuscaloosa: University of Alabama Press, 1991).

Aulock, H. von, *Münzen und Städte Phrygiens* (2 vols.; Tübingen: Wasmuth, 1980, 1987).

Aytaçlar, P. Ö., and E. Akıncı, 'A List of Female Names from Laodicea', *EA* 39 (2006), pp.113–16.

Bahat, D., 'The Herodian Temple', in Horbury, Davies, and Sturdy (eds.), *The Cambridge History of Judaism*, III, pp.38–58.

Bailey, K., *Poet and Peasant and Through Peasant Eyes: A Literary-Cultural Approach to the Parables in Luke: Combined Edition* (Grand Rapids: Eerdmans, 1983).

Bamberger, J., *Proselytism in the Talmudic Period* (New York: KTAV, 2nd edn, 1968).

Bar-Asher Siegal, E., 'Who Separated from Whom and Why? A Philological Study of 4QMMT', *RevQ* 25 (2011), pp.229–56.

Barclay, J. M. G., *Flavius Josephus: Translation and Commentary. X. Against Apion* (Leiden: Brill, 2007).

———. *Jews in the Mediterranean Diaspora: From Alexander to Trajan (323 BCE– 117 CE)* (Edinburgh: T. & T. Clark, 1996).

———. '"Neither Jew nor Greek": Multiculturalism and the New Perspective on Paul', in M. G. Brett (ed.), *Ethnicity and the Bible* (Leiden: Brill, 1996), pp.197–214.

———. 'Paul and Philo on Circumcision: Romans 2.25–9 in Social and Cultural Context', *NTS* 44 (1998), pp.536–56.

Barth, M., and H. Blanke, *Colossians* (AB 34B; New York: Doubleday, 1994).

Bassler, J. M., 'The Enigmatic Sign: 2 Thessalonians 1.5', *CBQ* 46 (1984), pp.496–510.

Bauckham, R., 'Apocalypses', in Carson, O'Brien, and Seifrid (eds.), *Justification and Variegated Nomism*, I, pp.135–87.

———. *Gospel Women: Studies of the Named Women in the Gospels* (London: Continuum, 2002).

Baumgarten, J., 'The "Sons of Dawn" in CDC 13:14–15 and the Ban on Commerce among the Essenes', *IEJ* 33 (1983), pp.81–85.

Beal, T. K., *The Book of Hiding. Gender, Ethnicity, Annihilation and Esther* (London: Routledge, 1997).

Berthelot, K., 'Grecs, Barbares et Juifs dans l'œuvre de Philon', in B. Decharneux and S. Inowlocki (eds.), *Philon d'Alexandrie. Un penseur à l'intersection des cultures gréco-romaine, orientale, juive et chrétienne* (Monothéismes et philosophie 12; Turnhout: Brepols, 2011), pp.47–61.

——. 'La notion de *ger* dans les texts de Qumrân', *RevQ* 19 (1999), pp.169–216.

Best, E., *Disciples and Discipleship: Studies in the Gospel according to Mark* (Edinburgh: T. & T. Clark, 1986).

——. *Following Jesus: Discipleship in the Gospel of Mark* (JSNTSup 4; Sheffield: JSOT, 1981).

——. *Mark: The Gospel as Story* (Edinburgh: T. & T. Clark, 1983).

Beutler, J., 'Greeks come to see Jesus (John 12:20f)', *Bib* 71 (1990), pp.333–47.

Binder, D. D., *Into the Temple Courts: The Place of the Synagogues in the Second Temple Period* (Atlanta: SBL, 1999).

Bird, M. F., *Jesus and the Origin of the Gentile Mission* (LNTS 331; London: T&T Clark International, 2007).

Birnbaum, E., 'Philo on the Greeks: a Jewish Perspective on Culture and Society in First-Century Alexandria', in D. T. Runia and G. E. Sterling (eds.), *In the Spirit of Faith: Studies in Philo and Early Christianity in Honor of David Hay (= The Studia Philonica Annual 13 [2001])* (BJS 332; Providence: Brown University Press, 2001), pp.37–58.

——. *The Place of Judaism in Philo's Thought: Israel, Jews, and Proselytes* (BJS 290; SPM 2; Atlanta: Scholars Press, 1996).

——. Review of T. L. Donaldson, *Judaism and the Gentiles: Jewish Patterns of Universalism (to 135 CE)*, *SPhA* 20 (2008), pp.213–21.

Black, C. C., *The Disciples according to Mark: Markan Redaction in Current Debate* (JSNTSup 27; Sheffield: Sheffield Academic, 1989).

——. *Mark: Images of an Apostolic Interpreter* (SPNT; Edinburgh: T. & T. Clark, 2001).

Bogaert, P. M., *L'Apocalypse de Baruch* (2 vols.; Paris: Cerf, 1969).

Boismard, M.-É., and A. Lamouille (eds.), *L'évangile de Jean* (Synopse des quatre Évangiles en français 3; Paris: Cerf, 1977).

Borgen, P., '"There Shall Come Forth a Man": Reflections on Messianic Ideas in Philo', in J. H. Charlesworth (ed.), *The Messiah* (Minneapolis: Fortress, 1992), pp.341–61.

——. '"Yes", "No", "How Far?": The Participation of Jews and Christians in Pagan Cults', in T. Engberg-Pedersen (ed.), *Paul in his Hellenistic Context* (SNTW; Edinburgh: T. & T. Clark, 1994), pp.30–59.

Boring, M. E., *Mark: A Commentary* (NTL; Louisville: Westminster John Knox, 2006).

Box, G. H., and J. I. Landsman, *The Apocalypse of Abraham* (London: SPCK, 1918).

Boyarin, D., *A Radical Jew: Paul and the Politics of Identity* (Berkeley: University of California Press, 1994).

Braude, W. G., *Jewish Proselyting in the First Five Centuries of the Common Era: The Age of the Tannaim and Amoraim* (BUS 6; Providence: Brown University Press, 1940).

Brooke, G. J., *Exegesis at Qumran. 4QFlorilegium and its Jewish Context* (Atlanta: SBL, 2006, originally published by Sheffield: JSOT, in 1985).

——. 'The Kittim in the Qumran Pesharim', in L. Alexander (ed.), *Images of Empire* (JSOTSup 122; Sheffield: Sheffield Academic, 1991), pp.135–59.

Brown, R. E., *The Community of the Beloved Disciple: The Life, Loves, and Hates of an Individual Church in New Testament Times* (New York: Paulist, 1979).

——. *The Gospel according to John* (AB 29, 29A; 2 vols.; New York: Doubleday, 1966, 1970).

——. *An Introduction to the Gospel of John: Edited, Updated, Introduced and Concluded by Francis J. Moloney* (ABRL; New York: Doubleday, 2003).

Brown, S., 'The Matthean Community and the Gentile Mission', *NovT* 22 (1980), pp.193–221.

Bryan, C., *A Preface to Mark: Notes on the Gospel in its Literary and Cultural Settings* (Oxford: Oxford University Press, 1993).

Buell, D. K., and C. J. Hodge, 'The Politics of Interpretation: The Rhetoric of Race and Ethnicity in Paul', *JBL* 123 (2004), pp.235–51.

Buitenwerf, R., *Book III of the Sibylline Oracles and its Social Setting* (Leiden: Brill, 2003).

Byrne, B., *A Costly Freedom: A Theological Reading of Mark's Gospel* (Strathfield: St Paul's, 2008).

——. 'The Messiah in Whose Name "the Gentiles Will Hope" (Matt 12:21): Gentile Inclusion as an Essential Element of Matthew's Christology', *ABR* 50 (2002), pp.55–73.

Cadwallader, A. H., 'Anniversary Overlap: Or What Happens When St Paul Meets the Universal Declaration of Human Rights', in P. Babie and N. Rochow (eds.), *Freedom of Religion under Bills of Rights* (Adelaide: University of Adelaide Press, 2012), pp.51–62.

——. 'Honouring the Repairer of the Baths: a New Inscription from Kolossai', *Antichthon* 42 (2012), pp.150–83.

——. 'A New Inscription [read: Two New Inscriptions]: A Correction and a Confirmed Sighting from Colossae', *EA* 40 (2007), pp.109–18.

——. 'Refuting an Axiom of Scholarship on Colossae: Fresh Insights from New and Old Inscriptions', in A. H. Cadwallader and M. Trainor (eds.), *Colossae in Space and Time: Linking with an Ancient City* (Göttingen: Vandenhoeck & Ruprecht, 2011), pp.151–79.

——. '"What's in a Name": The Tenacity of a Tradition of Interpretation', Festschrift for Victor Pfitzner, edited by P. Lockwood, *Lutheran Theological Journal* 39 (2005), pp.218–39.

Campbell, D., *The Deliverance of God: An Apocalyptic Re-reading of Justification in Paul* (Grand Rapids: Eerdmans, 2009).

Campbell, W. S., *Paul and the Creation of Christian Identity* (London: T&T Clark, 2008).

Carey, G. C., *Ultimate Things: An Introduction to Jewish and Christian Apocalyptic Literature* (St Louis: Chalice, 2005).

Carleton-Paget, J., *Jews, Christians and Jewish Christians in Antiquity* (WUNT 251; Tübingen: Mohr Siebeck, 2010).

Carson, D. A., P. T. O'Brien, and M. A. Seifrid (eds.), *Justification and Variegated Nomism. I. The Complexities of Second Temple Judaism* (WUNT 2.140; Tübingen: Mohr Siebeck, 2001).

Carter, W., 'Are there Imperial Texts in the Class? Intertextual Eagles and Matthean Eschatology as "Lights Out" Time for Imperial Rome' (Matthew 24.27-31), *JBL* 122 (2003), pp.467–87.

——. *Matthew and Empire: Initial Explorations* (Harrisburg: Trinity Press International, 2001).

——. 'Matthew and the Gentiles: Individual Conversion and/or Systemic Transformation?', *JSNT* 26 (2004), pp.259–82.

Charles, R. H., 'II Baruch: The Syriac Apocalypse of Baruch', in R. H. Charles (ed.), *Pseudepigrapha of the Old Testament* (2 vols.; Bellingham: Logos Research Systems, 2004).

Charles, R. H. (ed.), *The Apocrypha and Pseudepigrapha of the Old Testament* (2 vols.; Oxford: Clarendon, 1913).

Charlesworth, J. H., *The Pseudepigrapha and Modern Research* (SCSS 7; Ann Arbor: Scholars Press, 1981).

Chesnutt, R. D., *From Death to Life: Conversion in Joseph and Asenath* (JSPSup 16; Sheffield: Sheffield Academic, 1995).

Christensen, D. L., 'Nations', in *ABD*, IV, pp.1037–49.

Clark, K. W., 'The Gentile Bias in Matthew', *JBL* 66 (1947), pp.165–72.

Cohen, N. G., 'The Names of the Translators in the Letter of Aristeas: A Study in the Dynamics of Cultural Transition', *JSJ* 15 (1984), pp.32–64.

Cohen, S. J. D., *The Beginnings of Jewishness: Boundaries, Varieties, Uncertainties* (Berkeley: University of California Press, 1999).

——. 'Crossing the Boundary and Becoming a Jew', *HTR* 82 (1989), pp.13–33.

——. *From the Maccabees to the Mishnah* (Philadelphia: Westminster, 1987).

——. *Josephus in Galilee and Rome: His Vita and Development as a Historian* (CSCT 8; Leiden: Brill, 1979).

——. 'Respect for Judaism by Gentiles according to Josephus', *HTR* 80 (1987), pp.409–30.

Collins, A. Y., *Mark : A Commentary* (Hermeneia; Minneapolis: Fortress, 2007).

Collins, J. J., *The Apocalyptic Imagination* (Grand Rapids: Eerdmans, 2nd edn, 1998).

——. 'Apocalyptic Literature', in R. A. Kraft and G. W. E. Nickelsburg (eds.), *Early Judaism and its Modern Interpreters* (Atlanta: Scholars Press, 1986), pp.345–70.

——. *Beyond the Qumran Community: The Sectarian Movement of the Dead Sea Scrolls* (Grand Rapids: Eerdmans, 2010).

——. 'The Jewish Adaptation of Sibylline Oracles', in I. C. Colombo and T. Seppilli (eds.), *Sibille e linguaggi oracolari: Mito, storia, tradizione. Atti del Convegno Macerata-Norcia, Settembre 1994* (Rome: Istituti Editoriali e Poligrafici Internazionali, 1998), pp.369–87.

——. 'Sectarian Communities in the Dead Sea Scrolls', in T. H. Lim and J. J. Collins (eds.), *The Oxford Handbook of the Dead Sea Scrolls* (Oxford: Oxford University Press, 2010), pp.151–72.

——. *Seers, Sibyls, and Sages in Hellenistic-Roman Judaism* (Leiden: Brill, 2001).

——. 'Sibylline Oracles', in *OTP*, I, pp.317–472.

——. 'Testaments', in Stone (ed.), *Jewish Writings of the Second Temple Period*, pp.325–55.

Colson, F. H., J. W. Earp, R. Marcus, and G. H. Whitaker, *Philo of Alexandria* (10 vols. and 2 supplementary vols.; LCL; Cambridge, MA: Harvard University Press, 1929–62).

Colvin, S., 'Names in Hellenistic and Roman Lycia', in S. Colvin (ed.), *The Greco-Roman East: Politics, Culture, Society* (Cambridge: Cambridge University Press, 2004), pp.44–84.

Cope, O. L., *Matthew: A Scribe Trained for the Kingdom of Heaven* (CBQMS 5; Washington: Catholic Biblical Association of America, 1989).

Crossan, J. D., and J. L. Reed, *In Search of Paul: How Jesus's Apostle Opposed Rome's Empire with God's Kingdom: A New Vision of Paul's Words and World* (New York: HarperCollins, 2004).

Cullmann, O., *The Johannine Circle: Its Place in Judaism among the Disciples of Jesus and in Early Christianity: A Study in the Origin of the Gospel of John* (London: SCM, 1976).

Dabelstein, R., *Die Beurteilung der 'Heiden' bei Paulus* (BBET 14; Frankfurt: Peter Lang, 1981).

Darko, D. K., *No Longer Living as the Gentiles: Differentiation and Shared Ethical Values in Ephesians 4.17–6.9* (LNTS 375; London: T&T Clark International, 2008).

Das, A. A., *Solving the Romans Debate* (Minneapolis: Fortress, 2007).

Davies, A., 'Greek Personal Names and Linguistic Continuity', in S. Hornblower and E. Matthews (eds.), *Greek Personal Names: Their Value as Evidence* (Oxford: British Academy, 2000), pp.15–39.

Davies, P. R., 'The "Damascus Sect" and Judaism', in J. C. Reeves and J. Kampen (eds.), *Pursuing the Text: Studies in Honor of Ben Zion Wacholder on the Occasion of his Seventieth Birthday* (JSOTSup 184; Sheffield: Sheffield Academic, 1994), pp.70–84.

Davies, W. D., and D. C. Allison, *A Critical and Exegetical Commentary on the Gospel according to Saint Matthew* (ICC; 3 vols.; Edinburgh: T. & T. Clark, 1988, 1991, 1997).

de Boer, M. C., *Galatians: A Commentary* (NTL; Louisville: Westminster John Knox, 2011).

Deissmann, A., *Bible Studies* (Edinburgh: T. & T. Clark, 1909).

Derrett, J. D. M., 'Crumbs in Mark', *Downside Review* 102 (1984), pp.12–21.

Dmitriev, S., *City Government in Hellenistic and Roman Asia Minor* (Oxford: Oxford University Press, 2005).

Dodd, C. H., *The Interpretation of the Fourth Gospel* (Cambridge: Cambridge University Press, 1953).

Donahue, J. R., and D. J. Harrington, *The Gospel of Mark* (SP 2; Collegeville: Liturgical, 2002).

Donaldson, T. L., 'Introduction', in T. L. Donaldson (ed.), *Religious Rivalries and the Struggle for Success in Caesarea Maritima* (Waterloo: Wilfred Laurier University Press, 2000).

——. 'Israelite, Convert, Apostle to the Gentiles: The Origin of Paul's Gentile Mission', in R. N. Longenecker (ed.), *The Road from Damascus: The Impact of Paul's Conversion on his Life, Thought, and Ministry* (MNTS; Grand Rapids: Eerdmans, 1997), pp.62–84.

——. 'Jewish Christianity, Israel's Stumbling and the *Sonderweg* Reading of Paul', *JSNT* 29 (2006), pp.27–54.

——. *Judaism and the Gentiles: Patterns of Universalism (to 135 CE)* (Waco: Baylor University Press, 2008).

——. *Paul and the Gentiles: Remapping the Apostle's Convictional World* (Minneapolis: Fortress, 1997).

Dowling, E. V., *Taking Away the Pound: Women, Theology and the Parable of the Pounds in the Gospel of Luke* (LNTS 324; London: T&T Clark International, 2007).

Downey, G., *A History of Antioch in Syria from Seleucus to the Arab Conquest* (Princeton: Princeton University Press, 1961).

Draper, J. A., 'Children and Slaves in the Community of the *Didache* and the Two Ways Tradition' (paper presented to the International Meeting of the SBL at Kings College, London, August 2011).

——. 'First-Fruits and the Support of Prophets, Teachers, and the Poor in *Didache* 13 in Relation to New Testament Parallels', in A. Gregory and C. Tuckett (eds.), *Trajectories through the New Testament and the Apostolic Fathers* (Oxford: Oxford University Press, 2005), pp.223–43.

——. 'The Holy Vine of David Made Known to the Gentiles through God's Servant Jesus: "Christian Judaism" in the *Didache*', in M. Jackson-MacCabe (ed.), *Jewish Christianity Reconsidered: Rethinking Ancient Groups and Texts* (Minneapolis: Fortress, 2007), pp.257–83.

——. 'The Moral Economy of the *Didache*', *HTS* 67 (2011), Art. #907, 10 pages. DOI: 10.4102/hts.v67i1.907.

——. 'Ritual Process and Ritual Symbol in *Didache* 7–10', *VC* 54 (2000), pp.1–38.

——. 'Vice Catalogues as Oral-Mnemonic Cues: A Comparative Study of the Two Ways Tradition in the *Didache* and Parallels from the Perspective of Oral Tradition', in T. Thatcher (ed.), *Jesus, the Voice, and the Text* (Waco: Baylor University Press, 2008), pp.111–35.

Drew-Bear, T., C. M., Thomas and M. Yıldızturan, *Phrygian Votive Steles* (Ankara: Ministry of Culture, 1999).

Dunn, J. D. G., *Christianity in the Making*. II. *Beginning from Jerusalem* (Grand Rapids: Eerdmans, 2009).

——. *The Epistles to the Colossians and to Philemon* (NIGTC; Grand Rapids: Eerdmans, 1996).

——. *The Epistle to the Galatians* (BNTC; London: A & C Black, 1993).

——. 'The Incident at Antioch (Gal. 2:11-18)', *JSNT* 18 (1983), pp.3–57.

——. *The New Perspective on Paul* (Grand Rapids: Eerdmans, rev. edn, 2008).

——. *The Partings of the Ways between Christianity and Judaism and their Significance for the Character of Christianity* (London: SCM, 1991).

Ehrenkrook, J. von, *Sculpturing Idolatry in Flavian Rome: (An)Iconic Rhetoric in the Writings of Flavius Josephus* (EJL 33; Atlanta: SBL, 2011).

Elliott, N., *The Rhetoric of Romans: Argumentative Constraint and Strategy and Paul's Dialogue with Judaism* (JSNTSup 45; Sheffield: JSOT, 1990).

Elliott, S., *Cutting Too Close for Comfort: Paul's Letter to the Galatians in its Anatolian Cultic Context* (JSNTSup 248; London: T&T Clark International, 2003).

Engberg-Pedersen, T., *Cosmology and Self in the Apostle Paul: The Material Spirit* (Oxford: Oxford University Press, 2010).

——. *Paul and the Stoics* (Edinburgh: T. & T. Clark, 2000).

Engberg-Pedersen, T. (ed.), *Paul Beyond the Judaism/Hellenism Divide* (Louisville: Westminster John Knox, 2001).

Esler, P. F., *Community and Gospel in Luke–Acts: The Social and Political Motivations of Lukan Theology* (SNTSMS 57; Cambridge: Cambridge University Press, 1987).

——. *Conflict and Identity in Romans: The Social Setting of Paul's Letter* (Minneapolis: Fortress, 2003).

Fee, G. D., *Paul's Letter to the Philippians* (NICNT; Grand Rapids: Eerdmans, 1995).

Feldman, L. H., *Jew and Gentile in the Ancient World: Attitudes and Interactions from Alexander to Justinian* (Princeton: Princeton University Press, 1993).

——. 'The Omnipresence of the God-Fearers', *BAR* 12 (1986), pp.58–63.

——. *Studies in Josephus' Rewritten Bible* (JSJSup 58; Leiden: Brill, 1998).

Feldmeier, R., and U. Heckel (eds.), *Die Heiden: Juden, Christen und das Problem des Fremden* (WUNT 70; Tübingen: Mohr Siebeck, 1994).

Figueras, P., 'Epigraphic Evidence for Proselytism in Ancient Judaism', *Immanuel* 24/25 (1990), pp.194–206.

Finn, T. M., *From Death to Rebirth: Ritual and Conversion in Antiquity* (New York: Paulist, 1997).

Fitzgerald, J. T., 'Paul and Friendship', in Sampley (ed.), *Paul in the Greco-Roman World*, pp.319–43.

Fitzmyer, J. A., *The Gospel according to Luke: A New Translation with Introduction and Commentary* (AB 28, 28A; 2 vols.; New York: Doubleday, 1981, 1985).

Fleddermann, H., *Q. A Reconstruction and Commentary* (Leuven: Peeters, 2005).

Foster, P., *Community, Law and Mission in Matthew's Gospel* (WUNT 2.177; Tübingen; Mohr Siebeck, 2004).

Fowl, S. E., *Philippians* (THNTC; Grand Rapids: Eerdmans, 2005).

France, R.T., *The Gospel of Matthew* (NICNT; Grand Rapids: Eerdmans, 2007).

Frank, T., 'Race Mixture in the Roman Empire', *AHR* 21 (1916), pp.689–708.

Gagniers, J. des et al. (eds.), *Laodicée du Lycos: le Nymphée, Campagnes 1961–1963* (Quebec: L'Université Laval, 1969).

Gafni, I. M., *Land, Center and Diaspora: Jewish Constructs in Late Antiquity* (Sheffield: Sheffield Academic, 1997).

Gager, J. G., 'Jews, Gentiles, and Synagogues in the Book of Acts', *HTR* 79 (1986), pp.9–99.

García Martínez, F., *The Dead Sea Scrolls Translated* (Leiden: Brill, 1996).

Gärtner, B., *Temple and Community in Qumran and the New Testament* (SNTSMS 1; Cambridge: Cambridge University Press, 1965).

Gathercole, S. J., 'A Law Unto Themselves: The Gentiles in Romans 2.14-15 Revisited', *JSNT* 23 (2002), pp.27–49.

Geffcken, J., *Komposition and Entstehungszeit der Oracula Sibyllina* (Leipzig: Hinrichs, 1902).

Gese, M., *Das Vermächtnis des Apostels: die Rezeption der paulinischen Theologie im Epheserbrief* (Tübingen: Mohr Siebeck, 1997).

Gilbert, G., 'Gentiles, Jewish Attitudes toward', in J. J. Collins and D. C. Harlow (eds.), *The Eerdmans Dictionary of Early Judaism* (Grand Rapids: Eerdmans, 2010), pp.670–73.

Gillihan, Y. M., *Civic Ideology, Organization, and Law in the Rule Books: A Comparative Study of the Covenanters' Sect and Contemporary Voluntary Associations in Political Context* (STDJ 97; Leiden: Brill, 2011).

——. 'The *ger* Who Wasn't There: Fictional Aliens in the Damascus Rule', *RevQ* 25 (2011), pp.257–305.

Ginzberg, L., *The Legends of the Jews* (6 vols.; New York: JPS, 1942).

Goodenough, E. R., *By Light, Light: The Mystic Gospel of Hellenistic Judaism* (New Haven: Yale University Press, 1935).

Goodman, M., 'Josephus' Treatise *Against Apion*', in M. Edwards, M. Goodman and S. Price (eds.), *Apologetics in the Roman Empire: Pagans, Jews, and Christians* (Oxford: Oxford University Press, 1999), pp.45–58.

——. *Judaism in the Roman World: Collected Essays* (AJEC 66; Leiden: Brill, 2007).

——. *Mission and Conversion: Proselytizing in the Religious History of the Roman Empire* (Oxford: Clarendon, 1994).

Goudriaan, K., 'Ethnical Strategies in Graeco-Roman Egypt', in P. Bilde, T. Engberg-Pedersen, L. Hanestad and J. Zahle (eds.), *Ethnicity in Hellenistic Egypt* (SHC 3; Aarhus: Aarhus University Press, 1992), pp.74–99.

Grabbe, L. L., *Judaism from Cyrus to Hadrian* (2 vols.; Minneapolis: Fortress, 1992).

Green, J. B., *The Gospel of Luke* (NICNT; Grand Rapids: Eerdmans, 1997).

——. *The Theology of the Gospel of Luke* (NTT; Cambridge: Cambridge University Press, 1995).

Gruen, E. S., *Heritage and Hellenism: The Reinvention of Jewish Tradition* (HCS 30; Berkeley; University of California Press, 1998).

Gundry, R. H., 'The Apostolically Johannine pre-Papian Tradition Concerning the Gospels of Mark and Matthew', in R. H. Gundry, *The Old Is Better: New Testament Essays in Support of Traditional Interpretations* (WUNT 178; Tübingen: Mohr Siebeck, 2005), pp.49–73.

——. *Mark: A Commentary on his Apology for the Cross* (Grand Rapids: Eerdmans, 1993).

——. *Matthew: A Commentary on his Handbook for a Mixed Church under Persecution* (Grand Rapids: Eerdmans, 2nd edn, 1994).

Guterman, S. L., *Religious Toleration and Persecution in Ancient Rome* (London: Aiglon, 1951).

Hagner, D. A., *Matthew* (2 vols.; WBC 33A, 33B; Dallas: Word, 1993, 1995).

Hall, R. G., *Revealed Histories: Techniques for Ancient Jewish and Christian Historiography* (Sheffield: Sheffield Academic, 1991).

Hamm, D., 'What the Samaritan Leper Sees: The Narrative Christology of Luke 17:11-19', *CBQ* 56 (1994), pp.273–87.

Hare, D. R. A., *The Theme of Jewish Persecution of Christians in the Gospel according to St. Matthew* (SNTSMS 6; Cambridge: Cambridge University Press, 1967).

Harland, P., 'The Declining Polis? Religious Rivalries in Ancient Civic Context', in L. E. Vaage (ed.), *Religious Rivalries in the Early Roman Empire and the Rise of Christianity* (Waterloo: Wilfred Laurier University Press, 2006), pp.21–49.

Harnack, A. von, *The History of Dogma* (2 vols.; London: Williams & Norgate, 1894).

Harrington, D. J., *The Gospel of Matthew* (SP 1; Collegeville: Liturgical, 1991).

——. *Invitation to the Apocrypha* (Grand Rapids: Eerdmans, 1999).

Harrington, H., *The Purity Texts* (CQS 5; London: T&T Clark, 2004).

Hayes, C., *Gentile Impurities and Jewish Identities: Intermarriage and Conversion from the Bible to the Talmud* (New York: Oxford University Press, 2002).

——. 'Intermarriage and Impurity in Ancient Jewish Sources', *HTR* 92 (1999), pp.3–36.

Heckel, U., 'Das Bild der Heiden und die Indentität der Christen bei Paulus', in Feldmeier and Heckel (eds.), *Die Heiden*, pp.269–96.

Helyer, L. H., *Exploring Jewish Literature of the Second Temple Period* (Downers Grove: InterVarsity, 2002).

Henderson, S. W., *Christology and Discipleship in the Gospel of Mark* (SNTSMS 135; Cambridge: Cambridge University Press, 2006).

Hock, R. F., 'Paul and Greco-Roman Education', in Sampley (ed.), *Paul in the Greco-Roman World*, pp.198–227.

Hodge, C. J., *If Sons, Then Heirs: A Study of Kinship and Ethnicity Language in the Letters of Paul* (New York: Oxford University Press, 2007).

Hoffmann, P., 'Mutmassungen über Q. Zum Problem der literarischen Genese von Q', in Lindemann (ed.), *The Sayings Source Q*, pp.255–88.

——. *Studien zur Theologie der Logienquelle* (NTAbh 8; Münster: Aschendorff, 1972).

Honigman, S., 'Abraham in Egypt: Hebrew and Jewish-Aramaic Names in Egypt and Judaea in Hellenistic and Early Roman Times', *ZPE* 146 (2004), pp.279–97.

Hood, B. J., *The Messiah, his Brothers, and the Nations (Matthew1.1-17)* (LNTS 441; London: T&T Clark International, 2011).

Hooker, M. D., *The Gospel according to St. Mark* (Peabody: Hendrickson, 1993).

Hopkins, K., *Death and Renewal* (Cambridge: Cambridge University Press, 1983).

Horbury, H., *Jews and Christians: In Contact and Controversy* (Edinburgh: T. & T. Clark, 1998).

Horbury, W., W. D. Davies, and J. Sturdy (eds.), *The Cambridge History of Judaism*. III. *The Early Roman Period* (Cambridge: Cambridge University Press, 1999).

Horgan, M. P. *Pesharim: Qumran Interpretations of Biblical Books* (CBQMS 8; Washington: Catholic Biblical Association of America, 1979).

Horsley, G. H. R., *The Greek and Latin Inscriptions in the Burdur Archaeological Museum* (RECAM V; London: British Institute at Ankara, 2007).

——. 'Homer in Pisidia: Aspects of the History of Greek Education in a Remote Roman Province', *Antichthon* 34 (2000), pp.46–81.

——. *New Documents Illustrating Early Christianity*, I (North Ryde: Ancient History Documentary Research Centre, 1981).

——. *New Documents Illustrating Early Christianity*, II (North Ryde: Ancient History Documentary Research Centre, 1982).

Horsley, R. A. (ed.), *Paul and Empire: Religion and Power in Roman Imperial Society* (Harrisburg: Trinity Press International, 1997).

——. *Paul and Politics: Ekklesia, Israel, Imperium, Interpretation* (Harrisburg: Trinity Press International, 2000).

——. *Paul and the Roman Imperial Order* (Harrisburg: Trinity Press International, 2004).

Horst, P. W. van der, 'Two Short Notes on Philo', *SPhA* 18 (2006), pp.49–55.

Houten, C. van, *The Alien in Israelite Law* (JSOTSup 107; Sheffield: Sheffield Academic, 1991).

Hultgren, S., *From the Damascus Covenant to the Covenant of the Community* (STDJ 66; Leiden: Brill, 2007).

Humphrey, E. M., *Joseph and Asenath* (Sheffield: Sheffield Academic, 2000).

Iersel, B. M. F. van, *Reading Mark* (Edinburgh: T. & T. Clark, 1989).

Isaac, E., '1 (Ethiopic Apocalypse of) Enoch', in *OTP*, I, pp.5–89.

Iverson, K. R., *Gentiles in the Gospel of Mark: 'Even the Dogs under the Table Eat the Children's Crumbs'* (LNTS 339; London: T&T Clark International, 2007).

Jackson, G. S., *'Have Mercy on Me': The Story of the Canaanite Woman in Matthew 15.21-28* (JSNTSup 228; London: Sheffield Academic, 2002).

Jacobson, A. D., *The First Gospel: An Introduction to Q* (Sonoma: Polebridge, 1992).

Jervell, J., 'The Lost Sheep of the House of Israel: The Understanding of the Samaritans in Luke–Acts', in J. Jervell, *Luke and the People of God: A New Look at Luke–Acts* (Minneapolis: Augsburg, 1972), pp.113–32.

Johnson, L. T., *The Acts of the Apostles* (SP 5; Collegeville: Liturgical, 1992).

——. *Among the Gentiles: Greco-Roman Religion and Christianity* (AYBRL; New Haven: Yale University Press, 2009).

——. *The Gospel of Luke* (SP 3; Collegeville: Liturgical, 1991).

Johnson, M. D., *The Purpose of the Biblical Genealogies with Special Reference to the Genealogies of Jesus* (SNTSMS 8; Cambridge: Cambridge University Press, 2nd edn, 1988).

Kahlos, M., *Debate and Dialogue: Christian and Pagan Cultures c. 360–430* (Aldershot: Ashgate, 2007).

Kartveit, M., *The Origin of the Samaritans* (VTSup 128; Leiden: Brill, 2009).

Kasher, A., *Jews, Idumeans and Ancient Arabs: Relations of the Jews in Eretz-Israel with the Nations of the Frontier and the Desert During the Hellenistic and Roman Era (332 BCE–70 CE)* (TSAJ 18; Tübingen: Mohr Siebeck, 1988).

Kearsley, R. A., 'Women and Public Life in Imperial Asia Minor: Hellenistic Tradition and Augustan Ideology', in G. R. Tsetskhladze (ed.), *Ancient West and East* (Leiden: Brill, 2005), pp.98–121.

Keizer, H. M., 'Life Time Entirety: A Study of ΑΙΩΝ in Greek Literature and Philosophy, the Septuagint and Philo' (PhD diss., Amsterdam, 1999).

Kerkeslager, A., 'The Absence of Dionysios, Lampo, and Isidoros from the Violence in Alexandria in 38 C.E.', *SPhA* 17 (2005), pp.49–94.

Kingsbury, J. D., *Conflict in Mark: Jesus, Authorities, Disciples* (Minneapolis: Fortress, 1989).

Klawans, J., *Impurity and Sin in Ancient Judaism* (New York: Oxford University Press, 2000).

——. 'Notions of Gentile Impurity in Ancient Judaism', *AJSRev* 20 (1995), pp.285–312.

——. *Purity, Sacrifice, and the Temple: Symbolism and Supersessionism in the Study of Ancient Judaism* (New York: Oxford University Press, 2006).

Kloppenborg, J. S., *Excavating Q: The History and Setting of the Sayings Gospel* (Minneapolis: Fortress, 2000).

——. *The Formation of Q* (Philadelphia: Fortress, 1987).

——. *Q, the Earliest Gospel: An Introduction to the Original Stories and Sayings of Jesus* (Louisville: Westminster John Knox, 2008).

——. 'The Sayings Gospel Q and the Quest of the Historical Jesus', *HTR* 89 (1996), pp.307–44.

Koch, D., 'The God-Fearers between Facts and Fiction: Two Theosebeis-Inscriptions from Aphrodisias and their Bearing for the New Testament', *Studia Theologica* 60 (2006), pp.62–90.

Koch, D.-A., *Die Schrift des Evangeliums: Untersuchungen zur Verwendung und zum Verständnis der Schrift bei Paulus* (BHT 6; Tübingen: Mohr Siebeck, 1986).

Konradt, M., *Israel, Kirche und der Völker im Matthäusevangeliums* (WUNT 215; Tübingen: Mohr Siebeck, 2007).

Kossen, H. B., 'Who Were the Greeks of John XII.20?', in J. N. Sevenster (ed.) *Studies in John: Presented to Dr. J. N. Sevenster on the Occasion of his Seventieth Birthday*, (NovTSup 24; Leiden: Brill, 1970), pp.97–110.

Kovacs, J. L., '"Now shall the ruler of this world be driven out": Jesus' Death as Cosmic Battle in John 12:20-36', *JBL* 114 (1995), pp.227–47.

Kraabel, A. T., 'Afterward', in Overman and MacLennan (eds.), *Diaspora Jews and Judaism*, pp.347–57.

——. 'The Disappearance of the "God-Fearers"', *Numen* 28 (1981), pp.113–26.

——. 'The Disappearance of the God-Fearers', in Overman and MacLennan (eds.), *Diaspora Jews and Judaism*, pp.119–30.

——. 'The Roman Diaspora: Six Questionable Assumptions', *JJS* 33 (1982), pp.445–64.

——. 'Synagoga Caeca: Systematic Distortion in Gentile Interpretations of Evidence for Judaism in the Early Christian Period', in J. Neusner and E. S. Frerichs (eds.), *'To See Ourselves as Others See Us': Christians, Jews, 'Others' in Late Antiquity* (Chico: Scholars Press, 1985), pp.226–32.

Kugel, J. L., 'The Story of Dinah in the Testament of Levi', *HTR* 84 (1992), pp.1–34.

Kugler, R. A., 'Testaments', in Carson, O'Brien, and Seifrid (eds.), *Justification and Variegated Nomism*, I, pp.189–213.

Kulik, A., *Retroverting Slavonic Pseudepigrapha: Toward the Original of the Apocalypse of Abraham* (Leiden: Brill, 2005).

Labahn, M., *Der Gekommene als Wieder kommender. Die Logienquelle als erzählte Geschichte* (Leipzig: Evangelische Verlagsanstalt, 2010).

Lajara, I.-J. A., *The Carian Language* (Leiden: Brill, 2007).

Lampros, S. P., Μιχαὴλ Ἀκομινάτου τοῦ Χωνιάτου τὰ σωζόμενα (2 vols.; Groningen: Bouma, 1968).

Lane, E., *Corpus Monumentorum Religionis Dei Menis* (3 vols.; Leiden: Brill, 1971–76).

Langbrandtner, W., *Weltferner Gott oder Gott der Liebe: Die Ketzerstreit in der johanneischen Kirche* (BBET 6; Frankfurt: Lang, 1977).

Laufen, R., *Die Doppelüberlieferungen der Logienquelle und des Markusevangeliums* (BBB 54; Bonn: Hanstein, 1980).

LaVerdiere, E. A. *The Beginning of the Gospel: Introducing the Gospel according to Mark* (2 vols.; Collegeville: Liturgical, 1999).

——. 'Do You Still Not Understand?', *Emmanuel* 96 (1990), pp.382–89.

——. 'Jesus among the Gentiles', *Emmanuel* 96 (1990), pp.338–45.

Lawson, V., 'Tabitha of Joppa: Disciple, Prophet and Biblical Prototype for Contemporary Religious Life', in R. M. Chennattu and M. L. Coloe (eds.), *Transcending Boundaries: Contemporary Readings of the New Testament* (Biblioteca di Scienze Religiose 197; Rome: Libreria Ateneo Salesiano, 2005), pp.281–92.

Levine, A.-J. *The Social and Ethnic Dimensions of Matthean Salvation History: 'Go Nowhere among the Gentiles' (Matt. 10.5b)* (SBEC 14; Lewiston: Edwin Mellen, 1988).

Levine, L. I., *The Ancient Synagogue: The First Thousand Years* (New Haven: Yale University Press, 2nd edn, 2005).

——. 'The First Century Synagogue: Critical Reassessments and Assessments of the Critical', in D. R. Edwards (ed.), *Religion and Society in Roman Palestine: Old Questions: New Approaches* (New York: Routledge, 2004), pp.70–102.

——. 'The Second Temple Synagogue: The Formative Years', in L. I. Levine (ed.), *The Synagogue in Late Antiquity* (Philadelphia: American Schools of Oriental Research, 1987), pp.7–31.

Levinskaya, I., *The Book of Acts in its First Century Setting.* V. *Diaspora Setting* (Grand Rapids: Eerdmans, 1996).

——. 'The Inscription from Aphrodisias and the Problem of God-Fearers', *TynBul* 41 (1990), pp.312–18.

Lieu, J. M., *Christian Identity in the Jewish and Graeco-Roman World* (Oxford: Oxford University Press, 2004).

——. '"The Parting of the Ways": Theological Construct or Historical Reality?', *JSNT* 56 (1994), pp.101–19.

Lim, T. H., 'Kittim', in L. H. Schiffman and J. C. VanderKam (eds.), *The Encyclopedia of the Dead Sea Scrolls* (New York: Oxford University Press, 2000), pp.469–71.

Lincoln, A. T., and A. J. M. Wedderburn, *The Theology of the Later Pauline Letters* (NTT; Cambridge: Cambridge University Press, 1993).

Lindemann, A. (ed.), *The Sayings Source Q and the Historical Jesus* (BETL 158; Leuven: Peeters, 2001).

Lohse, E., *Colossians and Philemon* (Hermeneia; Philadelphia: Fortress, 1971).

Longenecker, B. W., *Remember the Poor: Paul, Poverty and the Greco-Roman World* (Grand Rapids: Eerdmans, 2010).

Lopez, D. C., *Apostle to the Conquered: Reimagining Paul's Mission* (Minneapolis: Fortress, 2008).

Lührmann, D., *Die Redaktion der Logienquelle* (WMANT 33; Neukirchen–Vluyn: Neukirchener, 1969).

MacDonald, M., *Colossians and Ephesians* (SP 17; Collegeville: Liturgical, 2000).

MacLennan, R. S., and A. T. Kraabel, 'The God-Fearers – A Literary and Theological Invention', *BAR* 12 (1986), pp.46–53.

——. 'The God-Fearers – A Literary and Theological Invention', in Overman and MacLennan (eds.), *Diaspora Jews and Judaism*, pp.131–43.

MacMullen, R., 'The Epigraphic Habit in the Roman Empire', *AJP* 103 (1996), pp.233–46.

——. *Romanization in the Time of Augustus* (New Haven: Yale University Press, 2000).

Malbon, E. S., *In the Company of Jesus: Characters in Mark's Gospel* (Louisville: Westminster John Knox, 2000).

——. *Mark's Jesus: Characterization as Narrative Christology* (Waco: Baylor University Press, 2009).

——. *Narrative Space and Mythic Meaning in Mark* (Sheffield: JSOT, 1991).

Malherbe, A. J., *Paul and the Popular Philosophers* (Minneapolis: Fortress, 1989).

Mánek, J., 'Fishers of Men', *NovT* 2 (1957), pp.138–41.

Manson, T. W., *The Sayings of Jesus* (London: SCM, 1949).

Marchand, F., 'The Philippeis of *IG* VII 2433', in R. W. V. Catling and F. Marchand (eds.), *Onomatologos: Studies in Greek Personal Names Presented to Elaine Matthews* (Oxford: Oxbow, 2010), pp.332–43.

Marcus, J., '*Birkat Ha-Minim* Revisited', *NTS* 55 (2009), pp.523–51.

——. *Mark 1–8 : A New Translation with Introduction and Commentary* (AB 27; New York: Doubleday, 2000).

Marks, R. G., *Image of Bar Kokhba in Traditional Jewish Literature* (University Park: Pennsylvania State University Press, 1994).

Martyn, J. L., *Galatians: A New Translation with Introduction and Commentary* (AB 33A; New York: Doubleday, 1997).

——. *The Gospel of John in Christian History: Essays for Interpreters* (New York: Paulist, 1979).

Mason, S., *Flavius Josephus: Translation and Commentary. IB. Judean War 2* (Leiden: Brill, 2008).

——. *Flavius Josephus: Translation and Commentary. IX. Life of Josephus* (Leiden: Brill, 2001).

——. 'Should Any Wish to Enquire Further (*Ant.* 1.25): The Aim and Audience of Josephus's Judean Antiquities/Life', in S. Mason (ed.), *Understanding Josephus: Seven Perspectives* (Sheffield: Sheffield Academic, 1998), pp.64–103.

Matthews, E., 'Names, personal, Greek', in S. Hornblower and A. Spawforth (eds.), *Oxford Classical Dictionary* (Oxford: Oxford University Press, 3rd edn, 1996), pp.1022–4.

McCane, B. R., 'Simply Irresistible: Augustus, Herod, and the Empire', *JBL* 127 (2008), pp.725–35.

McKnight, S., *A Light among the Gentiles: Jewish Missionary Activity in the Second Temple Period* (Minneapolis: Fortress, 1991).

McLaren, J. S., 'Going to War against Rome: The Motivation of the Jewish Rebels', in M. Popović (ed.), *The Jewish Revolt against Rome: Interdisciplinary Perspectives* (JSJSup, 154; Leiden: Brill, 2011), pp.129–54.

——. 'Jews and the Imperial Cult: From Augustus to Domitian', *JSNT* 27 (2005), pp.257–78.

——. 'Josephus on Titus: The Vanquished Writing about the Victor', in J. Sievers and G. Lembi (eds.), *Josephus and Jewish History in Flavian Rome and Beyond* (JSJSup 104; Leiden: Brill, 2005), pp.279–95.

——. 'A Reluctant Provincial: Josephus and the Roman Empire in *Jewish War*', in Riches and Sim (eds.), *The Gospel of Matthew*, pp.34–48.

Mendels, D., *The Rise and Fall of Jewish Nationalism. Jewish and Christian Ethnicity in Ancient Palestine* (Grand Rapids: Eerdmans, 1992).

Menken, M. J. J., *Old Testament Quotations in the Fourth Gospel: Studies in Textual Form* (CBET 15; Kampen: Kok Pharos, 1996).

Metzger, B. M., *A Textual Commentary on the Greek New Testament* (Stuttgart: Deutsche Bibelgesellschaft, 2nd edn, 1994).

Meyer, P. D., 'The Gentile Mission in Q', *JBL* 89 (1970), pp.405–17.

Milgrom, J., *Leviticus* (AB 3, 3A, 3B; 3 vols.; New York: Doubleday, 1991–2001).

——. *Numbers* (JPS Torah Commentary; Philadelphia: JPS, 1990).

——. 'Rationale for Cultic Law: The Case of Impurity', *Semeia* 45 (1989), pp.103–9.

——. 'Religious Conversion and the Revolt Model for the Formation of Israel', *JBL* 101 (1982), pp.169–76.

Miranda, E., 'La communità giudaica di Hierapolis di Frigia', *EA* 31 (1999), pp.109–56.

Mittag, F. P., *Antiochus IV Epiphanes. Eine politische Biographie* (Berlin: Akademie, 2006), pp.214–24.

Moloney, F. J., 'From Cana to Cana (John. 2:1–4:54) and the Fourth Evangelist's Concept of Correct (and Incorrect) Faith', *Salesianum* 40 (1978), pp.817–43.

——. *The Johannine Son of Man* (BSR 14; Rome: Libreria Ateneo Salesiano, 1978).

——. 'The Johannine Son of Man Revisited', in G. van Belle, J. G. van der Watt and P. Maritz (eds.), *Theology and Christology in the Fourth Gospel* (BETL 184; Leuven: Peeters, 2005), pp.177–202.

——. *John* (SP 4; Collegeville: Liturgical, 1998).

——. 'Who Is the Reader in/of the Fourth Gospel?', *ABR* 40 (1992), pp.20–33.

Momigliano, A., 'From the Pagan to the Christian Sibyl', in R. DiDonato (ed.), *Nono Contributo: alla Storia degli Studi Classici e del Mondo antico* (Rome: Edizioni di Storia e Letteratura, 1992), pp.725–44.

Monnet, J., 'The Symbolism of Place: A Geography of Relationships between Space, Power and Identity', *Cybergo: European Journal of Geography* 562 (2011). Online: http://cybergeo.revues.org/24747 (accessed 14 March 2013).

Moulton, J. H., and G. Milligan, *The Vocabulary of the Greek Testament: Illustrated from the Papyri and Other Non-Literary Sources* (London: Hodder & Stoughton, 1930).

Mussies, G., 'Jewish Personal Names in some Non-literary Sources', in J. W. van Henten and P. W. van der Horst (eds.), *Studies in Early Jewish Epigraphy* (Leiden: Brill, 1994), pp.242–76.

Netzer, E., *The Architecture of Herod the Great Builder* (TSAJ 117; Tübingen: Mohr Siebeck, 2006).

Neusner, J., 'The Doctrine of Israel', in J. Neusner and A. Avery-Peck (eds.), *The Blackwell Companion to Judaism* (Oxford: Blackwell, 2000), pp.230–46.

——. 'Explaining the Great Schism: History versus Theology', *Religion* 28 (1998), pp.139–58.

Neyrey, J. H., 'The Idea of Purity in Mark's Gospel', *Semeia* 35 (1986), pp.91–128.

Nickelsburg, G. W. E., *1 Enoch 1* (Hermeneia; Minneapolis: Fortress, 2001).

——. *Jewish Literature between the Bible and the Mishnah* (Minneapolis: Fortress, 1981), pp.212–14.

Niehoff, M. R., *Philo on Jewish Identity and Culture* (TSAJ 86; Tübingen: Mohr Siebeck, 2001).

Nolland, J., *The Gospel of Matthew* (NIGTC; Grand Rapids: Eerdmans, 2005).

——. 'Uncircumcised Proselytes?', *JSJ* 12 (1981), pp.173–94.

Noy, D., *Foreigners at Rome: Citizens and Strangers* (London: Duckworth, 2000).

Oakes, P., *Philippians: From People to Letter* (SNTSMS 110; Cambridge: Cambridge University Press, 2001).

O'Brien, P., *Colossians, Philemon* (WBC 44; Waco: Word, 1982).

Olender, M., 'Aspects of Baubo: Ancient Texts and Contexts', in D. M. Halperin, J. J. Winkler and F. I. Zeitlin (eds.), *Before Sexuality: The Construction of Erotic Experience in the Ancient Greek World* (Princeton: Princeton University Press, 1990), pp.83–113.

Overman, J. A., 'The God-Fearers: Some Neglected Features', in Overman and MacLennan (eds.), *Diaspora Jews and Judaism*, pp.145–52.

——. *Matthew's Gospel and Formative Judaism: The Social World of the Matthean Community* (Minneapolis: Fortress, 1990).

Overman, J. A., and R. S. MacLennan (eds.), *Diaspora Jews and Judaism: Essays in Honour of, and in Dialogue with, A. Thomas Kraabel* (SFSHJ 41; Atlanta: Scholars Press, 1992).

Parke, H. W., *Sibyls and Sibylline Prophecy in Classical Antiquity* (London: Routledge, 1988).

Paul, G. M., 'The Presentation of Titus in the *Jewish War* of Josephus: Two Aspects', *Phoenix* 47 (1993), pp.56–66.

Pearce, S. J. K., *The Land of the Body: Studies in Philo's Representation of Egypt* (WUNT 204; Tübingen: Mohr Siebeck, 2007).

Pleket, H., 'The Infrastructure of Sport in the Cities of the Greek World', *Scienze dell'Antichità* 10 (2000), pp.627–44.

Pokorný, P., *Colossians: A Commentary* (Peabody: Hendrickson, 1991).

Porton, G. G., *The Stranger Within Your Gates: Converts and Conversion in Rabbinic Literature* (CSHJ; Chicago: University of Chicago Press, 1994).

Price, J., 'Josephus and the Dialogue on the Destruction of the Temple', in C. Böttrich and J. Herzer with T. Reiprich (eds.), *Josephus und das Neue Testament. Wechselseitige Wahrnehmungen. II Internationales Symposium zum Corpus Judaeo-Hellenisticum 25.–28. Mai 2006, Greifswald* (WUNT 209; Tübingen: Mohr Siebeck, 2007), pp.181–94.

Priest, J., 'Testament of Moses', in *OTP*, I, pp.919–35.

Qimron, E., and J. Strugnell (eds.), *Qumran Cave 4 V. Miqsat Maʿase Ha-Torah* (DJD 10; Oxford: Clarendon, 1994).

Rajak, T., 'Greeks and Barbarians in Josephus', in J. J. Collins and G. E. Sterling (eds.), *Hellenism in the Land of Israel* (Notre Dame: University of Notre Dame Press, 2001), pp.244–62.

——. *The Jewish Dialogue with Greece and Rome. Studies in Cultural and Social Interaction* (Leiden: Brill, 2001).

——. *Josephus: The Historian and his Society* (London: Duckworth, 2nd edn, 2003).

Ratté, C., 'The Urban Development of Aphrodisias in the Late Hellenistic and Early Imperial Periods', in C. Bern, L. Vandeput and M. Waelkens (eds.), *Patris und Imperium: Kulturelle und Politische Identität in den Stadten in den römischen Provinzen Kleinasiens in der frühen Kaiserzeit* (Leuven: Peeters, 2002), pp.5–32.

Ravens, D., *Luke and the Restoration of Israel* (JSNTSup 119; Sheffield: Sheffield Academic, 1995).

Reddish, M. G., *Apocalyptic Literature* (Nashville: Abingdon, 1990).

Reid, B. E., *Choosing the Better Part? Women in the Gospel of Luke* (Collegeville: Liturgical, 1996).

——. *Parables for Preachers: Year C* (Collegeville: Liturgical, 2000).

Repschinski, B., 'Matthew and Luke', in D. C. Sim and B. Repschinski (eds.), *Matthew and his Christian Contemporaries* (LNTS 333; London: T&T Clark International, 2008), pp.50–65.

——. *Nicht aufzulösen, sondern zu erfüllen: Das jüdische Gesetz in der synoptischen Jesuserzählungen* (FzB 120; Würzburg: Echter, 2009).

Reynolds, J., and R. Tannenbaum, *Jews and Godfearers at Aphrodisias: Greek Inscriptions with Commentary* (Cambridge: Cambridge Philological Society, 1987).

Rhoads, D. M., *Reading Mark, Engaging the Gospel* (Minneapolis: Fortress, 2004).

Rhoads, D. M., J. Dewey, and D. Michie, *Mark as Story: An Introduction to the Narrative of a Gospel* (Minneapolis: Fortress, 2nd edn, 1999).

Richardson, P., *Building Jewish in the Roman East* (Waco: Baylor University Press, 2004).

Riches, J., *Conflicting Mythologies: Identity Formation in the Gospels of Mark and Matthew* (SNTW; Edinburgh: T. & T. Clark, 2000).

Riches, J., and D. C. Sim (eds.), *The Gospel of Matthew in its Roman Imperial Context* (JSNTSup 276; London: T&T Clark International, 2005).

Richter, G., 'Präsentische und futurische Eschatologie im 4. Evangelium', in P. Fiedler and D. Zeller (eds.), *Gegenwart und kommendes Reich: Schülergabe Anton Vögtle zum 65. Geburtstag,* (Stuttgart: KBW, 1975), pp.117–51.

Richter Reimer, I., *Women in the Acts of the Apostles: A Feminist Liberation Perspective* (Minneapolis: Fortress, 1995).

Riggs, J. W., 'The Sacred Food of *Didache* 9–10 and Second-Century Ecclesiologies', in C N. Jefford (ed.), *The Didache in Context: Essays on its Text, History, and Transmission* (NovTSup 77; Leiden: Brill, 1995), pp.256–84.

Robert, L., *Noms indigènes dans L'Asie-Mineure Gréco-romaine* (Amsterdam: Hakkert, 1991 [1963]).

Robinson, G., *A Change of Mind and Heart: The Good News according to Mark* (Revesby: Parish Ministry Publications, 1994).

Robinson, J. A. T., 'The Destination and Purpose of St John's Gospel', *NTS* 6 (1959–60), pp.117–31.

——. *The Priority of John* (London: SCM, 1985).

Robinson, J. M., P. Hoffmann, and J. S. Kloppenborg (eds.), *The Critical Edition of Q* (Minneapolis: Fortress, 2000).

Rocca, S., *Herod's Judaea: A Mediterranean State in the Classical World* (TSAJ 122; Tübingen: Mohr Siebeck, 2008).

Rordorf, W. '*Ta hagia tois hagiois*', *Irénikon* 72 (1999), pp.346–64.

Rosenblum, J. D., 'Food and Identity in Early Rabbinic Identity' (paper presented at the SBL Section *Meals in the Greco-Roman World Group*, San Francisco, 19–22 November 2011).

Royse, J. R., 'The Works of Philo', in A. Kamesar (ed.), *The Cambridge Companion to Philo* (Cambridge: Cambridge University Press, 2009), pp.32–64.

Rubinkiewicz, R., 'Abraham, Apocalypse of', in *ABD*, I, pp.41–43.

——. 'Apocalypse of Abraham', in *OTP*, I, pp.681–88.

——. 'Les sémitismes dans l'Apocalypse d'Abraham', *Folia Orientalia* 21 (1989), pp.141–48.

Ruden, S., *Paul among the People: The Apostle Reinterpreted and Reimagined in his Own Time* (New York: Pantheon, 2010).

Runesson, A., 'Judging Gentiles in the Gospel of Matthew: Between "Othering" and Inclusion', in D. M. Gurtner, J. Willitts and R. Burridge (eds.), *Jesus, Matthew's Gospel and Early Christianity: Studies in Memory of Graham N. Stanton* (LNTS 435; London: T&T Clark International, 2011), pp.133–51.

——. *The Origins of the Synagogue: A Socio-Historical Study* (Stockholm: Almqvist & Wiksell, 2001).

——. 'Particularistic Judaism and Universalistic Christianity? Some Critical Remarks on Terminology and Theology', *Studia Theologia* 54 (2000), pp.55–75.

——. 'Rethinking Early Jewish–Christian Relations: Matthean Community History as Pharisaic Intragroup Conflict', *JBL* 127 (2008), pp.95–132.

Runesson, A., D. Binder, and B. Olsson, *The Ancient Synagogue from its Origins to 200 C.E.: A Source Book* (Leiden: Brill, 2008).

Saldarini, A. J., *Matthew's Christian-Jewish Community* (CSHJ; Chicago: University of Chicago Press, 1994).

Salmon, M., 'Insider or Outsider? Luke's Relationship with Israel', in J. B. Tyson (ed.), *Luke–Acts and the Jewish People: Eight Critical Perspectives* (Minneapolis: Augsburg, 1988), pp.76–82.

Samkutty, V. J., *The Samaritan Mission in Acts* (LNTS 328; London: T&T Clark International, 2006).

Sampley, J. P., 'Introduction', in Sampley (ed.), *Paul in the Greco-Roman World*, pp.1–15.

Sampley, J. P. (ed.), *Paul in the Greco-Roman World: A Handbook* (Harrisburg: Trinity Press International, 2003).

Sanders, E. P., *Judaism. Practice and Belief 63 BCE–66 CE* (London: SCM, 1992).

Sandt, H. van de, 'Two Windows on a Developing Jewish-Christian Reproof Practice: Matt 18:15-17 and *Did.* 15:3', in H. van de Sandt (ed.), *Matthew and the Didache* (Assen: Van Gorcum, 2005), pp.173–92.

Sandt, H. van de, and D. Flusser, *The Didache: Its Jewish Sources and its Place in Early Judaism and Christianity* (CRINT III.5; Assen: Van Gorcum, 2002).

Schäfer, P., *Judeophobia: Attitudes toward the Jews in the Ancient World* (Cambridge, MA: Harvard University Press, 1997).

Schaff, P., *The Teaching of the Twelve Apostles* (New York: Funk & Wagnalls, 1885).

Schiffman, L. H., *Who Was a Jew? Rabbinic and Halakhic Perspectives on the Jewish-Christian Schism* (Hoboken: KTAV, 1985).

Schlueter, C. J., *Filling Up The Measure: Polemical Hyperbole in 1 Thessalonians 2.14-16* (JSNTSup 98; Sheffield: JSOT, 1994).

Schmidt, F., 'Gôral versus Payîs: Casting Lots at Qumran and in the Rabbinic Tradition', in F. García Martinez and M. Popovic (eds.), *Defining Identities: We, You, and the Other in the Dead Sea Scrolls. Proceedings of the Fifth Meeting of the IOQS in Groningen* (STDJ 70; Leiden: Brill, 2007), pp.175–85.

Schofield, A., *From Qumran to the Yahad: A New Paradigm of Textual Development for the Community Rule* (STDJ 77; Leiden: Brill, 2009).

Schottroff, L., *Lydia's Impatient Sisters: A Feminist Social History of Early Christianity* (Louisville: Westminster John Knox, 1995).

Schuchard, B. G., *Scripture within Scripture: The Interrelationship of Form and Function in the Explicit Old Testament Citations in the Gospel of John* (SBLDS 133; Atlanta: Scholars Press, 1992).

Schultz, B., *Conquering the World: The War Scroll (1QM) Reconsidered* (STDJ 76; Leiden: Brill, 2009).

Schulz, S., *Q – Die Spruchquelle der Evangelisten* (Zurich: TVZ, 1972).

Schürer, E., *The History of the Jewish People in the Time of Jesus Christ, Second Division* (4 vols.; Edinburgh: T. & T. Clark, 1890).

——. *The History of the Jewish People in the Age of Jesus Christ (175 B.C.–A.D. 135)* (rev. G. Vermes, F. Millar, M. Black and M. Goodman; 3 vols. in 4 parts; Edinburgh: T. & T. Clark, 1973–87).

Schwartz, D. R., 'On Sacrifices by Gentiles in the Temple of Jerusalem', in D. R. Schwartz, *Studies in the Jewish Background of Christianity* (WUNT 60; Tübingen: Mohr Siebeck, 1992), pp.102–16.

Schwartz, S., *Josephus and Judaean Politics* (CSCT 18; Leiden: Brill, 1990).

Schwiebert, J., *Knowledge and the Coming Kingdom: The Didache's Meal Ritual and its Place in Early Christianity* (LNTS 373; London: T&T Clark International, 2008).

Scott, J. M., *Paul and the Nations: The Old Testament and Jewish Background of Paul's Mission to the Nations with Special Reference to the Destination of Galatians* (WUNT 84; Tübingen: Mohr Siebeck, 1995).

Sechrest, L. L., *A Former Jew: Paul and the Dialectics of Race* (LNTS 410; London: T&T Clark International, 2009).

Segal, P., 'The Penalty of the Warning Inscription from the Temple of Jerusalem', *IEJ* 39 (1989), pp.79–84.

Senior, D., 'Between Two Worlds: Gentiles and Jewish Christians in Matthew's Gospel', *CBQ* 61 (1999), pp.1–23.

——. 'The Eucharist in Mark: Mission, Reconciliation, Hope', *BTB* 12 (1982), pp. 67–72.

Sheridan, R., *Retelling Scripture: 'The Jews' and the Scriptural Citations in John 1.19–12.15* (BIS 110; Leiden: Brill, 2012).

Sherwood, A., *Paul and the Restoration of Humanity in Light of Ancient Jewish Traditions* (AJEC 82; Leiden: Brill, 2013).

Shiner, W. T., *Follow Me! Disciples in Markan Rhetoric* (SBLDS 145; Atlanta: Scholars Press, 1995).

Sim, D. C., 'The "Confession" of the Soldiers in Matthew 27.54', *HeyJ* 34 (1993), pp.401- 24.

——. *The Gospel of Matthew and Christian Judaism: The History and Social Setting of the Matthean Community* (SNTW; Edinburgh: T. & T. Clark, 1998).

——. 'The Gospel of Matthew and the Gentiles', *JSNT* 57 (1995), pp.19–48.

——. 'The Gospel of Matthew, John the Elder and the Papias Tradition: A Response to R. H. Gundry', *HTS* 63 (2007), pp.283–99.

——. 'The Magi: Gentiles or Jews?', *HTS* 55 (1999), pp.980–1000.

——. 'Matthew, Paul and the Origin and Nature of the Gentile Mission: The Great Commission in Matthew 28:16-20 as an Anti-Pauline Tradition', *HTS* 64 (2008), pp.377–92.

——. 'Rome in Matthew's Eschatology', in Riches and Sim (eds.), *The Gospel of Matthew*, pp.91–106.

Şimşek, C., *Laodikeia (Laodikeia ad Lycum)* (Istanbul: Ege Yayınları, 2007).

Smallwood, E. M., *The Jews Under Roman Rule, from Pompey to Diocletian: A Study in Political Relations* (Leiden: Brill, 1976).

Smith, C. W. F., 'Fishers of Men: Footnotes on a Gospel Figure', *HTR* 52 (1959), pp.187–203.

Smith, M., 'The Gentiles in Judaism 125 BCE–CE 66', in Horbury, Davies, and Sturdy (eds.), *The Cambridge History of Judaism*, III, pp.192–249.

Smith, T. J., 'Votive Reliefs from Balboura and its Environs', *AS* 47 (1997), pp.3–49.

Spawforth, A. J. S., *Greece and the Augustan Cultural Revolution* (Cambridge: Cambridge University Press, 2011).

Spencer, F. S., *Acts* (Sheffield: Sheffield Academic, 1997).

Spencer, J. R., 'Sojourner', in *ABD*, VI, pp.103–4.

Spilsbury, P., *The Image of the Jew in Flavius Josephus' Paraphrase of the Bible* (TSAJ 69; Tübingen: Mohr Siebeck, 1998).

Stanley, C., '"Neither Jew nor Greek": Ethnic Conflict in Graeco-Roman Society', *JSNT* 64 (1996), pp.101–24.

Stanton, G. N., *A Gospel for a New People: Studies in Matthew* (Edinburgh: T. & T. Clark, 1992).

Stark, R., *The Rise of Christianity: A Sociologist Reconsiders History* (Princeton: Princeton University Press, 1996).

Steck, O. H., *Israel und das gewaltsame Geschick der Propheten* (WMANT 23; Neukirchen–Vluyn: Neukirchener, 1967).

Stenschke, C. W., *Luke's Portrait of Gentiles Prior to their Coming to Faith* (WUNT 2.108; Tübingen: Mohr Siebeck, 1999).

Sterling, G. E., '"Philo has not been used half enough": The Significance of Philo of Alexandria for the Study of the New Testament', *PRS* 30 (2003), pp.251–69.

Stern, M., *Greek and Latin Authors on Jews and Judaism* (3 vols.; Jerusalem: Israel Academy of Sciences and Humanities, 1974–84).

Stone, M., 'Apocalyptic Literature', in Stone (ed.), *Jewish Writings of the Second Temple Period*, pp.383–441.

——. *Fourth Ezra* (Hermeneia; Minneapolis: Fortress, 1990).

Stone, M. (ed.), *Jewish Writings of the Second Temple Period: Apocrypha, Pseudepigrapha, Qumran Sectarian Writings, Philo, Josephus* (Philadelphia: Fortress, 1984).

Stowers, K., *A Rereading of Romans: Justice, Jews and Gentiles* (New Haven: Yale University Press, 1994).

Strack H. L., and P. Billerbeck, *Kommentar zum Neuen Testament aus Talmud und Midrasch* (4 vols.; Munich: Beck, 3rd edn, 1951–56).

Strecker, G., *Der Weg der Gerechtigkeit: Untersuchung zur Theologie des Matthäus* (FRLANT 82; Göttingen: Vandenhoeck & Ruprecht, 1962; 3rd edn 1971).

Stroup, C., 'A Reexamination of the "Sons of the Pit" in CD 13:14,' *DSD* 18 (2011), pp.45–53.

Stuckenbruck, L. T., '"Protect Them from the Evil One" (John 17:15): Light from the Dead Sea Scrolls', in M. L. Coloe and T. Thatcher (eds.), *John, Qumran, and the Dead Sea Scrolls: Sixty Years of Discovery and Debate* (EJL 32; Atlanta: SBL, 2011), pp.139–60.

Stuehrenberg, P. F., 'Proselyte', in *ABD*, V, pp.503–5.

Swartley, W. M., *Mark, the Way for All Nations* (Scottdale: Herald, 1979).

Tagawa, K., 'People and Community in the Gospel of Matthew', *NTS* 16 (1970), pp.149–62.

Tannenbaum, R. F., 'Jews and God-Fearers in the Holy City of Aphrodite', *BAR* 12 (1986), pp.44–57.

Taylor, V., *The Gospel according to St Mark: The Greek Text with Introduction, Notes and Indexes* (London: Macmillan, 2nd edn, 1966).

Terian, A., 'Had the Works of Philo Been Newly Discovered', *BA* 57 (1994), pp.86–97.

Thomas, E., *Monumentality and the Roman Empire: Architecture in the Antonine Age* (Oxford: Oxford University Press, 2007).

Thompson, J. W., *Moral Formation according to Paul: The Context and Coherence of Christian Ethics* (Grand Rapids: Baker Academic, 2011).

Tisera, G., *Universalism in the Gospel of Matthew* (EUS 482; Frankfurt: Lang, 1993).

Tod, M. N., 'An Ephebic Inscription from Memphis', *Journal of Egyptian Archaeology* 37 (1951), pp.86–99.

Tomson, P., '"Jews" in the Gospel of John as Compared with the Palestinian Talmud, the Synoptics and Some New Testament Apocrypha', in R. Bieringer, D. Pollefeyt, and F. Vandecateele-Vanneuville (eds.), *Anti-Judiasm and the Fourth Gospel; Papers of the Leuven Colloquium, 2000* (Assen: Van Gorcum, 2001), pp.301–40.

Tov, E. (ed.), *The Texts from the Judaean Desert: Indices and an Introduction to the Discoveries in the Judaean Desert Series* (DJD 39; Oxford: Clarendon, 2002).

Trebilco, P., *Jewish Communities in Asia Minor* (SNTSMS 69; Cambridge: Cambridge University Press, 1991).

Trilling, W., *Das Wahre Israel: Studien zur Theologie des Matthäusevangeliums* (ETS 7; Munich: Kösel, 1959, 3rd edn, 1964).

Trümper, M., 'The Oldest Original Synagogue Building in the Diaspora: The Delos Synagogue Reconsidered', *Hesperia* 73 (2004), pp.513–98.

Tuckett, C. M., 'Matthew: The Social and Historical Context – Jewish Christian and/or Gentile?', in D. Senior (ed.), *The Gospel of Matthew at the Crossroads of Early Christianity* (BETL 243; Leuven: Peeters, 2011), pp.99–129.

——. 'On the Stratification of Q', *Semeia* 55 (1991), pp.213–22.

——. 'Q and the Historical Jesus', in J. Schröter and R. Brucker (eds.), *Der historische Jesus. Tendenzen und Perspektiven der gegenwärtigen Forschung* (BZNW 114; Berlin: de Gruyter, 2002), pp.213–41.

——. *Q and the History of Early Christianity* (Edinburgh: T. & T. Clark, 1996).

——. 'The Temptation Narrative in Q', in F. Van Segbroek et al. (eds.), *The Four Gospels 1992: Festschrift Frans Neirynck* (Leuven: Peeters, 1992), pp.479–507.

Umemoto, N., 'Juden, "Heiden" und das Menschengeschlecht in der Sicht Philons von Alexandrien', in Feldmeier and Heckel (eds.), *Die Heiden*, pp.22–51.

Uro, R., *Sheep among Wolves: A Study of the Mission Instructions of Q* (Helsinki: Suomalainen Tiedeakatemia, 1987).

VanderKam, J. C., *The Book of Jubilees* (2 vols.; Leuven: Peeters, 1989).

——. *Textual and Historical Studies in the Book of Jubilees* (HSM 14; Missoula: Scholars Press, 1977).

Vermes, G., *The Dead Sea Scrolls: Qumran in Perspective* (Philadelphia: Fortress, 1981).

Volz, P., *Die Eschatologie der jüdischen Gemeinde im neutestamentlichen Zeitalter* (Tübingen: Mohr, 1934).

Wainwright, E. M., *Shall We Look for Another? A Feminist Rereading of the Matthean Jesus* (TBLS; Maryknoll: Orbis, 1998).

Wander, B., Gottesfürchtige und Sympathisanten: Studien zum heidnischen Umfeld von *Diasporasynagogen* (WUNT 104; Tübingen: Mohr Siebeck, 1998).

Wardle, T., *The Jerusalem Temple and Early Christian Identity* (WUNT 291; Tübingen: Mohr Siebeck, 2010).

Watson, F., *Paul, Judaism and the Gentiles: Beyond the New Perspective* (Grand Rapids: Eerdmans, rev. and exp. edn, 2007).

Watts, R. E., *Isaiah's New Exodus in Mark* (Grand Rapids: Baker, rev. edn, 2000).

——. 'Mark', in G. K. Beale and D. A. Carson (eds.), *Commentary on the New Testament Use of the Old Testament* (Grand Rapids: Baker Academic, 2007), pp.111–249.

Weaver, D. J., ' "Thus You Will Know Them By Their Fruits": The Roman Characters of the Gospel of Matthew', in Riches and Sim (eds.), *The Gospel of Matthew*, pp.107–27.

Wefald, E. K., 'The Separate Gentile Mission in Mark: A Narrative Explanation of Markan Geography, the Two Feeding Accounts and Exorcisms', *JSNT* 18 (1996), pp.3–26.

Wegner, U., *Der Hauptmann von Kafarnaum (Mt 7,28a; 8,5–10,13 par Lk 7,1-10). Ein Beitrag zur Q-Forschung* (WUNT 2.14; Tübingen: Mohr, 1985).

Weissenrieder, A., *Images of Illness in the Gospel of Luke: Insights of Ancient Medical Texts* (WUNT 2.164; Tübingen: Mohr Siebeck, 2003).

Weitzman, S., 'Forced Circumcision and the Shifting Role of Gentiles in Hasmonean Ideology', *HTR* 92 (1999), pp.37–59.

Williams, C. H., 'Isaiah in John's Gospel', in S. Moyise and M. J. J. Menken (eds.), *Isaiah in the New Testament* (NTSI; London: T&T Clark International), pp.101–16.

Williams, M. H., 'The Use of Alternative Names by Diaspora Jews in Graeco-Roman Antiquity', *JSJ* 38 (2007), pp.307–27.

Wilson, S. G., *Related Strangers: Jews and Christians, 70–170 CE* (Minneapolis: Fortress, 1995).

Wilson, W. T., *The Hope of Glory: Education and Exhortation in the Epistle to the Colossians* (Leiden: Brill, 1997).

Winter, B. W., *After Paul Left Corinth: The Influence of Secular Ethics and Social Change* (Grand Rapids: Eerdmans, 2001).

Wintermute, O. S., 'Jubilees', in *OTP*, II, pp.35–142.

Wise, M. O., *A Critical Study of the Temple Scroll from Qumran Cave 11* (Chicago: The Oriental Institute, 1990).

——. 'Dating the Teacher of Righteousness and the *Floruit* of his Movement', *JBL* 122 (2003), pp.53–87.

Woolf, G., 'Becoming Roman, Staying Greek: Culture, Identity and the Civilizing Process in the Roman East', *PCPS* 40 (1994), pp.116–43.

——. *Becoming Roman: The Origins of Provincial Civilization in Gaul* (Cambridge: Cambridge University Press, 1998).

Yadin, Y., *The Scroll of the War of the Sons of Light against the Sons of Darkness* (Oxford: Oxford University Press, 1962).

Yegül, F., *Baths and Bathing in Classical Antiquity* (New York: MIT, 1992).

Zeller, D., 'Jesus, Q und die Zukunft Israels', in Lindemann (ed.), *The Sayings Source Q*, pp.351–69.

Zgusta, L., *Kleinasiatische Personennamen* (Prague: Czechoslovakian Academy, 1964).

Zuiderhoek, A., *The Politics of Munificence in the Roman Empire: Citizens, Elites and Benefactors in Asia Minor* (Cambridge: Cambridge University Press, 2009).

INDICES

INDEX OF REFERENCES

INDEX OF AUTHORS